otball than mere
ou will di
resses. If played
game brings out t
boy. It develops hi
It teaches him th
lice. It teaches hi
other game does, t
e cool, with a lev
ntial. It teaches hi
nly. All this

JOCK

THE STORY OF JOCK McHALE
COLLINGWOOD'S GREATEST COACH

GLENN McFARLANE

The Slattery Media Group
140 Harbour Esplanade, Docklands
Victoria, Australia, 3008
visit slatterymedia.com

National Library of Australia Cataloguing-in-Publication entry

Author: McFarlane, Glenn.

Title: Jock : the story of Jock McHale Collingwood's greatest coach / Glenn McFarlane.

ISBN: 9781921778292 (hbk.)

Subjects: McHale, James Francis, 1882-1953.
            Collingwood Football Club--History.
            Australian football players--Victoria--Collingwood--Biography.
            Australian football coaches--Victoria--Collingwood--Biography.
            Australian football--Victoria--Collingwood--History.

Dewey Number:
            796.336099451

Group Publisher: Geoff Slattery
Cover and page design: Daniel Frawley
Creative Director: Andrew Hutchison
Photo production: Natalie Boccassini, Ginny Pike
Production Manager: Troy Davis

Cover Photograph: Courtesy of Newspix

Images: Slattery Media Group archives, Australian Football League archives, Newspix,
Collingwood Football Club, Fairfax

Printed and bound in Australia by Griffin Press

This book is dedicated to Charlie Dibbs,
my grandfather, who won five premierships under
Jock McHale's coaching, and to Charlie's daughter, Dawn,
my mother, who taught me to love Collingwood.

Contents

A man revealed

At first the voice is barely audible above the din of the victorious Collingwood dressing room in the mad moments immediately following the 1953 Grand Final. It is quintessentially Australian in its drawl, yet there is an unmistakable hint of Irish brogue that first-generation immigrants often transferred to their children. The Magpies had just won their first premiership in 17 years, an eternity for a club so accustomed to regular success. For once the voice of 'Jock' McHale battles to overcome the raucous revellers committed solely to celebrating an end to the longest flag drought in the club's history to that stage. Typically, as he has done on countless occasions for almost half a century, he calls for order. He repeats the message with more purpose and the roar cuts back to a more sustainable level. For the briefest of moments, McHale's tone wavers, perhaps weakened by the strain of such a close match, his heart still beating rapidly. Standing on a bench, elevated and straining his eyes out to look at a sea of faces— many of them instantly recognisable; others less familiar—McHale tells the throng that the club's long-time benefactor John Wren has agreed to give the players £500 to mark their achievement. As soon as the words come out of his mouth, the boom of noise rises even more.

Wren has been handing out money to Collingwood and to its players for almost as long as the club has been in existence. But no one in the room, and certainly not Wren's good friend McHale, knows at the time this will be his final donation. By this time, Wren is escaping the crowd swelling out of the Melbourne Cricket Ground, stopped only for a quick question from a newspaper reporter about what Collingwood's premiership means to him. He answers briefly and to the point, and then moves on, content that the club he has always supported—and loved—had been restored to its rightful position.

McHale is content, too. He has made many thousands of speeches to Collingwood congregations over the years, but this one is special. It's also his last, but no one knows that either. The grey-haired, almost portly figure carries on. He is no longer the coach of Collingwood, having retired from the position three years earlier, after a staggering 38 seasons in charge. But, in many ways, he remains the patriarch of the Pies; the colossus of Collingwood. It's been that way for 50 years. Never mind the fact that he is less than three months away from his 71st birthday. McHale is as revered as ever. That respect extends from the precious still few living who were with him, shoulder by shoulder, in the early days when Collingwood crafted a history and a fame out of a desire to turn the socially deprived inner-city suburb into a sporting phenomenon; and from the youngest members of the 1953 premiership side who know the power that 'Old Jock' still wielded as a selector and vice-president.

The irony was that McHale wasn't from Collingwood. He never lived or worked in the suburb, unlike many of his contemporaries; but he came to love the football club that made the suburb famous with a passion almost unparalleled. And while he might well have been coach in the club's eight previous Grand Final wins, and a player in the one before that batch, this breakthrough 1953 flag meant so much to him, and to Collingwood. A bungled and divisive succession to his coaching tenure had almost brought the club to its knees. Back then, in April 1950, it seemed as if the foundations of the power club that McHale had helped to build had crumbled like so many empires had done before. His replacement as coach, former player and reserves coach Bervin Woods, lasted only a handful of days as a revolution swept through the club that had seemed to be immune from such bickering and bitterness. But somehow Collingwood had emerged from this predicament to win a premiership in the space of three years.

So it is little wonder that McHale is declaring to those present that he has never experienced a flag such as this one. Uncharacteristically, his voice crackles as memories of past premierships and past champions sweep through his mind as if they were still before him. The patriarch clicks himself back into action as he swears he rates this season the most enjoyable he had been involved in. A rare smile breaks across his face as he says he is so pleased for coach 'Phonsey' Kyne and for the next wave of Collingwood premiership players.

Eight days later many of those in the room that fading September afternoon are standing side-by-side at McHale's grave; the shock of his sudden departure etched on their faces; his farewell speech still ringing in their ears. For some, a half-century of memories had come flooding back, first at the service at St Therese's Catholic Church in Lincoln Road, Essendon, and later at the Coburg General Cemetery. At the gravesite, one of McHale's old sparring partners on the field, former Fitzroy captain Gerald Brosnan, then 76, tells those around him of a story dating back 50 years and one month, to a time when two warring suburbs—Collingwood and Fitzroy—met in the 1903 Grand Final. The outcome of the premiership rested on Brosnan's last-minute kick. Brosnan tells the mourners that McHale had been standing right beside him when he took the fateful kick. The shot started straight before veering to the wrong side of the goalposts if you were a Fitzroy supporter, and to the right side, if you were a Collingwood barracker. The kick left the Magpies as premiers for a second successive year.

But the truth was that McHale had not even played in that match. He was sitting on the wrong side of the fence, dressed in a suit with a Magpie emblem on it, watching helplessly thanks to an injury suffered in the previous game. He had played 14 games in his debut season, including seven in a row leading into the Grand Final, but could not play in the match that mattered most. As elated as he was for his teammates, and for the club that would play such a significant part for the rest of his life, it hurt to watch the game unfold without any direct involvement. He would have to wait another seven years to experience that premiership feeling.

Brosnan's blunder was, perhaps, understandable on closer inspection. In so many ways, McHale came to represent a personification of the Collingwood Football Club through the first half of the 20th century. It seemed everything, directly or indirectly, that happened to the club during that expanse of time was somehow related to him in one way, shape or form. It came first with McHale as a player, a person who overcame some early setbacks to carve a career out of his persistence, his commitment to being physically and mentally prepared for any challenge, and his resilience which would see him once go almost 11 years without missing a match. Second, it was as a playing coach when coaches were a relatively new concept in an era when captains controlled a large part of the direction and destiny of teams on the field. Then, most tellingly, it was as a non-playing coach, where he exercised his will and his workings on two generations of Collingwood footballers. All up as a coach, playing or non-playing, McHale was in charge of all Collingwood's matches—with the notable exception of one—from 1912 to 1949, a period that spanned two cataclysmic World Wars and a crippling Depression. In that time, Australia was presided over by 12 different Prime Ministers, including one, John Curtin, who had been a close friend and sports opponent of McHale when they were growing up. To put McHale's longevity into football context, the 11 other clubs that made up the Victorian Football League through most of those years had 173 different coaches in that time, with St Kilda and North Melbourne (who had only been competing in the competition since 1925) each having 20 individual coaches compared to Collingwood's. In that light, it is little wonder that, for so many people, Collingwood's history to that time would often be considered McHale's history.

The McHale legend was every bit as imposing as the reality. In a way, it still is. When Mick Malthouse became Collingwood's fifth premiership coach in 2010—a century on from McHale's first premiership as a player—he was surprised to learn that he had become the oldest premiership coach in league history—at 57 years and 46 days. "Jock McHale coached for so long that I just assumed that he was the oldest (to win a flag)," Malthouse said in the Grand Final afterglow.

In truth, McHale was yet to turn 54 when he tasted for the final time the ultimate success as a coach (in 1936), even though he toiled away for another 13 years. To this day, McHale remains one of the most imposing figures in Australian football history—almost 130 years on from his birth, almost a century on from his first year as coach and almost 60 years since his passing. But while the statistics and records surrounding McHale and the Collingwood teams he presided over are well-known, precious little is known about the man acknowledged as the 'Prince of Coaches', or 'the King of Coaches', and what made him tick. McHale's 50 years as service to Collingwood—as a player, a playing coach, a captain, a non-playing coach, a committeeman, and later as a vice-president and selector—came in the years before television. His playing career had concluded well before the game began to reach a wider audience on radio. There is no vision of him playing and only a few still shots of him as a player remain frozen in time. There is that precious audio recorded of McHale from the rooms after the 1953 Grand Final. That is all that is left of the voice and the penetrating oratory that helped to shape a football club that became the most loved—and simultaneously the most hated—in the country, and helped to shape the indigenous game that was a stranger to him as a child, but would become such an enormous part of his life.

But what do we really know about the man whose sobriquet was simply Jock? We know that he coached Collingwood a record 714 times for 467 wins, 237 losses and 10 draws over an astonishing 38 seasons. That's a 65 per cent winning record—only his arch rival 'Checker' Hughes and Tom Hafey come close to that record. We know that he coached the Magpies to a record eight premierships and 27 finals series and 59 finals, with four of those flags coming in succession from 1927-1930, with a team universally known as *The Machine*. We know the medal presented to the winning coach on Grand Final day bears his name, a belated tribute to the man who had no real official recognition or tribute in his lifetime from the competition he gave a lifetime's service. But if you set aside the facts and figures, and the sheer statistical magnitude of a lifetime in football, sadly there has been little sinew put on the bones of these statistics.

Perhaps that is why there are so many misconceptions about McHale. He wasn't the first coach. He wasn't even Collingwood's first coach. And he wasn't, as some would have you believe, successful simply because he had the financial support—and friendship—of Wren. McHale lost many good and great players because of a philosophy that all players were equal and should be paid as such, a belief that he and the club strictly adhered to. But he was, perhaps, one of the first of the systematic coaches, who developed strategies and styles well in advance of his rival coaches.

But if you set aside the facts and figures of his extraordinary time and experiences in the game, Jock McHale remains the "ghost of coaching", as he was once described by Kevin Sheedy, another coaching genius with Irish ancestry. Indeed, the publisher of this book, Geoff Slattery, correctly points out that McHale's football record is crystal clear, "but what power separated him from the rest of those who coached is a mystery and may well be a mystery that will never be solved."

This investigation into McHale's football and coaching career, and in a sense, of his life, does not profess to solve that mystery. Too much water has passed under Dights Falls to change this. Those close to him have gone. His children are dead; two of them lived tragically short lives and predeceased him and another was believed to be stillborn. All who played with him are long gone, and only a small group of players of those who were coached by him remain alive. Those who reported his era are gone too, but thankfully their detailed writings survive. During the research for this book, several mysteries were solved; others were not. But what this book has been able to do is to put some human elements to a man who was revered and feared—and loved—by most who knew him.

CHAPTER 1

The McHales of Mayo

1882-1888

S ydneysiders were busily preparing themselves for Christmas when James Francis McHale, the first-born child of Irish immigrants, came into the world on December 12, 1882. Early on, he would be known as James. In time, his parents and friends would call him Jim. Later he would almost universally be known as Jock. Looking back years later, McHale would say that he was born at Botany Bay, that most Australian of places, near where Captain James Cook first landed just over 112 years earlier. However, McHale's birth certificate reveals that it was not in Botany Bay where he took his first breath, but a few suburbs away in Alexandria. Part of this misunderstanding could have been that his parents, John and Mary, were at the time living in the hustle and bustle of Botany Road, Alexandria, a road that stretched its way through the central part of Sydney almost to the waters of Botany Bay.

The exact location of McHale's birth is made all the more difficult by the fact that street numbers were not used in Botany Road at the time. More confusing, too, is that McHale's birth was registered under the name of 'McKale', and much later, when electronically tagged, it was 'McKate'. As such, the birth certificate of one of Australian football's most famous figures and arguably the most recognisable name associated with the Collingwood Football Club has been hidden away under a variant surname for almost 130 years. No explanation survives for this error, but it was almost certainly the result of the registrar misunderstanding the Irish lilt of his mother, who was referred to in the document incorrectly as 'Mary McKale'. Neither two-month-old James, nor his father John, listed as 28 and a labourer, were in attendance on February 9, 1883 when Mary came to present details of the arrival of their first child.

The average life expectancy for males in Australia in 1882 was 47 years, two months and 12 days. For females, it was considerably better, at 50 years, 10 months and two days.[1] In a time in which there were no antibiotics, where childhood mortality was heartbreakingly high, where childbirth was predominantly at home and without medical assistance, and where men and sometimes women were routinely engaged in occupations that were hazardous, there were considerable obstacles to living a long and healthy life.

Fortunately, for John and Mary, James Francis grew fast and strong. By the time he had reached 47 years and two months, he was at the peak of his powers as coach of Collingwood, having just led his team to three successive premierships. He also had more than 20 years to live. Sadly, several of his siblings, and a few of his own children, would not be so fortunate.

On the day that McHale was born, one of Australia's worst mining disasters occurred at the No.2 shaft of the New Australasian Mine, near Creswick, in country Victoria. News of the "terrible catastrophe", as *The Argus* described it, was cabled throughout the colonies as an increasingly forlorn rescue operation was made: "The men engaged in one of the drives unexpectedly broke into the old workings of the No.1 shaft and immediately an immense body of water burst through,

---

1   *Australia Through Time*, Random House, 1994

flooding the lower level of the mine and rising in a very short space of time to a height of 30 feet in the shaft. The influx was so sudden and heavy that those working where the breach occurred had no time to warn others, being obliged to fly for their lives. The 27 engaged in the other part of the workings were unable to reach the shaft. The mothers, wives, children and friends of the men below assembled at the mouth of the shaft, waiting in an agony of distress for information regarding the result of the flooding."[2]

The news was appallingly bad. Only five of the 27 men trapped by the mass of water managed to reach ground high enough to survive. The bodies of the 22 drowned men were recovered days later, leaving 17 widows and many children without fathers, and the country with a stark reminder of how tenuous life could be in 19th century Australia.

December 12, 1882 was also supposed to be the day that the touring English cricket team, captained by Ivo Bligh, was to play against a team of 18 players in Tamworth. Unfortunately, the rain that had swept across New South Wales over the previous few days had rendered the pitch unplayable. *The Sydney Morning Herald* explained: "At 12 o'clock the game was, by common consent, given up. Play would have been impossible, as although the rain held off at half-past 11, the wicket was quite sodden. The Englishmen arranged to leave this morning. This was a great disappointment to everyone."[3]

Four months earlier, a mock obituary in *The Sporting Times* in London had announced the death of English cricket after the Australians had won a Test match at The Oval. Carrying on that theme, Bligh said his visiting team had come to Australia to "beard the kangaroo and bring back those ashes". Soon after the Tamworth wash-out, the England team travelled to Melbourne for the Christmas-New Year period

2   *The Argus*, December 13, 1882
3   ibid, December 13, 1882

ahead of the first Test of a three-match series. It was at Rupertswood, in Sunbury, on the eve of Christmas where Bligh was presented with a small terracotta urn from a group of Melbourne women following a social match. One of the women would later become his wife. That diminutive trophy would become the symbol of England-Australia Test cricket, the Ashes.

On the morning of James McHale's first Christmas Day, *The Sydney Morning Herald* proclaimed that Sydney was a much more joyous place to be than 12 months before. It claimed: "Never before have the streets of Sydney presented such a scene of life and gaiety as on Saturday evening (December 23). At the same period last year the city was still darkened with the shadow of a pestilence which had invaded the city and the suburbs, and there was, consequently, not the usual holiday influx of visitors. Life is dearer than friendship, and friends in the neighbouring colonies avoided Sydney by spending their Christmastide elsewhere, fearing to come into what was supposed to be in the domain of the Contagion. Scores of houses in the city were still displaying the habiliments of woe, and it was only natural that at such a period tradesmen should share in the general feeling of depression into which the city had been plunged."[4]

A smallpox outbreak, one that would have wide-ranging and beneficial ramifications for the young colony, had raged through the streets of inner Sydney, particularly in the Rocks district, from May 1881 to February 1882. The 220,000-strong population of Sydney, which had risen dramatically from about 45,000 in 1851, had been gripped by fear and panic that the highly infectious disease which had long been a death sentence in Europe, Asia and elsewhere would gain a deadly foothold in Australia. But somehow, fortunately, the outbreak never transformed into an epidemic.

A total of 163 cases led to 41 deaths, although it is believed the true figure would have been much higher given the subterfuge

---

4   ibid, December 25, 1882

of some loved ones to conceal the real reason for these deaths. Those survivors were afraid they would lose their accommodation. What the outbreak did achieve, however, was a change in health policies. The Infectious Diseases Supervision Act of 1881 brought about compulsory notification of small pox and other diseases, a hospital for infectious diseases was opened, and there was an overhaul of quarantine procedures.

James's father, John, had seen the fear arising out of illness and disease before, and had no desire to experience it again. On his arrival in Sydney in March 1880, he and the rest of the passengers and crew aboard the ship, *Norval*, were quarantined at sea for more than a week before finally gaining clearance to land. The end of McHale's long journey from his family home of Emlagh, in County Mayo, on the far western coast of Ireland, to his new home in Sydney, Australia had been delayed by a chicken-pox outbreak near the end of the trip. Prior to that, it had been a relatively incident-free voyage, with no births or deaths recorded. But when a few passengers started to show signs of sickness as they entered Australian waters, it became a worrying time for all of the passengers aboard.

The Sydney Morning Herald detailed: "The immigrant ship, *Norval*, from London, on the 6th December, and Plymouth six days later, arrived in Port yesterday morning flying the yellow flag. The ship is under the command of Captain (George) Halliday, and Dr Thomas Harrison is the medical officer on board. The captain reports that he has more than 300 adults and 66 children immigrants, and that he has two or three cases of chicken pox amongst them. The ship has been 81 days during the journey, and, with the exception of the illness above referred to, the health of those on board is first class."[5]

The 1445-tonne ship had "crossed the Equator on the 4th of January, the meridian of the Cape of Good Hope on the 31st, and was off Tasmania on the 23rd of February."[6] The journey was met

---

5   ibid, March 3, 1880
6   ibid, March 3, 1880

with mostly moderate weather and conditions before a heavy gale blew the ship about as it made its way up the coast. But just when McHale and the rest of those aboard were preparing themselves for dry land again, the chicken pox outbreak put a sinister conclusion to their journey.

The men and women of the *Norval* spent nine days anchored, waiting for permission to land. Of those struck down by the illness, one would not survive. She was a 15-year-old girl who had endured the rigours of almost three months at sea, only to succumb when she was within sight of what was meant to be her new home.

Finally, Captain Halliday was granted *pratique* (licence given to a ship to enter port on the assurance of the captain that it is free of contagious disease) on March 11, nine days after first trying to reach land. Slowly, but surely, the *Norval* was towed up into Neutral Bay where the arriving vessels docked. A report on the ship's release from quarantine said: "There are 386 immigrants on board, comprising 45 married couples, 86 single men and 124 single women ... the married couples and single men will be for hire on Monday and Tuesday next at the Immigration Depot, and the single women at 12 o'clock today in the same place."[7]

John McHale stepped off the ship that day with his cousin, Austin McHale, who had accompanied him on the journey. The immigration register claimed that John was 35, but it was once more a slip of the pencil. McHale was actually 25. He was listed as a labourer from County Mayo, in the west of Ireland, a Roman Catholic who could both read and write. He nominated a cousin, James McHale (Austin's brother) as a relative he had in Sydney.

The interest in the *Norval* immigrants as far as their job prospects went was strong. They had arrived in port on a Friday and yet by the

---

7   ibid, March 13, 1880

following Tuesday, it was reported that "all the immigrants have been engaged, or having arranged to proceed at their own wish into the country ... (and) there will be none for hire this day at Port Macquarie as previously advertised. The immigrants of the *Norval* seem a useful lot of people, and likely to make good colonists. An unusually large number left the vessel on their own account, a large proportion being those who had been sent for by their friends; so that, as Sir Henry Parkes said in Parliament the other day, there are many people here who do not think the country is overstocked with labour."[8]

John McHale's arrival must have been a bittersweet moment for him. He had come to start his new life in the colonies, and to chase opportunities that were not attainable in the land of his birth. But initially he would have to make do without his new wife, Mary, whom he had married only five months earlier. The pair had wed in the Roman Catholic Church in Louisburgh, in County Mayo, on October 12, 1879. On the marriage certificate, John's surname was listed in the old style of the family name, MacHale. He was aged 25, and a farmer from Emlagh, only four miles from where he was married. His wife, Mary Gibbons, was three years younger, and a farmer's daughter from a neighbouring village.

Both bride and groom were said to have descended from the first John MacHale to come to the district in about 1780. As one of Mary's long distant relatives, Mary Doyle, explained: "Intermarriage among succeeding generations makes our family tree very complicated. John and Mary grew up about a mile apart in a very beautiful place beside the Atlantic Ocean. Both families had small farms, but life was hard and many people emigrated to America and Australia."[9] John and Mary had known each other all of their lives. But, as a married couple,

---

8   ibid, March 16, 1880
9   Correspondence with Mary Doyle, 2010

they would only get to spend two months together before John headed to England, and Plymouth, to catch the *Norval*.

The plan was a daunting one. John was to try to set up a new home for the pair in far-off Sydney before sending passage back to Ireland for his wife. While there is clear evidence of John's pathway to Australia, there is no such trace for Mary's journey, other than a few anecdotes handed down over succeeding generations. The name of the vessel and the dates in which she travelled to Sydney—along with her sisters Winifred and Brigid—have been lost over time. Family folklore has it that she remained in Ireland for up to a year after John farewelled his family before he finally sent word to her to follow.

Given that her first child, James Francis, was born in December 1882, Mary must have arrived in Sydney by March of 1882. The likelihood is she arrived in 1881. Her sister Brigid would become homesick and return to Ireland after several years in the country. Mary Doyle recalled hearing stories of the heartache surrounding Mary's departure: "My mother said that her father often told her that he could remember his father crying all night long the night Mary left (for) Southampton on her long voyage to Australia. He (my grandfather) was about ten years old. Mary was his oldest sister. They never saw her again. Such was the story of so many people in Ireland. They must have had great courage and strength and a sense of adventure to go so far away in search of a living."[10]

The first John MacHale came to live in Emlagh a century before his namesake great-grandson left for Australia. According to a family history, *Kith and Kin*, written by Pat Joe McHale in 1988, John was granted about 400 acres in Emlagh in the late 18th century on the recommendation of a man named Jordan, for whom he had tended stock. The Jordans had garnered large portions of land and were accepted as tenants of the Browne landlords through the generations.

---

10   ibid

It was said: "Jordan built himself a house at Legaun on what James Berry describes in his *Tales of the West* as the bright sunny western slopes of the hill of Oldhead, which commanded a fine view of the valley of the great Anchill mountains, Clare Island, and the wild, western Atlantic. Both Browne and Jordan knew that this development was not welcome in that particular area, for while the O'Malleys, former lords of the territory, had lost much of their power, they were still able to cause great trouble to unwelcome settlers. Perhaps then, as a form of insurance, Jordan brought with him some Mayo natives who would be more acceptable and help to achieve a peaceful settlement in a hostile area."[11] John MacHale was one of these.

Kith and Kin detailed: "One can only imagine how he must have felt when on getting to Emlagh (probably about 1780) he surveyed his property on horseback for the first time. While 400 acres was a substantial property in those times, one must remember that the area was in a wild state, intersected with cuttings that brought water from the mountains to the sea. There were no roads then or for long afterwards, leading to the area. (But) doubtless also John saw the possibilities and was a courageous man."[12]

John MacHale was related to the man who would later become Ireland's Archbishop of Tuam, John McHale, a champion of the downtrodden, of which there were many spread out across Ireland throughout the 19th century. A sports ground named after the Archbishop—McHale Park—is famous in Castlebar, in County Mayo. As remote as Emlagh was at the time, where the wild Atlantic Ocean crashed into the western tip of County Mayo, John MacHale managed to create a home, and start a dynasty, with his wife, Cecilia O'Toole. The O'Toole family came from a small island off the coast called Inishturk and used to land on John's Emlagh Point, and it was said that "on one of these occasions John laid eyes on Cecilia ... She was a very pretty girl. Her family was so happy with the idea of John

---

11   *Kith and Kin*, Pat Joe McHale, An Choinneal, 1988
12   ibid

and Cecilia's marriage that (they) gave them the fertile land of Cahir (Island) six miles from Emlagh. Some time after the marriage, the O'Tooles found a treasure hoard of gold bars and other valuables on the island. The treasure was generously shared with John who took the bars by horseback to Dublin to get them valued. This must have been a formidable journey at the time."[13]

Life was tough in the early 1800s, but in a short space of time, John MacHale had acquired a wife, a large pocket of land and the means with which to develop it. Soon he would have a family of his own— a son, James, and three daughters, Ann, Sarah and Mary.

James was the male heir of the MacHale family. He married Catherine O'Malley—known as "Kitty above all"—near the turn of the 19th century. His wife's beauty was such that she won many prizes as the finest girl at many fairs in the region. While his father had produced only one son from four children, James would have an ample supply. He had five boys who, as *Kith and Kin* stated, made up the "the core of the family and who formed five natural divisions in the MacHale ancestry."[14]

James would eventually divide his properties at Emlagh between three of those sons—Austin, Patrick and James—in "roughly three parts". Our focus is on Austin, who would be the grandfather of 'Jock' McHale, though he would never meet him. Austin married Mary Joyce, started his own family, and constructed the first slate-covered home of the area on his share of 135 acres. A description in 1844 of the region said it was: "Characteristically a highland district, replete with grand and savage scenery, dashed over with the opposite touches of brown morass and of brilliant romance."[15]

---

13   ibid
14   ibid
15   *Parliamentary Gazette of Ireland*, 1844

But whatever wild romance existed in the first half of the 19th century, there was nothing but hardship that came out of one of the most heartbreaking chapters in Ireland's history, starting in 1845. The Great Famine, which was caused by a fungus that ruined the potato crop that season, and in subsequent years, would have devastating consequences for the country, and for the Parish of Kilgeever, of which Emlagh formed a part. Almost 90 per cent of the Irish population was dependent on the potato back then. There was, according to the Kilgeever parish history, "a total (and fatal) dependence on the potato"[16] and it made for "widespread devastation throughout the parish ... its most notable result was a sharp drop in population. Hunger, disease and emigration resulted in the population dropping by 50 per cent."[17]

Because of its remote location, the Kilgeever Parish suffered horrendously. John Garvey, the chairman of the Kilgeever Relief Committee, told a central relief commission in October 1846 that "the great distance of this parish from Westport and the almost total want of provisions renders such a measure (of urgent help) absolutely necessary to preserve the lives of the people. In many instances people have to travel a distance of 50 miles going and returning before they can procure a single stone of a meal or any other description of human food."[18] Two months later, Reverend Potter claimed that the Parish had been "grossly and shamelessly neglected". By early the next year, George Lynch, the secretary of the Kilgeever Relief Committee, said in a letter to a newspaper that the "deaths from want are daily increasing" and that many burials were taking place without coffins "in order to apply the price (of coffins) to the purchase of food".[19]

Starvation was not the sole cause of death. Fever and dysentery were rife. During the year known as "Black '47", records suggest

---

16 *A Glance at Our Past*, An Choinneal, 1980
17 ibid
18 ibid
19 ibid

that there were between seven and 10 deaths per day in Louisburgh alone. The population of Kilgeever Parish had been 14,105 in 1841. Within a decade, it was 7939. Almost half of those had perished because of the Great Famine, and the remainder had decided there was no alternative other than to emigrate. In Ireland, it was said that a million people died, and another million left the country for a new life as the Famine "cast its gaunt shadow over the course of future Kilgeever and Irish history".[20]

Pat Joe McHale's family history summed up the struggle of so many in this region: "Hidden behind the names are [sic] a bubbling cauldron of pain, heartache, joys, and happiness, which have been impossible to communicate."[21] Somehow, Austin and Mary's family grew through it all. They would have 11 children: Michael, James, John, Patrick, Sarah, Mary, Honor, Nancy, Maggie, Catherine and Brigid.

John, the father of future Collingwood coach Jock McHale, was born in Emlagh in 1854; he was baptised in the Louisburgh Catholic Church on June 10 of that year. He attended the national school at nearby Accony, which had opened six years before his birth.

A snapshot of the district taken a few years after he had left it for Sydney described the people of Louisburgh and Westport as "honest and hard working ... it would be difficult to find anywhere along the coast a district where energy and self-reliance are more apparent."[22] The isolation was evident, "all communication with Westport is by road, no steamers or sailing boats call at any place in the district ... there are no banks or loan funds ... during spring and summer credit is obtained by shopkeepers. Bills are generally paid by the following Christmas, with 10 to 15 per cent being charged. The people of this district take three meals daily, viz—Breakfast—at nine o'clock, tea and flour bread is always taken except for poor families, the latter using potatoes and milk or eggs; Dinner—consists of potatoes and fish, poor

---

20   ibid
21   *Kith and Kin*, Pat Joe McHale, An Choinneal, 1988
22   Report of Inspector Major Ruttledge-Fair, District of Louisburgh, 1893

families who have used potatoes for breakfast generally manage to have tea or flour bread for this meal; and Supper—at seven or eight o'clock, consists of potatoes and milk, with families in better circumstances again taking tea."[23]

Little is known of John's courtship of Mary Gibbons in the mid- to late 1870s. In a time when many marriages were arranged, the union of John and Mary was, according to an ancestor, "a love match."[24] They were married in October 1879. Another famine had hit Ireland that year, increasing the hardship for all but a lucky few. After one of the wettest periods on record, the country's potato crop failed for a third successive year. The west of Ireland suffered as badly as any other region.

As with the previous generation, there was widespread panic and fear amongst the general populace. But, fortunately, the lessons of the miserable 1840s had improved the chances of those most likely to suffer. There was still considerable hardship, but few fatalities arising out of this famine. There was undoubtedly hunger, but rarely starvation. But what the famine did do was to make young Irishmen and women consider their fate in their home country—as deep as the connections were—and contemplate moving to lands of supposedly greater opportunities. John and Mary McHale were two such people. Their new life—for better *and* for worse—would be in far-off Australia. For the remainder of their lives (and they would die in the same year, 1923), the pair would toy with the prospect of returning home to Ireland to visit their family and friends they had left behind. But they never did.

This dislocation would weigh heavily on both of them over the years, particularly on Mary, as it did for millions of Irish immigrants who had forged new lives and new stories across the seas. Mary betrayed some of those thoughts in a letter home to her sister Sarah three decades after she bade farewell to Ireland, writing in 1912:

---

23   ibid
24   Correspondence with Mary Doyle, 2010

"I often grieve at being so far away from you and my native land, and my loving parents whom I will never forget till I die. I wish often that I never left home."[25]

For John McHale, there was a bit of symmetry about the birth of his first child on December 12, 1882. Three years earlier—to the day—he had left Plymouth bound for Australia. But with the arrival of his son James, named after John's grandfather, and with plans for more children, John realised he needed a steadier income than the one normally provided for a labourer. As such, he signed on to be a probationary constable—No.4452—on May 17, 1883, with the New South Wales police force. His employment record describes him as he was, almost as if he was standing in front of you: "six foot, blue eyes, brown hair, (with a) fresh complexion."[26]

It also detailed that he was married, was previously a labourer, was a native of Ireland, and was a Roman Catholic. But there was one notable mistake. Perhaps it was an intentional one. John was listed as being born in 1858—four years after his actual birth—in a sure sign that he was worried that his 29 years might have been an age impediment to gaining a new career in the police force. Once in, he adapted to the position with relative ease. Within three months of signing on, he was appointed an ordinary constable on August 1, 1883.

A letter that arrived from Ireland in early 1884 only served to emphasise the tyranny of distance that stood between John and Mary's new life, and their families back home. Just as the McHale family was

---

25   Correspondence with Mary Doyle, 2010. An earlier attempt at a biography on
     'Jock' McHale confused John McHale with James McHale, the New South Wales
     policeman who was involved in the capture of bushranger Johnny Dunn, who was
     an associate of Ben Hall, in 1865. But John was only 11 then, and was still in Ireland.
     That was 15 years before Jock's father even arrived in Australia.
26   John McHale, police record, NSW Archives

starting to make a fist of their life in a new country, the news from Emlagh would be devastating. Two of John's sisters, Sarah and Mary, had married brothers Anthony and Michael O'Malley, who lived across the water on Clare Island. In late December 1883 the O'Malley brothers had sailed across to Emlagh, along with Sarah's nine-year-old daughter, Alice.

The patriarch of the family, Austin McHale, insisted that Alice stay until after the New Year, so that he could head to the fair, where he intended to buy some new shoes for his granddaughter. Years later, Alice's daughter, Ciss Salter, would document the tragedy that followed, as was passed down through the family lore over the years: "It was a showery day when the boat left Emlagh to return to the island, and included in the party now was Michael McHale, who was going to the island to buy some cattle. They had left some time when the weather developed into a very heavy squall. My great-grandmother, Mrs McHale, said to my mother that it was a very bad one, and that she hoped the men would be all right."[27] They were not all right. The boat went down in the squall and there were no survivors.

John McHale had lost a brother, and two of his sisters had lost their husbands, and their means of support. In a letter to Sarah almost 30 years later, he would write of the "the terrible calamity of the drowning of your dearly beloved husband (Anthony), and my dear brother Michael, and Michael O'Malley (may the Lord have mercy on their souls). It was the means of shortening the lives of my dearly beloved parents. My poor mother was so tender hearted she could not stand it."[28]

It has long been known that Jock McHale started life in Sydney, but what has never been revealed before was his family's move to Coonabarabran (450km north-west of Sydney) in either late 1883 or early 1884, and then to Warialda (almost 600km north of Sydney)

---

27   *The Clare Island Drowning,* Ciss Salter
28   Letter, John McHale to his sister Sarah O'Malley, July 24, 1912

almost four years after that. These moves came about because of his father John's postings with the New South Wales police force. He was appointed the acting gaoler of the Coonabarabran lock-up.

As much as the influx of people to the region brought about improved facilities and resources in the 1880s, it was still a "wild place"[29] when the McHales arrived in town. Liquor was a serious problem in the district, and this caused much of the patronage of the prison cells that John McHale tended. Coonabarabran, according to a local history, was known as "a drinking man's town ... the reputation of the hotels had not changed. The magistrates saw the same old faces for the same old offences. The new sly grog shops mostly managed to escape the eagle eye of the law. Occasionally the case of a travelling hawker with a few jugs of home brew hidden amongst his pots, pans and fancy goods came to the attention of the bench. Some of the more sober members of the community were not at all impressed by the amount of alcohol which the town seemed to consume. The wives of some prominent members of the community had already brought their husbands before court to have the sale of liquor to them forbidden."[30]

A temperance group from Gunnedah came to Coonabarabran in 1886 to try to set up a local branch to save the community from the five hotels, the countless sly-grog shops and the itinerant hawkers selling their potions to the public. But it never worked, and doubtlessly John McHale was kept busy in his line of employment.

When the McHales had taken the long coach ride to Coonabarabran, Mary was pregnant. On March 1, 1884, a second son arrived. He was named John Joseph, after his father, and came into the world with the assistance of a nurse, Mrs Rowland. James Francis was now 15 months old. John and Mary, and their two sons, would have been in attendance on the gala occasion when Coonabarabran officially became a town in the weeks after John's first birthday, on March 20, 1885.

---

29   Correspondence with Jewell Toynton, 2010

30   *Coonabarabran: As it was in the beginning*, Joy Pickette and Mervyn Campbell, 1983

Five months later, on August 26, 1885, the family welcomed a baby sister, Mary Winifred. In the fertile tradition of Catholic families of the time, Mary was back carrying another child by the middle stages of 1886. But expectation was interrupted when young Mary Winifred came down with whooping cough. The heavily pregnant Mary and John desperately called in one of the town's two doctors, Dr Loughnan, to try to save the life of their beloved daughter. There were also fears the highly contagious disease could be passed on to the other two children.

Described as "a tireless and energetic man,"[31] Dr Loughnan had developed a reputation for taking on, and sometimes curing, hopeless cases. On one such occasion he drove his buggy through the night to reach a seriously ill patient. By the time he had emerged from the house, his horse was dead from exhaustion in its shafts. He had saved the patient, but lost the horse. Locals had a saying in Coonabarabran in the 1880s: "Never fear, Loughnan's coming."[32] But, as well regarded and respected as Dr Loughnan was, there was nothing he could do to save Mary Winifred McHale. She passed away in the early hours of one morning late in November 1886, with her distraught parents by her side.

The headstone that still survives in the Roman Catholic section of the Coonabarabran Cemetery is a simple but stark reminder of the grief suffered: "In Loving Memory of Mary Winifred. Daughter of John and Mary McHale. Aged 15 months." James's fourth birthday, which occurred two weeks after his sister's death, would have been a solemn occasion. Infant mortality rates had fallen at that time to 115.9 per 1000 births.[33] But that meant nothing to the McHale family, who had lost a significant part of their lives. On Christmas Eve 1886, Mary delivered another baby girl, Sarah

---

31 ibid
32 ibid
33 *Australia Through Time*, Random House, 1994. According to the *Sydney Morning Herald* (May 24, 2010) for every 1000 children born in Australia now, 4.7 will die before the age of five.

Jane. As wonderful as it was to have a new baby in the household again, it could never erase the pain of losing a child.

Indeed, it may have been grief that played a role in why the McHale family left Coonabarabran. John gained a transfer to Warialda, on the banks of the Reedy Creek, which was less than 150km from the Queensland border. But if McHale thought the move would be a peaceful one, he would be sorely mistaken. The small town was the centre of a bizarre murder, and he would have to arrest the perpetrator. It happened in early March 1888—just six weeks after the centenary celebrations of the landing of the First Fleet—and it would shake the small community into fear.

As the *New South Wales Police Gazette* documented: "Alfred Merritt, alias Happy Jack, charged with the wilful murder of James Osborne, alias James Doherty, at Warialda on 3rd instant, has been arrested by Constable McHale ... Committed by the District Coroner for trial at Tamworth Circuit Court."[34] The case was a particularly messy one. Merritt, who had several other aliases, "plunged a sheath knife into the heart of a mate, a jockey named Jas Osborne or Doherty. Death was instantaneous. The diabolical deed, for which no motive could be assigned, has caused intense horror in this small community."[35]

It later emerged that that the pair had come to Warialda from Armidale, 190km away. Staying at the Royal Hotel, Osborne went into Merritt's room and it was supposed that he tried to rob his friend while he was on the bed. *The Sydney Morning Herald* said that "Merritt rose from his bed, and seizing the deceased, threw him on his back, his head against the footboard of the bed, and while having him in that position, stabbed him through the heart ... Merritt then got up, and coming out on to the verandah he held up his hand, the knife reeking with blood, and exclaimed: 'I have done for him, I have killed him'."[36]

---

34   NSW Police Gazette, March 14, 1888
35   *The Sydney Morning Herald*, March 6, 1888
36   ibid

Mary was pregnant at the time. A few months later, Michael Patrick McHale, the fifth child of the family, was born. At about this time, John decided he had had enough of the police force. He resigned on May 21—almost five years after joining. The McHales—father John, mother Mary, and children James, John, Sarah and Michael—were on the move again, this time to Melbourne, in Victoria. For five-and-a-half-year-old James, he was about to go on another adventure—where a football club that didn't even exist yet would ultimately change his life.

CHAPTER 2

Young James

1889-1902

Melbourne was hurtling along on an unprecedented economic boom when the McHale family landed on its doorstep in June 1888. What no one, least of all John and Mary, knew was that the city was at the back end of the period of unparalled prosperity. The city had undergone a transformation during the 1880s, a period in which its citizens had embarked on an ambitious building program that would earn it the title of 'Marvellous Melbourne'. It was claimed to be the seventh largest city in the British Empire and was widely considered, according to Don Garden's history of Victoria, to be "a fast, flashy, prosperous metropolis which dominated the colony's economy".[1]

In that decade, Victoria was "spiralling upwards in a heady boom ... without equal in Australian history. The confidence in the future of Victoria, especially Melbourne, brought British investors flooding in. Melbourne boomed as money became readily available for any purpose, public or private, soundly based or speculative."[2] There was

---

1   *Victoria, A History,* Don Garden, Nelson, 1984
2   ibid

seemingly no shortage of capital for construction of new buildings, many of them with ornate fixtures, on new facilities for the swelling populace, and for a transport infrastructure that would have been the envy of many more well-established cities around the world.

Victoria's population increased by 278,000 between 1881 and 1891, and 209,000 of them—almost 75 per cent—chose Melbourne as their home. The biggest single intake of the decade came in 1888, the year that the McHale family made their journey south. John and Mary and their children James, John, Sarah and Michael were part of an influx of 46,000 that year.

Sadly for John and Mary, just nine months after arriving in Melbourne, and only a few months after James's sixth birthday, the family's youngest child, Michael, died from a severe bout of gastroenteritis. He had lived for only 10 months.

It was not stated in the death certificate how long his body had fought the illness, but not even the presence of a Dr Wood at the family home on the day of his death could make a difference. The McHales were living at 78 Neill Street, Carlton, at the time. It was March 18, 1889.

John McHale, who listed his profession on the death certificate as a labourer, solemnly went in to register his son's death the following day, documenting all the details that were required to close a life that had barely begun. On the same day, the McHale family gathered at the nearby Melbourne General Cemetery to farewell their boy.

James had now lost two siblings. Sadly, there would be more tragedy to come.

James would have started his schooling in the early months of 1889. The first school that he went to was St Brigid's, on the corner of Nicholson Street and Alexandra Parade in North Fitzroy. It was only a few hundred metres from the family home. The bluestone St Brigid's church had been built in 1870, with two side aisles added in 1881 and 1885, and it was most likely the location for the funeral of Michael McHale on the day after his death.

There was a strong Irish connection in the area, and a speech from two visiting Irish nationalist MPs, John Deasy and Sir Thomas Esmonde, in July 1889 attracted more than 600 people and filled the classroom at St Brigid's. Deasy held the seat of West Mayo, the region of John's birth. His speech was one of great passion on the Irish issue of independence from Britain; the Irish wanted Home Rule. "He spoke about the condition of Irishmen. The tenant farmers, he contended, had reclaimed the land from bog, marsh and moorland, barren hillsides had been converted into productive homesteads, and these, not the landlord, deserved credit for the labour. If the effort of the sons of Ireland were united, there would soon be ushered in a new and a better era for the downtrodden nation."[3]

A month earlier, at Mrs Harriet Pryde's City Hotel in Johnston Street, Collingwood, there was a gathering that would play a major role in the future direction of the life of six-year-old James McHale. The gathering was designed to create a senior football team for Collingwood, a struggling inner-city working class suburb that had had enough of its residents leaving the district to play football. *The Argus* reported: "A large and influential meeting of the citizens of Collingwood was held ... to consider the advisability of starting a senior football club. The Hon. G.D. Langridge said it was a disgrace that Collingwood did not possess a senior football or cricket club; a number of the senior clubs of other suburbs were manned by Collingwood players, it having been the training ground for them. He trusted that the Britannia (junior) Club would see their way clear to start one. Cr Beazley, M.L.A., also spoke in favour of the motion and stated it was his firm opinion that the Collingwood Council would do its best to further the interest of the club and provide them with a suitable playing ground."[4]

---

3   *The Argus*, July 25, 1889
4   *The Argus*, June 13, 1889

George Langridge and William Beazley were appointed to approach the Britannia club with the proposal. The sentiment was strong. The Collingwood Football Club had a name. But it did not yet have a competition to play in. The hurdle came when the Victorian Football Association refused to grant the club permission to join the competition. Still, those associated with the push would not give in. The community spirit and civic pride that would become such a significant part of the Collingwood club in the future ensured that this setback was not an end. It was only a beginning.

Within three years, at the start of 1892, the club that would become known as the most famous football team in the country was finally granted admission to play. And within 14 years of that meeting in 1889, James, or 'Jim', McHale would start his association with Collingwood that would last for the rest of his life.

On November 10, 1889, Mary gave birth to a daughter, Margaret Eileen, this time at 28 Neill Street, Carlton, with the assistance of a Dr Fenwick. John had changed jobs. He was listed as a railway employee, an occupation that he would fill for much of the remainder of his life.

In the days leading up to Margaret's birth, Melbourne had enormous interest in a racehorse called Carbine, known as 'Old Jack', who would carry the heaviest impost of any horse in the 29-year history of the Melbourne Cup, already the country's most famous race. Ordinary people with little more than a passing interest in the sport of kings took it all in. In Collingwood, a young man with big dreams was revelling in the biggest moment of his 19 years.

He was also the son of Irish immigrants. But this one-time boot-maker from the Whybrows factory had followed an old racing maxim from journalist Nat Gould—"back a good horse and a good jockey, and damn the weight"[5]—to invest his savings on Carbine long before the weights had been announced for the race. His mates chided him when 'Old Jack' was burdened with 10 stone and five pounds (almost 66kg).

---

5   *John Wren: A life reconsidered*, James Griffin, Scribe, 2004

But the young man insisted that the race would be the foundation stone of his fortune, and when Carbine saluted, he was reputed to have won £180. (A five-room house in the inner suburbs cost £400 at this time).

Years later, the man would recall it was his "first substantial win on anything ... I wasn't quite twenty, but Carbine brought me good luck."[6] The young man's name was John Wren, and although he had never met James McHale—whom he would later call Jock—and would not for some years to come, their lives would interconnect until their dying days.

By the early 1890s, there was an ominous feel to the way in which the economy and business confidence was playing out. Truth be known, there had been worrying signs in the late 1880s that the economic prosperity was headed towards a none-too-palatable conclusion. There were rallies and a few recoveries, but from the early 1890s, there was serious trouble brewing.

The boom that had driven tens of thousands of people to make Melbourne their new home was well and truly over by 1892. Within a three-year period, the city's population had dropped by as much as 56,000 as people deserted, according to Don Garden, "the depressed city, with its hungry, workless men, its profitless industries, its timid government struggling to make the budget balance, no matter the cost in human values."[7]

The city was shaken by the collapse of a number of financial institutions. By then, the battle of the working class and, indeed, most of the middle class was to simply survive. What made matters even more perilous was the fact that there was no such thing as social security or welfare payments to ease the suffering of so many families. Fortunately for John McHale and his family, he was able to keep his job with the Victoria Railways for the duration of the depression.

6   *The Real John Wren*, Hugh Buggy, Widescope, 1977
7   *Victoria, A History*, Don Garden, Nelson, 1984

The job even facilitated a brief move to Centre Road, East Brighton, where another son, George Alfred, was born on August 22, 1892.

The effects of the 1890s depression would have far reaching ramifications for the people and the institutions of Melbourne. Garden's history of the state argued that many of those changes came about because of the economic obliteration of the time: "The depression of the 1890s was a pivotal point in Victoria's history. Before the economic calamity, Victoria was notable as being progressive, optimistic, probably the most advanced of the colonies and politically liberal. Afterwards, Melbourne, and perhaps Victoria as a whole, was greatly changed. Material progress was slower, the breezy optimism gone; they were chastened, quieter and in the future to become more staid and conservative. Sydney survived the depression much better and was to carry into the 20th century much of the confidence and drive lost in the collapse of marvellous Melbourne."[8] Some Sydneysiders revelled in the plight of their southern neighbour, referring to it as "Smellboom."[9]

In 1892, at the point where the bottom had fallen out of the economy, the Collingwood Football Club was founded. Just as organisations and institutions were going out of business, the Magpies were trying to gain a foothold in Melbourne's world of football.

Collingwood's acceptance as a team for the VFA was the culmination of three years of hard work. Just as the new club was readying itself for the challenge, the Britannia Football Club was disintegrating. At a bitter meeting at the Grace Darling Hotel, in Smith Street, in early 1892, the Brittania club effectively disbanded. Some of the remnants went to Fitzroy; only a handful of players and a sprinkling of supporters chose to support the fledgling Collingwood club.

8   ibid
9   ibid

Any fears that the actual support might not match the promised support were quashed at a meeting at the Collingwood Town Hall on February 12, 1892. There were so many people in attendance that some had to follow the events through an opened window. Beazley chaired the meeting, and he enthusiastically told the gathering that the Collingwood club would "draw immense crowds and be the cause of much money being spent in the district".[10] Another speaker, John Hancock, MP, claimed the club would soon be "the premier team— for the very name Collingwood would strike terror into the hearts of opposition kickers."[11]

On the same day as the meeting took place, the local newspaper *The Mercury* reported: "There were 60,000 men, the bone and sinew of the colony, walking the streets of the metropolis and suburbs, idle and penniless."[12] James McHale was not yet 10.

After almost 15 years of near-constant movement from abode to abode, the McHale family finally settled on a suburb to call their own in late 1893 or early 1894, and it would be the one where John and Mary would remain for the rest of their lives. Their eldest son James would only move as far as the adjoining suburb, Brunswick, and briefly, to Essendon, in his last years.

Coburg, described only a few years earlier as "a very pretty suburb with country lanes and charming little valleys everywhere ... the district is strictly dairy and poultry farming with cultivated paddocks and farm houses, giving it an English rural appearance,"[13] would be the place where the McHale family would settle. Initially, they would live in Sheffield Street, which was just off the main thoroughfare and

---

10   *Collingwood Illustrated Encyclopedia*, Michael Roberts and Glenn McFarlane, Slattery and Lothian Books, 2004

11   ibid

12   *Mercury*, February 12, 1892

13   *Almost Pretty, A history of Sydney Road*, Laura Donati, 2005

business district of Sydney Road, and only a few kilometres from Pentridge Prison. It was there that John and Mary welcomed another child, Dorothy Catherine, on September 26, 1894.

Coburg had initially been known as Pentridge before the citizens rallied to change the name in 1870 to rid themselves of the negative connotations relating to the penal establishment. Like most of Melbourne, Coburg and Brunswick had swelled with new residents throughout the 1880s. Brunswick's population rose from 6222 in 1881 to 21,955 a decade later; Coburg's went from 2659 to 5794.[14]

New estates were created, many of them feeding off Sydney Road, which was described as "a place of movement, commotion and bustle ... with late night trading on Friday nights, Sydney Road became a spectacle. In the late nineteenth century, shoppers used its footpaths to talk to friends and acquaintances as they made their way from shop to shop until their arms were laden heavy with parcels. Orators assembled on street corners to lecture and prophesise to anyone who wished to stop and listen. Political views and topical issues were aired, as well as religion."[15]

But the depression left a firm imprint on the two suburbs. Some of those homes in the new estates were left idle. To emphasise the struggle in the early to mid-1890s, the Coburg council prosecuted 325 people for non-payment of their rates; Whelan the Wrecker started as a demolishing company, knocking down disused homes; and a block of land was sold for less than what it had been purchased for 50 years earlier.[16]

James McHale transferred to the school at St Paul's, in Coburg, and it would become the education base for most of his family over the years. The school and the parish church had been in operation since 1850, the year before prisoners first began arriving at the newly created prison that stood alongside it.

---

14   ibid
15   ibid
16   ibid

The redeveloped and reworked St Paul's Catholic Church was opened in November 1894. It was a significant moment for the strong Irish-Catholic community of the Coburg district. *The Argus* recorded that the church was "opened and solemnly dedicated yesterday ... it is eight months since the foundation stone was laid, and by vigorous efforts the priests in charge have succeeded in erecting a beautiful church on a commanding site in Coburg ... the Archbishop concluded by congratulating the large congregation for having erected a suitable temple for the offering of the sacrifice, despite the lingering depression."[17]

In attendance that day was the Right Reverend Monsignor, Charles O'Hea, who gave his life to the region, but who would go down in history as the man who had baptised Ned Kelly, and who would minister to him just before he was hanged in 1880—eight months after John McHale arrived in Australia.

As was the case for families at the time, the McHales moved from house to house on a regular basis. In 1895, they were living in Hardwick Street, Coburg. A year later, John and Mary moved the family to Buckingham Avenue (now Cash Street) which was just one street across, close to Sydney Road. There they would stay. The pair would die in the house within 10 months of each other almost 30 years later.

It was a time of great divide between Catholics and Protestants. On July 19, 1896, a provocative plan to stage a march through Brunswick to commemorate the Protestant victory at the Battle of the Boyne— fought between the Catholic King James and the Protestant King William in 1690—met with significant resistance. It would lead to the suburb's "most violent Green and Orange clash."[18]

The Protestants were meant to march up Sydney Road to the Wesley Church. But the hundreds of marchers met with a crowd of almost 20,000 "Irish and Catholics"[19] who were holding their own rally on the

---

17   *The Argus*, November 26, 1894

18   *Almost Pretty: A history of Sydney Road*, Laura Donati, 2005

19   ibid

vacant land next to the Sarah Sands Hotel to "euphemistically discuss the 'Irish Question' ... Orange items of clothing were like red rags to the Green crowd and were violently torn off."[20] A crowd looked on as the violence escalated and the hopelessly undermanned police tried to calm a situation that was rapidly running out of control.

The Argus reported: "It is 50 years since the last Orange riot took place in Melbourne ... (but) yesterday a fresh outburst of violence at Brunswick, on a scale of far greater magnitude, and embracing a much larger number of participants, showed that the flame of the old rancour, so far from being extinct, still burns with undiminished fury. For about three hours yesterday the extraordinary spectacle was witnessed of Protestants and Catholics—the majority of whom were natives of Australia—fighting with the ferocity of wild beasts for a politico-religious principle that has no relevance outside of Ireland."[21]

The most optimistic of the 25,000 people believed to be in attendance—both participants and the onlookers (thousands had sought vantage points)—was a socialist who brought a red flag and urged Protestants and Catholics alike to join forces against the capitalists. According to The Argus, they "simply turned their backs on him, and shook their sticks in anticipatory ecstasy."[22]

One man, James Holland, was arrested for waving a knife about, and two others, Samuel Doyle and Jeremiah Slattery, were arrested for attempting to free Holland from custody. "On all sides there were cut heads and bleeding faces, but as long sticks and stones were the only weapons used the damage seemed to be comparatively unimportant."[23] It was only the clear-thinking of clergymen on both sides of the religious divide that stopped this dangerous incident from careering out of control.

---

20   ibid
21   *The Argus*, July 20, 1896
22   ibid
23   ibid

It's not known if 13-year-old James McHale was there. But what is certain is that plenty of young boys from the region were, given it was a Sunday. They formed a large part of the curious onlookers watching this age-old problem rear its head on the streets of the supposedly safe and serene suburb of Brunswick.

The Argus said that: "As far as the eye could see the street was crowded. All the upper windows opposite the church were full of heads, there were boys and men clinging to the parapets, and projecting cornices and the verandah roofs carried a dangerous load of excited and curious mortals. The pine-trees in the church grounds formed a roosting place for a lot of lads exulting over the prospect of a diversion, from whatever quarter it might come."[24]

By now, James was a student of the Christian Brothers' College in East Melbourne. The College had been started in Victoria Parade in 1871, and came to be known as CBC Parade after the street in which it was first housed. Enrolment records have long since been lost. One report had James attending the school from 1894-1896. But it is almost certain he didn't start at the school until 1895, and the likelihood is that he stayed for longer than 1896. In later life, James—who was then called Jim or Jock—would tell people that he started at the Christian Brothers' College when he was "12 and a half", which validates the 1895 start-time as he would have turned 12 in December 1894.

The official history of Parade listed two different accounts of his years there. In one, it says McHale attended during the mid 1890s. Another reference has him finishing in 1900, which is also possible. A few accounts of McHale's early life have suggested that he continued to study until he was at least 17, which was more than a little unusual for many people of his time. But if this is true, then it goes to show

---

24   ibid

that he must have had an aptitude for education. Certainly, in later life, he spent countless hours lecturing to students through the generations of the importance of combining school with sport. It was a perfect balance, he argued with some vigour.

Whatever the case, and however long he spent at Parade, McHale was undeniably moved by his experiences. It was there, on the hard gravel playground, that he would come to develop an affinity and bond with Australian football. As it was with most educational facilities at the time, sport was only a secondary pastime, far removed from the minds of most teachers. CBC Parade was no exception in those days. As P.C. Naughin acknowledges in a history of Parade College: "Boys might play their games, but sport was always suspected as likely to distract (students) from the really important matter of schooling."[25]

But there was a champion for the case for physical education and the playing of school sport at the school at the time, Brother McGee, who had been born in County Cavan, Ireland, before migrating to South Australia. After a teaching stint in New Zealand, he came to the College in 1894 and stayed until 1901. He actively encouraged students to compete physically in an array of sports—"Sport, he thought, should be cultivated for the development of character, the physical fitness it is supposed to engender and the entree it gives to the mixed world of Australian manhood."[26]

Bob Rush, who would go on to be a Collingwood teammate, official and friend of Jock McHale's for the next half a century, was a student at least a year ahead of McHale at Parade, and he marvelled years later at how powerfully Brother McGee's philosophy had resonated with many of the students who came into connection with him.

Rush said: "The wags called him 'Maggie', certainly not in derision, but more as a term of endearment, for no teacher ever so entirely won the hearts of his pupils ... The motto *Suaviter in modo, Fortiter in re'* (Latin for "gentle in manner, resolute in excellence") aptly describes

---

25   *The Parade Story, 1871-2001*, P.C. Naughin, Parade
26   ibid

his teaching, and the boys that made no progress had but themselves to blame."[27]

Rush provided an evocative look at the playgrounds at the school when he said in 1915: "The old schoolyard was not asphalted till late in the (1898) year and though slippery enough, it was even worse then. Coarse gravel formed the surface. It would be interesting to know how much of that gravel we carried away in our hands and knees during a football season. However, judged by results, it could not have been a bad training ground, for about twenty senior footballers of the future were scattered through the various classes of that year (1898)."[28]

James McHale would be one of them. But Rush would say years later that 'Jock'—as he would become better known as—had struggled to win a place in the best side from Parade. He had only just started to learn the game, but it wouldn't take him long to master it. He was a quick learner.

Rush also gave an insight to one of the pastimes of the more daring Parade students during the 1890s. In 1893 John Wren, that young man who had wagered on Carbine and won his fortune, set about the ambitious plan of starting up a "tote" thinly disguised as a "tea shop" in the heart of Collingwood, to allow punters to wager on the horses.

The front of the shop was in Johnston Street, and it backed on to Sackville Street: "(The) site of the tote was a two-storeyed brick shop just where Johnston Street drops rather steeply on to the river plain of the Collingwood flats ... in its early humble beginnings punters entered the tote from Johnston Street. Later, betting was conducted in a large yard behind the shop. That yard could be entered from Sackville Street. A solid fence twelve feet high, reinforced with iron staunchions, was run up on the Sackville Street frontage. A second fence of heavy timbers formed an inner defence rampart."[29]

---

27   *The Paradian*, 1915, Bob Rush
28   ibid
29   *The Real John Wren*, Hugh Buggy, Widescope, 1977

The mystery of who actually owned and operated the tote fascinated most Melburnians who knew of its existence, and perhaps led to the mystique surrounding John Wren for the remainder of his life. But the people of Collingwood knew. Many of them had a vastly contrasting view of the gambling man than did many of the wowsers of Melbourne who fought to have 'Wren's Tote', as it would become known, closed down for good.

The students of the College knew, as Rush would have you believe. He claimed that a number of pupils used to run the risk of getting in trouble from the Brothers by heading down Wellington Street and trying to get a wager on down at the tote.

Rush said: "Wren's totalisator was in the heyday of its career, and engendered a racing spirit in the boys from the nearer suburbs. One or two of us had the 'open sesame' for the famous Collingwood tea shop and wood yard, so many a sixpence or shilling was invested on 'certainties'. (Another schoolmate) Billy Devereux was chief commissioning agent, while the Flemington boys generally brought the latest racing gossip to school."[30] However, the Brothers found out and began to enforce a stringent rule about remaining on the school grounds during the lunch break.

The McHale family continued to grow, yet tragedy was never too far removed. Another daughter, Winifred Lillian, was born in June 1897, but she died in Buckingham Avenue 18 months later, on December 14, 1898, from double pneumonia. James had turned 14 two days before her death.

There would be two more children to come. Another daughter, Alice (or Alicia) Louisa, was born on May 25, 1899, and another son, Edward William, was born on August 16, 1902. When Edward was born, Mary

---

30   *The Paradian*, 1915, Bob Rush

was 45. Her span of producing children had fallen only four months short of 20 years. She had produced 12 children, eight of which were to survive childhood. John, still a railway employee, was almost 50.

The birth certificate of Mary's last child—filled in by her 15-year-old daughter Sarah—listed the ages of her children, as if they had all survived. Her daughter Mary would have been 16. Michael, or 'Mick', as it referred to him as, would have been 13. Winifred, or 'Lillian', would have been five.

In a letter home to her family a decade later, Mary documented her grief and revealed she had also given birth to a stillborn little girl who never had a name. She wrote: "I was in trouble at the time of her birth ... she was a lovely child, so you can see for yourself, dear (sister) Sarah that I had a bone to pick. I had a lot to contend with in Australia. My life was everything but happy."[31]

There was another member of the McHale household at the time, but he forms one of a number of mysteries surrounding Jock's story. He was Robert Paul McHale. No birth certificate can be found for him. His death certificate shows he was born in New South Wales in around 1890, and lived there until he was about six. All through that stage, John and Mary and their family were living in Melbourne. He came to live with the McHale family in the late 1890s and became a part of the family, living in Buckingham Avenue until he was married.

It is not known whether he was a blood relative or not. He was not mentioned as a child in two surviving letters written home to Ireland by John and Mary in 1912. But Robert listed John as his next of kin on a war enlistment form, and on his death certificate in April 1971, the mystery is maintained. It lists his father as "Unknown McHale" and his mother as "Unknown McHale". Whatever the case, he worked

---

31   Letter, Mary McHale to her sister Sarah, December 12, 1912

in the Victorian Railways, along with other members of the McHale family, including John, and he called himself Jock's "brother" for the rest of his life.

On leaving school, James McHale, or Jim, as he was being increasingly called, embarked on two new careers. Both of them would be long and fruitful.

The first was in regard to his employment. He started work in 1901 with one of the state's oldest breweries, McCracken's.

McCracken's Brewery had been a Victorian institution since 1851, when brothers Robert and Peter McCracken, along with James Robertson, founded the company and, according to *The Amber Nectar*, "moved [it] into the west end of Collins Street when it was just bush and scrub ... for half a century they produced some of the best beer in Melbourne, they had a huge Victorian Gothic establishment right opposite the Rialto building and just around the corner from St James' Cathedral before it was moved."[32]

At the time Jock got his start, the company was run by Alex McCracken, who was the son of Robert. He also held a high position in Melbourne society for a number of reasons, not the least of which being that he had been an Essendon Football Club secretary and later president, and was the first president of the newly formed (in October 1896) Victorian Football League, a position he held until his death in 1915, when he was replaced on an interim basis by Charles Brownlow.

Jock would work in a brewery into the last year of his life. It's likely that he would have used the cable tram from Coburg, where a terminus was established in 1887, to get to and from work. According to a history of Sydney Road, "the system suited densely populated Brunswick, as the fares were inexpensive, the service regular and the stops were frequent ... When a driver or gripman wished to stop, he simply pulled a lever which dis-attatched the cable once again."[33]

---

32   *The Amber Nectar, A celebration of beer and brewing in Australia*, Keith Dunstan, Viking O'Neill, 1987

33   *Almost Pretty, A history of Sydney Road*, Laura Donati, 2005

The second pertained to the game he had learned to love at school. He resolved to play for the new local junior team in Coburg. He started at the turn of the century, and was beginning to play some seriously good football with them.

The 1901 preview for Coburg was all positive. The *Coburg Advertiser* said: "The Coburg Football Club gives every indication of proving a strong and representative combination, as during the short existence of the club, which is competing for the Victorian Junior Football Association premiership, a large number of footballers, whose fame on the field is well known to the followers of this interesting winter sport have entered the club, who will on Saturday next open the season by playing the West Richmond club on the Recreation Reserve, where the controlling committee desire to see a large gathering of residents."[34]

Several weeks later, according to the *Coburg Advertiser*, the Footscray juniors ventured to Coburg and "adopted very questionable tactics and resorted to very rough play ... During the game the umpire took the names of several (Footscray) players with the intention of reporting them to the Association for bad language and rough play."[35] It didn't worry the 18-year-old Jim. He was "amongst those deserving of special mention", having kicked all three of Coburg's goals.

McHale also played cricket for a junior Coburg team, the Royal Stars. He would become firm friends with a young man three years his junior, who played with a Brunswick team. That man's name was John Curtin, who would later become one of Australia's greatest Prime Ministers at a time of crisis for the country during World War II. The pair would keep in contact for the rest of their respective careers, despite living in different states for much of the last few decades of their lives.

As much as McHale loved cricket, and had ambitions of one day playing for Australia, and as much as he fancied himself as a foot-runner, it was football that seemed to be his strength. He was making

---

34   *Coburg Advertiser*, May 4, 1901
35   *Coburg Advertiser*, June 8, 1901

a real impression for his local team, predominantly as a forward. In a game against Collingwood Juniors at Victoria Park, the *Coburg Advertiser* recorded: "In the first half of the match the Collingwood team completely run (sic) over their opponents."[36] But it was noted that "McHall (sic) was decidedly applauded ... (he) was Coburg's goalist."[37]

By 1902, McHale had designs on moving up to the VFL competition. He got his chance to show off his wares when he was selected for the VJFA representative side that was to play against Essendon, the team that had beaten the Collingwood side in the previous year's VFL Grand Final. He had attracted more than a few accolades and people were watching him closely, but some newspapers referred to him as 'McKale'. After another game, it was said "M'Hale, Coburg's champion goalkicker, is displaying his old form."[38] He would work hard for Coburg during the 1902 season, just waiting for his chance at the top level.

Football folklore has it that McHale was first spotted kicking a ball around at an inner-city wood-yard by former Collingwood committeeman Jack Duncan. It is not known if this was fact or apocryphal. If it did happen, it was likely to have occurred in late 1902, when the VFL season was already well under way. For McHale was undoubtedly offered the chance to try out with Collingwood late in that season. But he didn't make the team. He was rejected and returned to Coburg, to play out the season there.

---

36   *Coburg Advertiser*, June 22, 1901
37   ibid
38   *Coburg Advertiser*, May 31, 1902

The Magpies were on the way to their first VFL premiership. It would have been an exceedingly tough time to try and break into the Collingwood team. Having won the 1896 VFA premiership, the Magpies had been competitive in the early years of the VFL competition.

But Collingwood had stumbled on a remarkable new style of play on a "business holiday" to Tasmania in July 1902. The club had taken a mid-season trip across Bass Strait, and they returned with a new style that would not only hand them a decided advantage on rival teams, it would change the way the game was played. In one of two exhibition matches played there, the teams were so uneven that one of Collingwood's most controversial characters, Dick Condon, began to experiment with a series of short kicks. A few of his teammates, most notably Charlie Pannam and Ted Rowell, joined in the fun. When the side returned to Melbourne, the tricks became a tactic that the Magpies would fashion as their own.

The stab-kick, a new and inventive way of passing the ball to a teammate, ended the stop-start brand of football that had long been the style. Collingwood would claim for decades that this systematic style was the reason for the club's wonderful successes.

As the club's first history, written by renowned journalist Percy Taylor in 1949, explained: "A necessary adjunct of the stab was the ability to lead out for the pass, as the stab kick—a fast moving, half distance kick that rarely went higher than five or six feet—gave the man in front easily the best chance of taking the mark ... The new method was probably the greatest upward move football had received up to that period. Football as a science can be said to have begun with the discovery of the stab kick."[39]

So the fact that McHale was overlooked at his first shot is perhaps not surprising. But the characteristics that he had developed in his formative years, such as determination and persistence, meant that the next time an opportunity presented itself he would leave nothing to chance.

---

39   *Collingwood Football Club, 1892-1948*, Percy Taylor

CHAPTER 3

Becoming a Magpie

1903-1906

J im McHale made a resolution around the time of his 20th birthday. He decided to give up smoking. It was a tough call, but almost intuitively he knew he had to make it to further his sporting opportunities, and to chase the VFL dream that had eluded him at Collingwood in late 1902. Almost half a century later, he would look back on his extraordinary time in the game, and say his decision to quit smoking had played a significant role in his longevity in the game.

It's not certain how long McHale had been smoking, but if he was like many young Australians he would have started in his early teens. After all, it was only a decade earlier that Australian writer Henry Lawson made a statement that "the average Australian boy is a cheeky brat with ... a craving for cigarettes and no ambition beyond the cricket and football fields."[1]

Twice late in his life the significance of McHale's decision to quit cigarettes would be made. In 1950, *The Argus* wrote of him: "One of the

---

1   *Australia Through Time*, Random House, 2000

best things he did for his football was to give up smoking at 20 in the days when cigarettes cost 3d for (a packet of) 25. He took his doctor's advice and hasn't had a cigarette since. 'And it's harder to give up than beer', McHale added."[2] Then, on McHale's death in 1953, respected journalist Hugh Buggy recalled the time the legendary Collingwood figure told him: "You've got to be moderate in everything, especially smoking. I gave up cigarettes in 1902, when I was 20."[3]

McHale didn't mind a beer. As a brewery worker, it was one of the perks of his profession. He still worked for McCracken's Brewery, and remained living with his parents and siblings in Buckingham Avenue, Coburg.

But he knew that the smokes were not assisting him in becoming the best footballer he could possibly be.

McHale also had no issue with the fact that Collingwood had initially overlooked him. He explained later: "I first came to Collingwood in 1902, but was hardly good enough for the team that year."[4]

Just as he had the previous year, McHale was selected in a combined VJFA side to compete against the reigning premier in a match before the start of the season. This time that team was Collingwood, and he was determined to prove that he was more than up for the challenge.

As he recalled: "Next year (1903), however, I was down to training and had a good chance of gaining inclusion in the side. Playing for a combined junior team against Collingwood who were then champions, I was placed in the centre against the famous Fred Leach. Ordinarily I was placed (at) half forward, but (former Collingwood player) Billy O'Brien, a shrewd judge of football, told me to play in the centre as he

2   *The Argus*, April 6, 1950
3   *The Argus*, October 6, 1953
4   *The Sporting Globe*, May 19, 1923

considered that if I played well against Leach, I would be picked for Collingwood's training list."[5]

Leach, who was four years older than McHale, had made his VFL debut for Collingwood in 1897 and was described as "a football phenomenon around the turn of the century."[6] But facing adversity did not concern McHale, and, as nervous as he was, he performed above expectations.

In fairness to Leach, whom McHale admired immensely, he had carried an illness into the 1903 season. Leach would miss the first two home and away games and would only manage six for the season after a badly broken nose prematurely ended his year in Round 9. He would never play for the club again, and tragically would be dead before the end of the decade after contracting typhoid fever.

Modestly, McHale said later: "I played well, being in good nick with the (foot) running at the time."[7] It was better than that. He had competed well against a player who was the epitome of a class centreman. As McHale walked back to the pavilion with a sense of satisfaction etched on his face, he was greeted with the news he had long wanted to hear. He recalled: "The secretary, Mr E. Copeland, informed me that I was a certainty for the twenty five. There was no happier man in Melbourne than myself."[8]

A week after playing against Collingwood, McHale was named in two sides in the various newspapers: one with the Magpies in a practice game with Footscray; the other with the combined VJFA side against Richmond. There was never any doubt about which side he was going to play for.

---

5   ibid
6   *A Century of the Best*, Michael Roberts, Collingwood Football Club, 1991
7   *The Sporting Globe*, May 19, 1923
8   ibid

McHale had developed into a good athlete. He was a 'Collingwood six-footer', as the expression would be in the years to come. He stood at 180cm (about five foot 11 inches), just a fraction under his father's six foot, and he weighed in at about 78kg.

When he was reflecting on this initiation to Victoria Park, McHale would make the mistake of saying Condon was the coach when he arrived in 1903. The Magpies didn't have a coach that season. It wouldn't be until the following year when retired great Bill Strickland, who had captained the team to the 1896 VFA premiership, became Collingwood's first coach. But Condon would be the coach in 1905 and 1906.

Coaches were, like the motor car, a relatively new phenomenon, with an as-yet undefined importance. The legendary Jack Worrall was considered the first VFL coach when he took over as Carlton's "secretary" in 1902. In a book describing the history of leading VFL coaches, it was said that he "used to put on football gear and run instructional training on the ground, by 'moonlight', as one old-timer put it ... Nobody until Worrall had been given all of the modern coach's jobs—recruiting and rebuilding the team, supervising fitness and devising winning tactics."[9]

Worrall introduced iron discipline and structure. Later on, the Carlton coach famously said that: "Boys, booze and football do not mix. You have to cut back on one or the other. Players who prefer beer to eucalyptus will be struck off the list."[10]

The lack of a coach did not hinder Collingwood in 1903. The Magpies had a veritable wealth of experienced players. McHale, who was described by *The Herald* as a "good place (kick) man"[11] would reflect: "There were many great players in Collingwood (colours) at the time. Ted Rowell was in his prime and could kick a place kick fifty or sixty yards every time without difficulty. The Lockwoods (Ted

9   *Footy's Greatest Coaches*, Stephanie Holt and Garrie Hutchinson,
10 *This Football Century*, Russell Holmesby and Jim Main, Wilkinson Books, 1996
11 *The Herald*, May 1, 1903

and George) were great players, while a young man could not fail to pick up points from stalwarts such as Dick Condon, Eddie Drohan, G (eorge) Angus, (Alf) 'Rosie' Dummett, Bob Rush and (Bill) Proudfoot."[12]

Lawrence 'Lardie' Tulloch was the captain; Charlie Pannam the vice-captain. Jack Monohan had long been an important player. There were other players, too, who played key roles in the system that set Collingwood apart from the rest of the competition, and officials worked assiduously on ensuring that advantage continued on the other side of the fence. Collingwood was only 11 years old as a football club, but it was already playing like a hardy veteran well beyond its years and entrenched in the game. The support it had garnered, and the laurels that it had won (the 1896 VFA pennant and the 1902 VFL premiership) were already the envy of many.

McHale—at 20 years and 141 days—*did* win selection to make his debut in the opening game of 1903. It was the first of 261 games he would play for the Magpies, and fittingly, it came up against Carlton. He had lived in that suburb on the border with Fitzroy when his family had first come to Victoria 15 years earlier. Now he was playing with Collingwood, at Carlton's home ground, Princes Park, not more than a few kilometres from the Neill Street residence where the McHale family had first lived in Melbourne.

Worrall's Blues won by 21 points. As 'Observer' summed it up in *The Argus*: "The result was a sore blow for the followers of the 'Magpies', many of whom, however, declared it to be expected, as there were too many 'passengers' or 'has beens'. Carlton's forwards were too clever for Collingwood's defence. McHale, a new Collingwood player, is well worth his place in the team, but with one or two exceptions, the Magpies disappointed their supporters."[13]

It was a harsh assessment given the fact that Collingwood was missing four members of its 1902 Grand Final side. Fred Leach,

---

12   *The Sporting Globe*, May 19, 1923
13   *Collingwood Observer*, May 7, 1903

Con McCormack and George Angus were out injured, while, another, Frank 'Charger' Hailwood, had gone to Kalgoorlie for a season.

It had been a "lively contest" and the missing players proved "a handicap" to the side. *The Australasian* said the two "fresh men McHaile (sic) and (Billy) Spears (in his second game) acquitted themselves commendably."[14] Collingwood captain Lardie Tulloch had acknowledged to his Carlton counterpart Joe McShane after the game that "You beat us fair and squarely", to which McShane replied "We're going to beat many more this year."[15] McHale's first match ended in the Carlton changerooms after the Blues invited the Collingwood team in to have a few ales.

McHale spent much of his first month in black and white in the back pocket, but made an impression with some solid football. His fourth game, on May 23, 1903 was a history-making one, and one that would take the young Collingwood footballer back to the city of his birth. Collingwood and Fitzroy played the first match for premiership points outside Victoria. The Sydney match was played at the Sydney Cricket Ground, not that far from where McHale had been born, and it was meant to showcase all of the best attributes of a game that had ambitions of expanding to a bigger, national audience.

While Collingwood fans, unable to make the trip to Sydney, lamented the decision to "lose" a home game, the two clubs and the VFL rejoiced in the experience. As 'Markwell', of *The Australasian* recorded: "The trouble and expense to which Collingwood's and Fitzroy's executive had been put in connection with the undertaking were entirely lost sight of in the consequences of the immense support that had been achieved ... they (the teams) were taken by boat or by drags to all the beauty spots; they were banqueted and feasted to their hearts' content; and they were praised and thanked almost inordinately for their sacrifices in the interests of Sydney football."[16] It was said that

---

14   *The Australasian*, May 9, 1903
15   *The Herald*, May 1, 1903
16   *The Australasian*, May 23, 1903

"the certainty (was) that Australian football had found a secure footing in Sydney."

The Sydney Morning Herald said: "Special efforts are being made to assure the enjoyment of the visitors during their trip to Sydney."[17] Some of these engagements included a picnic around the Harbour, a night at Fitzgerald's Circus, a trip to Tooth's Brewery (which would have particularly impressed the brewery worker McHale), a drive to down to Sandringham with "10 drags complete with footballers" and a smoke concert at the Grand Hotel.

It was a noble quest, almost 80 years before a team would one day call Sydney home. For 20-year-old McHale, it was a memorable experience, one that made a lasting impression on him. It provided an opportunity to travel with his new teammates, and to get to know them better. He saw the camaraderie that the journey engendered; and for the rest of his days was a fierce believer in visits to other states during the season breaks.

He particularly gravitated to Ted Rowell, who became a close friend, and enjoyed the sightseeing in a city of which he had no memory. Four decades on, Rowell spoke with affection about the Collingwood side of 1903, and particularly their trip north.

As much as Collingwood enjoyed the trip, the result was not what it wanted. On the smaller, more congested SCG, Fitzroy emerged with the premiership points. Some of the game was lost on the crowd of somewhere between 18,000 and 20,000. But the enthusiasm of the fans could hardly have been denied. Even the Sydney reporters tried to paint a picture of the mood of the day.

'Onlooker', from the *Sydney Referee*, was allowed access to the rooms, giving a glimpse of what McHale experienced as he prepared for his fourth game. "While the spectators' impatience is soothed to a slight degree by the performance of an itinerant band of contortionists, keen on earning a few shillings, come with me to the dressingrooms of the gladiators. After becoming somewhat inured to the noise and flurry

---

17   *Sydney Morning Herald*, May 21, 1903

of trainers, bootmen and pungent fumes of the various embrocations which are the necessary impediments of the modern football team, turn we to the wall whereon is hung the plan of the coming battle ... a silence is presently demanded—the captain (Tulloch) jumps on a table and issues his final instructions as to the system to be pursued. 'Ere he finishes we leave the stirring scene, anxious to secure a good place to view, and shortly afterwards a hum, succeeded by a hoarse shout from thousands of throats, denotes the advent of one of the teams ... the great black and white bands of Collingwood first burst into view."[18]

The Magpies got off to an impressive start, kicking three goals to one in the opening term. But only three more goals would come for them for the rest of the game, and McHale had plenty to contend with as a wasteful Fitzroy booted 6.17 in the last three terms to win by 17 points. The Magpies were 2-2 after four rounds, but incredibly, they would not lose another game for the rest of the season, including a game against Rutherglen on the journey home.

Still, McHale was not considered for the Round 5 match against Melbourne. He returned against Geelong the following week and "defended admirably."[19] But then he missed a month before resuming in Round 12 to play for the first time on the MCG in a VFL match. Once more he was playing in defence, and Collingwood's strong win was because of the fact, according to *The Australasian*, that "their passing, foot and hand, was miles ahead of Melbourne's and their marksmanship was of a distinctly higher grade."[20]

Essendon challenged Collingwood in Round 14, leading at half-time before the powerful Magpies stormed over the top of them. *The Australasian* contended: "(Essendon's) skill, forcefulness

---

18 *The Sydney Referee*, May, 1903
19 *The Australasian*, June 13, 1903
20 *The Australasian*, June 25, 1903

and resource went nearer to demolishing Collingwood's system than anything that happened to the same company for months."[21] But the final margin in Collingwood's favour was still 27 points.

A closer challenge came from Carlton a fortnight later. Late in the contest, Carlton's Mick Grace took a mark 20 metres out, directly in front, with little time left: "With breathless interest, the multitude awaited the outcome of the kick, and Collingwood supporters in the reserve were keenly agitated, for it was almost time for the bell and a goal meant victory for Carlton."[22] But the kick—as another more famous one would later in the year—missed its target, and the winning streak rolled on.

Carlton and Fitzroy loomed as the only dangers to back-to-back flags. Having finished as the minor premier, the Magpies met the Blues in the semi-final. Under *The Argus* finals system, established in 1902, the team which finished on top of the ladder at the end of the home and away season had the right to challenge for the premiership if defeated in either the second semi-final or the Final. The Magpies had utilised that advantage a year earlier, but hoped they wouldn't have to this time around.

In the lead-up to the game against Carlton, *The Australasian* said: "Reports from the headquarters of the 'Woodsmen' go to show that, with the exception of F. Leach, who definitely relinquished the game two months ago, the whole of this season's playing strength is available and every man is in perfect condition."[23] By the end of the match, those pre-game words would have been cold comfort to McHale, who had impressed, only to be injured in the penultimate match.

In that semi-final, he had been among "a fine body of defenders,"[24] with *The Herald* saying "in their defence, McHaile (sic), right back, and Monohan, on the half line, saved their side from many a serious

---

21   *The Australasian*, August 15, 1903
22   *The Australasian*, August 22, 1903
23   *The Australasian*, September 5, 1903
24   *The Australasian*, September 12, 1903

menace."[25] It was a dour struggle, with the Magpies defenders under intense pressure "in every part of the game they (Carlton) forced the pace so hard that the much-talked of Collingwood system was entirely thrown out of gear and the Woodsmen were compelled all the time to battle (for) dear life."[26]

The Blues led by seven points going into the final term. But, like a champion team should, Collingwood rallied. A two-goal to nil last half an hour saved the match, and they closed fast to win by four points. One of the negatives of a tight, tense match was a knock suffered by McHale late in the game. He kept playing, as was the necessity in those days without an extra player as a reserve. But it would cost him the chance of playing in his first Grand Final.

The exact nature of McHale's injury has been clouded by more than a century. In those days, unless an injury was serious, it was rarely defined. The reason for absences was often left unrecorded, unless that injury had left a team short on a Saturday, or if it was of a serious nature.

McHale learnt the importance of attending training that year, saying later that "every man on the training list had to turn up for practice regularly and participate in it strenuously if he desired inclusion in the team."[27] He had attended training on 32 of the 33 nights in 1903, a feat that earned him 10/6 from the club for his dedication.[28] It would be a trait that he would follow through his years as a player, and he would demand of his players as a coach.

Perhaps the night that McHale missed was the one before the Grand Final. In the lead-up to the clash with Fitzroy, *The Herald* explained: "There has been something in the nature of 'staling' observable in the condition of the Collingwood team lately, and the committee has eased the men in their training operations during the week. Some little time ago the team went in for vapour baths as a limb loosener

---

25   *The Herald*, September 7, 1903
26   *The Australasian*, September 12, 1903
27   *The Sporting Globe*, May 19, 1923
28   Collingwood Annual Report, 1904

and general improver of condition, but this week the steaming process was discontinued. On the Tuesday night general ground practice was indulged in as usual but it was then decided that for the remainder of the week the team should rest and conserve all their energies for the match tomorrow ... on the Collingwood side, G(eorge) Lockwood had to take the place of McHale in the team."[29] McHale had played 14 games in his debut season, but would watch the Grand Final from the other side of the fence.

The Australasian described the combatants for the 1903 Grand Final between Collingwood and Fitzroy as primed and ready for action. It recorded: "Men never took to the football field in better fettle ... A glimpse into the team dressingrooms revealed men bubbling over with life and health."[30] As one of the 32,263 non-participants, McHale watched uneasily as the two teams fought out an excruciatingly close contest.

The Magpies held sway narrowly for most of the game, leading by one point at the first change, five points at half-time, and four points at the last change. *The Australasian* said that "as an exposition of artistic football the engagement fell a trifle below others in the season; but this was only to be expected in a conflict in which so much was involved."[31]

The premiership came down to the last kick, when Fitzroy's captain, Gerald Brosnan, marked and had the chance to secure the pennant for his team as the last seconds ticked before the final bell. "The premiership literally hung upon the last kick taken in the match; for if ... Brosnan had driven the ball a few further inches to the left, he would have gained a goal instead of a behind, and snatched from Collingwood their second successive premiership. And it was a shot which, in ordinary circumstances, the player would have negotiated with the greatest of certainty."[32]

---

29   *The Herald*, September 11, 1903
30   *The Australasian*, September 19, 1903
31   ibid
32   ibid

Brosnan's shot was perilously close. Ted Rowell said in *The Sporting Globe* in 1943: "The day was hot and the ground was hard, and it was a terrific battle from start to finish. The pace was fast, but the scoring low, with Collingwood always a little bit ahead. The ball was rushed forward and G. Brosnan, the most deadly of Fitzroy forwards, marked it. From where I was, it looked like a goal, but a slight current of air deflected it in the last few yards. One flag went up and the bell rang."[33]

Brosnan said he had never been "as sure as anything in his life (that it was going to be a) 'goal' ... I got my toes fairly onto the ball and the distance was just mine. But the wind got onto an almost spent ball and puffed it aside."

Full-back Bill Proudfoot was one of those closest to the ball when it made its trajectory towards goal. He would reveal years later how the lace of the ball had come so close that it grazed the post. Collingwood had won by two points to claim a back-to-back triumph, and, as the annual report would say months later: "These successes have been due in a measure to the superior class of players secured, but more so to the systematic and regular training which the players have willingly undergone."[34]

Such was Collingwood's dominance of football in 1902-03 that some critics claimed that the Magpies were pushing the professional boundaries of what was meant to be an amateur sport. In the wake of the 1903 win, *The Australasian* claimed Collingwood was "widely talked of as a team amongst which the cloven foot of veiled professionalism is permitted to freely tread. For the sake of Collingwood; for the sake of its players; for the sake of the League; and then all for the sake of football, the honour that is above winning the flag. If the rumours are true, I can forecast the alienation of the manlier elements in the club, the quick decline of football in the district, and a very serious injury to the league as a body and to the game itself through the length and breadth of Australia. There are players in the Collingwood team who

---

33   *The Sporting Globe*, June 5, 1943
34   Collingwood Annual Report, 1904

will, I feel certain, take steps to disprove the rumours that are current, and tend to discredit the club; and I am content to leave it to them to prove to the suspicious public that there is not amongst them a single individual who looks for and receives any payment for his playing."[35]

Richard Stremski's *Kill For Collingwood* documented: "Player payments at Collingwood can never be clearly delineated precisely because the club always manipulated or concealed some aspects of its expenditure. The evolution of player payments at Collingwood was unique. After 1895 Collingwood compensated its payments by providing testimonials, gifts, loans, travelling allowances, employment, team trips and a retirement scheme."[36]

Some claimed that John Wren was responsible for payments to players in those 1902-03 years. That was not correct, as Wren, having been a patron and donor in the late 1890s, appeared to be distant from the club from the end of 1901 until about 1914. Stremski's *Kill For Collingwood* said this could have had something to do with the fact that he may have had an issue with the brother of another of the club's patrons, Sir John Madden.

Wren had a few more serious things on his agenda a few months after the 1903 premiership. In November of that year, the police occupied Wren's famous Johnston Street "tote" on the morning that the lightweight Lord Cardigan beat the champion mare Wakeful to win the Melbourne Cup.

Just before the start of the 1904 season, one momentous occasion would not have escaped Jim McHale's attention. Three years on from the Federation of Australia, John Christian Watson—known as Chris Watson—became Prime Minister of Australia. He was the first Labor Prime Minister of Australia, and the world's first labour head of Government. It mattered little that Watson's time in charge was brief—only 112 days—or that he could never hope to achieve anything of great note given the party's lack of seats to implement change.

---

35   *The Australasian*, September 19, 1903
36   *Kill For Collingwood*, Richard Stremski, Allen and Unwin, 1986

After back-to-back flags, Collingwood's start to 1904 was just as promising, but by season's end they too had fallen short after a solid if inconsistent season. For McHale, it was a significant one. Having arrived at Collingwood as a forward from Coburg, and having played in defence in his first season, he would soon move to the centre. With Fred Leach gone, the Magpies were looking for a replacement, and McHale fitted the bill. He was named full-back in the opening game against Geelong at Victoria Park, where he "kicked in with great power and got his side out of difficulty."[37] On a day when the club's secretary, Mr E. L. Wilson, unfurled the pennant won the previous year, and a Collingwood brass band played, according to *The Australasian*, "choice selections" during the afternoon, McHale was an important player.

A week later, Charlie Pannam was "restored to his old place on the wing"[38] allowing the kid from Coburg to play in the centre. He filled the breach in the Round 2 win over Melbourne, and a week later in the shock loss to South Melbourne, *The Australasian* reported, he was "brilliant in (the) centre."[39] It would become his preferred position for much of his career.

That Round 3 loss ended a 17-game winning streak for Collingwood. Before that loss, McHale had been on the winning side in 14 of his first 16 matches. The result was a major surprise, as South Melbourne had lost 13 games in a row leading up to it. While McHale was a hit in the centre, the 26-point loss gave a hint of a vulnerability that had been missing from the Magpies' make-up in the preceding two years. After opening the season with successive wins, the next lot of back-to-back wins would not come until the tail end of the home and away fixture.

That inconsistent form led to the appointment of the club's first coach, Bill Strickland, late in the season, and it appeared to pay dividends. Collingwood won four games in a row from Round 14.

---

37   *The Australasian*, May 14, 1904
38   *The Australasian*, May 21, 1904
39   *The Australasian*, May 28, 1904

The 10-point win over Carlton on August 20 had black and white fans believing the season may not be a dead issue. *The Australasian* summed up the feelings of many at Victoria Park that afternoon, saying: "Collingwood had, by diligent practice and study, under Mr Strickland's capable direction, developed their system to a pitch of excellence not approached by them previously for the year."[40]

In one of those four wins, McHale kicked his first goal in black and white in his 30th game for the club. It came in a 61-point win over St Kilda that had nine goalkickers. In that game, *The Australasian* said, it was said that "Collingwood's work was systematic and intelligent; St Kilda, the reverse ... The pick of the centre line was (Eddie) Drohan, but McHale, in the centre, was good throughout."[41]

McHale continued to improve in his role as the centreman. He might not have been as aesthetic to watch as Fred Leach, but he was effective and had fashioned himself into an important player. Dedication and a commitment to training played a role. He didn't miss a training session in his second season, along with six other players, and it not only honed his skills, it lined his pockets with an extra guinea for his commitment to attending. He was in a ballot for a gold medal for the most attendances, but lost out to another former Parade College student, Bob Rush.

Despite Strickland's influence, and the turnaround in Collingwood's fortunes, Fitzroy proved too strong in the 1904 semi-final at the MCG. The Maroons led from start to finish, and despite a late rally from Collingwood, the result was never seriously in doubt. The final margin was 11 points. *The Herald* said McHale "played a telling game" in the centre.[42] His task was made easier by the fact that Fitzroy's centreman Harry Clarke was "rendered almost useless through injury sustained before the (half-time) interval."[43] That result didn't appear

---

40   *The Australasian*, August 28, 1904
41   *The Australasian*, August 20, 1904
42   *The Herald*, September 17, 1904
43   ibid

as bad when Fitzroy made easy work of Carlton in the Grand Final, winning the premiership decider by four goals.

♣

There were a few personnel changes at Collingwood in 1905. The sometimes erratic, never conservative Dick Condon was appointed as the club's coach; 'Lardie' Tulloch retired and wanted to take up umpiring, so Charlie Pannam was elected captain.

The challenge of meeting last year's premiers Fitzroy came in Round 1, and it showed the Magpies had some work to do. After a one-goal to nil first term in their favour, Collingwood slowly was overtaken by Fitzroy, and the Maroons held on to win by three points. It was a "stubborn struggle", and McHale formed part of a "strong and efficient centreline" that included George Green and Percy Gibb, a new player from Richmond.[44]

McHale was prominent a week later when he helped to set up the first goal kicked in the game against Carlton. It was one of 10 goals the Magpies kicked that day (six to Charlie Pannam) and the centreman played a role in setting many of them up in the 32-point win.

A big crowd had squeezed into the ground for the 3pm start, and it had some suggesting that a 2.30pm start might be better, given that darkness was starting to set in late in games. Most footballers still worked on the Saturday morning before heading to the football, and McHale was no exception in his ongoing role with McCrackens. One reporter from *The Australasian* wrote: "Everyone recognises that the average footballer is a worker, whose employer grinds him down to long hours for poor pay."[45]

That win over Carlton was the start of three months without a loss, and the system that had vanished for a period the previous year was clearly back. *The Australasian* said: "There was not a man on the side

---

44   Richmond did not join the VFL until 1908
45   *The Australasian*, May 20, 1905

but filled the post assigned to him as if he were born to it; and their individual and collective resourcefulness commanded the admiration of all unbiased onlookers ... they must, unless they break down, have a big say for the premiership."[46]

The Australasian pinpointed McHale as the most improved player in the team. He had adapted to the Collingwood system and the team with relative ease. It was said: "Finer football than was shown by their centreman, McHale, has not been seen at Victoria-park (sic). From end to end of the tussle he made no mistake, and on the ground, in the air, with hand and with foot, he was a brilliant and consummate artist. The champion centreman of the year will have to be a marvel to beat McHale on last week's form ... McHale had nominally for (his) immediate opponent in the centre, (Bob) Boyle, who was, I think, Carlton's first performer. As a matter of fact, the two rarely met during the afternoon and each did their finest work when the other was out of reach."[47]

After the first-round loss, 12 successive wins followed, including an important one over Fitzroy in Round 8. Condon's coaching was clearly making an impression. The system was back to its devastating best, and the training had lifted up a gear or two. The *Weekly Times* gave readers a rare pictorial insight into the club's regime during the week, with a series of images showing players engaged in various drills, practising high marking with a medicine ball placed high on the ceiling, working with a punching bag and skipping ropes, and importantly it showed how the players had practised the system of half-passes that had played such a key role in the club's early successes.

Collingwood was two games ahead of Fitzroy atop the VFL ladder heading into Round 14, just before the sectional rounds. In a surprising result, Essendon upstaged the Magpies, who kicked poorly. The final score was 10.6 (66) to 7.11 (53).

---

46 ibid
47 ibid

Perhaps the loss had something to do with the fact that the club had just returned from a mid-season sojourn to Adelaide and Broken Hill, where the team played two matches. Three more wins came in the sectional rounds, against Carlton, Melbourne and South Melbourne. It was enough to ensure the Magpies finished as minor premiers. This provided Collingwood with the security of a challenge match if it was to lose its first final. *The Argus* finals system provided the right of challenge for the team that finished on top. Few thought they would need it.

But some meticulous planning from Carlton coach Jack Worrall was responsible for a shock semi-final win over Collingwood. It started during the week when Worrall took into account every scenario that was likely to confront the Blues. *The Argus* revealed after the Blues' 46-point win over the Magpies that "Carlton had played the match several times during the week with wax matches on a table—the way in which some of the greatest battles in history are fought."[48]

Part of Worrall's strategy was to ensure that no Collingwood player was to be left unattended. Collingwood failed to kick a goal for the entire first half. The deficit was 32 points at the half-time interval, with the game effectively over.

From the early stage of his playing career, McHale was a student of team styles and strategies and he would likely have noted about how the Blues followed Worrall's plans to the letter. But Fitzroy comfortably accounted for Carlton in the following match, to set up a Grand Final contest with Collingwood able to exercise the challenge.

For McHale, it promised to provide a special moment. He had missed the Grand Final two years earlier. This time, though, he would get the chance to run out on the most important occasion of the season in what would be the first of 20 Grand Finals he would contest as a player or coach.

The supporters were excited, too. To the tune of *Little Dame Trot*, there was a popular song designed for their heroes, which gained some note in 1905. It went:

---

48   *The Argus*, September 18, 1905

So hurrah for the Magpies, for the 'Woods we will sing,
Who play the game of football the premiership to win
For they have beaten all comers in all shapes and form,
Hurrah for Collingwood who left the League to mourn.
For their Pannam, Angus and Pears play forward with fame,
And Strahan, Drohan and Incoll half-forward, play the game
While Green, McHale and Gibbie (sic), the premiers centre play;
And Monohan, Fell and Fraser, half-backs win all day.
There's Proudfoot, Rush and Dummett, the back fort in the team;
And Nash, Leach and Condon, the greatest followers. When ever seen,
All play with Collingwood Eighteen, the Eighteen of great fame,
So there's honour to those Magpies, the premiers at the game.

Special trains came from Ballarat and Bendigo for the 1905 Grand Final. Collingwood's Harry Pears needed to travel, too, as 'Kickero' from *The Herald*, observed: "(He had) signed for the shearing in the Western District recently, but he will come to Melbourne to take part in the game tomorrow, though he will have a long journey."[49] In the preparation for the contest, the Magpies sought to go in with a heavier team than the one that took the field against the Blues a fortnight earlier. They also went for experience.

The three least experienced players—George Marsh (seven games), Percy Ogden (four games) and Fred Stancliffe (seven games)—gave way to a trio of men who had played in the 1903 premiership side, Bill Proudfoot (who was 37 years and 111 days old and about to play his 107th VFL game), Matthew Fell (30, 116th VFL game) and Jack Incoll (26, 61st VFL game).

On the Thursday night before the game, said *The Herald*, "the Collingwood team talked over the situation. They were addressed by Messers (E.W) Copeland, (Bill) Strickland, (Charlie) Condon and (Dick) Condon. Each player criticised the other players' style of play,

---

49   *The Herald*, September 29, 1905

and suggested improvements. Some were very candid critics, too, but everyone accepted the criticism in the proper spirit."[50]

McHale was to be opposed to 'Tammy' Beauchamp in the middle. Rain had fallen on the morning of the match and the crowd swelled to more than 30,000 by the time Collingwood "came through the gate with a rush and at once indulged in a little practice. They spun about two balls and played their half-length kicking, marking and sprinting."

Fitzroy won the toss after Gerald Brosnan went to the Collingwood rooms and spun a "lucky" sovereign given to him by Tom Banks, and the Maroons took first use of the breeze. But Collingwood was able to restrict them in the opening stanza, with neither side scoring a goal. At the first change of ends, Fitzroy led 0.3 to 0.1.

The Australasian claimed: "Collingwood's tactics throughout the quarter were as legitimate as they were successful and rendered practically useless Fitzroy's winning of the toss."[51] But the biggest handicap the Magpies had to endure was an injury suffered by Dick Condon.

McHale would later say that Condon was one of the greatest footballers he had even seen. On this day, though, Condon was "lamed" late in the first term, which meant "keeping up with Fitzroy (in the second term) was highly creditable."[52] The score was locked together on 1.3 each, and the scales seemed to have swung in Collingwood's favour when Fitzroy defender Jim Sharp emerged almost as lame as Condon.

Fitzroy scored three goals to one in the third term, as the game and the premiership seemed to be slipping away from Collingwood. The Magpies' sole goal for the term came in the dying seconds when Pears passed to Drohan, who place kicked it through. The difference at the last change was 14 points.

That was enough to have the Maroons go on the defensive. *The Australasian* recorded: "They put into practice the lesson taught to them by Collingwood in the opening term, and if truth be told,

---

50   ibid
51   *The Australasian*, October 7, 1905
52   ibid

they rather bettered the instruction. They hugged the wing with the ardour of earnest lovers."[53]

In shutting down the game, Fitzroy also shut down Collingwood's premiership hopes. 'Observer' from *The Argus* said: "In the last quarter there was not so much vim to Collingwood's attack. Their dashes were spasmodic and, giving all their energies to defence and defensive tactics, Fitzroy met every Collingwood advance with effect."[54] Only a behind to Drohan troubled the scoreboard for the term, which was the lowest collective last quarter score-line in a Grand Final, and remains so to this day.

Captain Charlie Pannam summed up the mood in the Collingwood camp in *The Herald* on October 2: "Well, I really think we could have won the game. The bad luck was ours throughout, and we suffered severely from the crippling condition of Condon. He strained the muscles of his knee so badly that today he has to walk with a stick. (Percy) Gibb, too, was disabled. The ball hit the top of his fingers of his right hand and knocked two of them badly out of place. So you see we practically had two men out of it. My opinion is if Condon had remained sound—for up until the time his leg went, he was doing magnificent work—we would have beaten them. Anyway, we are a good second."[55]

No doubt revelling in the premiership win after what had happened two years earlier, Brosnan said in *The Herald*: "I see that it has been stated that Collingwood could not get their system into play owing to a wet ball, but the ball and the ground were as dry as we could wish."[56] Then he added that "we beat them chiefly across the centre, where young (Barclay) Bailes and (Tammy) Beauchamp were very fine in their work."[57] That last assessment would not have sat well with McHale, who was opposed to Beauchamp throughout the game.

---

53   ibid
54   *The Argus*, October 2, 1905
55   *The Herald*, October 2, 1905
56   ibid
57   ibid

If McHale's first three seasons at Collingwood had been characterised by harmony and camaraderie, he was about to see the other side of the coin in 1906. What happened at Victoria Park that season is still unclear, but a few schisms within the playing group, involving coach Dick Condon and captain Rosie Dummett, put paid to any hopes that Collingwood had of seriously challenging for the premiership.

McHale would never forget what happened, and would always maintain the only way to attain success at a club was to do so with discipline and unity. Those two words were in short supply at the club in 1906. As Richard Stremski documented: "Jealousy over the captaincy and team selection (possibly involved the issue of localism) seem to have been at the centre of a dispute between players, in which Condon was involved."[58]

There were few external signs of it early in the season, other than an inconsistent start that had a win-loss, win-loss, win-loss first six weeks. McHale kicked a goal—his second career goal—against Geelong in the comfortable Round 1 win. But *The Australasian* argued that Bill Mackinlay had the better of him in the centre.

A loss to South Melbourne followed, with some suggesting too many of the Magpies were on the wrong side of 30. There were five who were 30 or more: George Angus, Dick Condon, Arthur Leach, Charlie Pannam and Jack Monohan. There were also two 29-year-olds in Ted Rowell and Eddie Drohan. McHale was 23 at the time, and one of the youngest in the team.

But a strong win over reigning premiers Fitzroy came next where, according to *The Australasian*, Collingwood "showed form that equalled their finest of last year; and their most seasoned players were again conspicuously and consistently able." McHale was one of

---

58   *Kill For Collingwood*, Richard Stremski, Allen and Unwin, 1986

the best players in the 43-point win over the Maroons. But that win would only cover up the cracks. Against a more formidable Carlton in Round 4, Collingwood was no match. McHale was opposed to Blues centreman Rod McGregor in a solid duel that would be replicated for years to come.

The real shock came when Collingwood chose to stand Condon down "for club reasons" ahead of the Round 6 clash with Essendon at East Melbourne, a match that the Magpies lost by 17 points.

'Markwell', from *The Australasian*, documented the dissension at a club normally devoid of it: "As in the happiest of families there sometimes arises discord ... a question upon which differences of opinion are held, and when divergent views are obstinately preserved in, and harmony is for the time upset. With Collingwood, the trouble is more deeply seated. The executives believe that players opposed to this year's captain are playing below form and have reluctantly arrived at the conclusion that these players have frequently and purposefully neglected to pass the ball to certain of their club-mates, when the passing could easily have been done, and would have resulted in benefit to the team. This pettiness of spirit has, probably, caused the club to lose a match or two which through concertedness might have been saved.

"It is gratifying to note that the Collingwood committee are taking very radical steps to bring the discontented members to their sense. Fortunately, the executive have kept in reserve several very capable recruits, and these are being brought in to fill the places that are being compulsorily vacated by men who in the past have been star performers but whose club patriotism has succumbed to trivial disappointment. Possibly a few weeks spent in cool reflection outside the pickets will have a curative effect on the disordered players."[59]

One of those young lads played his first game a week after the Essendon loss, against Melbourne. Despite the inner turmoil that

---

59   *The Australasian*, June 23, 1906

had taken place, Collingwood beat Melbourne by 44 points and the 17-year-old forward kicked three goals. His first name was Walter, but he would become known as Dick Lee, to have a point of difference from his father, Wal, who had long been Collingwood's head trainer. Dick Lee would become one of the greatest players in the history of the club.

By the end of June 1906, Condon had resumed training. The following month Dummett stepped down as captain "and the committee thanked him for the sportsmanlike spirit he had shown."[60] *The Herald* said that "the ruffles that have upset the serenity of the Collingwood atmosphere have been smoothed out and happiness reigns supreme."[61] That wasn't entirely correct.

But at least the coach was back playing. Jack Monohan filled in briefly as skipper before Arthur Leach was elected as the new captain, and the Magpies set about trying to right the ship.

After playing in the Round 10 game against Fitzroy, McHale missed the next two matches with injury. That was a rarity for him. Up until then, he had played 61 of the club's previous 66 games since his debut. Incredibly, he would not miss another game for almost another 11 years.

He returned to fitness in time for the club's trip to Tasmania in August, where it was hoped the past angst could be wiped clean. The Annual Report recorded: "The trip to Tasmania was one that will long be remembered ... most of the time was spent with Hobart as headquarters—many of the interesting places mentioned in *The Term of his Natural Life* were visited and proved full of interest. A two day's trip was taken to Franklyn (sic) and a visit also paid to Oatlands in the midlands. Launceston, with its gorge and power station, and Cora Lynn contributed largely to the first two days' pleasure."[62]

---

60   *The History of the Collingwood Football Club, 1892-1948*, Percy Taylor, 1949
61   *The Herald*, June 29, 1906
62   Collingwood Annual Report, 1907

The trip was precisely the tonic the team required. Previous interstate trips had bonded the players, as had been the case with visits to Tasmania in 1902 and Sydney in 1903—both premiership years.

The Australasian said: "Perhaps no team on the league list knows better than Collingwood the value of going (away) together; and certainly no team requires less coaching in that regard. Their unanimity and system have been (except for a brief period in the early part of the year when two or three of them kicked over the tracks) the admiration and envy of antagonists. They, least of all clubs, required a holiday trip to Tasmania to make them pull together. Nevertheless they have had their happy outing and they have come back with friendship and harmony more closely cemented than ever; and are prepared to face the ordeal of the final games full of confidence in their ability to win the premiership."[63]

Collingwood rallied late in the season. One of the first-year players used in three games late in the 1906 season was a recruit from Williamstown, Tom Nelson. He took part of the Boer War tune *Goodbye Dolly Gray* and added 41 words to make the most famous theme song in Australian football, *Good Old Collingwood Forever*. Nelson was dropped after the sectional game win over Melbourne the week before the finals and he would never play in the black and white again. But the words which he penned would go down in Australian sporting history.

That left Collingwood to meet Carlton in the semi-final. The Blues had taken professionalism almost to a new level under Worrall. The Magpies were without Pears, who this time had "gone away (to Queensland) for the shearing season" and Bob Rush, who had not played since Round 10, and had a seriously broken finger that "had to be wired."[64] Bob Strachan was also in doubt. He had missed the previous game due to an injured knee that came from him "springing on a tram-car in the morning, (where he) banged his leg against the

63   *The Australasian*, August 25, 1906
64   *The Herald*, September 14, 1906

seat on the dummy with such force as to lame him."[65] Strahan would prove his fitness, but George Green could not be considered due to his sore knee.

McHale, in his 67th game, was one of the most prominent players in the semi-final, driving the ball from the centre on a number of occasions early in the game. Carlton had control initially with five goals to two in the first term. The difference at half-time was 12 points in the Blues' favour. But a strong third term, in which the Magpies kicked 3.2 to 0.5, gave Collingwood a chance.

The Magpies clung to a three-point lead at the last change. But the Blues kicked three goals to one in the final term to put the issue—and Collingwood's season—beyond doubt. The only consolation was that McHale had been one of his team's best players.

---

65   ibid

CHAPTER 4

A Star
is Made

1907-1911

An advertisement placed in newspapers across Australia in 1906 and 1907 extolled the virtues of Dr Morse's Indian Root Pills. Promising to curb a range of ills—from tired limbs to headaches, from the common cold to skin irritations—one of the more convincing endorsements came from a mother from Coburg.

The housewife claimed: "For some three years I was a great sufferer from severe pains in the head, and I also had developed varicose veins, and running sores around the ankles. I tried many medicines and consulted several doctors. A St Kilda lady advised me to try Dr Morse's Indian Root Pills, and sure enough I found an appreciable improvement in my health. I am now able to get about, and do my household work. At present, I am better than I have been for years, and I attribute the sole cause to the wonderful medicinal properties of Dr Morse's Indian Root Pills. They are now our family medicine for all general complaints."[1]

---

1   *Hobart Mercury*, August 28, 1906

The testimony came from "Mrs Mary McHale, Buckingham Avenue, Coburg," who happened to be the mother of one of the VFL's leading footballers, Jim McHale. Given that Jim was still living with his family at the time it is tempting to suggest that the pills might have played a part in his appetite for hard work. But that would have been unlikely. Jim's capacity to work hard seemed ingrained.

McHale was a hardy soul. Perhaps his work ethic came from his Irish heritage, where family members he had known by name only had toiled tirelessly for modest returns. He thrived on his work at the brewery, starting work not long after first light and carrying on until darkness rolled in. Then he would make a dash to Victoria Park. Football training was every Tuesday and Thursday nights in the winter months.

In his first five VFL seasons, McHale missed only one night of more than 200 sessions the club undertook. That blemish came in his first year, in 1903. Collingwood demanded that commitment from its players and in time McHale would insist on the same from his players. The 1907 Annual Report highlighted those requirements: "Our best players are keenest in their training. The small awards given annually are not the reason that players put everything else aside two times a week to have the necessary exercise, but it is their wholeheartedness and enthusiasm for the game."[2]

As a centreman, McHale proved resilient and resourceful, capable of putting aside aches and ailments, and even the occasional injury, to turn out in black and white each week. After missing two games in Round 11 and Round 12 of 1906, McHale embarked on a remarkable stint of 191 consecutive games, stretching across 11 years to 1917. It set a record that would last a quarter of a century. There must have been an element of luck associated, but his ability to play beyond the pain threshold set him apart from many contemporaries.

In an era when training for football—at least outside Collingwood—was often haphazard and irregular, preparation was everything to

---

2   Collingwood Annual Report, 1907

McHale, and to Collingwood. He used the summer months to work on his speed by doing foot-running, and he played cricket until about 1906, once even harbouring an ambition of playing for his country. But football won out.

He had defined strengths, particularly his capacity to read and understand the play. From an early age, he dissected styles and systems, and worked tirelessly on the areas he believed needed attention. More than 20 years after his retirement, *The Age* said: "His ability as a foot runner, combined with a clever turn either way, made him an elusive but doughty opponent, while he always played the game with the ball as his objective and was never guilty of unfair tactics."[3]

An examination of McHale's attributes that came in *Footy's Greatest Coaches* said he was "strong, had big hands, ran hard, had an enormous work-rate, and very quickly provided evidence of a prodigious football brain. He read the ball—and opponents—with precision. He worked on his speed with summer sprints, becoming quick for his size. An excellent ball-handler, he was capable in the air and strong on the ground, but sometimes lacklustre in disposal, punting too high for forwards who were beginning to appreciate more precise passing."[4]

McHale watched individuals, and opposition teams. One of them was Collingwood star Dick Condon, a controversial character possessing more flair than McHale, yet who also could be unpredictable and erratic. Condon had a capacity for individuality, in contrast to the philosophy that McHale would favour, first as a player and later as a coach. Yet when asked long after his retirement to nominate the greatest footballer he had seen, McHale replied without hesitation: "Why, Dick Condon, of course!"[5]

As much as he would have been tempted to emulate Condon's many tricks, most were unattainable as teammate Eddie Drohan

---

3   *The Age*, May 13, 1944
4   *Footy's Greatest Coaches*, Stephanie Holt and Garrie Hutchinson, Coulomb
      Communications, 2002
5   *The Age*, May 13, 1944

acknowledged. Drohan once said: "When at Collingwood I studied Condon's movements and tricks, but he held sole world's patent rights for most of them."[6]

Change played a role in McHale's life in 1907. A merger between six Victorian breweries, including McCracken's, formed one of the most famous companies in Australian business, Carlton and United Breweries. There had long been talk of a consolidation. In 1871 there were 126 breweries in the state.[7] That was not sustainable, especially after many failed to survive the calamitous final decade of the 19th century.

In 1903, the year that McHale first played for Collingwood, representatives of the leading brewing companies sought closer cooperation, and decided to form the Society of Melbourne Brewers. Within three years, six breweries—Carlton Brewery Ltd, McCracken's City Brewery Ltd, Castlemaine Brewery Co (Melbourne), Shamrock Brewing and Malting Co Ltd, the Foster's Brewing Co Pty Ltd, and the Victoria Brewery Pty Ltd—announced an intention to merge.

On May 7, 1907—on the 10th anniversary of the first round of VFL football in 1897—Carlton and United Breweries was formed. The link between these great entities led to more than a century of sponsorship, which was beneficial for both.

According to *The Amber Nectar*, a book on Australian brewing, there was a sense of sadness among employees of the companies, as well as beer drinkers around the state who had long been accustomed to their preferred brews. The *Australian Brewers' Journal* lamented: "No Victorian beer drinker will think, without a pang of regret, that the days of McCracken's are numbered. And never in the history of City

---

6   *A Century of the Best*, Michael Roberts, Collingwood Football Club, 1991

7   *The Amber Nectar, A celebration of beer and brewing in Australia*, Keith Dunstan, Viking O'Neil, 1987

Brewing did it turn out better beer than it is brewing today. There is no beer in Melbourne which has a better finish than McCracken's."[8]

McHale was a McCracken's man to the core, but would come to serve the new entity with distinction and loyalty for the rest of his working years. Back then, the "beer was still delivered by horses, and magnificently ... Bottles had tie-down corks, and beer pulls were splendid with ivory handles ... there were more than six hundred employees in the six breweries; some retired but many others were employed to deal with increased production at Carlton and Victoria. All operations were consolidated at the Carlton and Victoria breweries within 18 months."[9]

McHale would shift to the Carlton Brewery in Bouverie Street, Carlton. In the decades to come, he would spend almost as much time there, and at Victoria Park, as at home.

Having endured a splintered season in 1906, Collingwood also underwent its own transformation in 1907. Condon left for Tasmania, where he intended to do some coaching and explore umpiring options. The irony was not lost on those who knew him. Just seven years earlier, Condon had been banned "for life" for informing an umpire that "Your girl's a bloody whore". The suspension was lifted, after persuasion from Collingwood in 1902, and he returned in time to help pioneer the stab-kick.

Other mainstays who had played in the club's breakthrough 1896 VFA premiership and the 1902-03 VFL flag sides were also gone. Defender Bill Proudfoot retired after 15 seasons. Charlie Pannam played the first two games of 1907 before transferring to Richmond in the VFA as playing coach. Another veteran, Jack Monohan, joined

---

8   *The Australian Brewers' Journal*, November 20, 1907
9   *The Amber Nectar, A celebration of beer and brewing in Australia*, Keith Dunstan, Viking O'Neil, 1987

Brunswick in the VFA after one game in 1907. They were significant losses in personnel and personality. All four had been critical to the club's success, and were powerful characters within the dressingroom.

The Annual Report acknowledged: "The names of Messrs Condon, Monohan and Pannam have been so associated with the success of Collingwood that a team without them a few years ago would have been an absurdity. Still, this had to be the last season. Mr Condon accepted a position in Hobart as coach and umpire, Mr Monohan joined the Brunswick club and Mr Pannam, the Richmond club. To each, your committee donated £20, which sums were increased by donations from members who remember with pleasure the grand games they fought for their club."[10]

The subsequent leadership vacuum meant other players needed to step up. Ted Rowell was appointed playing-coach, and Arthur Leach was reappointed captain. Eddie Drohan, George Angus and McHale were going to have to play roles in the transition. All five played in the 18 games Collingwood contested in 1907.

The club's most exciting young player, Dick Lee, played 17 games, booting a club record 47 goals, the most in the VFL, in his second season. Importantly, Collingwood had to inject new players, while striving to retain the proud tradition of making the finals in every VFL season it had contested.

Collingwood started promisingly enough in 1907, with an eight-point win over Fitzroy, blooding two new players, including Tom Baxter, from Maldon. Fitzroy had six debutants. One of them, Harold 'Lal' McLennan, would become one of McHale's great rivals in the centre. *The Australasian* said: "An assemblage of more than 10,000 ... left the scene at the conclusion feeling that (they) had received full value for (their) sixpence."[11]

There was another change that day: the Collingwood players first appeared in bare-kneed trousers. *The Australasian* said: "As the team

10   Collingwood Annual Report, 1908
11   *The Australasian*, May 4, 1907

filled out for the start, it was observed that the local 18 presented a greatly improved appearance from previous years. They seemed a brighter, smarter and more thoroughbred body of athletes; and the gain in appearance was due to the becomingness of their new uniform. Often has the charge of dowdiness been laid against our football costumes and it has not been unwarranted. Mr E. W. Copeland, Collingwood's attentive and able secretary, has shown it is possible to turn out a team dressed in a style at once comfortable and becoming."[12]

'Observer', from *The Argus,* believed it "gives the impression of increased height and weight."[13] Having his bare knees exposed for the first time did not worry McHale. He formed a "particularly capable centre-line" with George Green and Percy Gibb.

But an improving St Kilda halted Collingwood in a "hard, slogging game"[14] in Round 2. Rowell chose to play in the centre, pushing his good friend McHale to half-back, where he was adjudged one of the club's best players. McHale was restored to the pivot the following week, but for the second week in a row Collingwood failed to score a goal in the opening term. McHale was listed as his team's best player in the 28-point loss to South Melbourne at the Lake Oval.

The loss to Melbourne a week later, at Victoria Park of all places, made it a hat-trick of defeats. This left the new-look Magpies sitting in sixth spot, just off the bottom on percentage.

Just when the season appeared precariously placed, the Magpies reeled off six straight wins from Round 7 to Round 12. The most unusual came against Fitzroy at Brunswick Street. The Maroons dominated the first term, kicking 7.0. Then Collingwood stopped them from scoring for the next two terms before powering on to a nine-point win.

The Herald said: "How well the (Collingwood) side played during these middle terms is seen in their amassing 57 (points) to Fitzroy's

---

12   ibid

13   *100 years of Australian Football, the complete story of the AFL,* John Ross and Garrie Hutchinson, Penguin, 1996

14   *The Australasian,* May 11, 1907

nothing, a record that has, I think, never before been approached by any team at the expense of the Maroons. Their all-round display was the best they had given for the year, and it was marked by a return to the accuracy in passing, at half-distance, and to the excellence of the system that made them formidable in previous seasons."[15]

McHale's form was strong. Against South Melbourne in Round 10, according to *The Australasian*, "very skilful play and the best marking in the match came from McHale in the centre".[16] A week later against Melbourne, Collingwood kicked its highest score of the season to win by 79 points. *The Australasian* said: "They have succeeded in getting their system of quick, accurate passing into thorough working order, their freshmen for the year having become, every one of them, expert at the business."[17]

One of the other reasons for the return to form was the efforts of its centreline: "Green, McHale and Gibb across the centreline, made hacks of the men immediately opposed to them ... (Herbert) Hill did fairly in the centre, but McHale knew too much for him."[18]

Later, *Punch* described McHale as a player who "combines speed, grace and science. Those who know him well say 'Mac' would make a great explorer, as he always discovers the leather when it appears lost."[19]

Carlton dented that confidence in Round 13. In the "the most forceful, determined battle of the year",[20] as *The Australasian* termed it, the Magpies led by six points leading into the last term. Such was the pressure that "there was not a man in either company but played as if his future prospects, here and hereafter, depended on the issue."[21]

The Argus said: "The centreline was of McHaile (sic) alone, maintaining his form and playing very fine football."[22] But as

---

15   *The Herald*, June 22, 1907
16   *The Australasian*, July 13, 1907
17   *The Australasian*, July 20, 1907
18   ibid
19   *Punch*, September 30, 1907
20   *The Australasian*, August 10, 1907
21   ibid
22   *The Argus*, August 5, 1907

industrious as the Magpies had been, "the Collingwood system did not withstand the strain".[23] The Magpies failed to score in the final term, and lost by 11 points.

The Australasian gave an evocative description of the crowd at the Geelong game in Round 14: "Despite important counter attractions in the racing and lacrosse fixtures, and notwithstanding that a heavy shower of rain fell about 2 o'clock, the heavy attendance was unusually good, and included the customary percentage of ladies, whose presence and bright, attractive costumes added charm and picturesqueness to the proceedings. In fact, at no previous period of the game's history, has football been as universally popular as at present."[24]

McHale had his admirers, but more attention was paid to 18-year-old 'Dick' Lee, who kicked seven of the club's 15 goals. A number of these came in the last term, when Collingwood had seven shots at goal—six through the big sticks, with a seventh striking the post. *The Australasian* said: "Against such shooting (or such luck), no team in the world could have a hope. Look to it, Carlton. The Magpies may deal with you in similar fashion in the final go for the premiership."[25]

Collingwood never got the chance to challenge Carlton. It lost its last three home and away games, and fell at the first finals hurdle, losing to South Melbourne in the semi-final. 'Observer' from *The Argus*, recorded: "For some reason not easily explained, but chiefly, perhaps, because so many of the crack Collingwood men failed to play up to form, it was a disappointing game."[26] By three-quarter time, the difference was 21 points. A five-goal to three-goal final term was enough to see South Melbourne win by 34 points.

It was noted that "Collingwood's failure is largely explained by the fact that players like McHaile (sic), Rowell, Lee, Drohan, Angus, (Albert) Pannam, Green and Rush were a long way under their form."[27]

---

23   ibid
24   *The Australasian*, August 17, 1907
25   ibid
26   ibid
27   ibid

McHale was presented with his five-year certificate at the annual meeting at Victoria Park on March 30, 1908. Three teammates (Ted Rowell, Eddie Drohan and George Green) received the same hand-painted reward, while Arthur Leach was presented with one for 10 years and Jack Monohan for 15 years.

The Annual Report explained: "One has to only read over this list to appreciate immediately the skill, energy and perseverance the several players named have shown on many a stubbornly contested field and to wish for those of the five years standing the same success that has attended those of the 10 and 15 years."[28]

Loyalty was something that Collingwood preached, and McHale valued. But there had been other offers. It was around this time that he received interest from Brunswick to become a playing coach. He considered it, before knocking it back. How the course of history might have changed for him—and for Collingwood—had he traded Collingwood's black and white for Brunswick's!

It is incredible to think that half a century of football went by without coaches. Tactics and team selection were left in the hands of captains and senior players. Fitness and preparation were often the domain of designated trainers, or done on a more *ad hoc* basis.

It wasn't until Carlton appointed Jack Worrall as secretary in 1902, and he fashioned the role of coach, that football would take a leap into the unknown. He would come to cast an eye over all of the operations of the football club, including strategy and selection, recruiting and the rebuilding of the team.

Worrall would have outstanding success in the role at Carlton, and later at Essendon, although his iron-will discipline was not to everyone's liking.

---

28   Collingwood Annual Report, 1908

Over the next decade, other clubs would follow in appointing coaches: Collingwood (1904), St Kilda (1906), Melbourne (1907), Essendon (1908), South Melbourne (1909), Geelong (1910) and Fitzroy (1911).

McHale would have noticed the impact of coaches. It was an area he intended to pursue, but not yet. Collingwood was the focus of his sporting intentions, and recognition of his talents meant he was soon appointed to the selection committee. In 1908 he attended all 19 meetings to help choose the side.

Again he was diligent at attending training, but for the first time since his 1903 debut season, McHale missed a session (one only), yet he was still rewarded for his consistency with a trophy worth half a guinea for his attendances.

—

Two new teams came into the VFL in 1908, Richmond and University. The season also signalled the 50-year anniversary since Australian football's birth in 1858, a year in which another NSW-born sportsman Tom Wills penned his famous letter to *Bell's Life in Victoria and Sporting Chronicle*; the Melbourne Football Club was formed; and the first recorded match between Scotch College and Melbourne Grammar took place. To mark the occasion, the VFL arranged a carnival late in the season that brought in teams from the various states, as well as one from New Zealand.

The introduction of Richmond brought some angst from Collingwood. The Magpies had been supportive of the new team, and was accepting of the fact that Charlie Pannam, who had crossed there the season before, would be playing against his old side. But the Magpies were not prepared for the return of Condon from Tasmania, or his decision to become the playing coach of Richmond in early April. A clearance was granted because "he had obtained a situation through that club (Richmond) that Collingwood could not find for him."[29] But there was more than a little ill feeling, and Condon's name would barely be uttered at Victoria Park for years to come.

Losses to Geelong at Corio Oval by 47 points and Fitzroy at Victoria Park by 31 points made for a tough start to the 1908 season. In the first game, the Magpies blooded five players, including a gangly 24-year-old from the Collingwood Trade League called Les Hughes. His teammates would call him 'Flapper' or 'Lofty'.

The omens for the Geelong game were not good when the train from Melbourne was delayed by more than 15 minutes, meaning the match had to be pushed back and ended almost in darkness. In the Fitzroy game, Collingwood managed only one goal for three quarters, before losing by just over five goals.

McHale was "very much in evidence for Collingwood in the centre"[30] but *The Australasian* wondered if the slow start had something to do with strategy: "They had, apparently, refrained from rushing their preparations for the heavy season they have in front of them. Possibly their policy in this regard is not as short-sighted as it appears: for it is seldom that a team trained to the limits at the start of a year succeeds in keeping in form to the finish. There are men of sound experience on the club's executive who may be trusted to have their team in trim sufficiently early to give them a fair chance of getting into the first four when the end is approaching."[31]

Only once before 1908 had Collingwood ended a round on the bottom of the ladder: Round 3, 1900, three years before McHale first donned black and white colours. But the Magpies were at the tail for four consecutive rounds in 1908, from Round 2 to Round 5. Collingwood managed only three wins from its first nine games, with two of them coming against the new sides.

The win over Richmond was a comfort to those who wanted to make a statement about Condon's questionable loyalty. McHale was

---

29 *The History of the Collingwood Football Club, 1892-1948*, Percy Taylor, 1949
30 *The Herald*, May 9, 1908
31 *The Australasian*, May 16, 1908

one of his team's best where, "in the early part of the afternoon, (he) was prominent in the centre."[32] He helped to hold out a fast-finishing Richmond which booted five goals to one in the last term to miss out by 15 points.

After indifferent form, Drohan resigned the captaincy ahead of the Geelong game. His replacement, Bob Nash, switched roles with McHale for the Round 10 clash, with the club's regular centreman heading to full-back. *The Australasian* observed: "(Nash) directed affairs from a point of vantage in the centre whence McHale was despatched to take care of goal. The exchange proved a double benefit; it greatly helped the side and it suited the men themselves to a nicety. McHale saved his goal often with timely dashes out."[33]

Rowell was coach, but later in the year Bill Strickland was appointed "director to the team, with power to direct the play, confer with the captain, and instruct players during the interval."[34]

McHale's versatility meant his brief switch to defence had not stopped him from consistently being named among the best players. Several times in the following game against Fitzroy, which Collingwood won by two points, he saved the day for his team with his guile. Early on he "dashed in and put play to the wing". Then, in the second term, "the Roys made another attack on the Collingwood goal, but ... McHale met them at the right moment and quickly transferred play to the other end."

On another occasion when the ball went "into the teeth of (Fitzroy's) goal, McHale had it away in a flash."[35] In that time, he played his 100th game, against Richmond, making him only the 12th Collingwood player to reach the three-figure tally.

The Argus described it as "a fine, hard game, as becoming of neighbours; and there was nothing given in the way of bumps that was

---

32 *The Argus*, June 8, 1908
33 *The Australasian*, July 4, 1908
34 *The History of the Collingwood Football Club, 1892-1948*, Percy Taylor, 1949
35 *The Herald*, July 4, 1908

not returned."[36] As scrupulously fair as McHale was, he received howls of disapproval from the Punt Rd crowd for an incident in the first term, though it was almost certainly an accident. "Passed out to the centre, (Billy) Schmidt went for a high mark, just as McHale ducked and the 'Richmondite', falling heavily on top of his head, was carried from the ground."[37]

After trailing by 19 points at half-time, Collingwood scored six goals in the third term to be only eight points in arrears at the last change. At that time, according to *The Argus*, "Collingwood looked like winners ... gradually they forged ahead."[38] But, with Condon and Pannam (three goals) adding experience, the Richmond side wrestled back the lead, and held on to win the match by five points.

Wins over St Kilda and Melbourne left Collingwood percentage points behind South Melbourne in the battle for fourth spot, and with the two teams scheduled to play in the final round it meant the victor would lock in a finals berth. But, first, there was a break of competition matches for the Jubilee Carnival.

It coincided with the arrival in Melbourne of the United States Fleet, on a worldwide tour that President Theodore Roosevelt used to demonstrate the capabilities of its naval forces. Both events attracted the citizens of Melbourne in incredible numbers. One newspaper said: "Immense public enthusiasm has been awakened by the visit of the American battle fleet. Never in the history of Melbourne have so many people been congregated in the city."[39] Hundreds of thousands of people lined the streets for a procession; and two teams from the ships *Minnesota* and *Kentucky* played a game of "football" where "padded knickers, jerseys with padded elbows and shoulders and shin-guards" fascinated sports fans at the MCG as they watched one of the more unusual curtain-raisers.

---

36   *The Argus*, August 3, 1908
37   ibid
38   ibid
39   *Kalgoorlie Western Argus*, September 8, 1908

The arrival of the fleet had editorialists wondering if the fleet might one day be needed to safeguard Australia; with one saying: "The United States of America will be our first line of defence against Asia."[40]

The last round took place on the day that the US fleet sailed out of Melbourne for Albany, with Collingwood needing to beat South Melbourne in the rain at Victoria Park to make the finals. McHale was back in the centre. *The Argus* said: "At the start of the game, played on a slippery turf, the embankment looked as if it had been thickly planted with umbrellas, while the players' hands were white with resin, to give them the best chance of holding the ball."[41]

Collingwood fielded a strong side, including veteran Arthur Leach, who had returned in the previous match for his first game of the season, and George Angus, after injury had kept him out of three matches. South attacked the ball—and the man—hard early. Leach was a target, with an act that 'Observer' of *The Argus* said was one of the worst he had seen on a football field: "Every impartial was amazed and indignant to see (Bert) Franks hitting Leach time after time. Twice he just missed him; the third time Leach was knocked down. Leach's fine self-control prevented trouble; for the crowd were roaring with anger, and had they got hold of Franks at that moment, the game might have had an early and unpleasant ending."[42]

It didn't help South Melbourne. They could muster only two goals to Collingwood's 10 by three-quarter time. The final margin was 66 points.

The semi-final against Essendon could not have been more contrasting. The rain held off for the duration of the game, and the 'Same Old' were more than a match. McHale was "sound and reliable"[43], according to *The Australasian*, despite one disappointing early passage of play. After an early behind scored by Essendon, Rowell

---

40   *Australia Through Time*, Random House, 2000
41   *The Argus*, September 7, 1908
42   ibid
43   *The Australasian*, September 19, 1908

booted the ball back into play to a contest that McHale was involved in. He gave the free kick away to Paddy Shea, who passed the ball over to Alan Belcher, resulting in Essendon's first goal. After a close first half, in which Collingwood trailed by only five points, Essendon dominated the final hour of the game. The opposition booted 6.7 to 2.1 in the second half, winning by 35 points.

There may have been some excuses on Collingwood's side, with reports that some of the Magpies stars were under a cloud.[44] At one stage of the game, 'Observer' of *The Argus* said: "For a time the ball was Essendon's private property—though it was a Collingwood ball, and one of (T.W.) Sherrin's best, made expressly for the match ... Sherrin is making them now less of an oval than formerly, and the result is that the players are no longer puzzled for half a match by strange boomerang flights."[45]

Collingwood's inconsistent form had led to its decline. It wasn't just the number of games that the Magpies lost—they even lost members due to poor early season form, leading to a plea from 'Bud' Copeland ahead of the 1909 season. He urged: "For several years Collingwood's membership exceeded that of any club, but last season (1908) it retrograded ... It is to be hoped members will push the club along once more. And keep it in the van. Your committee are expected to be always on the lookout for better players—and if they please you in this respect, you can all do your part in gaining new members. Let the motto of every member at the commencement of this, our 18th year, be, 'I will add one'."[46]

Jim McHale had an important engagement in the week leading up to the 1909 season—getting married. It's not known how long

44   *The History of the Collingwood Football Club, 1892-1948*, Percy Taylor, 1949
45   *The Argus*, September 14, 1908
46   Collingwood Annual Report, 1909

McHale had known Violet Mary Angel Godfrey for before their wedding on Wednesday, April 28, 1909. The Annual Report stated: "One remarkable feature about Collingwood's players is their willingness to enter into the married state. Whether it is the presence of so many fair and enthusiastic supporters at their matches, or their superior form of training that they experience at the hands of Wal Lee, their trainer, which makes them so attractive, we are not prepared to say. Probably it is both. Mr J. McHale (is) now off the list of the eligibles. To each player and his partner in life we offer sincere congratulations and earnest hopes for future happiness and prosperity."[47]

The club made a presentation to him and his new bride. Violet, who was 27 and a machinist, came from Brunswick. Her parents were listed as labourer William Godfrey and June Godfrey (nee Randall), though family folklore suggests that Violet had been adopted. No birth certificate exists for her, even though she noted that she had been born in Carlton.

McHale was 26 and listed as a cellarman who lived in Coburg, where he lived with his parents, John and Mary, and his siblings. Clergyman Joseph McCarter conducted the service at St Ambrose's Catholic Church in Sydney Road, Brunswick on April 28, 1909.

It would become Jim and Violet's church for the next four decades— through the good times and the heartache yet to come. After the wedding, the couple moved into 111 Talbot Street, Brunswick, in the hope that they might start a family of their own soon.

Just three days after his marriage, McHale ran out for the 105th time in the game against Fitzroy. The Magpies had a new coach, George Angus, and Bob Nash was elected captain on a popular vote. It was a significant day, with the opening of the club's new grandstand. The old 1892 stand had been moved to the south-west corner to make way for a new one to be built on its site. The foundation stone had been laid on March 13 (on a day when a man was projected from

---

47   Collingwood Annual Report, 1910

a cannon as part of the bizarre ceremony), but the reality was that construction had been under way for some time.

In the old stand, players were known to receive rubdowns while standing for the sheer lack of room. The new stand provided two dressingrooms, a committee room, a gymnasium, and bathrooms and toilets for the home and visiting team.

The Herald also said it provided players with the best possible protection from abuse or projectiles: "The players pass straight from their dressing rooms to the arena via a tunnel, thus avoiding the passing among an excited perhaps offensive crowd of barrackers."[48] But the celebrations ended there. The Maroons' capacity to spoil the party for their old rivals once more came to the fore. They defeated Collingwood by 11 points, with McHale getting plenty of work after being selected at full-back. He was, according to *The Australasian*, "ranked highest for Collingwood for persistent excellence".[49]

The following week Collingwood had a narrow six-point win over St Kilda at the Junction Oval. A deluge was so heavy in the first half that "the spectators only had a blurred view of the game, as if they were looking at flickering cinematograph pictures."[50] Only three years earlier, the world's earliest-known feature length narrative, *The Story of the Kelly Gang*, had been released.

Despite the weather, *The Australasian* said, the Magpies had good support away from their home base, with "a demonstrative section of the 'Woods' barrackers (who came) ... in all kinds of conveyances from their populous city, and the going home in the rain of these exulted supporters in wood and coal carts, furniture vans, pony barrows, etc, was a diverting spectacle."[51] The Magpies had "snatched a bare win ... in a fresh, strong game that was closely contested until the final bell."[52]

48 *Collingwood At Victoria Park*, Michael Roberts and Glenn McFarlane, Lothian, 1999
49 *The Australasian*, May 8, 1909
50 *The Argus*, May 10, 1909
51 *The Australasian*, May 15, 1909
52 ibid

Carlton, the team that had won three consecutive premierships under Jack Worrall, was having its own problems. Talk of bickering over Worrall's stern discipline had been rife. Ahead of the Round 3 clash with Collingwood, *The Australasian* reported that: "Rumour was busy late in the week concerning the continuance of trouble in the ranks at Carlton. It was generally believed that certain prominent players were holding out for more 'liberal' expenses and that the executive of the club were determined they would not increase allowances beyond what they knew to be legitimate." Moreover, *The Australasian* claimed that: "The dissatisfied players had been informed that unless they turned out against Collingwood their places would be filled by other men and that League football would know them no more."[53]

Despite the bickering, the Blues managed to overcome the Magpies by 17 points. McHale was back in the middle, and he did "brilliant and valuable work in the centre."[54] After five rounds, and a loss to South Melbourne, Collingwood was 2-3 with plenty of work to do.

Two wins in three days came next, with victories over Essendon (42 points on Saturday, June 5) and University (36 points on Monday June 7), on the Prince of Wales birthday public holiday. Both games were played at Victoria Park in a boon for the local side and nearby shopkeepers. "Business thrives hugely just now with the Magpies," *The Australasian* said. "After downing Essendon mercilessly they had no misgivings concerning University. Collingwood's briskness and system commanded undoubted mastery ... McHale showed superb form in the centre."[55]

The victory over Essendon was the start of a nine-game winning streak. The closest Collingwood came to defeat in this time was a draw with Melbourne in Round 9. Even that game had the feel of a win, given the Magpies had trailed by 23 points at the last change on a muddy MCG. At times the Magpies' plight looked forlorn, but "all the white feather Collingwood ever show is confined to the bird

---

53   *The Australasian*, May 22, 1909
54   ibid
55   *The Australasian*, June 12, 1909

they have taken for their crest ... as one man, they rose valiantly to the occasion, and with avalanche-like rushes they swooped again and again on goal."[56]

Bill Heatley kicked the levelling goal, and the bell sounded on the first draw in Collingwood's history. After going without a draw for so long, the Magpies would have a second—against University—in Round 16. Again, it came after the club trailed deep into the last term, before a goal to Les Hughes just before the final bell levelled the scores.

McHale was one of the Magpies' best players against University, kicking a vital goal for his team. His form had been strong all season. By season's end, he would gain 230 votes from readers of *The Argus* as the football champion of the VFL, third overall in terms of Collingwood—behind Dick Lee (942 votes) and Tom Baxter (441). The winner of the popular vote, though, was Essendon's Bill Busbridge, with 16,500 votes.[57]

There were other close contests, including a one-point win over a fractured Carlton, which was soon to lose its coach Worrall, who had little choice but to resign "for the sake of the club and for peace and quietness".[58] McHale, said Percy Taylor in his club history, was a "telling factor" in the game, and was "in rare form for this year."[59]

A win over another premiership contender in South Melbourne in Round 14 saw Lee carried from the field after kicking six of the club's eight goals. This win put Collingwood on top of the ladder, and McHale dared to believe that the premiership that he had craved might finally be in the offing. But a loss to Essendon in Round 15, followed by the draw with University, hurt.

The draw could perhaps have been forgiven because the previous week the club had travelled to Sydney for an exhibition clash with Geelong and another one against a combined NSW team, both of

---

56   ibid
57   *The Argus*, September 27, 1909
58   *100 years of Australian Football, the complete story of the AFL*, John Ross and Garrie Hutchinson, Penguin, 1996
59   *The History of the Collingwood Football Club, 1892-1948*, Percy Taylor, 1949

which resulted in wins. But the loss to Essendon and the draw with University cost Collingwood the minor premiership, which South Melbourne managed to steal back.

The pressure was on Collingwood heading into the semi-final. It had endured a recent lack of finals success and "the committee decided to spare no effort to enable their team to beat South Melbourne. It was felt that the ruckmen would need all the strengthening and recuperating influences that could be obtained, and the committee decided to try the effects of oxygen on their men. It accordingly secured some, and at the half-time interval, players and committee, instead of saying 'Will you have a drink?' asked 'Will you join me in oxygen?'"[60]

The club's doctor, Dr Maurice MacGillicuddy, obtained two cylinders of oxygen, and it was on hand in the rooms for the half-time interval, though there is some dispute as to how many players used it. In most reports, and in most historical accounts, it has been recorded that only one player, Jim Shorten, used it.

The Argus, though, quoted Dr MacGillicuddy as saying the followers, George Angus, Les Hughes and Dick Vernon "sat with the cups over their mouths" and took part in the process. Regardless, it had no impact. The Magpies led by two points at half-time. But, after the oxygen was used, South Melbourne kicked six goals to one in the third term, and stole a break. The final margin was 21 points.

Frustration at a lack of recent success meant there was a "growing anxiety"[61] within Collingwood. The Annual Report was emphatic in its plans for 1910, saying: "We confidently expect—and with a young, manly and vigorous team such as we have, and the addition of some

---

60   *The Argus*, September 19, 1909
61   *The Magpies, The Official Centenary History of the Collingwood Football Club*, Brian Hansen, 1992

promising recruits, we have every right to expect—that Collingwood, if it cannot command success, will at least deserve it."[62]

McHale was as frustrated as anyone. He had played in a winning final in his first season, yet had since played in seven successive losing finals. In 1909 he had once more attended all training sessions, and after a ballot, had won "the prize of a suit of clothes"[63] donated by Mr J.F. Treadway, from the clothing store in Smith Street, Collingwood.

'Old Boy', from *The Herald*, said Collingwood "had a reputation to lose ... it has always been in the final four and it intends to stay there."[64] But the club wanted much more than that.

A loss to Carlton in the opening game of 1910 was hardly the most opportune start. Neither was a mid-season slump that saw the Magpies lose three consecutive games, something that the club had not done since the end of the 1907 season. At one stage, the Magpies dropped to sixth, but the club never gave in to the belief that they could match it against any team in the competition.

McHale played a big role in this. Now into his eighth season, the brewery worker was considered one of the club's best players, along with captain-coach George Angus and champion forward Dick Lee, and was more than adept at matching it with the other great centremen of the competition.

That defeat to Carlton in the opening round brought out a few doubters. *The Argus* argued: "We generally anticipate good system from a Collingwood team, but on this occasion the general-ship was all on the other side. It was soon evident that a footballer like Angus, who is always in the stress of it rather than looking on, cannot be an efficient captain."[65]

It was a harsh assessment. In the next breath the same reporter highlighted that Angus was Collingwood's best player in the 28-point

---

62   Collingwood Annual Report 1910
63   Collingwood Annual Report, 1910
64   *The Herald*, April 30, 1910
65   *The Argus*, May 2, 1910

loss. McHale was said to have played "fairly" in the centre, and he booted his fifth career goal in the third term.

An event from across the other side of the world saw the Round 2 matches postponed from May 7 until the following week. News filtered through to Australia that King Edward VII had died.

'Markwell', of *The Australasian*, detailed the mood of Melburnians: "The sad event of King Edward's death has moved to deepest mourning the millions that make up the Empire. The dire intelligence reached the city about midday on Saturday, and the suddenness of the calamity shocked the community, for although everyone had been apprised for a day or two before that the indisposition was serious, no one could have anticipated so rapid a fatal ending. Upon business, the effect was paralysing, and in common with the rest of their fellow citizens, those whose Saturday afternoons are usually devoted to sport, lost no time in evidencing their inability and utter disinclination to carry out their customary programmes. Sportsmen generally have been wont to regard the departed monarch as a personal friend, as much as a ruler of the Empire."[66]

There was a push to suspend football for an extra week, but "the sacrifice was not demanded ... since telegrams from the Motherland had intimated that it was the wish of His Majesty, King George V, that the amusements of his subjects should not be unduly interfered with."[67]

When football resumed, Collingwood defeated the previous year's premier, South Melbourne, by 41 points. "On the form that had been shown ... there seemed very little chance of Collingwood winning ... on this occasion, however, (they) were at home (invariably a matter of moment to them) and they had, in the interim, added unmistakably to the strength, speed and general efficiency of their team."[68] First-year player Joe Scaddan was mentioned, as well as second-year players Richard Daykin, Percy Wilson and Jack Shorten.

---

66   *The Australasian*, May 14, 1910
67   *The Australasian*, May 21, 1910
68   ibid

Frustration crept into South's game. One incident saw "what seemed like a deliberate blow on the chest of McHale, his opponent in the centre, by (George) Bower ... McHale claimed equality with his antagonist, Bower, who was very fine in the centre. (He) is an accomplished player, and needs to use no illegal methods in disposing of an adversary."[69]

Two days before Collingwood's next fixture, a clash with St Kilda at Victoria Park, another momentous occasion beckoned. Earth passed through the tail of Halley's Comet. Unfortunately, cloud cover made visiblity of the comet near impossible, but on the Saturday night—just hours after Collingwood had beaten the Saints by 73 points—more than a few Melburnians managed to catch a glimpse of the phenomenon.

In Durban, South Africa, "natives connected the King's death with Halley's Comet ... they expressed the belief that the comet is a chariot sent to carry the King's soul to heaven."[70] Closer to home, in Shepparton, sections of the Chinese community feared it was a bad omen, saying the comet's appearance "foretold all sorts of trouble, such as war, pestilence, drought and famine of rice".[71]

A two-point loss to Essendon in Round 4 was a game that got away after the Magpies kicked a woefully inaccurate 4.17 (41) to 6.7 (43). In the last term, said *The Australasian*, "Collingwood peppered away ... eight tries, all within range, and several of them easily so, produced but a single point each, and altogether the 'Woodsmen's luck was out. With less than two minutes to go, (Dick) Lee snapped Collingwood's last goal ... (but) it was the mere inaccuracy in marksmanship that brought about the 'Woodsmen's defeat."[72]

---

69   ibid
70   *Camperdown Chronicle*, May 12, 1910
71   *Sydney Morning Herald*, May 25, 1910
72   *The Australasian*, June 4, 1910

Prime Minister Andrew Fisher was at the game just days after winning a federal election, having failed in an earlier stint. McHale was a Labor voter. *The Australasian* said: "For his initial view of Melbourne football, it was a pity the Prime Minister was shown a game that fell far below the customary standard. Mr Fisher would have carried away with him a bad impression of Australian Football. I doubt if any previous meeting (of Collingwood and Essendon) furnished more roughness and bullocking, or was so lacking in attractive incidents ... As the roughness increased, there came reprisals ... the man who seemed to suffer the most was Angus, the Collingwood captain, who lay on the slab for several minutes. His collapse had been due to a succession of shocks."[73]

This was symbolic of a theme of the 1910 VFL season. Violence on and off the field became prevalent. "From every ground on which League football was played, the majority of players carried away painful reminders of the severity of the ordeals through which they had passed."[74] By mid-season, it was enough to have administrators and even the state government concerned. There was an "announcement that the Premier (Sir John Murray) and the Chief Commissioner of Police had decided to take proceedings against unruly players. Your footballer is no fool. He recognises the fact that there is a power above him."[75]

McHale's form was outstanding in the bracket of four successive wins that followed the Essendon loss. After the game against Melbourne, which the Magpies won by 48 points, *The Australasian* said: "Collingwood's brightest star was McHale, who was in his element where nothing unsportsmanlike was attempted. Collingwood played with splendid concert, each man fitting his position like the several parts of a smoothly-running machine."[76]

---

73   ibid
74   ibid
75   *The Australasian*, June 11, 1910
76   ibid

Wins against Fitzroy, Richmond and University followed. In the last of those wins, "Collingwood's most brilliant and useful player was McHale, who has from the opening of the year, invariably shown tip top form in the centre."[77]

Then, inexplicably, three weeks of losses followed, throwing a serious doubt on the club's premiership prospects. Angus missed all of them with injury, leaving his vice-captain Lee as a reluctant stand-in, with McHale assisting. Collingwood managed only two goals against Carlton; and only four against South Melbourne. It was feared that "they had lost their run of system."[78] Rowell and Angus returned the following week against St Kilda, and it, too, was a close call, with victory of 11 points being assured only late in the game. Perhaps a turning point came against Essendon in Round 13, where the club had only kicked one goal to three-quarter time before finishing with a match-winning four goals in the last term in atrocious conditions at East Melbourne. According to *The Australasian*: "Men, in their hunt for the ball, plunged often into pools that not only covered their boot-tips, but that splashed so high as to momentarily hide from the view of onlookers bodies as well as boots."[79] McHale was a key player, defeating Busbridge, who broke his finger in the battle. "They were largely indebted to McHale for their success ... for their crack centreman played a wonderful game in the slush."[80]

Collingwood used its weekend off football to travel to the western half of Victoria. The Annual Report said: "Apart from the pleasure derived, the few days' rest relaxes the hardened muscles often resulting from the stern course of training necessary for the modern-day footballer and braces him up generally for the final contests."[81] The club visited Hamilton, Warrnambool and Colac, playing and winning against local teams.

---

77   *The Australasian*, June 26, 1910
78   *The Australasian*, July 16, 1910
79   *The Australasian*, July 30, 1910
80   ibid
81   Collingwood Annual Report, 1911

The winning streak continued on arrival home, and the final round win over Geelong at Victoria Park saw Collingwood "comported ... like a team of champions ... one of (their) strongest points just now is pace. They have been speedy for the majority of teams they have encountered this year."[82] The win saw the club finish the home and away season in second spot to Carlton, and with a real chance to break the seven-year drought.

McHale and Collingwood threw themselves into training with gusto in the lead-up to the semi-final against Essendon. One observer on the final night of training before the game said: "In the closing stretches of the Thursday, one looked upon the scene of briskness and enthusiasm ... Nearby every player of the team was at work trying to perfect himself in picking up, handling, passing, running, dodging, marking and kicking, not one of them failed to test himself."[83]

The Magpies were confident, but when the heavens opened up shortly after noon, it perhaps squared the ledger somewhat. "The opinion of the public was that, with fine weather something classy in the way of football would have been seen, but with rain-soaked ground, and the slippery ball it was felt as if it was anyone's game."[84] For a time, it even looked as if the authorities would postpone the match. But Collingwood was desperate for the match to go ahead.

Such was the Magpies' eagerness that the players waited impatiently around the boundary for the junior curtain-raiser between Leopold and South Yarra to finish. Collingwood held sway from the earliest stages of the game, with McHale getting his hands on the waterlogged ball with regularity. He even kicked a goal in the opening term, the only goal he ever kicked in a final.

---

82   *The Australasian*, September 9, 1910
83   *The Australasian*, September 17, 1910
84   ibid

The Magpies led by 28 points at half-time, but no one felt safe or secure. However, nine goals to four followed in the last hour of the game, with Collingwood's first finals win since 1903 coming by 58 points. Weaknesses, according to Taylor's history of Collingwood, were near impossible to pinpoint, as the team came together: "A premier team must be evenly and excellently manned in all points, and to my mind, Collingwood fits the both in both requirements ... Every man was a star, with McHale the brightest."[85] Lee kicked six goals.

The ease of the win provided confidence that Carlton could be beaten. That received further validation the following week when an extraordinary set of circumstances arose before the Carlton-South Melbourne semi-final. Three Blues were withdrawn from the game after allegations of bribery cast a shroud over the competition. One of the players, Doug Gillespie, was later cleared, but two, Alex 'Bongo' Lang and Doug Fraser, were banned for five years.

It was not known how this would impact on the spirit of Carlton, but it clearly had an impact in the semi-final as South Melbourne won the match. Given the Blues were the minor premier, they had the right of challenge. Collingwood had to win its way past South Melbourne in a preliminary final before it could tackle Carlton in the Grand Final.

For the second game in a row, McHale was the adjudged by most people as the best player on the field. Taylor wrote: "In an attractive and stubborn game, all helped, but McHale must be accorded the place of highest honour."[86]

Collingwood led narrowly throughout before gradually drawing away to win by 11 points. McHale was finally going to play in a Grand Final. It would prove to be one of the most controversial premiership play-offs in VFL history.

A crowd of 42,790 turned up to the MCG on October 1 to see Collingwood and Carlton compete for the premiership, and much

85   *The History of the Collingwood Football Club, 1892-1948*, Percy Taylor, 1949
86   ibid

of the partisan support was with Collingwood, given the betting controversy associated with Carlton, and because the Magpies had been "repeatedly in the finals without of late years getting actually on top."[87] Fate was also on Collingwood's side. "A coincidence was noted as the teams came out ... in every one of the finals this year the first team on the ground had won the match."[88]

After a season of controversy involving betting and brawls, the VFL must have surely been hoping for a smooth finale. A portent came on the morning of the match, when *The Herald* ran a cartoon depicting Collingwood and Carlton players trading punches. In a few hours, the image would become an embarrassing reality.

There was tension almost from the time the two teams arrived at the ground. When the umpire, Jack Elder, went into the rooms to inspect the players he noticed a "sullen hostility".[89] He was right. *The Argus* reported ominously that "it was clear in the first five minutes that the game was going to be desperately hard. No one gave any thought about the possible consequences."[90]

In the richest vein of form in his career to date, McHale played a key role. He was 27, and playing in his first Grand Final in his 144th game. No other Collingwood player in the team had played more games. He had a hand in the club's first goal, which was highlighted by a spirited run from defence to attack. "Collingwood's retaliating charge was more effective, for McHale, (Tom) Baxter, and Angus took the ball the length of the ground, and with a fine drop kick, Angus set his side a goal-kicking example by landing the first (goal)."[91]

Collingwood booted another three goals in an opening term, seeing them lead with a score of 4.3 to 1.2. The early lead came about from "some very brilliant football ... McHale, (Percy) Gibb, Baxter

---

87   *The Argus*, October 3, 1910
88   ibid
89   *This Football Century*, Russell Holmesby and Jim Main, Wilkinson Publishing, 1996
90   *The Argus*, October 3, 1910
91   ibid

and (Dick) Vernon working well together".[92] Oddly, though, this "dazzling rush of success" was followed by a bizarre switch in tactics in the second term, as Angus instructed his team to go on the defensive to restrict Carlton as the primary motivation, *The Herald* said. "Angus massed his men wholly for the defence and, as a consequence, Carlton began to show up, and with anything like the same luck and skill that Collingwood were able to command, the Blues might have recovered their position."[93] The margin at half-time was 15 points.

But there were some concerns. Joe Scaddan had been seriously injured, but gamely fought on. Dave Ryan hurt his elbow and had to play forward as a result, while Angus and Percy Wilson also suffered injuries that would restrict them.

Dick Lee increased Collingwood's lead when play resumed, and for a time it seemed as if the Magpies were destined to run away with the contest. But the Blues kept working hard, and a late goal in the third term made it 20 points at the last change.

The two teams gathered themselves for some respite before resuming the battle. Most of the Carlton players stood in their huddle; many of the Collingwood players lay the on the turf. A photograph shows Angus receiving a rub down from a trainer from a bottle of an unknown source, while the club's master conditioner Wal Lee watches on. Beside Angus, crouching down, is McHale, who is taking his "lemon" and gathering his thoughts for the challenge ahead.

What followed in the last quarter was described by *The Argus* as the "the most disgraceful scene witnessed on a Melbourne football field."[94] In the middle stages of the final term, a fight broke out in front of the Harrison Stand. It started between Carlton's Jack Bacquie and Collingwood's Tom Baxter.

The Argus documented the clash: "Bacquie … rose for a mark. Baxter rose a second later. As the two men regained their feet, their arms

---

92   ibid
93   *The Herald*, October 1, 1910
94   *The Argus*, October 3, 1910

locked about the ball. Bacquie wrenched and twisted. Baxter hung on tenaciously. Bacquie fell back and Baxter was still gripping the ball. Bacquie released one hand and Baxter freed one of his hands. Bacquie, hot with rage at his possession being so obstinately disputed, raised his hand and in a second the two men fell to the ground fighting."[95] Then Jim Shorten hit Bacquie with "an all-mighty punch". Les Hughes was knocked out and Richard Daykin came to the aid of his teammate in what was a "period fraught with sensational possibilities."[96]

The only way that umpire Elder managed to stop the all-in brawl from degenerating further was to bounce the ball. He said later: "The whistle and the bounce did the trick. Suddenly players remembered that there was a ball to be chased. The sparring and the grumbling and the swinging rights and lefts stopped like magic. I feel certain that if I failed to get the game going again that day the crowd would have swarmed onto the ground and rival camps of barrackers would have been at each other's throats."[97] The game was played out. McHale's wish was granted. Collingwood had won by 14 points. If Lee was Collingwood's best player with four of the club's nine goals, then McHale was the next best. But just as many people were talking about the brawl as the Collingwood victory.

Angus had become Collingwood's first VFL premiership coach; McHale was finally a premiership player. The coach praised his players for their resilience. Angus told the waiting media: "I am satisfied that my team is better, and in today's go, we were heavily handicapped, for three of us—Wilson, Ryan and I—were crippled after half-time. They played magnificent."[98] It was the first time these two teams had competed in a Grand Final. The next five would be in Carlton's favour.[99]

---

95   ibid
96   ibid
97   *This Football Century*, Russell Holmesby and Jim Main, Wilkinson Publishing, 1996
98   *The Premiership's A Cakewalk*, Glenn McFarlane with Richard Stremski, Spicer's Papers, 1998
99   Carlton would defeat Collingwood in the next five Grand Final meetings—1915, 1938, 1970, 1979 and 1981

There were two interesting postscripts. Tom Baxter was one of four players suspended, and he received a year's ban. But the VFL received a letter from Baxter's teammate, Daykin, who was about to retire from the game. Daykin claimed it was him, and not Baxter, who had struck Bacquie. Incredibly, the VFL found in his favour, and overturned Baxter's decision, despite umpire Elder's insistence on who the culprit was.

The other postscript concerned the club's treasurer, Bob Rush, who had retired from the game in 1908, but who would serve the club in administration for decades. He used his knowledge of Latin from his time at CBC Parade to come up with *Floreat Pica* as the club's motto. Roughly translated, it means "May the Magpies prosper", and given what occurred in 1910 it seemed wholly appropriate.

The win was a popular one, and the celebrations sustained. "The cheers of the vast crowd assembled on the MCC ground, which greeted the success of your players in the final match, had hardly died away when congratulatory messages began to pour in from all parts of the Commonwealth; and you have every reason to be proud of the hearty felicitations extended to the club by offices of the other league teams, including the Dark Blues, our doughty opponents in the final game."[100] There were two functions at the Collingwood Town Hall—one organised by the club and another by "the ladies of Collingwood."[101] The president of the South Melbourne Football Club, Henry Skinner, even entertained the players and the committee at a "sumptuous dinner at Hosie's Cafe" where the Collingwood team was "greatly praised for skilful players and sportsmanlike behaviour on the field."[102]

McHale, according to the club's 1911 annual report, "won the admiration of all for his fine play in the centre position, and (he)

---

100 ibid
101 Collingwood Annual Report, 1911
102 ibid

was presented with a kit bag by Mr A. Oakman."[103] The club took the team on an end-of-season trip to Adelaide, where they met in a match with the South Australian premier, Port Adelaide. The VFL champions lost the clash, as "about half the regular players were unable to make the trip". In keeping with his durability, McHale was one of those still out there playing.

After one of the most controversial seasons in the VFL's short history, there was always likely to be some change heading into 1911. The most contentious centred on a proposed payment to players after years of "shamatuerism", where football clubs worked in a clandestine way to compensate their players. For years clubs had flouted the VFL's Rule 29 which stated: "Any player receiving payment directly or indirectly for his services as a footballer shall be disqualified for any period the league may think fit, and any club paying a player either directly or indirectly for his services as a footballer shall be dealt with as the League may think fit."[104] It all came to a head in February when 68 VFL players met at the Orient Hotel, in Bourke Street, to discuss a number of proposals that had been put forward concerning the future of the game. McHale was one of them. In fact, such was his commitment to the cause that he was elected to a committee comprising nine players appointed to approach the VFL with their recommendations. South Melbourne's Dick Casey moved a motion that declared: "That its interest would be best served by open professionalism, leaving to each club its own management."[105] The motion was carried 65 to three. But the VFL could not reach an agreement despite delegates holding a vote several times.

---

103   ibid
104   *The Argus*, March 1, 1911
105   *The Argus*, February 7, 1911

Believing that Rule 29 would be deleted, Collingwood officials met with the players in May to formalise an arrangement in the event that the VFL would head down the path of professionalism. It would form the cornerstone of Collingwood's egalitarian financial arrangement with its players for generations.

The Argus reported: "The Collingwood executive, who has always been on the best of terms with its players, has formulated a definite scheme whereby the executive takes 25 per cent of the takings for administrative purposes, and the other 75 per cent is to be divided amongst the players. The arrangement has been agreed to by the players, each of whom will in future play under signed agreement with the committee."[106]

The players selected in the seniors were to earn a flat rate of one pound as their expenses for the week. Each player was to earn the same amount, a philosophy that would become so important to McHale. *The Argus* explained: "Whether a man lives 100 yards or 100 miles from the ground, he gets his allowance of one pound." The Collingwood players went further, stating a policy that "they have decided that they will not have in their team, to share in the profits, any man who wants to live on the game. A man must have a trade or other honest profession."[107]

Finally, on Friday, May 12, the night before Collingwood's Round 3 clash with Geelong, the VFL finally secured the three-quarter majority vote needed to repeal Rule 29, and usher in one of the biggest changes in the game.

Not everyone agreed. One of the founding fathers of the game, H.C.A. Harrison, had earlier stated: "For nearly 50 years the game had been amateur, but now it was degenerating ... Clubs could do no greater damage to young men to make them professional."[108] Even the president, Alex McCracken, admitted he had not supported it. But the majority of delegates did.

---

106   *The Argus*, May 2, 1911
107   ibid
108   *The Argus*, March 1, 1911

McHale's involvement in the debate over professionalism in football was an indication of just how comfortable he felt of his role within the game. On the field, he had become an industrious and sometimes inspirational centre-man; one of his side's important players. Off it, he was also playing a bigger role in the fortunes of the club. Dick Lee was vice-captain, but in keeping with his penchant for preparation, McHale was appointed as an assistant to the club's playing coach George Angus. The unpaid role was as a supervisor of training. They must have made for a formidable duo: Angus, the former Boer War soldier with the neat moustache who was once described by a teammate as a man who had never been seen smiling;[109] and McHale, with a similarly serious countenance who believed implicitly in being as physically prepared as possible.

They were both there in the front row of the grandstand as the Collingwood team assembled to watch the unfurling of the 1910 premiership pennant ahead of the Round 1 clash with Richmond at Victoria Park. McHale is in long sleeves, leaning against the rail, and his mouth is open in a half-smile. In the grandstand the fans have risen to their feet and in front of the stand men and women in hats look on proudly.

The Herald described the moment: "Collingwood supporters cheered and cheered again when the premiership pennant was run up the flag staff ... They won it last year and as it fluttered when shaken out against the north wind, there were many shouts ... 'We will win it again this year'."[110]

The recruitment of a number of young players, as well as the continued good form of the premiership players from the previous year meant the Magpies were always going to be a chance in 1911.

Some of those recruits would have long-lasting impacts on McHale's life at Collingwood. One was a young man from Bendigo called Dan Minogue. Such was the belief that Collingwood officials had in him

---

109   *A Century Of The Best*, Michael Roberts, Collingwood Football Club, 1991
110   *The Herald*, April 29, 1911

that he had accompanied the side on their trip to Adelaide at the end of the previous season. Minogue fractured his collarbone only minutes before the end of his first game in Round 1, but he showed enough to suggest he was going to be a star—and a leader.

Jim Sharp, the former Fitzroy captain, transferred to Collingwood, and would become one of McHale's great friends.

Meanwhile, two players from different backgrounds but who became the closest of friends made their debuts that season. One was a Collingwood native, Malcolm Seddon, known to his mates as 'Doc'. The other was Percy Rowe, who used 'Paddy Rowan' as his football name for dual reasons: it was a pseudonym he had used in boxing to ensure his mother did not know of his pugilistic endeavours; and also because he had played football with South Bendigo under his actual name earlier in the season. The pair would be inseparable until an event halfway across the world would separate them from Collingwood, one of them permanently. Others to commence careers in 1911 and have long-term careers at Collingwood were George Anderson, Jack Green and Alec Mutch.

The Magpies opened the 1911 season with two wins, against Richmond and Fitzroy; McHale was nominated in newspapers as one of the best in both. But then there were successive losses to Geelong (by three points) and Essendon (by a massive 85 points). The loss to Geelong was at least close, and there was the caveat that Dick Lee had missed the game with injury. It was a game in which the visiting side to Victoria Park wore red socks to prevent a clash in the uniforms.

But the loss to the 'Same Old', which was now being coached by Jack Worrall, was embarrassing. Still without Lee, the Magpies could manage only seven goals to Essendon's 21. It was the club's most embarrassing performance in almost 20 years of competing. *The Australasian* said: "Never since Collingwood became a senior team (in 1892) has such a crushing defeat been inflicted upon the club. The best that could be said for Collingwood was that if their skill failed them, their hearts never faltered."[111]

There were concerns about Collingwood. One supporter, who called himself 'Black and White', wrote to *The Herald*: "As an old supporter of the 'Magpies', it appears to me that their attack is very weak ... (and) the defence is even weaker than the attack. The fact is the past reputation of a club won't bring players; they have to be looked for, and the sooner the committee emerge from the seclusion of their luxuriously appointed room under the grandstand and hustle a bit like the officials of other League clubs, the better for Collingwood."[112] It was a harsh assessment, although the Magpies did make a considerable number of changes the week later. That loss was followed by three tight wins against South Melbourne, Melbourne (in McHale's 150th game) and University.

Lee was back in the team by this stage, but even he couldn't help when the Magpies went down to the Blues in Round 8 after a lacklustre performance at Princes Park. A scoreless first quarter meant the team was always on the back foot. Two goals—one of them to Lee—came in the second, but Collingwood did not score another one for the rest of the game, losing by 33 points in difficult conditions.

In the lead-up to the St Kilda game a week later, the Coronation Honours were announced and it led to a quaint example of just how feted the Collingwood players were at the time. When the list was declared, the story goes that a young lad on a train bound for Victoria Park station noted the honours in *The Herald* and explained: "What! No Dick Lee!"

Old rivals Fitzroy proved another hurdle in Round 11, and *The Australasian* stated that "Collingwood are not having the best of fortune or luck so far. That the team on paper is a good one, there can be no denying, but there is something astray, and that something cannot be explained."[113] This was compounded by a suspension to Lee,

---

111   *The Australasian*, May 20, 1911
112   *The Herald*, May 26, 1911
113   *The Australasian*, July 1, 1911

who had received a "severe thump" in the second quarter and responded with a "hard blow" on Bill Walker. The crack forward would not play again until Round 16, and two losses in that period that placed more pressure on the club.

Through it all, McHale's form was outstanding. He was arguably Collingwood's most consistent player of the season, and was rarely out of the best players. He was rewarded by being chosen to play for Victoria in the national championship in Adelaide, and such were his leadership qualities that he was chosen as vice-captain of the team. Other Collingwood players selected were Dick Lee, Ted Rowell and Jim Sadler.

There was a reception on arrival for the teams. According to *The Adelaide Advertiser*, "the party were driven in a drag" to the league rooms where the "father of the game", H.C.A Harrison, then almost 75, gave a response. He said he hoped to live long enough to "see a team come to Australia from far-off America (cheers) ... and looked forward some day to the visit of a Japanese team ... if the Japanese could only play football as they could fight, they would prove to be a tough proposition for an Australian team ... he was proud of the fact that the rules as he had drawn them up had never been materially altered and still stood as a foundation of their game."[114]

Victoria had won the carnival three years earlier and was expected to do the same. But a number of injuries to the Victorian side and a competitive South Australian team made things very difficult. The issues started as early as the first game against New South Wales. In that game, Lee (who had already kicked four goals) suffered an injury that would have serious implications on the carnival, but also for Collingwood, which could ill afford to be without the champion goalkicker. Such were the injury woes that the Magpies team that happened to be visiting Adelaide during the time of the carnival had to offer up Jim Sharp as a call-up.

---

114   *The Adelaide Advertiser*, August 2, 1911

The NSW team also pushed the Victorians all the way, with their coach Mick Grace urging them to "slam into them harder" at the long break. It was a four-goal win, but hardly an impressive one. The same could be said for the next clash with Tasmania, although the final margin was 31 points. In the match against Western Australia, they were further affected by injuries. The match was a one-sided one, with the final margin being 56 points, but there were genuine fears about the South Australian side.

Given the hard state of the Adelaide Oval, the local curator poured almost a million litres of water onto the ground before the game because it had been "like concrete."[115] And then the heavens opened and the players faced a "sodden, greasy" playing surface. It was supposed to suit the Victorian side; it didn't.

The South Australians gained an early advantage and took a nine point lead into half-time. But the Vics could only add two behinds in the last hour of play, as the home side dominated, winning by 43 points. Even though McHale fought hard and was clearly one of the Victorian players of the carnival, his team was outplayed.

The losing captain, Bill Eason, said: "We got what we thought we wanted ... a wet, heavy ground, but they beat us. I think they would have beaten us by more if the ground was dry. (At least) our centreline held their own."[116] He listed McHale as one of the best players for his state over the duration.

When the Magpies returned to Melbourne—minus first year player Alec Mutch, who had appendicitis while he was in Adelaide and would not play again that season—the team sparked into action with four successive wins. It started with the massive 89-point win over University in Round 16. Collingwood kicked 14 goals (Lee kicked three, but Percy Wilson was out with an ingrown toenail) and kept University without a goal for the duration of the match. The University side was weakened with students missing because of examinations, but it was a rout regardless.

---

115 *The Argus*, June 19, 1952
116 *The Adelaide Advertiser*, August 14, 1911

McHale was able to replicate his white-hot form of the carnival on his return. Against Carlton, according to *The Australasian*, McHale "played one of his very best games ... full of sterling merit. Seldom when he got the ball did he fail to make good use of it, and most of the Collingwood goals were obtained as a brainy play on McHale's part."[117] The 15-point win that day elevated the Magpies into the four. They held on to their place, by two games, and squared off against South Melbourne in the semi-final.

South went into the game as favourites, but Collingwood was "the cooler team", going on to win the match by five goals. A week later Worrall had a modicum of revenge on his old side, Carlton, when he coached Essendon to a win in the other semi-final. It set up a Grand Final between Essendon and Collingwood. The Magpies had to be prepared to beat the 'Same Old' twice, as the latter was the minor premier with the right of challenge. But the real worry for Collingwood was that Lee had aggravated his knee again in the semi-final.

As resilient as McHale had been, the Collingwood side had numerous injuries in 1911 highlighted by two major injuries early in the Grand Final. First, Lee was hurt, and then by the end of the first quarter, Minogue had badly injured his shoulder. As *The Herald* noted: "It was a misfortune for Collingwood ... Lee's leg crossed an Essendonian on the run, but it was enough to jar a weak knee; whilst Minogue was jammed in a crush in front of goal ... It was apparent that Lee was not able to do justice to himself at all, and it would have been far better to have given the injury a further rest, and for a player sound of limb to have played."[118]

The rain that arrived just before the game had made it difficult. In the opening term, said *The Herald*, Collingwood "looked smart and athletic with bare, muscular arms the size one would have fancied in a tug-of-war, but Essendon were wiser in wearing sleeves to their

---

117   *The Australasian*, August 26, 1911
118   *The Herald*, September 23, 1911

jackets—a fact which Collingwood realised long before half-time."[119] By that stage, after a scrappy first hour of play, the Magpies trailed by 16 points, but were still in the contest. Minogue was gamely playing on, and Lee had been dispatched at times to defence as he tried to offer something that his wounded knee could barely allow.

Collingwood was forced to wait around for an extra 10 minutes after the half-time break, with Essendon's late arrival being blamed on them putting longer nails into the stops on their boots. The Magpies barely believed them, and in a response, played their way back into the match. They managed two goals for the term, while restricting their opponents to only two behinds. One of the Magpies' goals came from the courageous Minogue. Almost incapacitated, he took an unlikely mark that "he could never have got with the least opposition ... one of the chivalrous things of the game was to see some of the Essendon backs trying to keep off him."[120] The goal reduced the difference to four points. By three-quarter time, it was only three points, and the game and the premiership was in the balance.

But the focus in the final term centred on one player, and it would make for a controversial conclusion to the Grand Final. Tom Baxter was a 27-year-old playing his 89th game for the club. He had been one of Collingwood's premiership heroes a year earlier; it was a different story 12 months on. The rover did manage his club's only goal for the term. But it was his misses, and the way in which they happened, which threw much of the attention back on him.

The Australasian reported that: (Baxter) "though playing a fine game roving, somehow could not do right when in a place forward. Especially in the last quarter did he fail to realise expectations. Twice he kicked into the man at his mark when shooting for goal within easy range (at least one was a place kick with a heavy ball) and twice was he free kicked in the same term for holding the ball too long.

---

119   ibid
120   ibid

"Then, on another occasion, he missed the goal with a quick snap not many yards away from the post. Supporters were surprised to see this usually reliable and clever player making mistakes at a critical stage of the match."[121] It was said that Baxter's misses were the reason for Collingwood's inability to reel in Essendon, and it was "hard to account for those failures."[122] In the end, Collingwood fell only six points short when the final bell sounded.

Some alleged that Baxter had "played dead". At the conclusion of the game "a demonstration was made by a section of the spectators against Baxter, of Collingwood."[123] The Collingwood player protested his innocence, almost from the moment he walked off the MCG into the dressingroom. Baxter's performance in the last quarter was peculiar, but as historian Richard Stremski noted that he was one of the few Collingwood players capable of scoring in a tense last term, including kicking his side's only six-pointer of the last half hour. Certainly one of his teammates, Ted Rowell, who had been wrongly accused of "playing dead" in 1902, had some sympathy. Rowell wrote: "The most disappointed player was Tom Baxter, who although he kicked the only goal for Collingwood in the last quarter, missed several opportunities to win the game, and be the hero of the day. The ball was very heavy and sodden. Many people considered Baxter had not given his best. That was added bitterness to his cup of sorrow. He asked for an inquiry by the Collingwood committee, of which I was a member, and there being absolutely no foundation for the irresponsible talk, the committee exonerated him and expressed confidence in him."[124]

Baxter fought for the inquiry to take place and contended that he had "indisputable proof" that he was an innocent man. Stremski contended that there had to be some doubt about the allegations. Baxter left Collingwood for St Kilda at the end of the year, and it also gave rise to speculation that the rover was no longer wanted,

---

121   ibid
122   ibid
123   ibid
124   *The Sporting Globe*, June 5, 1943

with the first history of the club suggesting he left because he was an "unwilling player."[125] The reality was that he was "unwilling" to play for Collingwood after the controversy that surrounded his final game with the club.

It's not known what McHale made of it all. But what was certain was that he had fought to lift his team after being beaten in the first half. He had been "cool and resourceful". After being beaten by Bill Sewart in the first half, and twice being penalised when he ran too far without bouncing, and held on to the ball too long, he responded strongly. McHale, according to *The Herald*, "made amends by keeping with his opponent in the two concluding quarters. On the day, 'Mac' was not so brilliant as usual, but it can be said he proved a very useful player. One cannot be expected to play a champion game every Saturday."[126]

It had been a big year for McHale, and the loss of the Grand Final was one of the few negatives. He had been vice-captain of his adopted state; the 1912 Annual Report said he had won "unstinting praise for his fine centre play."[127] He had taken on a training role that suited his coaching aspirations, and had—once again—attended every training session in 1911, earning for himself another suit from Treadways.

There was, said the 1912 annual report, also the presentation of a "handsome silver hotwater kettle" placed at the committee's discretion, from the licensee of the London Hotel. It was "unanimously awarded to your brilliant and consistent centre, Mr Jim McHale, for his fine record of 165 matches in his nine years of service."

---

125   *The History of the Collingwood Football Club*, 1892-1948, Percy Taylor, 1949
126   *The Herald*, September 23, 1911
127   Collingwood Annual Report, 1912

CHAPTER 5

Becoming 'Jock'

1912-1914

The portents were not good. In April, just a few days after Collingwood's first practice match of 1912 between a team of "Magpies" against a side of "Bluebirds" at Preston Park, one of the world's most remarkable engineering achievements came to a sad, distressing and almost lonely end in the middle of the Atlantic Ocean. The *Titanic*, at the time the largest and heaviest ship ever constructed, struck an iceberg four days into her maiden voyage from Southampton to New York. News of the disaster was cabled around the world even as ships were steaming to rescue the small number of lifeboats that harboured those lucky enough to find sanctuary on that freezing night, after the White Star liner broke apart and was sucked to its icy grave.

By the time news of the disaster reached Australia, the casualty figures were so distressing that they were hard to comprehend. More than 1500 souls perished; only 706 survived. There were six Australians on board: four crew members and two passengers. Only two survived. *The Argus* mused solemnly: "Never has there been a more appalling disaster at sea than that which has just befallen the *Titanic*. It has generally been supposed that a vessel constructed with such cunning could not sink, no matter what she might collide with. The Titanic, however, had the dire misfortune to smash into a yet greater and more solid leviathan than herself."[1] It was, as Thomas Hardy penned in the *Convergence of the Twain*, a moment "where consummation comes, and jars two hemispheres."[2]

The Collingwood Football Club would refer to disasters in its summation of the 1912 season. Although admittedly there were no fatalities, there were injuries and issues aplenty in a season in which few things went right from start to finish. It marked the first year that Jim McHale—who was increasingly being called 'Jock' by some people around the club—took over as coach of the Magpies. It was the first of 38 seasons that he would act as coach (either playing or non-playing), and given the manner of that inconsistent season, it could so easily have been his only one. At other clubs, it might have been.

In describing the football year, the committee declared in the Annual Report: "Season 1912 will probably be long remembered as the most disastrous in the club's history, and for the first time since the inception of the League—sixteen years ago—our team failed to secure a place in the final four."[3] Given the club's short but proud history, this was an enormous shock, not only for those intimately involved, but also the growing band of supporters inside and outside of the suburb's boundaries. There were a few reasons for this failure: the loss of several senior players leading into the season, including the man who had led the club to its 1910 premiership; a series of shocking injuries which weakened the team, particularly in attack; and a rare, brief crisis of confidence from McHale himself.

It started when George Angus, who had coached the club for the previous two seasons, decided to seek a clearance to Williamstown in the VFA. Wearing a red rose in his coat, Angus told a hearing of

---

1   *The Argus*, April 17, 1912
2   *The Convergence of the Twain*, Thomas Hardy, 1915
3   Collingwood Annual Report, 1913

VFL delegates in April: "I don't think I'd be of much further use to the (Collingwood) club. I'm going to Williamstown. They want me to coach the side. I don't suppose I will play much owing to this old foot of mine."[4] Collingwood offered no objections. Angus was rising 37, and injury had cost him the chance to play in the previous year's Grand Final. Dick Lee had captained the club that day with assistance from McHale, while Angus oversaw tactical issues from the other side of the fence.

Tom Baxter, as previously mentioned, sought a move to St Kilda. It was granted, with Collingwood's secretary, Bud Copeland, explaining that Baxter "leaves the club with the good wishes of two-thirds of the players, and a big majority of the members of the club."[5] He "believed Baxter had done his best" in the game. It was an unfortunate set of circumstances, more so when considering Baxter's revelation at his clearance hearing that he had wagered £32/10/- on the outcome of the 1911 Grand Final—and lost. He declared that he had backed Collingwood. To put that bet into context, just a few years later, £2/8/- was considered sufficient for a family of four to live on for a week.[6]

One of the biggest concerns centred on Dick Lee. His playing future was in doubt, owing to the injury he had aggravated in the 1911 Grand Final. He was only 23, and had kicked 191 goals from his 99 games. *The Argus* said: "His leg is giving him trouble ... Yesterday he was placed under the care of a surgeon."[7] There was considerable doubt whether the brilliant aerialist and goal-kicker would ever reach 100 games, and doubts over his career surely must have been a weight on the new coach's mind.

As experienced as McHale was as a player, and as prepared as he believed he was for every eventuality, his first season as coach proved a tough initiation. Strangely enough, he was not elected captain prior

---

4   *The Herald*, April 26, 1912
5   *The Football Record*, May 11, 1912
6   *Australia Through Time*, Random House, 1999
7   *The Argus*, April 26, 1912

to the start of the season. At the time captains were the result of a popular vote amongst the playing group, and that was not always going to favour a person who was already considered a hard-task master, as McHale was. The players' decision must have come as a surprise to the man in whom the committee had placed great faith as coach.

When the Collingwood players gathered to cast their selections, Jim Sharp was elected as the skipper. Magnanimously, Sharp declined the offer, and maintained that McHale deserved to have the honour. *The Football Record*, in its first year of publication in 1912, summed up the situation at Victoria Park: "Fine sportsmanship was shown at the Collingwood players' meeting for the election of the captain and vice-captain. Jim Sharp was nominated for captain, but declined and proposed J. McHale, who he said deserved the honour and he would do all in his power to assist him. Dick Lee, last year's vice, then proposed Jim Sharp for that position. When such fine sporting feeling is shown at the outset of a season a pleasant and happy season is assured, even though not so successful as anticipated from a playing point of view."[8] McHale had become close to Sharp since his move across from Fitzroy (where Sharp had captained the Maroons for three seasons), and he would have no doubt appreciated the gesture from his friend.

An *Argus* feature article on the role of a captain made for interesting reading on the eve of the 1912 season. It read: "The captains are chosen by the players, and although it sometimes happens that the choice lies with the good-natured, sociable champion, with little capacity for leadership, it more frequently happens that the teams show good judgement in selecting as their commanders men who know how to act and to act properly in an emergency, and can think calmly while playing a dashing game."[9]

The Argus noted a good captain "should command first the respect of his men. His conduct must therefore be manly on and off the field, and he must live cleanly. He must be a sterling player. He must not only tell

---

8   *The Football Record*, May 4, 1912
9   *The Argus*, April 27, 1912

his men what to do, but he must be able to do it himself. He must be quick brained, and keen and observant. He must see the weakness of his side and weakness of his enemy. And he must note those features once and act accordingly. He must think for himself and plan moves in an instant. And if he changes the positions of his men, he should be careful not to give offence to his followers, for even sturdy, 'bullocking' footballers can be as sensitive as artists. He must persuade his men that he is making the changes because they are playing so well that he wants to take full advantage of their splendid efforts. He must cry out loud and gesticulate wildly, but he must give his orders coolly, without any fuss, and save the situation with so little demonstration that his leadership is unnoticed, save by the most observant critics in the crowd."[10]

Another salient point was that captains tended to be players under 30, given the "fast game" being played in 1912. That was "unfortunate" as "their judgment is scarcely matured when the speed of the game necessitates their retiring, and instead of players, they become onlookers, with an ever-lasting regret as they view a match that ripened experience is so seldom in accord with pace and vigour and vim."[11] McHale was under 30, but only just. He was about to enter his 10th VFL season, and was an experienced player of 164 games.

His *Argus* profile read: "James McHale, who will lead Collingwood, is as good a centreman as there is playing today. He is a fine mark, and when he gets the ball he always kicks it into the danger zone—for the enemy—well forward where the crack goalkickers are waiting. He can twist and turn, big man as he is, like a hare. All centremen must be able to turn with the suddenness of lightning flashes. If he has one fault, it is that of punting the ball high, instead of sending it through with the swift, low, sure flight, which follows the skilful drop kick, but although the ball soars high from the punt, it invariably lands in a good position and with such a smart (forward) as Lee about, the disadvantages of

---

10   ibid
11   ibid

the punt are unnoticed. A fine mark is McHale, always fair and cool. He should make a fine skipper."[12]

McHale always maintained that he could not recall how the nickname 'Jock' started. But it has long been accepted as fact that he garnered the name from *The Herald's* leading sporting and political cartoonist, Sam Wells, in the early 1920s. Wells' depiction of McHale dressed in a kilt, and sometimes a Scottish hat, helped to popularise it to the point where some people during Collingwood's halcyon years of the 1920s and '30s believed it was his real name, though few dared to call it to his face. While it would become a name that would strike fear and envy into rival teams, the irony was that McHale was of Irish extraction, not Scottish. The truth was that McHale had been called Jock by some teammates—and perhaps even a few supporters—long before Wells picked up his ink pen.

The first known reference to McHale as Jock comes in the club's Annual Report of 1912. It was made in reference to McHale's performance in the 1911 interstate carnival in Adelaide: "'Jock' McHale won unstinted praise for his fine centre play, and was acclaimed as one of the stars of the Carnival."[13] That came a decade before the time Wells— who would later be responsible for Geelong's Cats nickname in 1923— started with *The Herald*. In many of his later interviews, McHale would continue to plead ignorance about how it started, other than to say it had been with him for as long as he could remember.

There were significant changes for the VFL ahead of the 1912 season. *The Football Record* was introduced at a price of one penny with the stated ambition of giving readers "the very latest items of intelligence ... with every point of interest in the football world."[14]

---

12   ibid
13   Collingwood Annual Report, 1912
14   *The Football Record*, April 27, 1912

The VFL president, Alex McCracken, who had been McHale's old brewing boss, pleaded for a good, clean season after the scandals of the previous few years, and with a short-lived experiment of on-field stewards being introduced. He stated: "I hope this year will be equally as prosperous as the last; that it will be fertile in good games, and good sport, and absolutely sterile of unpleasantness."[15] McHale was not overlooked in the inaugural edition of *The Football Record*. He graced the pages with a powerful photograph.

Another innovation—something that made The *Football Record* a much needed commodity for those attending the football—was the introduction of numbers on the backs of the players' guernseys. Newspapers were not allowed to list them. Numbers had first been used as far back as the Collingwood-Fitzroy match in Sydney in 1903, McHale's fourth game. Then, in the 1911 finals series, they were used with minimal success as many of the numbers were indistinguishable. The *Football Record* explained: "Players are to wear numbers conspicuously displayed on each man's back. This will facilitate the identification of players by the general public, and to know who's who when one is watching the proceedings."[16]

But unfortunately the decision to make it happen ahead of the 1912 season came too late for the first edition of the Record to carry all the names and numbers. "There has been an extraordinary rush in the preparation of the numbers, and the work incidental to the innovation. Lists of the names were not supplied in time to permit the fulfilment of ideas that were contemplated, and the proprietor craves the indulgence of readers for any shortcomings in that regard in this, the opening issue."[17] *The Football Record* did briefly acknowledge that, "Collingwood has appointed Jim McHale coach to the team."[18] He would be wearing No.16 in his first year as playing coach.

---

15   ibid
16   ibid
17   ibid
18   ibid

There was plenty of excitement heading into the new season. Not only did it mark 20 years since the birth of the football team that had made the working-class suburb of Collingwood famous, but the club believed it had a strong-willed, tactically astute playing coach, enough good senior players to remain competitive and a host of young prospects eager to make their mark. A series of practice matches had been hotly contested. As *The Herald* suggested: "The crowds of young players who have gathered night after night reminded one not of bluebirds or magpie country, but a swarming of mutton birds or quails or something like that. A place in the Collingwood team is always sought after, for the reason it is a well-managed club, seldom ruffled by any bickering or unpleasantness."[19]

Dan Minogue, so frustrated by injuries in his first year, was considered by *The Herald* to be a "top notcher", Paddy Rowan was said to be a "much improved player", Doc Seddon was "coming along nicely", Alec Mutch had recovered from his appendicitis, George Anderson had quit farming to be closer to Melbourne for his football, and newcomer Charlie Laxton looked a likely type.

The first of Jock McHale's 714 games as a coach would come on April 27, 1912, against Melbourne, at the MCG. Many Collingwood supporters had already pencilled it into their expectations as a likely win. The Melbourne side had not beaten Collingwood since 1907. But surprisingly, it provided a tight and tense opening half, with the home side carrying a three-point lead into the half-time break.

The Argus said that after half-time: "A complete change now came over the game. Collingwood seemed to lose all their dash; they played without any system and looked like a beaten team."[20] Compounding the problem for the new captain-coach was the fact that his opponent in the centre had led much of the play for Melbourne. "McHale's

---

19   *The Herald*, April 19, 1912
20   ibid

football before half-time was all that could be desired ... but (Jim) Fitzpatrick, in the centre, was now playing all over McHale."[21] 'Kickero', of *The Herald*, brought another interpretation in McHale's sudden loss of form in the second half, saying "'Mac' doubtless was somewhat hampered by his new responsibility as skipper."[22] It's unlikely the highly respected respected 'Kickero', whose actual name was Tom Kelynack, would have made such an assertion without being confident it was correct, and he clearly would have gleaned some of that information from either talking with McHale directly, or with one of the Collingwood insiders.

In the end, Melbourne won the contest by 29 points, with Collingwood's forward line appearing barren without the injured Lee. It was hardly an excuse, but some critics believed Collingwood was a fair way off peak condition in the early weeks of the 1912. This was surprising given McHale's obsession with preparation. *The Argus* stated: "The Collingwood men have not yet got into proper condition, but the end of the season is a long way off, and there are many hard games to be played before the semi-final stage is reached."[23]

Two moments in the following match against Essendon at Victoria Park characterised Collingwood's lack of confidence at the time. Both resulted in goals in the Same Olds' 17-point win over the Magpies. The first came when Ted Rowell, for whom McHale did some summer pencilling work in Rowell's time as a bookmaker, came to grief in incredible circumstances, costing Collingwood a goal, much to the disbelief of the black and white faithful. *The Herald* described: "Towards the end of the first quarter Essendon made a rush for the Collingwood goal. The ball went to Ted Rowell, who stopped it but did not hold it. Then it rolled about five yards from him, (with) no Essendon player being nearer than 20 yards. Everyone was wondering why Ted did not get to the ball. It was afterwards found that the

---

21   ibid
22   *The Herald*, May 2, 1912
23   *The Herald*, May 3, 1912

toe of his boot was stuck in a drain pipe and before he could extricate it, (Percy) Ogden dashed up and kicked the ball through."[24] The loose drain pipe had cost Collingwood a goal, and a few moments of embarrassment for the normally unflappable Rowell.

The other moment was worse, because it was said to have cost Collingwood the match. After leading early, the Magpies faltered and Essendon took a three-point lead into the last term. Then, a passage of play involving McHale hurt the Magpies dearly. *The Herald* recorded: "The game ... resulted in a grand and exciting battle with the result in doubt until three minutes before the final bell, when Jim McHale, in making a dash for goal, missed the bounce, an Essendon player luckily kicked the ball off the ground, and thence it went through goal, settling Collingwood's chance."

The Herald summed up the playing coach's feelings about his "little misadventure", saying: "McHale feels sore, and blames himself for losing the game, but it was purely an accident that he failed to get the bounce which he would have done nine times out of ten." Luck was seemingly in short supply that day, particularly for Collingwood. But Essendon's ruckman Fred Baring had his fair share of ill-fortune, too. "Not only did he (Baring) get a bad fall, but when his clothes were carried out (of the Victoria Park dressing rooms) to the motor car, in which he was taken home, a valuable diamond ring dropped out. Despite advertising and the offer of a handsome reward, he has not recovered it."[25]

If those two on-field mistakes were almost comical, a far more serious incident occurred in Collingwood's third successive loss to start the 1912 season. The 57-point loss to St Kilda—with Baxter opposing his old teammates—at the Junction Oval was described by *The Herald* as "one of the most disappointing displays ever given by a Collingwood side."[26] But as bad as the Magpies were, it was the

---

24   *The Herald*, May 10, 1912
25   *The Herald*, May 17, 1912
26   *The Herald*, May 17, 1912

broken leg suffered by Sharp that stood out—quite literally. Sharp, just 209 days older than McHale, had been one of the most popular players in the VFL, and had been adopted by the Collingwood faithful after coming out of retirement in 1911, following a dispute with his old club Fitzroy.

The collision with a St Kilda player was accidental, but it ended up breaking Sharp's shinbone "almost halfway through ... Collingwood and the football world, generally, were similarly shattered."[27] The injury was so bad that *The Herald* quickly deduced that it "may have the effect of keeping him out of the game altogether."[28] It was Sharp's 17th game with Collingwood. He would play one more—five years later—when filling in when the club was short of a player because of a late withdrawal. The injury on the day had a massive impact on the Collingwood players and McHale. *The Herald* said: "It helped to rattle the team, but (even) before he was injured, the play was very amateurish and the Magpies never got going properly."[29]

Collingwood had lost the first three games of 'Jock' McHale's coaching career—the first time this had happened to the club to start a season. McHale's own form mirrored that of his side. Against St Kilda, he was "second fiddle to his opponent ... Collingwood's skipper could not do anything right and was clean off his game"[30], according to *The Football Record*. Some fans wondered whether the loss of the stern, calculating Angus had been a reason for the inconsistent form of the Magpies. Others were beginning to privately and even publicly express concerns about whether Collingwood needed more change, and whether McHale was the right man for the job.

The talk of Collingwood's decline was rife along bustling Johnston Street, and especially on the dividing battle lines of Smith Street, where the Fitzroy and Collingwood borderlines intersected. McHale

---

27   *A Century of the Best*, Michael Roberts, Collingwood Football Club, 1991
28   *The Herald*, May 17, 1912
29   ibid
30   *The Football Record*, May 18, 1912

would have been aware of this. Several reports refer to his difficulties in adapting to the captaincy, as well as the task of being coach. There was even talk of a reform group. *The Football Record* noted: "Does it not strike you that they (Collingwood) have been badly beaten—nay, positively walloped and out—in two of the three (games)? It looks now as if Collingwood will not gain a place as one of the final four. The defeat on Saturday (against St Kilda) has brought out a section of so-called supporters who are blaming the management and hinting at 'reform'. As reform goes nowadays, it seems to me that half of those who raise the yell do not know what it means. It is a very poor sportsman who in a time of reserve does not remember with some sense of gratitude the fine work done in the past by men who had brought the club up to the proud position it has held ever since foundation."[31]

One Collingwood barracker was so incensed with the talk of reform that he penned a letter to *The Herald*, saying: "A week or two ago there was an article in *The Herald* concerning football wowsers. It looked to me if there was some of the kind at Collingwood. Fair-weather barrackers, I am convinced, are wowsers. They are the curse of every club, for if a team is not consistently successful they attack the management and they seize a chance of bringing themselves into the light as reformers. Such people never give a thank you to those who have spent time, energy and money, in keeping the team in the front rank. They knew very little about football, and the wonder is that level-headed members take notice of their clamour."[32]

But not everyone was against the club. Club secretary, 'Bud' Copeland, was "inundated with letters from enthusiastic supporters sending names of recruits and some of them may turn out well ... at any rate, they will be tried ... The form against St Kilda was too bad to be true, as one old player put it—'They are only imitations of players'."[33]

---

31   ibid
32   *The Herald*, May 17, 1912
33   *The Argus*, May 17, 1912

On the Thursday night before the Round 4 game against Carlton, McHale made a stand. After a strong training session at Victoria Park, he gathered his team in the dressingrooms under the grandstand, and implored them to lift their performance. It was arguably the first of his "rallying" speeches, one of the hundreds he would deliver over almost four decades. Given the pressure that was being applied from forces outside of the club, it was also one of the most important of his early years as coach. As he stood there before the playing group— his deep-set eyes never leaving them as he spoke—McHale may have been aware of the importance of the message he was about to deliver. According to *The Herald*, he urged: "Now lads, for the club's sake, for your own sake, and for my sake, go out and win against Carlton."[34]

In the lead-up to the game, the club was said to be in the doldrums. But from the moment the players emerged from the dressingrooms that night, and headed towards their pushbikes, or the train, or the cable trams, for their journey home, there was a sense that Collingwood's dismal start to 1912 was about to turn for the better. With McHale's words ringing in their ears, the players turned out at Princes Park two days later seeking the club's first win at the venue in seven years, since 1905. It would be no easy task.

While, according to *The Herald*, the "the great football public jumped to the conclusion that it was virtually the beginning of the end of the successful career of the Magpies", Collingwood reproduced its best form with a "dashing" and "smart" performance in an exceptionally tight contest. Carlton appeared to hold sway in the first 15 minutes of the second term when it rattled off three goals. "The cry went up, 'The Magpies are beaten again', but the cry was premature."[35] It was then that Collingwood fought back to kick three goals of its own, and led by a point at half-time.

Three more goals to one came in the third term, as the three-quarter time margin stretched to 13 points in Collingwood's favour. *The Football*

34   *The Herald*, May 24, 1912
35   Ibid

Record noted that an unnamed Collingwood committeeman "who one would not be ordinarily consider superstitious" was concerned with the figure, given the ill fortune that had followed the club that year. He said: "I wish it was 12 or 14 points; I don't like the number (13). It is unlucky."[36] What the committeeman, and the rest of the almost 10,000 fans, had not reckoned with was a mistake in the scoreboard calculations that would have implications later in the day. The real margin was 14 points, not a seemingly ill-fated 13.

In a tight and tense conclusion, Carlton battled valiantly to make up lost ground, while Collingwood defended determinedly. It was a thrilling contest, with *The Football Record* saying that "if anybody wanted more exciting entertainment, I don't know where it is obtainable unless on the broken wing of a flying machine 3000 feet in the air."[37] Flight was a new phenomenon; it had only been two years since Harry Houdini had delighted the residents of Diggers Rest, just north of Melbourne, with a powered flight in March 1910.

In that match against Carlton, McHale was one of the hardest working players, desperately trying to lift his players with words and deeds. As a player, he fought out a classic duel with Rod McGregor, and had the better of him. As coach, he had moved Rowell to attack in the third term. As captain, he tried to lift his players over the line.

Carlton scored two goals in the last term; Collingwood could not manage one in return. The Magpies' final score was a behind from Doc Seddon, as the Blues put on a few more behinds before the final bell. Incredibly, it looked to almost everyone at the ground that the game had ended in a sensational draw. The reality was very different, as 'Kickero', of *The Herald*, reported: "The (score) board showed 6.10 all, and thousands of spectators left for home under the impression that a draw was the outcome of the great struggle. The scoreboard is fortunately not the official record of the day's proceedings. I say fortunately for a reason that on some of the grounds the work of

36   *The Football Record*, May 25, 1912
37   ibid

hoisting the figures is left to small boys whose attention to the business is very often not what it should be. On Saturday, a behind was wrongly credited to Carlton in the second quarter ... and the error was allowed to stand until the finish."[38]

McHale had coached his first winning game, but hadn't realised it until he got back to the sanctuary of the "away" dressing room at Princes Park. *The Argus* explained: "It was only after the majority had left the ground well satisfied with a drawn game that it was officially announced that Collingwood had won by a point."[39] It would not be until 1927—15 years later—that goal umpires were required to compare scorecards at the conclusion of each quarter, and alert the scoreboard of any errors.

For a time it looked like Collingwood's, and McHale's, luck had changed. Dick Lee was exercising again. Collingwood's inefficient attack desperately needed him, but "the committee do not wish to take any risks and he will not be playing without a searching test."[40] That came sooner rather than later. Lee was selected in the Round 5 game against Richmond, a match in which Collingwood dominated from start to finish. Five goals to nil set the scene in the first term, and Lee ended up kicking two goals in the club's 32-point win.

But the misfortune rolled on. Just as the forward everyone wanted to see was back, he was gone again, and this time it looked like it might be forever, according to *The Argus*. "The mishap to crack forward R. (Dick) Lee ... will probably end his football career. Until within 10 minutes of the close of the game ... his knee, which had previously caused him trouble, stood all right and the executive were congratulating themselves on the fact. Then, however, in going for a mark near goal, he struck the behind post and fell with his football in the gutter just outside the playing space, and wrenched his knee again."[41]

---

38   *The Herald*, May 24, 1912
39   *The Argus*, May 20, 1912
40   *The Argus*, May 24, 1912
41   *The Argus*, May 31, 1912

With Lee gone, McHale barely had a side to choose from for the next game with Geelong. Dave Ryan's foot was poisoned. Ted Rowell was away on business. Others were not in a position to be considered. "The smile of Mr E.W. Copeland has gone and now as he glances over a long list of casualties, he wears a worried look, and says, 'We have a team of cripples'."[42] The fans were just as fatalistic. *The Herald* said: "One of the Collingwood members is thinking of teaching a magpie to whistle, 'There's nae luck about the house'."[43]

The team ventured to Geelong more in hope than expectation. The result was a 64-point loss. But you would not have known it from the train trip back from Corio Oval. *The Herald* said: "They share their defeats in the same sporting spirit as they display when they are victorious. On the return journey to town they sang their war song and glees with great gusto ... (Committeeman) Jack Joyce's tenor soaring high above all others, and (committeemen/delegates) Bill Strickland and Ernie Copeland nicely balancing the singing with deep base melody."[44]

The themes of inconsistent form and injuries prevailed. Before the Fitzroy win in Round 8, Copeland reeled off in *The Herald* the list of those unavailable as a doctor would his patient's list. "(Jim) Sharp still in bed, Lee's leg in plaster, (Les) Hughes badly sprained thumb—it may be fractured; (George) Anderson's knee injured, (Charlie) Laxton poisoned leg (no chance). How many is that? Five. That is all so far."[45] Still, against the odds, the Magpies beat the Maroons, and McHale was one of the catalysts for the 15-point win, despite almost becoming a casualty himself. *The Herald* claimed: "It must be said of Jim McHale, the Collingwood captain, that he is a good sportsman. He was buffeted on Saturday, his nose bled, he was kicked accidentally on the back of one hand and one shoulder was damaged. The Magpie captain did not squeak, but accepted the knocks as a part of the manly game."[46] While his team was being decimated on a weekly basis, the captain-coach just kept fronting up game after game. He hadn't missed a game since 1906 and remained as resolute as ever.

It was cold comfort to McHale, said *The Argus*, that "Collingwood's list of wounded must surely be a record. They had hoped that their hospital box was closed for awhile."[47] Early in the struggle with South Melbourne, Percy Wilson broke a bone in his foot. His season was over. After another significant injury setback, Strickland raised the issue of the VFL instituting a substitute rule, telling *The Herald:* "I am inclined to think that it would be a fair and reasonable thing to do if a substitute were allowed to take the place of an injured man up, say, to half-time. The substitute would not be as good as the injured man, or he would have been included in the team at the start."[48] Losses to South Melbourne, Essendon and Carlton left the club in eighth place, two games and percentage out of the four.

Three successive wins between Round 14 and Round 16 gave hope. By the end of Round 16, McHale's team was only percentage outside the top four with two games left. McHale had also turned his season's form around. In the loss to Carlton, *The Herald* said he gave a "masterful exhibition ... apparently the recovery of his form has come to stay."[49] He was among the best in the Round 14 win over Richmond and against Geelong a week later.

Three days after the win over Richmond, on July 30, 1912, Jock and Violet McHale had their first child—a son—at their family home in Talbot Street, Brunswick. Family folklore has it that Jock and Violet had another child—perhaps even earlier—but it was stillborn. No record exists to verify this as stillbirths were not recorded in Victoria at the time. If it did happen before the birth of little James Francis

---

46   *The Herald*, June 14, 1912
47   *The Argus*, June 21, 1912
48   *The Herald*, June 21, 1912
49   *The Herald*, July 27, 1912

McHale—known to his parents as Frank—then one can only imagine the sense of relief and responsibility that accompanied the safe arrival of their son.

Just three days before the birth, Jock's father, John, wrote home to County Mayo, Ireland, to his widowed sister, Sarah, with a sense of nostalgia, pride and yet regret about the passing of years, and the distance between the families. John informed his sister, who he had not seen for 33 years, that he had worked for the Victorian Railways for 24 years after an early job with the New South Wales police, and even reserved a sting for the Government, saying it was "crowding out Australia with immigrants from all parts of the world ... They are a patchy lot, a very poor lookout for them over here at the present time."[50] He spoke of his children "eight alive and four dead, who died in infancy", and detailed what those children were now doing as young adults.

There was a sense of affection in the assessment when describing Jock. "My eldest son James Francis ... is married about three years. He married a girl from Brunswick, Victoria. Her name is Violet Angel, a very nice young lady. He is a famous footballer in Australia and an all-round athlete. He has been chosen to represent Victoria all over Australia. At the present time he is captain and coach for a leading Melbourne team called Collingwood. He is very popular over here."[51] Then he added with a hint of hope: "Some of my sons are very anxious to go home for a trip. Myself and Mrs (McHale) are also very anxious and would be delighted to see you all once again."[52] John and Mary would never get the chance, and nor would their eldest son.

The form of McHale, now a proud father, had turned significantly. In the week that his son was born, *The Football Record* paid tribute to McHale with a ditty that was surely bandied around the Victoria Park outer:

50   Letter, John McHale to his sister Sarah O'Malley, July 24, 1912
51   ibid
52   ibid

Jim McHale, the never fail
His play oft stems the tide;
Good headwork, too, when things look blue,
Brings victory to the side.[53]

McHale's form had improved so much, and his reputation was so strong, that he had the honour of leading the Victorian team that played in Ballarat in August. The team also included Dan Minogue and Paddy Rowan, who were having fine seasons.

But just as Collingwood appeared set to strike for an unlikely finals berth, successive losses came in the last two rounds, to Fitzroy and South Melbourne. *The Herald* summed it up: "Collingwood is out in the cold."[54] It had missed the VFL finals for the first time since the League was formed in 1897. It was little wonder, given the lack of goalkicking power the club had without Lee. The club's leading goalkicker for the year was follower Les Hughes, with 13. It remains the lowest season tally for a leading goalkicker in the club's history.

Missing the finals would have been a bitter blow for all, especially McHale, who would have seen playing finals as something akin to a birthright. *The Football Record* didn't blame McHale personally, saying that "throughout his long career (he) has been a fair and manly player ... one of those who might, with advantage, be taken as a pattern by young players."[55] But others were voicing their disapproval. Still, the threatened reform group seeking to make changes at Victoria Park—perhaps even with the coach—never eventuated.

At the Collingwood annual meeting early in 1913, it was noted that "Collingwood paid (a) heavy tribute to the grim harvester: death."[56] The club's founding president, state parliamentarian W.D. Beazley, had died the previous June, and "a full muster of your players and committee walked at the head of the (funeral) cortege." Tom Sherrin,

---

53   *The Football Record,* August 3, 1912
54   *The Herald,* August 31, 1912
55   *The Football Record,* August 31, 1912
56   Collingwood Annual Report, 1913

whose name had become synonymous with football, and whose factory in Wellington Street, Collingwood, had become legendary, also passed away in November.

There was a bright note for McHale on the night of the annual meeting. He and his great friend Ted Rowell received their long-service certificates, according to the 1913 Annual Report, "having stood the storm and the stress of ten years' play". McHale had won the 1912 training award, once more earning him a suit from Treadways, as part of a ballot. But the most important thing to happen over the pre-season was a "redoubled" effort by the committee to restore Collingwood's pride. The Annual Report explained: "A sub-committee has been working during the summer, and a number of promising 'colts' will be tried out in the practice matches ... With the experience gained by our younger men, and the promise of likely juniors, Collingwood will make a bold bid to recover its proud position in the football world."[57]

The annual smoke night was brought forward to February, according to the 1913 Annual Report, "for the purpose of introducing the aspirants for inclusion in your team of the coming season to the last season players ... a most enjoyable evening, interspersed with advice from the club's old captains to the young players, and a capital musical programme was spent." Jim Sharp had retired, and Dick Lee also indicated that he would not play on. The committee accepted Lee's resignation with regret, and immediately set about trying to organise a testimonial. But they were not giving up on him, with the committee saying: "The hope (is) that at some future date, he will don the colours again."[58]

---

57   ibid
58   ibid

In McHale's second season as captain-coach (he was finally elected skipper outright by the players), Collingwood started with wins over Melbourne, Geelong, Essendon, Carlton, Richmond, University and St Kilda. McHale had made modifications to the Collingwood system. *The Australasian* referred to the changes: "Collingwood made their name in their palmy days by perfecting a class of play that had hitherto been undeveloped. It devolved upon other clubs to evolve a scheme that would break down the Magpies' almost perfect system—hence, the extraordinary modern pace, strength and dash. The Woodsmen are endeavouring to assimilate the two styles, still keeping to their short passes, while not sacrificing pace. The winners were a more even style, excelling in the air, and shining by comparison in the art of passing by hand and foot."[59] McHale was working hard to modernise the Collingwood system, while retaining its good points.

The same publication said a week later: "The dash of Collingwood was remarkable. As a general thing, the side year in and year out has not been noted for dash. I question whether Collingwood has ever shown greater dash as at present, and it augurs well for future success."[60]

By late May, it had gone further: "Collingwood's play has so far been a revelation. They were not quite in the first rank class last season but a few alterations and strict attention to business has (sic) worked wonders. The present combination has, of necessity, adopted the modern style of play, pioneered by Carlton, and is capable of holding their own against the best. They are a well-balanced side, and are bound to have a big say in this year's proceedings."[61]

Collingwood was "adapting to circumstances like a well-trained band" and was "a fast, good, weighty side, brimful of confidence though rather weak forward and they beat their opposition in judgement, picking their men out and long passing. Short passing,

---

59   *The Australasian*, May 3, 1913
60   *The Australasian*, May 10, 1913
61   *The Australasian*, May 24, 1913

not so very long ago, was one of the commandments ... but (Collingwood) has been responsible for moving with the times."[62] Brian Hansen in his club history said: "Players were told they had a tradition to uphold, they were good enough and nothing short of their best was good enough."[63]

Such a rich vein of form left Collingwood on top of the ladder for six straight weeks, from Round 2 to Round 7, and had *The Football Record* saying: "Look at the premiership table—Question: what is the first thing that strikes the eye? Answer: The Magpies are carolling on top, theirs is the only team that has scored a full 100 per cent."[64]

While the previous year McHale had endured a slow start, and internally it was feared his elevation to captaincy might have had an impact on his form, it was a different story in 1913. According to *The Football Record*, in Round 1, "Captain McHale set his men a fine example by getting rid of the ball quickly, passing accurately to the forwards and doing sterling work about the centre."[65] Against Essendon, in Round 3, *The Australasian* declared: "McHale's centre play for the 'Woods was one of his very best performances. Hardly once did Collingwood's captain make a mistake, his brainy play being of assistance to the forwards."[66]

It wasn't just the skipper. The team had quickly gelled back into a competitive force. Dan Minogue and Les Hughes had formed into a strong combination as followers, with Percy Wilson performing well as a rover. McHale, now wearing No.20 (Collingwood players were allocated numbers alphabetically), continued to play to a high

62   *The Australasian*, June 14, 1913
63   *The Magpies, The Official Centenary History of the Collingwood Football Club*,
      Brian Hansen, 1992
64   *The Football Record*, May 17, 1913
65   *The Football Record*, May 10, 1913
66   *The Australasian*, May 17, 1913

level in the centre. Paddy Rowan and Doc Seddon were making an impression, too. From being barely competitive only a year earlier, Collingwood was being spoken about as a premiership contender in the early months of the 1913 season. *The Football Record* suggested: "Collingwood's flag is still flying above all others. Collingwood's system and splendid unity of action were once again demonstrated."[67]

The win over Richmond in Round 5 brought about a nasty incident involving McHale. A scrupulously fair player, who made the ball his object at all times, McHale had a collision with Les Oliver that raised the ire of Oliver's teammates, and the Richmond supporters who had travelled up Punt Road and Hoddle Street to see the match at Victoria Park. *The Argus* insisted there was no malice in McHale's actions, saying that those who tried to remonstrate with him afterwards had not truly witnessed what had taken place. "As Oliver, the Richmond half-back, who fairly dazzled the crowd with some of his runs, was passing McHale, the Collingwood captain made a desperate grab to stop him. The result was that he caught Oliver just in the wind, and he dropped as if he were shot. Some of the Richmond followers, who clearly could not have seen what happened, were annoyed, but it was a pure mischance. McHale is not *that* kind of footballer and many creditable seasons have shown it. However, the incident seemed to wake up a bit of the devil in the players."[68]

During the week the VFL's permit and umpiring committee questioned the steward from the Richmond-Collingwood match, Dick McKay, about it. McKay said: "Ayles, the umpire, agreed with him that McHale tried to grab Oliver, who was running quickly with the ball, and that the Collingwood captain snatched the Richmond dasher's wind. There was nothing unfair in the incident and the committee accepted the explanation."[69]

---

67   *The Herald*, June 6, 1913
68   *The Argus*, May 26, 1913
69   *The Football Record*, July 7, 1913

But after seven straight wins Collingwood "met its Waterloo"[70], according to *The Argus,* on the public holiday for King George V's birthday, with a 10-point loss to Fitzroy. Just two days after the Magpies disposed of St Kilda, the Maroons proved too strong, and had the added incentive of displacing Collingwood on top of the ladder. Some of the activities that interested the populace of Melbourne on that day included the two football matches on offer, a "motor reliability run" from the city to Ballarat and back, a motor boat race from Williamstown to Sorrento, countless activities in the heart of the city, as well as matinee shows at the theatres and picture halls. But an "immense" crowd of around 30,000 crammed into Victoria Park. The *Argus* described the scene: "Beginning with the promise of a glorious day, the holiday weather turned raw and cold ... but nothing could stop the rush to Victoria Park where long before the match between Collingwood and Fitzroy started, the ground literally spilled over with onlookers."[71]

But Fitzroy had Collingwood's measure. *The Australasian* explained: "Collingwood fought gamely in the last term, doing most of the pressing, but for the weakness forward which has been apparent all season, must have won."[72] Those same issues were evident a week later when South Melbourne made it two losses in a row for Collingwood, booting five goals to two in the last quarter to win by 24 points. *The Australasian* said: McHale played "a clever game". Rowell was also one of his team's best players with his kick-ins a feature—"Only once did Ted fail to land the ball in the centre on the kick off, and that was in the second quarter when a dog interfered with him as he was kicking."[73]

Some were wondering if Collingwood's season had started to waver. That wasn't the case in the middle stretch of the season when it won six games in succession. In the last of those six wins, the Magpies

---

70   *The Argus,* June 13, 1913
71   *The Argus,* June 10, 1913
72   *The Australasian,* June 14, 1913
73   *The Australasian,* June 21, 1913

welcomed back champion goalkicker, Dick Lee. Lee had always hoped to play again. He did, against University in Round 15, and his three goals were the difference between the two teams. Collingwood won by 17 points. Lee won a "flattering reception" from the crowd, according to *The Australasian*, and "the champion forward has not forgotten how to kick goals."[74] He had taken to the field in a "special kneecap support" specifically designed by Syd Sherrin, the late Tom Sherrin's nephew, who was now running the company. It was designed to give greater protection to Lee's knee, and "minimise the effects of any knock which he may receive on the injury."[75] It had appeared as if "the Students" were a chance of causing an upset, especially as first-year Magpie Alan Cordner had been injured. But Collingwood steadied to win the match.

Lee had returned just in time for the "country" tour to Stawell, Ararat, Hamilton and Ballarat. The players, led by McHale, played matches at Hamilton and Stawell, winning both, and furthering the cause of football in the country zones as well as enjoying the hospitality. The Annual Report said: "The able management of your worthy secretary ('Bud' Copeland), the smoke nights, dance socials and pleasure drives arranged by the football enthusiasts at the places visited, all tended to make the trip a most pleasant reflection for those who participated."[76] Such was the enjoyment that *The Australasian* stated: "Collingwood vote their recent trip to the Western District one of the most enjoyable undertaken by the club."[77]

The club would bring back fond memories, as well as two boomerangs with black and white ribbons on them. The boomerangs were presented to the club from a group of 15 Aborigines from the Lake Condah Mission at the game in Hamilton. At the half-time interval there was a display of boomerang throwing. It would give

---

74   *The Australasian*, August 9, 1913
75   *The Australasian*, August 2, 1913
76   Collingwood Annual Report, 1913
77   *The Australasian*, August 23, 1913

rise to an idea. Boomerang throwing would become part of the half-time entertainment at Victoria Park for up to a decade. In the second half of the decade, an Aboriginal buckjumper and showman from Lake Condah, 'Mulga Fred', treated the Collingwood crowd to his incredible skills, where he could "whistle a boomerang over the crowd and they gasped as it returned to him."[78]

But Collingwood lost its three remaining home and away games on return from the "tour". In the first game back, against St Kilda at Junction Oval, the home side booted five goals to nil in the opening term, and won by 48 points. The Saints and the Magpies had been big improvers from the previous year, but it was cold comfort to a frustrated McHale. Too much was left to too few, and 'Observer' from *The Argus* documented this when he recorded: "Between the first half-dozen men on the Collingwood side and the rest of their team, there was a big gap."[79] One of the few who had an excuse was Jim Shorten, who dislocated his shoulder before half-time yet had to play on.

Losses to Fitzroy and South Melbourne in the last two rounds brought a vulnerability to Collingwood. In the game against the Maroons, the Magpies controlled the game for much of the first half, but their inaccuracy in front of goal proved fatal. *The Argus* said: "During the first half it seemed a certainty that Collingwood, who were passing the ball at long range with wonderful accuracy, playing the open game with far more skill and certainty than their opponents, and failing only when it came to shooting for goal, must win." Collingwood's half-time score of 4.8 included three posters. Its lead was 11 points. But that's where it ended. Despite the brilliance of Minogue, who was said to have no equal in the ruck in that game, and in that season, Collingwood failed to kick another goal. Fitzroy added six goals after half-time and won by 27 points. To make matters worse for McHale, his opponent, Lal McLennan (another Parade graduate), was the best player in his team.

---

78   *Kill For Collingwood*, Richard Stremski, Allen and Unwin, 1986
79   *The Argus*, August 11, 1913

That left a final-round clash with South Melbourne at Victoria Park, with the winner to avoid a clash with premiership favourite Fitzroy in the first final. There was a good turnout for the game, with the "big crowd instinctively knowing that (the two teams) would be playing for their lives in order to escape meeting Fitzroy'."[80] It also happened to be McHale's 200th match, the first time a player had reached that figure with the one club. It was a desperately close encounter. After leading by nine points at quarter-time, Collingwood was stunned in the second term when South Melbourne put on four goals to one. The visitors kept the momentum up in the third term, pushing out to a 14-point buffer at the last change.

It was only at this stage that McHale sought to change the Collingwood plan. *The Australasian* said: "It was not until three parts of the game had concluded that Collingwood, recognising the futility of kicking the ball into the air, adopted different tactics, keeping the ball low and making for ground play. At times the tactics looked like madness, but there was a method in it."[81] Collingwood added three goals to one in the last term, and for a time looked as if it would cap off McHale's milestone with a win. But a missed chance to Les Hughes late in the last term helped South Melbourne hold on for a two-point win.

'Observer' from *The Argus* recorded: "In the last quarter the ball was forced across the goal from a crush, Hughes being the only man in the vicinity. If he had kicked the ball as it rolled slowly in front, he would have in all probability have scored the goal; but making assurance doubly sure he endeavoured to pick it up, when his long legs slipped from under him, and he performed a most graceful slide on his back in the mud."[82]

Collingwood had made the finals in McHale's second year as coach, but it went into September without the form that had swept it to

80   *The Australasian*, September 6, 1913
81   ibid
82   ibid

13 wins from its first 15 games of the season. And it had to face, in Fitzroy, the team that had displayed such consistent form through the season. Collingwood's two goals to one against a slight breeze in the opening term at the MCG was a solid start, to the point where *The Argus* suggested: "Collingwood was playing a faster, cleaner, a more clever game, and looked like winners for some time."[83]

But Fitzroy kept Collingwood goalless in the second while adding four goals of its own. Then, as rain swept over the MCG, the Maroons dominated the third stanza, kicking 5.6 to 1.1. "When the heavy rain came on, and the ball became slippery and heavy, and the turf became insecure, the weight and force of the Fitzroy men told its tale instantly, and thereafter Collingwood were never in the hunt."[84]

The final margin stretched out to 37 points in the end, and a season that had started so promisingly for McHale, and for Collingwood, had petered out to a damp and disappointing climax.

While Collingwood looked optimistically to the 1914 season, as described in the that year's Annual Report: "As there is the likelihood of all last year's players being available again, the outlook for this season appears to be particularly bright, for they contain the nucleus of a Premier side ... (hopefully) we will be able to strengthen the few weak spots in last year's side and produce a team capable of annexing the 1914 premiership."[85] One of the new players was Harry Curtis, who had played for Carlton with little success, but would be an important player—and an even more important administrator—at Collingwood in the years to come.

At the annual meeting in early March, Jim Sharp, who had replaced Alf Cross as president, spoke buoyantly, saying: "There was every

83   *The Argus*, September 15, 1913
84   ibid
85   Collingwood Annual Report, 1914

prospect of even better things in the coming season (hear, hear) …
the play of the team had been consistently good, and the players had
done all their level best to uphold the honour of the Magpies."[86]
At the meeting, Jock McHale and Ted Rowell were bestowed with
life membership of the Collingwood Football Club. On the same
night Dan Minogue, who had been an outstanding performer for the
previous two seasons, was announced as the winner of a new suit from
Treadways for his dedication to training.

Minogue caused a shock on the eve of the season when he made
a "personal application for a clearance to Essendon Town, where he
had been promised a lucrative coaching position."[87] By that stage,
Essendon Town was known as Essendon A, and played in the VFA.
Minogue was only 22, and had played only 45 games over three seasons.
The application was, according to Taylor's history of Collingwood,
"unanimously refused."[88] Given the club's rigid policy of paying each
of its players the same amount—something McHale championed—
there was nothing that could be done in terms of money. But Minogue
was elected captain by the Collingwood players, with Paddy Rowan
vice-captain. Almost 100 years on, it is not known if McHale was
a candidate.

The 1914 season started in strange circumstances with two draws
on the opening day. Collingwood and Carlton were locked together at
Victoria Park, as were Geelong and Essendon at Corio. The Magpies
were lucky to secure the two premiership points as the Blues kicked
6.20 (56) to Collingwood's 8.8 (56).[89]

The Argus said: "With only a minute to go Collingwood made one
desperate dash. (Percy) Gibb got it in front, scored a beautiful eighth

---

86   *The Argus*, March 3, 1914
87   *The History of the Magpies*, by Percy Taylor, 1949
88   ibid
89   ibid

goal, and made the points even—56 apiece. For nearly a minute both sides made frenzied efforts to rush the winning point."[90]

Some black and white supporters were happy with the escape, with *The Australasian* saying some of them were "giving vent to the cry 'Ring the Bell'."[91] But with neither side able to score in the allotted time left, Collingwood timekeeper Jim Manning brought an end to the game with a clanging of the bell. McHale had been "as good as ever in the centre."[92]

Consecutive wins against Melbourne and Richmond followed. In the latter game, a kid called Frank Hughes played his first match for the Richmond. The kid's nickname was 'Checker', and he and McHale would have many heated battles as coaches in the years to come. Dick Lee was seemingly back to his best, and his five goals against Richmond in Round 3 was his best return since 1910. In the first three games of the season, he booted 14 goals. The on-field relationship between the coach and the key forward was strong. *The Sporting Globe* said: "When he (McHale) played centre for Collingwood he had a great understanding with Dick Lee, the famous goalkicker, and the pair put on many goals for the Magpies ... 'I have never seen another forward like Lee,' stated McHale, 'for he could anticipate exactly how you would kick the ball and would be well away from an opposing back man'."[93] Lee's greatest single performance would come later that season, in the game against University. He kicked 11 goals of Collingwood's 15, equalling the record for an individual performance set by Geelong's Jim McShane in 1899. It was the last time the Magpies would meet the Students, who left the VFL competition at the end of the 1914 season having won 27 games and drawn two from their 126 games since joining in 1908.

The Magpies' first loss came against reigning premiers Fitzroy in Round 4. After a slow start Collingwood led by four points at

90   *The Argus*, April 27, 1914
91   *The Australasian*, May 5, 1914
92   ibid
93   *The Sporting Globe*, May 19, 1923

half-time and a goal at the last change. But Lee was restricted to one goal for the game and, according to *The Argus*, "the forward line of Collingwood was noticeably weak."[94] Still, the Magpies and Maroons fought a close encounter that was a "whole-hearted struggle from start to finish, with both sides so intensely eager to win that the only faults in the match were those which invariably arise from over eagerness."[95] Trailing by eight points late in the game, *The Herald* said Collingwood made one last move when "(Gus) Dobrigh passed the ball to (Dan) Minogue, who scored (the club's) seventh goal." But the final bell left the club two points short.

Two weeks later, St Kilda inflicted another defeat on Collingwood, running out 38-point winners. McHale was best for the losing team, but there was criticism of his tactics. Les Hughes was used at centre half-back on the brilliant Dave McNamara, and it was considered "a mistake ... in keeping Hughes so long off the ball, especially when the Saints were having the best of the ruck work."[96] The speed and pace that had been a part of Collingwood's game a year earlier was gone, with *The Herald* saying "while systematic (they are) a trifle on the slow side ... Collingwood played without team play or decision, and this, combined with the erratic shooting of their forwards, left them little opportunity to become at any times dangerous."[97]

Just two days later, on the public holiday Monday, McHale was "a tower of strength" against Essendon, according to *The Herald*, as Collingwood returned to a winning frame of mind. "McHale and (Charlie) Laxton were superb, McHale's performance stamping him as a marvel."[98] It was a classic encounter, said *The Herald*: "Essendon's dash and pace in the first half was most pronounced, while Collingwood's brilliancy in the second portion was one of the best things of the year.

---

94 *The Argus*, May 18, 1914
95 ibid
96 *The Herald*, May 30, 1914
97 ibid
98 *The History of the Magpies*, by Percy Taylor, 1949

In the last term Essendon tired, the Magpies putting on all steam, and finishing like champions."[99]

But the loss of "five of their fastest men" for the Geelong game at Corio—George Anderson, Alec Mutch, Jim Jackson, Jim Sadler and Harry 'Ginger' Matheson (who had transferred from Carlton after an earlier stint at St Kilda)—saw the Magpies "at the mercy of the home men."[100] Then Carlton tipped Collingwood out of the "four", beating them by seven points at Princes Park. McHale was locked in a battle with Rod McGregor. "The two Macs were at home in the centre ... the one from the 'Wood was good in dashes and passing," wrote *The Herald*."[101]

In a book written by St Kilda great Dave McNamara that year, McHale was featured dressed in a fine suit: "'Divan' McHale is the centre of attention. He plays like a German band and is quite as persistent."[102] It was probably not the most appropriate description given the events of 1914, when a European war loomed.

A day and a half after Collingwood had defeated Melbourne in late June, an event on the other side of the world helped to sow the seeds of the conflict that would change the world. The assassination of Austrian Archduke Franz Ferdinand and his wife, the Duchess, in Sarajevo, on June 28, pushed the world to the brink of war. Prayers were offered up by the Archbishops of Canterbury and York and parishioners at St Ambrose's Catholic Church in Sydney Road, Brunswick, where Jock McHale, his wife, Violet, now pregnant with a second child, and their two-year-old son Frank attended each Sunday.

Against this uneasy backdrop, a meeting of VFL footballers at a city hotel on July 25 forecast an exciting adventure that McHale wanted

99   *The Herald*, June 13, 1914
100 *The Herald*, June 20, 1914
101 *The Herald*, June 27, 1914
102 *Football by David McNamara*, Page and Bird, 1914

to be a part of. The Collingwood coach had been one of his team's best players earlier in the day when the Magpies easily accounted for St Kilda at Victoria Park. That night he "enthusiastically supported" a proposal to take Australian football to an international audience. Former St Kilda captain Jimmy Smith had an idea to take 45 players on a world tour from January 1915 for a series of 25 exhibition games in Vancouver, San Francisco, England, France, and perhaps Ireland. McHale had previously expressed a wish to travel back to his parents' homeland in Ireland, and the prospect of such a venture would mean he could afford it. *The Herald* forecast that: "At least 25 matches would be played, with the tour occupying about five months."[103]

There were doubts about the business model of such a project, but to McHale it made for an opportunity too good to pass up on. It was not known how this venture would affect the VFL season—whether it would have to be delayed until the men returned from overseas. Smith had stated that the 45 men would be paid allowances of £70 each, along with payment for 20 weeks of £3 per man. The board and lodging would be met for 12 weeks at £3 per man. *The Herald's* football correspondent, 'Kickero', was initially a sceptic. "The proposal has been up in the air for some time, and I must admit that, prior to my conversation, I regarded the scheme as a wildcat one; but the promoter is an enthusiastic one, and has gone into details and probabilities so thoroughly that one is forced to admit that the scheme might, after all, prove a sound business investment."[104] McHale was joined at the meeting that night by his former teammate Bob Rush, who was Collingwood's treasurer, as well as other leading VFL players.

The ambitious plans to spread the Australian Football gospel internationally ended when a few days after the meeting Austria-Hungary declared war on Serbia. It was inevitable that Great Britain would be drawn in, and as a consequence Australia would share part of the burden, despite its geographical isolation. Australia was in

---

103   *The Herald,* June 16, 1914
104   ibid

the middle of an election campaign at this tenuous stage of world history. On July 31, 1915 the Opposition Leader, Labor's Andrew Fisher, made a famous speech at the Victoria Hall in Colac, in western Victoria. Fisher said: "I sincerely hope that international arbitration will avail before Europe is convulsed into the greatest war of any time. But should the worst happen after everything that has been done that honour will permit, Australians will stand beside our own to help and defend her to our last man and our last shilling." At the time Prime Minister Joseph Cook said: "I want to make it clear that all our resources in Australia are in the Empire, for the Empire and for the preservation and security of the Empire."[105] Fisher would be Prime Minister within a month.

By August 4, Great Britain and Australia were at war with Germany. On that day, McHale and the Collingwood team—"the Fighting Magpies on tour", as they were dubbed—arrived in Sydney as part of their 16-day sojourn to the northern states during the break for the 1914 Australian football carnival. A civic reception was held for the visiting footballers at the Sydney Town Hall. The chairman of the NSW League, H.R. Denison, spoke to the gathering, with *The Argus* saying: "What should have been a festive gathering and a joyous occasion was clouded by a shadow stealing over them in the shape of war. But he (Denison) found that those who took a lively part in the manly sports were foremost in defence, and he doubted not that Australian footballers, if called upon, would do their part on the battlefield."[106]

The Magpies enjoyed a fine fortnight, spending time in Sydney and Brisbane before returning to the city of Jock's birth for the final match of the carnival. The Annual Report acknowledged: "Your club, ever foremost to foster our national game, visited Brisbane for that purpose and played two games ... the match with South Adelaide ended in a draw, and the one against Cananore (Tasmania) was won by your club.

---

105   *The Argus*, August 1, 1914
106   *The Argus*, August 5, 1914

Amongst the many kindnesses rendered to your team, special mention must be made of a theatre party at Sydney; an invitation to the Sydney Stadium by J. Wren Esq.; and a launch trip by Mr "Dally" Messenger, the famous Rugbyite."[107]

Wren's re-emergence at Collingwood after more than a decade's absence was significant. The businessman's links to the Collingwood Football Club had gone back almost to the birth of the club in 1892— his famous tote started a year later in Johnston Street—and he had been one of the patrons of the Magpies between 1897 and 1901. But from that time on, he had kept his distance—at least officially. He was not associated with the Collingwood club in 1903 when McHale joined it.

Various theories abound for his absence between 1901 and the early years of the next decade. The most credible comes from Stremski's *Kill for Collingwood:* "Wren was not the most important patron or donor of the club at this time. The foremost supporter was Sir John Madden, who was then vice-chancellor of Melbourne University and chief justice of Victoria. Madden's brother, who was secretary of the VRC (Victoria Racing Club) and speaker of the legislative assembly after 1904, was reputed to be an implacable foe of Wren. The rivalry with the Maddens, whose mansions in Kew were near to his own, may well have prompted Wren to terminate his donations to the club in 1901. Thus, he was dropped as patron, and was not even a member at Collingwood for those 13 years (with the exception of 1911). Wren's football club support resumed during World War I as Madden's was ending."[108]

Wren contributed to Dick Lee's testimonial in 1913 and, as mentoipned, significantly treated the Collingwood team to that night at his Sydney Stadium a year later. From this moment on, the relationship between Wren and McHale would develop, to the point where, for almost the next 40 years, they would become close friends, discussing football and Collingwood on a regular basis.

---

107   Collingwood Annual Report, 1915
108   *Kill For Collingwood, Richard Stremski,* Allen and Unwin, 1986

The Magpies arrived home on August 19, desperate to defend their position in the top four. The Melbourne they returned to was a different one from the city they had left just over a fortnight earlier. On the day they arrived back at Spencer Street Station, there were enthusiastic crowds assembling in the city to join the "Australian Imperial Expeditionary Force" (AIF). The following day's edition of *The Argus* ran a photograph of the latest batch of new recruits signing up for the war as they made their way from Victoria Barracks to the camp at Broadmeadows. The accompanying story said: "In a sense it was a dress rehearsal of the real farewell ... from now onwards they will sink their identity, their occupation, their rank and their social status in the common service of their country ... A few weeks from now, the difference between bank clerk and bricklayer, public school man and navvy, will be swallowed up in the universal khaki."[109] A hundred 100 officers and 3000 men spent that night at the camp.

There was, indeed, a clerk amongst the returning Magpies: Alan Cordner, a player whom Jock McHale and his selection committee had chosen in 10 games in 1914, the same number as he had played the previous year after joining the club from Geelong. Two days after Cordner had returned to Melbourne from the trip north, he went to Victoria Barracks for a medical. A day later, on August 22, 1914, he enlisted in the AIF. That afternoon he played his last game against South Melbourne at Victoria Park. He had eight months to live.

The match against South Melbourne was always going to be a struggle, given Collingwood had endured a long train journey home just a few days earlier. South Melbourne narrowly held sway for most of the day, but Collingwood was still in striking distance—only 14 behinds—at the final change. McHale urged his team to lift in

---

109   *The Argus*, August 20, 1914

the last half hour. But the leg-weary Magpies could find no more. The Magpies failed to kick a goal in the last term, losing by 21 points.

It came down to a simple equation: defeat Geelong at Victoria Park in the last game and make the finals; lose and miss out for the second time in three years. Captain Dan Minogue, who was Collingwood's most important player, was suffering from influenza and missed the match. He was sorely missed. "In one of the best games of the year", said *The Herald*, Geelong managed to secure a narrow lead in the third term, before pushing away to a 24-point win. For the second week in a row, the Magpies did not kick a goal in the last quarter.

The critics believed the long journey home from their trip north had flattened the team. *The Herald* observed: "Prior to the carnival, they were regarded as certainties for one of the places, but the long and weary journey to Brisbane and back slowed them down, and took all the ginger out of them. Perhaps the players consider the trip worth the sacrifice, for there is no doubt that for the sake of a holiday, the premiership chance was thrown away."[110] McHale remained a firm believer in the "holiday" trips, and the team-bonding benefits associated with them. He would not abandon the interstate trips, and maintained that the benefits outweighed the negatives.

Collingwood's 1914 season was over. No one knew how the war in far-off Europe, or the enlistment of more than 50,000 young Australians by the end of the year, would impact on football, or the country. This was a time without precedent. Bob Rush believed that "there was practically no possibility of football declining in popularity."[111] It was hardly an isolated thought, with many believing that the war might well be over by the time the first contingent of Australian soldiers reached the battlefields. Although the season had ended in disappointment, Collingwood took the time to make a presentation to the first two players of the club to enlist.

110   *The Herald*, October 10, 1914
111   *Kill For Collingwood*, Richard Stremski, Allen and Unwin, 1986

The Herald detailed: "The executive of the Collingwood Football Club made a presentation to two of their players—A.Cordner and H. Matheson—who have enrolled in the service with the Australian Expeditionary Force. (President) J. Sharp handed the men two gold wristlet watches, wishing them success and good luck."[112] The brother of treasurer Bob Rush, Bryan, who had played 17 games in 1913 and '14, also enlisted shortly after. The painful years that lay ahead would test the resolve of not only the football club, but also the Australian community as it had never been tested before.

---

112   *The Herald,* September 12, 1914

CHAPTER 6

A Different Sort of Struggle

1915-1918

t was April 24, 1915. As the distant guns of war ground to a bleak and brutal stalemate in far-off Europe, the men yet to hear the "call of the Empire", and those who had no intention of doing so, went about their business as they had before. On that day, Jock McHale was urging his men on to victory over Essendon in the opening game of the VFL season that would become one of the most contentious in history. McHale proved himself "as nimble as ever"[1] as one of Collingwood's good contributors in the 26-point win. *The Herald* said: "Collingwood's ex-captain was nearly always in the van of successful dashes on Essendon's goal."[2] Dan Minogue had been re-elected captain, while Paddy Rowan was appointed vice-captain. As playing-coach, McHale had not sought election for either post.

The margin over Essendon had only been a solitary goal in the Magpies' favour at the three-quarter time break."[3] But McHale, who

---

1   *The Herald*, May 1, 1915
2   ibid
3   *The Argus*, April 26, 1915

was now 32, didn't want to leave anything to chance. He instructed his team to rise to the occasion, and it was precisely what they did in the last half-hour. Collingwood kicked the only three goals of the final term, one of them set up by the playing-coach. *The Argus* detailed: "Rowan, securing, passed to McHale, who sent it on to (Harry) Curtis, the latter getting (the club's) sixth goal."[4] Such a win meant that "there is an air of confidence at Victoria Park, which augurs well for the team's success."[5]

As Collingwood players celebrated their first win of the season, one of their former teammates, Alan Cordner, was contemplating a very different challenge almost 15,000km away from Victoria Park. He was preparing to go into battle with his 6th Battalion mates. Cordner, 25, and the rest of the Australian Imperial Force had been transferred from Egypt to the small Island of Lemnos, which would be the launching pad for the assault on Turkey's Gallipoli peninsula.

As Les Carlyon's *Gallipoli* explained, the scheduled date for the landing of British, French, Australian and New Zealand troops had been April 23, but fate—and the weather—was to play a role in delaying it for two more days. Carlyon wrote: "The Armada at Mudros (a port on Lemnos) grew and grew; battleships; converted liners; chartered tramps; destroyers; lighters that had been hurriedly bought in Mediterranean ports; tugs; cruisers; colliers; transfers from the North Sea and tugs from the Thames. Then the gales came and the landings were postponed until the 25th."[6]

On that last Saturday of innocence before the landings at Gallipoli, there were plenty of things to do in Melbourne. There were "performing seals and sea lions, performing dogs and monkeys" at the

4   ibid
5   *The Argus*, April 23, 1915
6   *Gallipoli*, Les Carlyon, Pan MacMillan, 2001

Aquarium. There was dancing at St Kilda Town Hall where practice was encouraged but "failure is impossible". There was "the home of the moving pictures", Hoyts, where a host of silent movies screened on a rotational basis, with the latest war news from Europe flashed on the screens as the only hint of a reality check.

One of the most popular pastimes was the commencement of the VFL season. Matches across Melbourne attracted strong crowds, only slightly down on the pre-war opening round of 1914. 'Observer' of *The Argus* noted: "The form shown and the interest displayed were in keeping with similar occasions, though on the whole the attendances were not up to the numbers of recent seasons."[7]

There had been a push—tepid at first—to ban VFL football for the duration of the war. But in the days to come, and with the news that would accompany the Gallipoli landings, the call would gain momentum. Already, University—which Collingwood had beaten on all 14 occasions over seven seasons, with McHale playing in all of them—had withdrawn from the competition, because of its high number of enlistments, as well as complications caused by exams and the club's inability to field a regular 18. To that stage, Collingwood had only three current players signed up: Cordner, Harry Matheson and Bryan Rush. But there was the promise of more to come, including some past players who were eager to enlist.

In the week leading up to the Round 1 matches, Wesley College's headmaster, L.A. Adamson, made a widely reported speech to his students, calling for an end to football until the cessation of hostilities. He argued: "Why not Iron Crosses for the premiers, instead of medals?" Then he added pointedly: "Any day now you may open the morning paper to read the first list of Australian casualties—that first list will rouse all the slumbering manhood of this young nation ... because we are so far from the agony, and from the cheerful crucifixion of those who are at the heart of things. Every additional man helps to

---

7   *The Argus*, April 26, 1915

lessen the price of lasting peace. What if the fatal paper is a Saturday issue? Would you still go to see the paid football circus ... you would not, you could not."[8]

Three days after Adamson's speech was reported in *The Argus,* the first boatloads of Australian soldiers landed in the half-light of dawn on a beach—the wrong beach, as it would turn out—on a small cove on the Gallipoli peninsula. It would become known as "Anzac Cove". The first boats landed to some resistance, a resistance that would progressively become fiercer as more boats rolled in through the morning. They were met with a terrain as imposing and impossible as any army could hope to overcome. They were met with insurmountable odds from the first moment Lismore's Corporal Joseph Stratford of the 9th Battalion—said to be the first Australian soldier to rush ashore— "threw himself on a machine gun and was riddled with bullets."[9]

Confusion and chaos reigned as freely as the bullets fired on the Anzacs—as the Australian and New Zealanders had become known. Patsy Adam-Smith's *The Anzacs* summed up the first 24 hours: "At the end of the first day 16,000 men had been put ashore, 2000 of them had been killed. And instead of driving a mile and a half inland with a front of four miles, our troops were clinging to a bare foothold on the Second Ridge, little more than half a mile inland on a front of one mile. Both sides had fought each other to the point of exhaustion. That 'baptism of fire', as the men called it, was to set the pattern for the next eight months."[10]

Alan Cordner was one of at least five VFL footballers killed that day, although he would not officially be pronounced dead for almost a year. His body was never recovered. He was two weeks short of his 26th birthday. Cordner's family would write forlorn letters for months, pleading for good news that would never arrive.

---

8   *The Argus,* April 22, 1915
9   *National Archives of Australia, papers,* testament from Private W. Kean
10 *The Anzacs,* Nelson, 1978

News of the landings reached Australia before the following weekend. By Thursday, April 29, McHale and most of Melbourne first became aware of the reports filtering through, even though there was nothing of the casualties mentioned. *The Argus* reported: "The announcements that the Australians were in the thick of their first engagement caused great excitement in the city, and filled several young men with martial ardour that carried them as far as the enlisting office. There was quite a rush of applications in the afternoon."[11]

The early reports were positive in a way that no one who was there would have recognised. *The Argus* said: "The Allied Expeditionary Force, including the Australian and New Zealanders, has been engaged on both sides of the European and Asiatic shores of the Dardanelles ... despite continual opposition by the enemy, the Allied troops succeeded in establishing themselves across the peninsula of Gallipoli. News reaches us that the action is proceeding satisfactorily."[12]

It wasn't until Saturday, May 1, that the extent of the casualties first started to emerge. It was the day that Collingwood took on Richmond at Punt Road. There were scenes of distress all across Melbourne as people congregated outside the offices of Melbourne's leading newspapers, with *The Argus* being inundated with mothers and fathers, sisters and brothers, family and friends trying to get a Saturday "special edition" that carried the names of the dead and the casualties.

A "pathetic incident", according to *The Argus*, happened out of the front of the office on the Saturday afternoon when a mother collapsed after reading her son's name among the list of those seriously wounded in the fighting. *The Argus* declared solemnly that "with the issue of the first list of Australians killed and wounded in the fierce fighting on the shores of the Dardanelles must come to all of us the realisation that the

---

11   *The Argus*, April 30, 1915
12   ibid

grim reality of the great struggle in which the Empire is engaged."[13] The holding pattern was no more. The grim reality would last for another 42 months.

Jock McHale never made a public statement about the war. While he had been prepared to consider a trip overseas in early 1915 for the proposed series of football matches (something which was effectively killed by the war), he had no intention of enlisting in the AIF. We can only speculate on the reasons for this. He was 32 years and 134 days old when the Australians landed on Gallipoli.

Did he feel as if he was too old? Perhaps. Did it have something to do with his family circumstances? He had been married to Violet for six years, and now had two sons. At that stage of the war, there was considerably more pressure on single men joining the army than married ones. That would change, as sacrifice became the prevailing mood of the community. Later, when the re-enforcements slowed to a trickle, there was greater pressure being applied to married men and fathers to enlist. Advertisements would tug at the heart strings, with some showing children asking fathers: "What did you do in the Great War, Daddy?"

Perhaps it had also something to do with McHale's Irish Catholic heritage. There is little doubt that the "slumbering manhood", as Adamson had called it, in Collingwood, as well as other suburbs such as Coburg and Brunswick, had been slow to heed the call. Suburbs with working-class, predominantly Irish-Catholic populations were often reluctant to enlist, and were slow in terms of their initial enlistment numbers.

According to historian Gillian Hibbins's book *A Short History of Collingwood*: "The working class was confused by what constituted their duty to 'King and Country' and the suspicion that somehow they would bear the brunt of it all."[14] Irish Catholics comprised a

---

13   *The Argus*, May 3, 1915
14   *A Short History of Collingwood*, G.M. Hibbins, Collingwood Historical
     Society, 1997.

quarter of the Australian population during the period of the First World War, and more than their fair share enlisted. Others though were less inclined to fight for an Empire that had never shown much compassion for those back in the homeland. It is not known whether McHale was in this mix.

As the appalling casualty lists filtered back to Australia on a daily basis, and as it became increasingly obvious that there would be no quick resolution to the conflict, pressure began to be applied—subtly and not so subtly—on able-bodied men of all denominations and dispositions. For those who hadn't enlisted, and also happened to be footballers, it was doubly so.

Tom Kelynack, better known as 'Kickero', from *The Herald*, wrote: "Football may be left to those who are unable to become soldiers—this is the time for all fit men to fall in for the sterner game. My own son left with the first contingent and I feel prouder of the part he has already played than if he were the finest footballer the world has ever seen."[15] His son, Charles, had enlisted almost as soon as war was declared. He would end up with the measles on Gallipoli and a Military Cross in France for gallantry in October 1917.[16] McHale would have known the journalist and would likely have known his son, given the Kelynacks lived in Shaftsbury Street, Moreland, just a few hundred metres on the other side of Sydney Road to his parents' home in Buckingham Avenue.

'Old Boy', from *The Argus*, asked his readers—and no doubt directed it to those many footballers who habitually read his columns—"Which game to play, football or war? Many hundreds have asked the question in the only way commensurate with loyalty to the nation. Those who

---

15 *Collingwood at Victoria Park*, Michael Roberts and Glenn McFarlane, Lothian, 1999
16 National Archives of Australia, papers of Charles James Kelynack. FOOTNOTE: The citation said Lieutenant Charles James Kelynack for conspicuous gallantry and devotion to duty. He worked through the engagement; establishing and maintaining communication in the face of great difficulty and under heavy shell fire. When a dug out was blown in he succeeded in rescuing two severely wounded men. He showed the greatest initiative and courage throughout.

have not, evidently, placed their clubs first, prefer to struggle for a Premiership before the prospect of a military cap."[17]

But McHale's old coaching rival, and the man who had done more to further the cause of coaching than any other person to that stage, Jack Worrall, had a more balanced view. Writing for *The Australasian*, he argued: "The idea of what constitutes a moral duty depends almost entirely on the individual, and the abolition of football would drive more men to drink than to war. The war news has more intense interest now that our brave boys are giving up their lives for the cause of freedom, rendering it more than ever necessary that there must be some relaxation from the mental strain of poring over the news from the seat of war. It would be a sign of decadence and funk to show the white feather in stopping all sports and amusements at this critical part of our nationhood."[18]

McHale was one of the club's best players in that 53-point win over Richmond at Punt Road—on the day that the first casualty reports from Gallipoli was released. *The Herald* said: "It is wonderful to watch the way in which Collingwood's old skipper, Jock McHale, without much apparent effort, manages to steer clear of danger and get the ball to the forwards. Time after time on Saturday, he was the pivot of Collingwood's assault on goal."[19] Collingwood's form was so strong early in the season that "spectators have seldom been treated to such an exhibition of handballing ... even allowing that sometimes the ball was thrown, it was all done so cleverly and neatly, and the players got out of difficult positions, that applause from around the ground was bestowed on the Woodsmen concerned."[20] This report would be the best indication yet that McHale was now known to all as Jock, and that the name had well and truly stuck.

---

17   *Collingwood at Victoria Park*, Michael Roberts and Glenn McFarlane, Lothian, 1999
18   *The Australasian*, May 15, 1915
19   *The Herald*, May 8, 1915
20   ibid

Even though he was considered a veteran, McHale had a strong start to the 1915 season, and played a role in Collingwood's unbeaten first five games. In one of those games, the 20-point win over the Saints, *The Herald* said one "enthusiastic admirer remarked, after Jim had beaten two opponents, 'There, what do you think of him? Been playing the game for 15 years without missing a game!'"[21] That wasn't entirely correct. He had been playing VFL since 1903—12 years. And he had not missed a game since 1906—nine years. In the win over Geelong, *The Herald* said: "McHale's clearances were a feature ... his heady work was the means of extricating the Magpies from difficult positions. Altogether his performance was in keeping with his grand reputation."[22]

With Minogue as captain, and McHale as coach, the Magpies had a near perfect combination. They were considered premiership contenders, along with Carlton. The first loss of the season came against the Blues, by two points, at Princes Park. If the news reports from Gallipoli were starting to have an impact on crowds, the Carlton-Collingwood game was an exception. *The Herald* described: "All roads led to Carlton and there must have been 30,000 people in the reserve or lining the banks ... the exhibition being the grandest that has been seen in Melbourne for the last three years."[23] It was noted that Collingwood had been "notoriously unsuccessful at Carlton", but the signs were good at half-time with the Magpies leading 6.4 to 4.5. Dick Lee, who was "in a deadly mood", had kicked all of Collingwood's first-half goals.

McHale was locked in yet another duel with his Carlton counterpart in the centre, Rod McGregor. *The Herald* said: "Each of them was frequently under notice on various occasions for smart and clever play.

---

21   *The Herald*, May 15, 1915
22   *The Herald*, May 29, 1915
23   *The Herald*, June 12, 1915

Taking the game right through, perhaps the Magpie representative gave the better account of himself."[24] Carlton kicked five goals to one in the third term, and ran out to a 17-point lead at one stage of the last term. But Collingwood, and Lee, kept coming. For a time it looked as if he would kick all of the Magpies' goals but Harry Kerley kicked a late one. Lee finished with nine of 10 goals. The Magpies finished two points short.

But as Collingwood started on another string of wins, the pressure was mounting on the VFL to bring an early end to the season owing to the distressing news from the war front. The Magpies, according to Stremski's *Kill for Collingwood*, were insistent that the game needed to go on. The club's secretary, 'Bud' Copeland, claimed football was "the workingman's relaxation on his half-holiday. It is a cheap amusement for thousands of people."[25] Copeland, according to *Collingwood at Victoria Park*, also argued that "membership tickets had been sold giving (fans) the right of entry to 16 matches, and if the season were curtailed we could not keep that contract."[26]

In many ways, Collingwood appeared to be championing the working-class, and those whose desire it was to retain the sport to create a diversion to the events of the war. But it also knew that if the competition was curtailed, the club risked seriously financial consequences. Attendances were dropping at an alarming rate as the season wore on, prompting some clubs to call upon the VFL to bring an early end to the season, as had been the case with the Victorian Football Association.

It all came to a head at a meeting on July 21, 1915 when a motion to cut the VFL season by five weeks was raised by Geelong, and seconded by Melbourne. Essendon, St Kilda and South Melbourne supported it. Those who voted to continue the season were Collingwood,

---

24 ibid
25 *Kill For Collingwood*, Richard Stremski, Allen and Unwin, 1986
26 *Collingwood at Victoria Park*, Michael Roberts and Glenn McFarlane,
    Lothian, 1999

Carlton, Richmond and Fitzroy—three of the top four teams on the ladder, with Richmond being the exception. The motion was lost, as a three-fourths majority was required. But the VFL did resolve to hand over 10 per cent of the match takings to the war effort in an effort to appease those who had insisted on more definitive action.

At a meeting of the Collingwood players, and the committee, in July, it was agreed that payments were to be cut in half and deferred until the end of the season. The club's annual report said that: "When it was decided that each club should give 10 per cent of each Saturday's gate receipts (to the war effort), our players unanimously agreed to accept smaller payments, so that the club would be able to contribute to its full quota."[27] But according to Stremski, "the altruism of Magpie footballers was negated when they discovered the trainers' wages were only deferred, and not reduced. Thus the club had to amend its footballers' wages in accordance with the same formula."[28] Since being appointed as coach in 1912, McHale had been receiving a double wage—one drawn as a player and the other as a coach.

The Herald suggested: "In the dressingrooms during the last few weeks, war and duty have been the chief topic of conversation; the question of the premiership has been relegated to the background. Practically all clubs, with the exception of those in the running, are losing men every week. As a prominent footballer remarked last Saturday, 'I tried to finish the season out, but my heart is not in the job, and I am off to fill one of the gaps and take my chance.' It must be remembered that footballers have no more moral obligation to enlist than any other section of the community, but they are grand raw material and the makings of ideal soldiers."[29]

The article urged restraint from Australians in regard to non-soldier footballers, of which McHale was one of its more prominent. It said: "Yet strange as it may appear, a man may be a splendid footballer and

---

27   Collingwood Annual Report, 1916
28   *Kill For Collingwood*, Richard Stremski, Allen and Unwin, 1986
29   *The Herald*, July 17, 1915

athlete, yet not fit to be a soldier. Many players have been anxious to serve their country, but a hammer toe or some bad teeth barred their glorious aspirations ... The atmosphere in the dressingrooms is very different from what it was a month ago. The men are more serious and the usual light-hearted gaiety has practically disappeared."[30]

After the loss to Carlton in Round 7, Collingwood won seven matches in succession. All wins were by considerable margins. In the 39-point victory over Melbourne at the MCG, *The Herald* claimed: "The pronounced superiority of Collingwood stood out like a beacon—the strength of their defence, the power of the pack, combined with the confidence and knowledge of a team as a whole being unrivalled."[31] In that game, however, there was criticism of the club's strategy in trying to slow the game up against quick opponents. This was clearly a McHale strategy, to not allow teams to play a free-flowing game against Collingwood.

The Herald said: "In every case their players unhesitatingly walk yards over their opponents' mark. The chief culprit was McHale, who erred all day, repeatedly cribbing five yards. They were repeatedly brought back and whistled off, but it made no difference as they persisted in the tactic all through the piece. It not only delays the game unnecessarily, but annoys the spectator and causes ill feeling among the players. The second fault is that whenever an opponent is given a free mark a Collingwood man holds the ball until every man on the other side is closely guarded. It is certainly not the duty of a player on one side to help the other side by immediately giving him the ball, but he has no right, either as a sportsman or a footballer, to place an obstacle in the way of the man getting the ball who is entitled to it."[32]

July and August 1915 were two of the biggest enlistment months of the entire war for Australians, with 36,575 and 25,714 men signing on.

---

30   ibid
31   *The Herald*, July 24, 1915
32   ibid

The increased numbers came as new offensives at Gallipoli brought about even more appalling casualty numbers. It was at this time that a few of those people close to McHale decided to join the army. Robert McHale was one of them, enlisting on July 13, three days after Collingwood's 98-point win over St Kilda. It gave Jock his closest personal connection to the war. On the enlistment form, Robert listed John McHale as his next of kin and father.

The irony is that the McHale we know the least about was the only family member to ever make the visit to Ireland, the land of John and Mary's birth. On a furlough from the front in December 1916, Robert McHale travelled to Ireland. This was confirmed by a letter from James Fergus (later a Bishop), a nephew of Mary McHale (nee Gibbons), to his Aunt Winifred, who lived in St Kilda. In January, 1917, Fergus wrote: "Tell me whether there is one of my Aunt Mary's (Mrs McHale's) sons at the front. The reason why I ask you is this: when I was home at Xmas, we heard that there was an Australian soldier named McHale (whose parents were from County Mayo) at home from the front in Castlebar. He was trying to find his friends but did not succeed and it was only when he had gone away again, that a person from our parish living near Castlebar suspected who he was. We were all sorry when we heard it. We would have enjoyed seeing him. But perhaps it was not meant to be."[33]

Two of Collingwood's most important players in the 1915 season, best mates Doc Seddon and Paddy Rowan, enlisted on the same day—one day after Robert McHale—on July 14. Officially, the club was supportive, saying that the executive and the players "influenced by the unsettled war condition prevailing and whilst doing their utmost to maintain Collingwood's prestige in the football world, they unselfishly made their desires and ambitions subservient to the national needs. Many of our players, who by their brilliant performances early in the season when all the team had their full strength, were proclaimed

---

33   *Letter, from James Fergus, January 17, 1917*

prospective premiers for 1915, covered themselves with greater honour than yet attained on the football field by answering the country's call at a time when their sacrifice was greatest. All honour to them and our earnest wish is that they may be spared to come back and add further lustre to careers which will be considerably enhanced in the harder game in which they now participate."[34]

Rowan and Seddon would be big absentees, with *The Herald* suggesting that "the loss of two such champions must affect their (Collingwood's) prospects. They comprise the second ruck and in the opinion of football followers are a stronger and better combination than ever (Dan) Minogue and (Les) Hughes."[35]

Collingwood sought approval to use the men who had enlisted in games until their departure. Other clubs sought the same assurance. *The Herald* reported: "The Military authorities are being approached with the objective of making arrangements for those League players who have enlisted to get the necessary leave each week to play with the respective clubs. Approval has been given to this course, so that, until they embark for the front, all players enlisting will be able to play when they desire."[36]

After being "severely" missed in the win over Geelong on July 24, Rowan and Seddon were back for the much-anticipated clash with Carlton at Victoria Park, though they did not play a big part in the outcome. Just as the last time these two teams met, it was a classic encounter, with only one point separating them at the conclusion, in Carlton's favour—again. Seddon kicked two of his club's nine goals, but he and his great mate did not make much of a difference. It was said: "Another factor that told against Collingwood was that Rowan, Seddon, and (Jim) Jackson, who had been granted military leave from Seymour, they were not anything like in their form. The training that is evidently necessary for a soldier is not of the kind for football,

---

34 Collingwood Annual Report, 1916
35 *The Herald*, July 31, 1915
36 ibid

and they not only died away in the run home, but were at times out of touch with the surroundings."[37]

On the day before Collingwood's next match, against Fitzroy, one of the suburb's most famous faces, John Wren, walked into the Melbourne Town Hall and said to the recruiting officer in charge: "Want to enlist, lad."[38] While some thought it was a good-meaning publicity stunt designed to promote recruiting, one of the state's leading Irish Catholics was earnestly backing the Australian war effort. He had earlier offered to give the family of the country's first recipient of the Victoria Cross, Albert Jacka, £500. Wren was 44— eleven and a half years older than McHale. The August 15 issue of *Labor Call* predicted: "If Jack entrenches himself in Gallipoli as he did in Collingwood when he defied the whole Police Force of Victoria to enter his Tote establishment, then the Blanky Turk will have Buckley's chance of shifting Wren."[39] It was a short-lived exercise. By December of the same year, Wren was ruled medically unfit and returned to civilian life.

Collingwood finished the 1915 home and away season on top of the ladder, with only two losses, both to Carlton by a collective three points. They completed the regular season with a win over South Melbourne, minus Rowan, Seddon and Jackson, who had been unable to attain the leave due to a meningitis outbreak at the Seymour camp. But the performance was not one that inspired most football reporters. *The Australasian* said: "Fully armed, they have only one weakness. Their centreline is not quite up to the quality of the rest of the competition. And a great deal depends on whether the quarantine regulations will allow the soldier players to compete in the remaining matches, for unless Rowan, Seddon and Jackson obtain their necessary leave, Collingwood can scarcely win."[40] It was also said: "On recent

---

37   ibid
38   *John Wren, a life reconsidered*, James Griffen, Scribe, 2004
39   ibid
40   *The Australasian*, August 28, 1915

form, Collingwood have been showing signs of the season's wear and tear, and are not nearly as fresh and convincing a side as they were a month ago."[41]

That malaise came to a head against Fitzroy in the semi-final, when rain and the absence of a few key players hurt Collingwood. There were reminders of the war effort everywhere, as wounded soldiers back from the front were admitted to the game without charge. Others in khaki "tried to carry the position at the turnstiles without paying and were turned back ... then they sang in chorus *Australia Will Be There*. A large number left this gate and went around to one near the Frank Grey Smith stand. The gate was forced open by one of the soldiers and hundreds streamed into the members' reserve laughing and shouting. The League had intended to admit them, but the men were impatient and took matters into their own hands."[42]

McHale had the services of his three soldier-footballers, but had lost three key other players in Les Hughes (broken rib), Alec Mutch (fluid on the knee) and Gus Dobrigh (influenza). Collingwood led by five points at half-time, 4.8 to 3.9, but the club did not kick another goal for the game. Inexplicably, it lost by 34 points.

It led Jack Worrall, writing in *The Australasian*, to question Collingwood's recent finals record. Worrall wrote: "Although Collingwood rarely misses inclusion in the final quarter, they always possess one undoubted weakness. Year in and year out, almost without exception, they rarely give of their best in the final games ... when the serious part of the business commences, there is more often a labouring than a dashing side. Evidently, they neglect the necessary easing in training at a vital part of their preparation with the evitable result that they get a bit on the stale side, where spring and elasticity are the essential of the hour. It is strange that they have never learnt the secret."[43]

---

41   ibid
42   *The Australasian*, September 11, 1915
43   ibid

But there was an element of truth to what the former Carlton and Essendon coach had said. McHale had trained his men hard and often in the first few years of his tenure. In time he would come to learn the secret that Worrall had alluded to and would come to heed Worrall's advice. More often than not in the years to come, he would ease up the training heading into the finals, often to the chagrin of concerned fans.

Once more the Challenge Rule allowed Collingwood to meet the winner of the Fitzroy-Carlton final, and it was seemingly fated that the Magpies would meet the Blues after their close encounters early in the season. Ahead of the Grand Final, McHale swung a shock. Looking for an edge, he chose his old mate, Ted Rowell. Rowell had retired after the end of the 1914 season. But the 39-year-old accepted the offer of his playing coach to don the boots one last time. Incredibly, he was listed amongst the best players on the day.

Rowan and Seddon were selected to play, but McHale was stunned to find on the morning of the 1915 Grand Final that his two key players had not returned to Melbourne. They were stuck in an army camp. One newspaper had the camp as being in Broadmeadows; another had it in Seymour. Whatever the case, their leave appeared to have been declined. So McHale sent secretary 'Bud' Copeland to fetch them in his motor car. Incredibly, as reported in *The Herald*, Copeland "found the soldier-footballers had had to take part in a 10-mile march this morning."[44]

Twenty-three years later, the next time Collingwood met Carlton in a Grand Final, Seddon would think back to the occasion with a hint of suspicion and sentiment. He told *The Argus* in 1938 how he and his mate Rowan were "ordered out on a route march by an adjutant who, they thought, must have been a Carlton supporter. (They) duly tramped the 10 miles, came back to a large meal of Irish stew, went on to the field to play for Collingwood—and lost."[45] With their legs aching from the march, and their tummies full of Irish stew,

---

44   *The Herald*, September 18, 1915
45   *The Herald*, September 21, 1938

the pair was "whirled" into the heart of the city just after one o'clock. The adjutant was never named, nor would it ever be proven that he had been a Blues fan.

In McHale's first Grand Final as a coach, up against Carlton's Norman Clark, the Magpies threw themselves into the contest and for a time looked as if they would win the game. Three goals in the opening term gave them a slight ascendancy, but the Blues responded with four goals to one in the second term to take a 16-point lead into the half-time break. Again, Collingwood's downfall came from its players holding on to the ball for too long, and McHale was one of the worst offenders. *The Australasian* observed that McHale's "play was devoid of the finish that characterised (Rod) McGregor's work, and the Collingwood man would have to get the ball six times to his opponent's three to make up for his deficiency and accuracy in kicking."[46]

McHale clearly sensed the game was slipping. At half-time, he instructed his team to be more direct. It brought about a "startling transformation in the play of the Collingwood men. Evidently their mistakes had been pointed out, for they swung into the game with refreshed vigour and determination, did less messing around with the ball, and kicked it fairly and strongly on every occasion."[47] But the advantages of having more of the ball did not translate into goals. Collingwood kicked 1.7 to 0.2 in the third term. The difference at the last change was five points.

An early goal to Dick Lee, after a chain of play from George Anderson, Tom Clancy and Harry Curtis, put Collingwood back in front. It was, however, a false dawn. Despite the fact that Collingwood went forward on a few more occasions, it could not manage another score. A couple of umpiring decisions raised the ire of McHale and the Magpies, but Carlton piled on five goals in the last 15 minutes. It was an "astonishing collapse". Seddon and Rowan stopped almost

---

46   *The Australasian*, September 18, 1915
47   ibid

to a walk—no thanks to their early morning march. Seddon would not play another VFL game for almost another four years. Rowan would never wear the black and white jumper again. McHale's hopes of being a premiership coach had been foiled—for the time being at least. The final margin was 33 points.

McHale's frustration was expressed in the 1916 Annual Report: "His heart and soul is in the club with which he has been such a prominent player for 13 years and there was no one more disappointed than he when the team failed to secure victory in the final match. Throughout another year, Mr Jas F McHale has worked assiduously and carried out his duties as coach to the team with satisfaction both to players and executive; and at the same time retained his position in the centre as a player."[48]

The year of 1916 would be a terrible year. By the time the next season had come around, the Anzacs had staged their most successful mission on Gallipoli—a remarkable, casualty-free mass withdrawal—and were now in France, where they would soon die in numbers even more distressing than in Turkey. For a time, it appeared as if the VFL would be abandoned. Five clubs voted not to compete in the season—Essendon, Geelong, South Melbourne, Melbourne and St Kilda. The remaining—Collingwood, Carlton, Fitzroy, and Richmond—agreed to stage an abbreviated 24-game home and away season, where each side would play the other four times.

For a time, recruiting footballers was harder than recruiting soldiers. If the enlistments had been slow initially from the Collingwood club in the first year of the war, the second year would add many more names. So the Magpies—with McHale clearly searching for new players—made a plea in the Annual Report for more local recruits to come forward. It said: "Many players are needed and a hearty invitation is extended to any married men who have not yet felt it their duty to enlist and youths who have been rejected or cannot receive parental

---

48   Collingwood Annual Report, 1916

authority. We feel there are numbers who love the game and will be willing to play to give enjoyment to thousands who must have a little pleasure on a Saturday afternoon, knowing at the same time their efforts result in hundreds of pounds being raised for the benefit of those who are risking their lives for their fellow men."[49]

There was no payment on offer for anyone. Due to the grave war situation, the payment of players was suspended. Only out of pocket expenses were to be drawn, and Collingwood did its best to limit that as well. McHale had been "unanimously re-appointed coach, but he announced he would act only in an honorary capacity."[50]

One of those who had enlisted was the captain Dan Minogue, who had been such a key performer for the club since his 1911 debut. Like McHale, he was Irish Catholic. But the former miner was unmarried and possessed a sense of adventure. In the first game, Collingwood's clash with Richmond, at Punt Road, *The Herald* reported: "two of the most popular men ... were Dan Minogue and Hugh James, who will shortly be leaving to uphold the honour of our country in the greater game."[51] The loss of Minogue, on top of Rowan and Seddon, meant that Collingwood—and McHale—had to work on building a new ruck brigade. Only Les Hughes remained of the "famous" four.

On the same weekend it was mentioned that a letter from Tel-el-Kabir, in Egypt, detailed Paddy Rowan's 20-round boxing contest with a fellow soldier. He had been knocked down, struck his head, but the "gong" had saved him. In the end, he survived the fight and emerged from the contest the winner. Sadly, it would not be as easy to escape from what awaited him in France.

Having played for the great bulk of his time in the centre, McHale spent the first four games of the season at half-forward, allowing George Anderson to take over his slot. In the Round 2 loss to Carlton, he booted a career-best three goals in the game, not only outshooting

---

49   ibid
50   ibid
51   *The Herald,* May 6, 1916

Dick Lee (two goals), but also being the highest goalkicker of the match. He would also spend time in the backline later in the year before resuming his role in the centre.

Collingwood got one back over Carlton three weeks later with a one-point win at Princes Park. Incredibly, the two teams met again on the holiday Monday in Ballarat in aid of Red Cross, and that match (not for premiership points) ended in a draw. It was the second draw the Magpies had played out that season, after an earlier one against Fitzroy.

Unfortunately, the Magpies could not give Minogue the send-off that it had wanted to. In Round 8, against Carlton at Princes Park, he played his last game for the club, as Collingwood went down by 12 points. There was a sense of theatre about the farewell. *The Argus* described it: "At the close of the match a band of soldiers, who had been cheering on Minogue, carried him off the ground."[52] One can only wonder at what McHale had made of this. His captain was seemingly more popular than he was. And McHale was about to lose his best and most popular player to the war, and there was nothing he could do about it. On the eve of his departure to the front, Minogue was presented with a gold wrist watch, and was told that there would always be a place for him when he returned safe and well.

Collingwood finished the abbreviated 1916 season in second place to Carlton, winning six of its 12 games. Fitzroy finished last, with only two wins and a draw against Collingwood. But remarkably, the Maroons found their form at the right end of the season. In the last home and away match, they had led the Magpies by nine points at half-time before Collingwood staged a revival. But there was no coming back the next week when in the semi-final—before a crowd of only 9638, according to *The Argus*—Fitzroy ended Collingwood's season with a six-point win.

It was meant to be a celebration for Jock McHale. On that day, he became the first VFL player to reach 250 games. In keeping with

---

52   *The Argus*, June 26, 1916

his desire to always put the team ahead of the individual, there was no mention of it at the club or in the press during the lead-up to the game. But it was an admirable lesson in longevity and durability. He was 33 years and 244 days old. His age and his milestone were in stark comparison to the majority of that 1916 semi-final side. Percy Taylor's history of Collingwood suggested that the team had "too many fresh men lacking experience".[53]

But the blow of missing the finals was nothing like the blow that hit Collingwood in December 1916 when the word came through that Paddy Rowan—Percy Rowe from the army's perspective—and Tom Wright (who had played 12 games with McHale in 1906 and '07) had been killed in the space of a week. A letter from a soldier to Collingwood detailed the story behind Rowan's death: "I am enclosing details of how Pat Rowe 'Rowan', Collingwood's crack follower, got fatally wounded. I was with Pat and some more chaps in a bombing post, in one of the hottest corners of the Somme firing line. It rains shells and bullets here. About half an hour before we got relieved Pat got hit. Pat was stooping down doing up his equipment getting ready to leave the line, when a shrapnel shell burst on the parapet about three feet above our heads. Pat gripped his side and fell. Turning to me, he exclaimed: "I'm gone, goodbye lads, let's shake hands."[54] He was dead the next morning. Wright, three and a half months older than McHale, was dead within the week.

The year of 1916 has often been described as a "melancholy year" for Australia. There was a "growing bitterness against those who stayed at home."[55] Whether this had some impact on McHale will never be known. He was admired and respected on the football field, and had

53   *The history of the Collingwood Football Club, 1892-1948,* Percy Taylor, 1949
54   *Fallen, the ultimate heroes,* Jim Main and David Allen, 2002
55   *Up Where Cazaly?,* Leonie Sandercock and Ian Turner, Granada, 1981

been so for more than a decade, but the men who were winning much of the laurels were those who were enlisting or fighting at the front. Still, only 10 per cent of Brunswick's male population had enlisted by 1916.[56] So McHale was far from alone in his decision to remain at home.

The pressure of the Government, and Prime Minister Billy Hughes, pushed the issue of conscription onto the agenda when reinforcement numbers dipped. It would become the most divisive issue of the war on the home front. In October, a plebiscite was conducted for the citizens of Australia to decide whether it could send men off to fight in France compulsorily. It gave rise to bitterness and sectarianism that divided Australians.

Daniel Mannix became the main opponent to the "Yes" vote, and the Irish-born Catholic Archbishop of Melbourne denounced conscription at nearby Clifton Hill in the lead-up to the vote as "a hateful thing, and it is almost certain to bring evil in its train. The present war could never have assumed such horrors if conscription had not prevailed in Europe. I have the impression, and I still retain the conviction, that Australia has done her fair share."

McHale's visits to Sunday Mass at St Ambrose's in Sydney Road, Brunswick, would have placed him right in the middle of the anti-conscription debate. As Laura Donati's history of Sydney Road, *Almost Pretty*, detailed: "In Brunswick, Catholicism and anti-conscription sentiments were closely intertwined, as demonstrated by St Ambrose's, which became the unofficial headquarters for the Brunswick antis."[57] Sydney Road became one of the many sites where the debate raged, as it would have been in most suburbs. There were jinkers with "Yes" and "No" daubed across them. Shops along the street were sometimes painted with anti-conscription slogans—"For King and Country, Vote No" and "Yes Spurts Blood."[58]

---

56   *Almost Pretty, A History of Sydney Road*, Laura Donati, 2005
57   ibid
58   ibid

The first vote was rejected, but only by a margin of less than 72,000 across more than 2.5 million votes. That was approximately 48 per cent for, and 52 per cent against. In McHale's suburb of Brunswick, it was more one-sided, with the vote going 36 per cent for and 62.5 against. When the debate was over (at least temporarily) St Ambrose's Church, Brunswick even got a visit from Dr Mannix in November 1916 where he spoke against the claims that Catholicism had halted conscription. "People now talked as if Catholic voters had really, as Australians termed it, 'turned down' conscription. But such people forgot that there were roughly some 1,200,000 votes cast against conscription. He took it that the 200,000 votes would go very nearly towards accounting for the Catholic vote against conscription, leaving a million Protestant votes against it."[59] Then Mannix added with a sting: "Most Catholics voted against conscription because most of them were sensible people."[60]

The ramifications were enormous. Hughes walked out of the Labor Party, taking with him many of his key people, and formed the Nationalist Party, with non-Labor forces. He won an election the following year, then called a second conscription plebiscite for December 20, 1917—eight days after McHale's 35th birthday. After a 46-word question for the first vote, Hughes kept it simple in the second attempt. The question was: *"Are you in favour of the proposal of the Commonwealth Government for reinforcing the Commonwealth Forces overseas."* The referendum was defeated by an even bigger margin.

The Victorian Government sought to introduce six o'clock closing for hotels in 1916 after pressure from the temperance groups and those eager to be seen to be making more of a sacrifice for the war

---

59   *The Argus*, November 20, 1916
60   ibid

effort. According to Keith Dunstan's *The Amber Nectar,* Victoria's Chief Secretary of the time said: "The demand everywhere is for sobriety; and when you try to enforce that on the troops, should not the people who do not go to the front be cheerfully willing to display equal abstinence."[61] Premier Sir Alexander Peacock put the issue to a vote and it was passed in October 1916. Six o'clock closing was meant to last for the duration of the war. It would last for almost another 50 years, and would even outlive McHale. What it meant though was a boom in the sale of bottled beer, and it meant that jobs were secure in the brewing industry.

In a time where death was a grim harvester, reeling in so many young men of different race and religion, there was another cruel blow to Jock's parents in February 1917. Having already lost four babies in childhood, they were about to lose a teenager. Edward William McHale, Jock's youngest sibling, was only 14 when he died at the family home in Buckingham Avenue of exhaustion from chronic nephritis (inflammation of the kidneys). He was laid to rest at Melbourne General Cemetery a day later.

Having lost another sibling, and with his wife Violet pregnant again, Jock McHale steeled himself for what he thought might be his last season of VFL football. He had long been a student of the club's history and wanted to join Jack Monohan and Bill Proudfoot as the only Collingwood footballers to play for 15 seasons. Payment to players was suspended in 1917, with the entire team limited to weekly expenses of £5. Only one player ('Gus' Dobrigh, who had to travel from Mentone to Victoria Park) was allotted "tea money". It went further than this. According to Stremski's *Kill for Collingwood,* five players refused to take any expenses: Harry Curtis, Charlie Laxton, Matt Cody, 'Pen' Reynolds and Maurie Sheehy.

The competition had grown by two teams, with Geelong and South Melbourne returning, and there was a further push to spruik for

---

61   *The Amber Nectar, A Celebration of Beer and Brewing in Australia,* Keith
      Dunstan, Viking O'Neil, 1987

recruiting soldiers at the opening matches of the season. It would have little success. Collingwood had no trouble accounting for Richmond in the Round 1 match, winning by 49 points. But the recruiting officers had considerably more trouble in preaching to the crowds before the game started. Sergeant W.H. Durand told *The Argus* that he had been well treated by the committee, but that the "crowd was hostile, and it was hard to get a hearing, and, therefore, we abandoned the attempt."[62]

Collingwood fell to Carlton in week two of the season before rallying to secure five wins as well as a draw with Richmond over the following six weeks. For McHale, something unusual happened in that game against the Blues. His body started to fail him. After a record 191 consecutive games that stretched back to Round 13, 1906, McHale finally suffered an injury—the type of which was unrecorded by newspapers—and missed the Round 3 and Round 4 games against Fitzroy and South Melbourne. It had been an extraordinary run of matches. But his issues with his body provided for a frustrating year for him personally, while the season was rolling on well for the team as a whole. After returning for two games in Round 5 and Round 6, McHale missed all six games from Round 7 to Round 12. Percy Wilson captained the team in his absence. McHale would have to watch the game from the sidelines, and he would have to try to lift the players in speeches before the game and, most notably, at half-time. Such would become his forte.

By the time McHale returned to the team, in August against Fitzroy at Brunswick Street, he was a father once more. Violet had had a girl, Mary Jean, at the family home in Talbot Street, Brunswick on July 5, 1917, two days before the club's second loss of the season, to South Melbourne by 17 points at the Lake Oval. He had three children now—his new daughter, as well as Frankie, who was five, and John, two.

---

62   *The Argus*, May 19, 1917

Collingwood's season had been a remarkably consistent one, though several injuries to key players had made life difficult. The club had been on top of the ladder for all but two weeks of competition, and it retained the minor premiership, despite a last-round loss to Geelong, by two points at Corio Oval. Incredibly, as documented in *A Century of the Best*, big man Les Hughes missed a bus that would have taken him to the train station to meet the Collingwood contingent bound for Geelong. That meant the club's president, and McHale's good friend, Jim Sharp had to don the black and white one last time. He had not played since badly breaking his shin bone in McHale's first year as coach, 1912. The comeback ended as soon as it started, with Sharp injuring his knee, and leaving Collingwood one player short for the rest of the game.

McHale had returned to the backline by this stage and it seemed as if the premiership that he craved as a coach was a step closer to reality when Collingwood thrashed South Melbourne by 60 points in the semi-final. Collingwood's 8.4 to 0.1 third term, described by *The Argus* as a "burst of success which robbed the match of further conviction."[63] The club's seven-year premiership drought appeared to be close to an end.

But Fitzroy had other ideas. The previous time the two teams had met—in Round 13—Collingwood had doubled their score. This time, though, the Maroons overpowered the Magpies in the last half-hour, to win by six points. *The Argus* called it "one of the keenest, closest struggles seen for a long time".[64] Despite a pre-game plea from McHale, who was rested for the game with another niggling injury, not to take the game lightly, Collingwood led at every change, but could not hold on. Their task was made difficult without their captain-coach, without their great goal-kicker in Dick Lee, who had weeks earlier become the first man to kick 500 goals in the VFL, and, for the great part of the game, without Charlie Laxton, who was injured earlier in the match.

---

63   *The Argus*, September 10, 1917
64   *The Argus*, September 17, 1917

It left Collingwood with the right of challenge. As Jack Worrall, of *The Australasian*, said: "By virtue of being leaders in the competition in the first round, Collingwood are entitled to the privilege of another match."[65] Worrall had been critical of the club's more recent finals record in the past, but this time he believed they would win the Grand Final, saying: "I am still of the opinion that, fully manned and barring accidents, Collingwood is the most skilful side of the season."[66]

McHale and the Magpies carried a talisman as they headed into the Grand Final. A horseshoe fashioned out of a German shell from the Western Front had arrived at the club. It was inscribed with "Good Luck" and "To CFC. From Doc. France 1917." It had been sent from former Collingwood footballer Malcolm 'Doc' Seddon, who had played in the losing 1915 Grand Final. A letter that accompanied it was simple yet inspirational. It said: "I hope this shoe will bring the boys to the top of the tree this year." They had achieved that through the season, and now McHale was urging them on to achieve the ultimate in football.

He got his wish for a two-pronged forward attack of Dick Lee and Harry Curtis, when Lee proved his fitness for the Grand Final. McHale would also be back in black and white, stationed in the back half, for what he considered could be his final game. Laxton also proved his fitness, so Collingwood was well placed to turn the tables on Fitzroy.

McHale again warned against complacency. Importantly, he told his players that, owing to the greasy conditions of the MCG, they needed to play body-on-body football across the ground, and attempt to out-muscle the Maroons as much as possible. Stremski described the coach's tactical nous heading into this game: "Convinced that Fitzroy's forwards were too light to withstand buffeting, especially on a ground as soggy as the MCG was that day, McHale instructed his players to hit as hard as possible."[67]

---

65   *The Australasian*, September 22, 1917
66   ibid
67   *Kill For Collingwood*, Richard Stremski, Allen and Unwin, 1984

The Magpies had eight scoring shots in the opening term, but could only muster 2.6 to the Maroons' solitary 1.0. A goal apiece came in the second quarter and the margin as the two teams headed into the main break was only 12 points. On a resumption of play, *The Argus* said: "For 10 minutes, there seemed to be every promise of Fitzroy recovering, and then the hope suddenly disappeared."[68] Collingwood kicked three goals to one in the third term, to open up a comfortable 28-point lead at the last change.

The Argus noted that: "In their previous engagement, when refreshments were being distributed, the great majority of players laid (sic) full length on the grass, not so on this occasion. With one exception [the correspondent did not name him]; they were all standing, ready and eager for the fray." They took that energy into the last term, kicking 3.6 to 2.5 to win by 35 points. Harry Curtis kicked his third goal, and Lee kicked two more goals in the last quarter to take his tally to four for the game—the same as he had kicked in the 1910 Grand Final. *The Australasian* noted: "It was fitting their champion forward Lee should, in the greatest match of all, give the side a lead by kicking the first goal, and conclude the argument with the last."[69]

The Magpies were "top of the tree" again, just as Seddon had predicted from the other side of the world. McHale had become a premiership coach for the first time, after some early lean years which had some observers, including the great Jack Worrall, wondering whether Collingwood had a premiership in its make-up. The club's review of the 1917 premiership season—its fourth VFL triumph— claimed: "Many games produced determined contests, but none more so than the final with Fitzroy. The Grand Final, with our full strength in the field, proved Collingwood the best team of the year and it was generally admitted it deserved the honours."[70]

---

68   *The Argus*, September 24, 1917
69   *The Australasian*, September 29, 1917
70   Collingwood Annual Report, 1918

A special celebratory "smoke night" was organised by the president Jim Sharp. The players were each presented with a "handsome gold medal", courtesy of businessman and benefactor John Wren, whose return to the club in the past few years had been a boon for the club.

McHale was presented with a hand-coloured framed photograph for his achievements of playing 15 seasons with the club, as well as becoming only the club's second premiership coach. On a more sombre note, the first premiership coach, George Angus, died two months after the 1917 triumph, aged 42. This time it was not war that claimed the life of a former Magpie. He had been a soldier in the Boer War before he joined the club, but it was a brain tumour that brought about his premature and sudden end.

McHale was content to chase back-to-back flags from the other side of the boundary line. He was 35 and had pushed his body through 15 seasons with barely a rest. He aimed to remain fit and active, just in case he was needed to don the jumper again—if injuries hit the club.

The 1918 season—the last of the war years—welcomed back St Kilda and Essendon. Only Melbourne remained out of the competition. Over the previous five years, Collingwood had recruited some important players, including Harry Curtis (1914), Con McCarthy (1915), Charlie Pannam jnr (1917) and Bill Twomey snr (1918). McHale was confident the team could retain its position at the head of the ladder, though they would have a serious new challenger in South Melbourne in 1918.

The Herald said: "Collingwood last season were composed of a fine, dashing, even band ... Their team would have held their own in the pre-war days so well were they balanced and so quick and accurate were they in all departments."[71]

The unfurling of the 1917 premiership flag was meant to be a celebratory moment. To a degree, it was. However, it came against Carlton in the opening round of the season, and the Blues were mourning

---

71   *The Herald,* May 11, 1918

the loss of their captain Rod McGregor's brother in the war. *The Herald* observed: "The principal match of the day was played at Collingwood where the premiership flag won last year— the silver anniversary of the formation of the club—was unfurled. Collingwood's supporters were delighted when Mrs Sharp, wife of Mr J. Sharp, the president of the club, unfurled the flag won by Collingwood. The pennant was (then) lowered to half-mast as a sign of mourning for R. McGregor's brother and Mr George Elmslie MLA, who died today."[72]

The compassion ended soon after. Despite not scoring a goal in the opening term, and kicking a woefully inaccurate 1.10 in the first half to trail by five points, Collingwood responded with a strong second half to secure the opening round win by 35 points.

Collingwood's first blemish came against South Melbourne in Round 3. Minus Lee, the Magpies had trailed by three goals at half-time before wresting back the lead—narrowly—at three-quarter time. In that time, it was a "black and white triumph ... they looked like the dominant teams of old."[73] But South Melbourne rallied and kicked five goals in the last 12 minutes of the game to win by 18 points.

McHale was back for his sole game of the season in the Round 7 game against Essendon at East Melbourne. He played forward that afternoon, and didn't trouble the scorers, but Collingwood did kick 10 goals to nil in the second half to record a 65-point win. A week later, Collingwood fell to Carlton. Again, the Princes Park hoodoo had defeated the Magpies, where it was suggested that "it may be that the ground, being so much more roomy than Victoria Park (which is on the small side) hampers them more than is generally supposed."[74]

South Melbourne beat Collingwood a second time—this time at Victoria Park by seven points—in Round 10, and then a fortnight later St Kilda edged them out by 13 points at the Junction Oval. But McHale

72   ibid
73   *The Herald*, June 1, 1918
74   *The Herald*, July 6, 1918

rallied his players—despite some injuries which kept key players. *The Herald* commented that: "A marked feature of Collingwood's play is their wonderful handpassing ... looking on, a lot of it seems doubtful, the distance carried at times being astounding. But it must also be remembered that what looks extremely doubtful from a distance bears a different aspect altogether when one is close at hand."[75] McHale had been working on it with his men at training, and it seemed to be successful. The Magpies, with a 10-4 record, finished the home and away season in second position behind South Melbourne, which had dropped only one game.

As the war appeared to be turning in the Allies' favour with a series of key victories in Europe, Collingwood was meeting with St Kilda in the semi-final. It was a tough encounter on the field, and just as willing in the outer when larrikins responded to the VFL's decision to raise the price of a glass of beer at the football to sixpence Garrie Hutchison and John Ross reported a comment at the time: "It is notable that the colourful language and riotous behaviour that sometimes erupts at football matches can usually be traced to the area around beer booths."[76]

For a time it looked as if St Kilda would pull off an upset, as it took a seven-point lead into the last term. But Collingwood steadied in the final half-hour, kicking 2.5 to 0.1 to regain the lead and win by nine points. Hughes was outstanding, as was Percy Wilson, while 19-year-old Bill Twomey—the youngest player on the field—was described as being "one of the best first-season men that has ever appeared in league football."[77] (Twomey played for Collingwood for five seasons, 1919-22, before retiring to become a pro-runner and a playing-coach in the country. He returned to League football a decade later for a short stint with Hawthorn. Later he became famous as the father of the three Twomeys, Bill, Pat and Mick, who distinguished themselves with Collingwood in the 1950s.) After South Melbourne narrowly

---

75   *The Herald,* August 3, 1918
76   *100 years of Australian football,* Garrie Hutchison and John Ross, Viking, 1996
77   *The Herald,* August 24, 1918

beat Carlton in the other final, it came down to a clash between the two best sides of the year for the premiership.

McHale came agonisingly close to coaching back-to-back premierships. With a team that was "weightier and more solid than their rivals",[78] Collingwood led the game narrowly for three quarters of the contest. It was four points at quarter-time, 16 points at half-time, and 12 points at three-quarter time. *The Herald* acknowledged Collingwood "maintained their form, the result being a grand exhibition of the game, played by thoroughly trained men."[79] But, before 39,262 fans, South Melbourne finished harder than its opponent. The Southerners clawed their way back into the contest, with two goals as scores were locked level with only a handful of minutes to go.

When Dick Lee passed to Snowy Lumsden the game looked to be back in the Magpies' favour as McHale nervously watched on from the sidelines. *The Herald* recorded: "The yelling and screaming stopped, as Lumsden carefully placed the ball and let drive. The kick was an excellent one, though just missed, but it put Collingwood a point in the lead with four minutes to go."[80] Lee marked on an acute angle and his missed shot was claimed by veteran Vic Belcher, who cleared the ball out of the danger zone for South Melbourne. The Herald continued: "With half a minute to go, (Mark) Tandy getting possession, raced past three opponents and let drive. The ball dropped a yard short, with two opponents fighting fiercely for possession, when (Chris) Laird applied his boot, and South won 'on the post' by five points ... (it was) the most remarkable victory ever witnessed in a league final."[81]

For McHale, it was a heartbreaking end to his first year as non-playing coach (barring the one match he filled in for). The game had looked in Collingwood's reach until the last 30 seconds of play. But the end of the war two months and four days later put everything

---

78   *The Herald*, September 19, 1918
79   ibid
80   ibid
81   ibid

into context. After more than four years of war, the guns fell silent on November 11, 1918. When the armistice was announced, *The Australasian* declared that "from henceforth, November 11, 1918, will be regarded as the greatest day in history."[82] *The Argus* rejoiced: "The end, at last, what words can tell you adequately of the wave of relief that will sweep the civilised world. Heads that for years have been bowed with suffering will be raised with thanksgiving."[83] Australia was a country that had fewer than five million people in it. Incredibly, as the Australian War Memorial would record, "416,809 enlisted, of which over 60,000 were killed, and 156,000 wounded, gassed or taken prisoner."[84]

According to AFL records, there were 94 known VFL League players to have given their life during the First World War. Seventy-eight of them were one club players, while another 16 played for two clubs. Collingwood lost eight past and present players: Sam Campbell, Alan Cordner, Fred Fielding, Charlie Langtree, Peter Martin, Paddy Rowan (Percy Rowe), Tom Worle and Tom Wright. University and Melbourne lost the most, with 19 and 16 respectively.[85]

There were mass celebrations in the heart of Melbourne. *The Argus* pondered: "To the men who have so nobly borne the brunt of the fighting come victory and rest; to their loved ones at home comes a deep content; and to the world the prospect of an early, and it is fervently hoped, a lasting peace ... In Melbourne last night the glad news that the German delegation had signed the armistice terms spread like wildfire. It reached the country almost as quickly as the more distant suburbs, and it kindled a blaze of feeling such as the State has never known before."[86]

People from the suburbs poured into the city when the news broke late in the day. Thousands rejoiced in the heart of Melbourne that memorable Monday night.

---

82   *The Australasian*, November 12, 1918
83   *The Argus*, November 12, 1918
84   Australian War Memorial website, www.awm.gov.au
85   AFL records, Courtesy of Col Hutchinson and Cameron Sinclair
86   *The Argus*, November 12, 1918

CHAPTER 7

Tragedy Strikes

1919-1926

Jock and Violet McHale were meant to celebrating their 10th wedding anniversary on April 28, 1919. Instead, they were watched helplessly as their eldest son lay dying before them. When he contracted bronchial pneumonia on April 22 it gave rise to a fatal combination. There was hope that he would pull through but sadly, those hopes were extinguished on Wednesday, April 30, when he died exactly three months before his seventh birthday—with his parents and his siblings John and Mary Jean (known mainly as Jean) beside him—at the family home at 111 Talbot Street, East Brunswick.

For all the trials and traumas that had affected McHale in his life, including the loss of five siblings long before their time, nothing could have prepared him for the death of his beloved son. Before Frankie took ill, Jock's mind would have centred heavily on how Collingwood was going to respond from its near miss in the 1918 Grand Final, or on maintaining his long tenure with the Carlton Brewery. Suddenly nothing seemed as important anymore, after losing the son who had been named after him.

For a football identity who was by now one of the most well-known names in the game, Jock McHale was an intensely private person. So was Violet. It was in keeping that they spoke to few people about the almost unbearable loss that had befallen them. There were no references in the newspapers to the death of McHale's son just three days before the start of Collingwood's 1919 season. There were no public notices filed to detail the family's heartache. A small funeral was held a day after Frankie's death in the church that Jock and Violet had been married at a decade earlier—St Ambrose's Catholic Church in Sydney Road, Brunswick—followed by a burial ceremony conducted by Catholic priest M. Palbett at Coburg Cemetery.

Collingwood had elected Con McCarthy as captain and he and other officials had to carry much of the load in the early stages of the 1919 season. McHale's mind was understandably elsewhere, at least in the first month or so. Incredibly, he was not listed as being on the club's selection committee for that season, as documented in the annual report published just before the start of the 1920 season. It is almost inconceivable to think McHale would not have attended at least some of those meetings, given he was coaching the side. But what it does say—at least in the early period after his son's death—is that he was frequently missing from the club, particularly when it came to meetings.

He continued to take training, but would likely have relied heavily on those listed on the selection committee: Jim Sharp (president), E.W. 'Bud' Copeland (secretary), as well as former players Jack Joyce and Alf 'Rosie' Dummett, and current players McCarthy, Les Hughes and Alec Mutch.

As the season progressed McHale would have attended some of these meetings, and he was recorded as having attended 21 of the 31 general committee gatherings in 1919. The mystery is that McHale was not listed as being on the match committee in seasons 1920 or 1921, either, before he returned to the listings for the 1922 season.

He was also absent for the official team photograph taken in the second half of the 1919 season. It would become the standard photo to mark the premiership achieved later that season. He and star wingman Tom Drummond were unavailable for the team sitting. Insets of both were used outside the borders of the photograph published in the annual report. But photographic licence allowed the club to super-impose images of McHale and Drummond into the back corners of the famous shot to mark their contribution. You could hardly have had a photograph of the premiership team without the coach, and one of its stars.

But although he might have missed a few backroom meetings, and perhaps even a handful of training sessions, McHale would not miss a match through the season. Just as he had been resilient as a footballer, he would prove the same as a coach. He did miss the last training session before Round 1—on the day he buried his son—but he was there at the Lake Oval when the Magpies started their 1919 campaign in the Grand Final rematch against South Melbourne. It is impossible to know how effective he was as a coach that day, but the fact that he was there after such a personal trauma said much to his players about what the club—and the game—meant to McHale.

Collingwood started off with a win, defeating South Melbourne by 13 points. *The Australasian* reported the Magpies had "a better method"[1] than their opponents—"they found their men more frequently and regularly, doing the double pass, repeatedly nonplussing the Southerners ... South excelled in the air, in dash and in long kicking; while Collingwood went in for the short, low passing."[2]

But the first round win was forgotten within a week when St Kilda broke a 24-game losing streak at Victoria Park, dating back to the start of the VFL in 1897. What made the win even more incredible was that the Saints achieved this without three key players who had been left out with influenza. Much to McHale's annoyance, St Kilda had

1   The Australasian, May 3, 1919
2   ibid

restricted Collingwood to only one goal in the first three quarters and had carried a 28-point lead into the final change. It looked like being a procession.

However, McHale's three-quarter time speech, and a quick revision of the team, made the difference. *The Argus* commented: "A sudden and sensational change came about with the re-arrangement of the Collingwood's ruck. (Les) Hughes and (Con) McCarthy went into the pack together, and in an instant the game swung around in Collingwood's favour."[3] It would not be the last time that the combination of McCarthy and Hughes would make an impact that season. This day, though, it took the Magpies to the brink of a sensational comeback win. Four goals to nil in the final term cut the margin and when Gus Dobrigh marked the ball just before the final bell, he had the fortunes of the game in his hands. Sadly, for McHale, and for Collingwood, the kick after the siren missed. St Kilda had won by three points. The Saints would not win another game at the ground for the remainder of McHale's life (the second Saints' win at Victoria Park would be in 1962).

Just as the country was trying to immerse itself in the sort of normality it had missed through the war years, the arrival of the 'Spanish flu' was a sobering reality check to the euphoria in the months after the end of the First World War. It was serious enough to shut schools for a period, to close public institutions, to have people travelling to the city or its surrounding suburbs wearing facemasks for protection, striking fear in the populace, particularly in the inner suburbs.

According to *Victoria, A History*, the first recorded case in Melbourne was on January 22, 1919. There would be several waves of the outbreak. By October, the epidemic was deemed to be over, with almost 12,000 deaths. There were 3,530 deaths in Melbourne, with 2,391 coming from "the more densely populated metropolitan area, especially the industrial suburbs".[4] The death toll worldwide showed

---

3   *The Argus*, May 12, 1919
4   *Victoria, A History*, Don Garden, Nelson, 1984

the extent of the impact of the virus. It was estimated that somewhere between 20 million and up to 100 million people died, between 2.5 and 5 per of the world's population. The true figure will never be known.

Collingwood won three games in succession after the St Kilda loss. The Magpies had regained Dick Lee for the game against Melbourne in early June. Lee was essential to McHale's forward plans. McHale had always believed in the importance of a good full-forward. In the Kevin Sheedy-inspired book of 2004, *The 500 Club*, it was noted, in an essay on tactics within the game: "It was he (McHale) who first saw the importance of how to move the ball forward to provide the best opportunity to score. At Collingwood training, McHale drilled his players relentlessly on their movement of the ball up the ground, with particular focus on giving the full-forward clear space 30 metres out from goal."[5] The philosophy would start with Lee in McHale's early years of coaching, and would continue to be worked on in the coming two decades with two other players considered among the greatest forwards to have played the game.

Having played in the previous two Grand Finals, Collingwood expected to play in a third. Part of that confidence came from the belief that at least two of the men who had left for the "greater battle" would be rejoining them now that the war was over. Dan Minogue, who had led the club so well in the two and a half seasons before his departure, and Doc Seddon, who had signed up with his best mate Paddy Rowan but had returned without him. Both were expected back in the country by the middle of the year. There were plans afoot to honour the Collingwood "footballer-soldiers" with a grand welcome home. It was even suggested that the club was planning to pay tribute to Minogue with a special parade down Smith Street on his return home.[6]

Seddon arrived back first. Having inspired the club by sending a horseshoe back from France as a good luck charm before the 1917

---

5   *The 500 Club*, Kevin Sheedy and Warwick Hadfield, News Custom Publishing, 2004
6   Interview with Minogue's grandson, Peter French

Grand Final, he was prepared to do it with his actions in 1919. He returned to Australia on the steamer *Cluny Castle* on May 22, two days before Collingwood's win over Richmond in Round 4. He started training almost immediately, and would be honoured at season's end with the presentation of a guinea "because he did not miss one training occasion after his return from the front."[7] Within 23 days, Seddon had satisfied McHale—and the selection committee—that he was ready to play, and he was back in Round 7, at Princes Park against Carlton. His return was memorable, booting a goal in the dying stages to cut the deficit to six points. But the fairytale result was not to be. The Blues steadied to win by 11 points.

Minogue arrived back on the steamer *Barambah* on July 26, two days before Collingwood's three-point loss to Fitzroy. It was assumed he would swap his khaki for black and white, as Seddon had done. But Minogue was about to shock the club by announcing his intention to join Richmond. Plans for the parade were torn up. A bitter new rivalry with Richmond was about to be born off the back of this defection. For McHale, who held loyalty so dearly, the decision bordered on treachery, even though Minogue maintained it was the right course of action.

Minogue's motivations can only be speculated. Several reasons have been espoused. Firstly, he was an outstanding leader and had plans to coach; something that would not have happened in the short term at Collingwood, with McHale entrenched in the job. Given McHale was still at the helm at Collingwood 30 years later, if that was the reason, that call was prescient. Then there was the close friendship he had formed with Richmond's Hugh James when fighting abroad. Both had played in the famous ANZAC match in London on October 28, 1916.

There was another more likely cause, as revealed in *A Century of the Best*. Minogue may have been persuaded to move by a feeling of dissatisfaction over the treatment of his former teammate Jim Sadler,

---

7   Collingwood Annual Report, 1920

by Collingwood—and coach McHale. Sadler had last played for the Magpies in Round 15, 1917, but was not selected in the club's finals or Grand Final side that season. Whatever the rationale, Minogue had no regrets about his decision to leave Collingwood. As he said years later in *The Sporting Globe:* "I may have allowed sentiment to sway my feelings in that case—I don't know. But I have never had cause to feel sorry for my action."[8]

Predictably, Collingwood vehemently opposed Minogue's move with a passion reserved for those who had wronged the club. McHale never spoke publicly about the defection, but he was said to have been incensed. Minogue was not welcomed back to Collingwood in a social forum again until the mid 1950s[9]—when McHale was dead.

The Magpies ensured that Minogue would not be granted his transfer to Richmond in 1919, and for good measure the club would refuse to pay him the money he was duly entitled to from his retirement fund.

Collingwood wanted to make an example of him, excommunicating the one-time captain and the man who some believed could be the long-time successor to McHale. Collingwood—and McHale—fervently believed in the loyalty of the players. No one was going to change that philosophy, or the club's policy that all players deserved to be paid the same.

As fate would have it, Richmond had emerged as one of the main threats to Collingwood's premiership prospects in 1919, and when the two teams met at Victoria Park on August 9, there was plenty of ill-feeling. Early in the last term, when Richmond shot out to an 11-point lead, McHale would have been extremely concerned. The Magpies were also down a man, as McCarthy, who had been the best player on the ground, strained the muscles in his back just before three-quarter time. Then, Dick Lee, once again showing the value of a great full-forward, turned the game with three quick goals, before

8   *A Century of the Best*, Michael Roberts, Collingwood Football Club, 1991
9   ibid

giving another one off to Harry Curtis for Collingwood to win the game by 13 points.

Collingwood secured the minor premiership—thus winning the right of challenge—when South Melbourne lost to Geelong in the final round. It had been the only week of the season that the Magpies would sit on the top perch. A week after Richmond stunned the previous year's premier, South Melbourne, in the first semi-final, Collingwood started brilliantly against Carlton in the second semi-final. Four goals to nil—4.7 (31) to 0.2 (2)—came in the first term, and by three-quarter time, the difference was 43 points. By game's end, the Blues had whittled the margin to 18 points. *The Argus* reported: "They (Collingwood) jumped out to the lead in the first furlong, had the race won at the home turn and it was only long after the distance was passed that Carlton put in its last run ... In the language of the moving pictures, Saturday's game might have been advertised Collingwood v Carlton—featuring Dick Lee."[10] Lee kicked four goals, but what was of concern to the coach was the loss of Percy Wilson to a broken arm.

Only Richmond, which had never won a VFL premiership or even played in a VFL Grand Final, stood between the Magpies and a fifth VFL premiership—and McHale's second as a coach. Many were predicting it was a *fait accompli* for the more seasoned, more experienced Magpies in the Final, but a prescient warning came from *The Herald*: "There is such a condition as overconfidence."[11] Whether it was overconfidence or overpowering from Richmond, the Magpies were no match and lost by 29 points. *The Argus* concluded: "They (Richmond) were the better side in the air, and Collingwood's famous system appeared once only as a flash in the pan ... they were beaten on their merits without room for excuse."[12] The right of challenge gave Collingwood a second chance, and Richmond its first Grand Final after one of the biggest shocks of the football season.

---

10   *The Argus*, September 29, 1919
11   *The Herald*, October 3, 1919
12   *The Argus*, October 6, 1919

The Collingwood coach's influence was telling in this time of unexpected crisis. His planning and strategy leading into the Grand Final turned the tide. The Collingwood Annual Report said: "The result of the final match was certainly a great surprise for everybody connected to Collingwood. However, a respite from training, the complete restoration of health of two or three of our players, who had been suffering injuries, the alteration of the team, and the disposition of others on the field brought about the desired result."[13]

McHale made several decisions that would have a significant impact. Mindful of the criticism that had come from people such as Jack Worrall that Collingwood failed to freshen itself for past finals, McHale gave his team a light week on the track. The Annual Report was glowing in its assessment of the principle: "It was mentioned that rest, except for a little gentle exercise on Thursday afternoon, was another essential to success; advice that was acted upon, with gratifying results from a Collingwood point of view."[14]

The coach had also set a plan in motion to curb the influence of Richmond big man Dave Moffatt, who had overpowered Les Hughes in the final. *The Australasian* said: "The authorities at Collingwood set to work to devise a means of nullifying Richmond's great strength in vital positions, and they succeeded beyond anticipations, even if luck aided them."[15] McHale chose McCarthy as the man to tackle Moffatt and to keep him far enough away from Hughes as to let the Magpie big man have a clear path to the ball. "Perhaps the most important factor in the (Grand Final) was that McCarthy, soon after the commencement of play, went into the pack to save Hughes from Moffatt's attentions. This has much to do with Collingwood's success as anything in the game."[16] The Magpies had eight players who were 29 and over, in a team whose average age was 27 years and 91 days. Those veterans

---

13 Collingwood Annual Report, 1920
14 ibid
15 *The Australasian*, October 11, 1919
16 ibid

were Doc Seddon (31), Flapper Hughes (35), Bert Colechin (32), Bill Walton (31), Dick Lee (30), Alec Mutch (30), Charlie Laxton (29) and Ernie Lumsden (29). The only teenager in the side was 18-year-old Ernie Wilson. This bunch was as close to a home-grown product as could be expected. Half of the 1910 premiership team had been recruited from the country zones, and two others were from outside of the Collingwood municipal boundaries, but this 1919 side included only two players not from the local zone.

After an even first half, Collingwood led at the main break by four points. The Tigers grabbed the lead briefly before Lee put the Magpies back in front. Goals to Walton and Bill Twomey stretched the margin at three-quarter time to 16 points. Then McHale produced another masterstroke. When he gathered his players around him, he implored the team to play aggressive, attacking football, and to not fall into the trap of trying to defend a lead. The ploy perplexed the opposition. In an era of football in which teams frequently opened up a lead and settled back trying to defend it, McHale knew the best way ahead was to push the scoreboard. It was said that Collingwood's "hand-passing, legitimate or otherwise—and it was principally otherwise—was perfection."[17]

Any chance of a Richmond revival was snuffed out in the opening minutes of the final term when Lumsden helped Seddon to a goal. In his 13th game back since returning from the war, Seddon was doing his best to taste premiership success. He had played in the club's losing 1915 Grand Final and he had been in France when the Magpies had won in 1917. This time he wanted to win it not just for himself, but as a tribute to his fallen mate, 'Paddy Rowan'.

The final margin was 25 points. McCarthy and Hughes played their roles in tandem; Charlie Pannam jnr was outstanding, Lee's three goals took his tally for the season to 56; Seddon (two goals) and Curtis (one) were strong in attack; defenders Colechin, Mutch and Walton

---

17   ibid

were key players; and Ernie Wilson, four days before his 19th birthday, received an early present.

It was also a triumph for McHale, who had won his first premiership as a non-playing coach. Sitting on the sidelines watching as his team powered away from Richmond, the team that had seduced Minogue away from them, McHale might have been forgiven for rubbing it in. But he didn't. He, and the club, had triumphed in the most trying year of McHale's life to date, and that was enough. In nominating McHale as a "Life Governor of the Melbourne Hospital" after the Grand Final victory, the club's 1920 Annual Report said of the coach: "It could not have been more worthily bestowed than on Mr. J. F. McHale, who, now that he has retired from the arena as a player, acts as a coach to the team, and rightly deserves commendation for his part of the work which led the club to gain two of the last three Premierships, narrowly missing the third."[18] It was a double premiership for Collingwood as the VFL had introduced a reserves competition for 1919, and the Magpie Juniors had won it in the early game.

Given the trauma he and his family had been through the previous year, it was of little surprise that Jock chose to leave the committee in early 1920. Seddon was one of those who would take his place. It was agreed, too, as Richard Stremski documented, that the pre-war scale of match payments would be restored, at "essentially one pound per match."[19] The Annual Report said: "The coach's salary was increased to £2."[20] McHale was getting more than the players at this stage, but that would change—of his own volition—in the coming years.

As he prepared for his team to take on Essendon at Victoria Park in Round 1, 1920 circumstances meant McHale was forced into a brief

---

18   Collingwood Annual Report, 1920
19   *Kill For Collingwood*, Richard Stremski, Allen and Unwin, 1986
20   Collingwood Annual Report, 1921

comeback at the age of 37 years and 141 days. *The Australasian* explained: "The new men chosen for Collingwood did not put in an appearance until too late. Thus the team was short-changed, necessitating the re-appearance of McHale, the old champion centreman. The veteran, who has been coaching Collingwood for years, deserves every credit for his prompt assistance in filling the gap, though youth outpaced and outplayed him."[21] For once, McHale was not at the peak of fitness, but he was still able to contribute to the club.

Collingwood lost the opening game of the season on a day in which the crowd was presented with the 1919 premiership flag fluttering in the breeze and the shock return of their coach for his 261st and last VFL game. He had played his first game in Round 1, 1903, and his last game in Round 1, 1920—17 years on, minus one day. He had played one game in 1918 (Round 7 against Essendon at the East Melbourne ground, having returned after the 1917 Grand Final win over Fitzroy.)

It was to be a slow start to the season for the Magpies with three losses coming from their first five games, with wins over Geelong and Melbourne, the only two successes in the first five weeks of competition.

The loss to Richmond in Round 5 was the hardest felt. It was a bitter blow to Collingwood, for it came against a team that now had Dan Minogue as its captain and coach. It was unusual as it was played on a Wednesday morning, to coincide with the arrival of the Prince of Wales, who was in the country to thank the country on behalf of his father, King George V, for the part Australia played in the Great War. A Collingwood member's ticket was even forwarded to the future King, although the Annual Report noting that he replied that he had regretted "he could not accept membership of any club except those which he could visit or have some connection."[22]

Not surprisingly, the first meeting of Minogue and Collingwood—and Minogue and McHale as coaches—attracted plenty of attention.

---

21   *The Australasian,* May 1, 1920
22   Collingwood Annual Report, 1921

The Australasian observed: "There was a huge crowd present and it overtaxed the accommodation. About 40 young men watched the play from the roof of the veranda of the old stand. Towards the finish of the game, when the excitement became intense, those on the roof began to move about. A moment before the bell rang H. James took a mark that placed Richmond in a position to win. Those on the roof stepped forward and the heavy weight caused the veranda roof to give way. For an instant, it looked as if those under the roof would be crushed."[23] Fortunately, the people on top were able to slide to safety.

Collingwood was not so fortunate. It ended up going down to the Tigers by seven points. McHale hated losing at the best of times. To do it against a team harbouring a player who he considered had committed a slight on the club would have bitten deep into him. A clutch of six successive wins followed which kept the Magpies in the top three on the ladder, behind only Fitzroy and Richmond.

But Minogue and Richmond would do it again, on Minogue's return to Victoria Park for the first time in four years. The Tigers ended Collingwood's run, and increased McHale's frustration. Collingwood were without Ernie Wilson, Twomey, Pannam, Lee and Dobrigh for the game. Collingwood led by 10 points at the last change, but had been forced to play with 17 players after Mutch strained his knee in the opening minutes of the match. The Magpies had led by four points with "half a minute to go" when a free kick against Maurice Sheehy went to Richmond's George Bayliss. *The Australasian* said: "Four men danced on the mark as he was about to take his kick, the ball falling short. (Charlie) Laxton had encroached over the line. Bayliss was awarded another kick, and his effort this time was straight and true."[24]

Minogue had made a difference to his new team. *The Australasian* claimed Richmond was "benefiting by (Minogue's) great ability as a coach, captain and player. He already has a strong influence over the team, which was unanimous in their praises in regard to leadership

---

23   *The Australasian*, May 22, 1920
24   *The Australasian*, July 31, 1920

and coaching ... (he) wished to play for Richmond last season, but the League refused. However, he was persistent and came up again this season."[25]

With Lee out injured for the Round 15 clash with St Kilda at the Junction Oval, and his career in its twilight, the club wanted to try a new forward to see whether he would be up to the task. Gordon Coventry, a teenage kid from Diamond Creek with big hands and a painfully shy disposition, was included for his first game. *The Australasian* called him "a trifle stage-frightened, for he did not shine. He is a good kick and may come along with experience of the rough and tumble of league life."[26]

Years later, Coventry, who kicked one goal on debut would say: "I saw hundreds of young lads having their first League games thereafter, but none was as inglorious as mine."[27] He was dropped the next week. In time, he would break every record in the game, and kick another 1298 over the next 17 years.

A few other notable players made their debuts in 1920. One of them was Charlie Tyson, from Kalgoorlie Rovers; another was Percy Rowe, from Rutherglen, who had initially come to Collingwood to play cricket with the legendary Jack Ryder. It must have been strange for Seddon. He had played in the second ruck with his great mate 'Paddy Rowan' before the pair went off to war. As has been noted, 'Rowan's' real name was Percy Rowe, and that was the name he died under at war in December 1916. And now Seddon had the chance of teaming with another Percy Rowe.

Lee was back and so was Coventry (who had kicked three goals in his Round 18 return against South Melbourne at Victoria Park) for the club's semi-final against Fitzroy. The Magpies proved too strong, kicking 4.17 to 3.5, to win by 18 points. But Lee's finals series looked in doubt when he suffered another knock to his suspect knee.

25 *The Australasian*, June 6, 1920
26 *The Australasian*, August 28, 1920
27 *A Century of the Best*, Michael Roberts, Collingwood Football Club, 1991

The victory set up a clash with Carlton, who had knocked off minor premier Richmond in the other semi-final. Richmond, with the right of challenge, moved through to what would be the Grand Final. Without Lee, McHale started regular centre half-forward Harry Curtis at full-forward before requisitioning Coventry to the role. It worked a treat as the teenager celebrated his 19th birthday—on the very day—with a five-goal performance in Collingwood's 24-point win.

For the second year in a row, Collingwood was to meet Richmond in a Grand Final. This time, the Tigers had Minogue, as well as an extra year's experience. *The Herald* declared October 2, 1920 as "a day that drew people out of doors, they swarmed towards the Melbourne Cricket Ground."[28] There were a few selection shocks; importantly, Dick Lee was missing. It was said that he "had given a trial to his injured leg yesterday evening and although he felt he could punt, he was unable to drop kick with any confidence. Like the true sportsman that he is, he decided not to run any risk, which might have had the effect of incapacitating himself early in the game and consequently he thought he should not play."[29]

Richmond included a first-game player, Bill James, from Kyabram, in the place of the ill George Bayliss. It would be the only game of his career. After kicking a goal in the Grand Final, a shooting accident on his foot over the summer months would render it impossible for him to play VFL football again. Witnessing his first Grand Final as a guest of the VFL, was Sir Arthur Conan Doyle, the famous author and creator of Sherlock Holmes.

Collingwood was the first team onto the field, but Minogue devised a tactic to leave Richmond in the rooms for as long as possible "lest the wait should get in their nerves and make them anxious."[30]

A speech from Richmond president, Jack Archer, as revealed in *Richmond Football Club: A century of League football*, detailed the

---

28   *The Herald*, October 2, 1920
29   ibid
30   ibid

ill-will that existed between Richmond and Collingwood. Before the players made their long-awaited entrance on to the ground for the Grand Final, Archer said: "The Collingwood Football Club we used to hold up as a pattern for sportsmanship. Yes, they were good sports at social gatherings, after the matches they won, but the scene changed at Collingwood this year when we beat them, and we're going to beat them today."[31]

He said Collingwood's shunning of war-hero Minogue had been a travesty. Archer stirred emotions: "At Collingwood, I was admiring their beautiful room and its appointments, and I noticed a nice souvenir sent by Danny Minogue to the club while away fighting for his country." The inference was that some at Collingwood—McHale among them—had not volunteered to fight for their country. He continued: "When I was admiring the souvenir, the secretary of Collingwood (E.W. Copeland) advised me that they had a fine photo of Minogue which used to adorn their walls but it was now relegated to obscurity with its face to the wall on the top shelf of a cupboard. Is that sportsmanship? I've come to the conclusion that it is all self, self, self with the League clubs, and the Richmond club from now on is going to be the same."[32]

There was a hint of antagonism even before the first bounce. *The Herald* said: "Both teams submitted themselves to a swarm of photographers and telegraph operators. (One player said) 'It's better to do it now; our faces might not look quite so well at the finish."[33] The events over the past year and a bit—since Minogue had returned from war—boiled over in the third term, by which stage Richmond had got on top of Collingwood. "Play became exceedingly rough," *The Herald* reported. "Trouble had been brewing for some time."

---

31   *Richmond Football Club, The Tigers*, A Century of League football, Rhett Bartlett, GSP Books, 2007

32   ibid

33   *The Herald*, October 2, 1920

After a 1.2 each stalemate in the first term, the Richmond side had led by nine points at both the end of the second and third terms. At three-quarter time McHale could sense his team was feeling the effects of the previous week's game against Carlton. *The Australasian* noticed it: "It was an omen sign that a majority of the Collingwood men, after lemon time, seemed tired and loath to resume. Richmond, on the contrary, was fresh and eager and was waiting expectantly for the bounce of the ball."[34]

Jack Worrall, writing in *The Australasian,* believed the impact of the tough game against Carlton had killed any chance the Magpies had of upsetting Richmond: "The team had not recovered from the strenuous trial at Carlton. The contest was so severe that several of the most notable Collingwood players performed at a disadvantage against Richmond. They were stiff and sore and consequently deficient in pace."[35]

Worrall added: "Collingwood has been a battling more than brilliant side, and was very lucky in being one of the final quartet. Several of their older players are decidedly on the down grade, and are getting slower, which is especially noticeable on a fine day."[36] To make matters worse, he said Richmond "practically owes its position to the leadership of Minogue".[37]

Collingwood made a few dashes early, but there was nothing McHale or his players could do to stop Richmond. The Magpies managed two goals in the last term, but their opponents kicked three. Minogue and Richmond had won the match—and the premiership—by 17 points.

---

34   *The Australasian,* October 2, 1920
35   ibid
36   ibid
37   ibid

Despite the Minogue affair, leaving Collingwood didn't always guarantee angst. When Percy Wilson decided to take up a second offer from Melbourne to captain-coach the side from the start of the 1921 season, the Magpies allowed the 32-year-old to depart. As the Annual Report suggested: "Mr Percy Wilson has played with us for twelve years ... Mr Wilson's whole heart and soul has been bound up with Collingwood, by recognising he cannot play much longer, finally concluded he would ask for a transfer. Your club has granted him a clearance with willingness, but a lot of regret."[38]

The supporters had no issue with Wilson's decision, unlike that of Minogue. In the club's Round 2 win over Melbourne, *The Australasian* noted: "A nice compliment was paid by Collingwood supporters to Percy Wilson as he led Melbourne onto the field ... they cheered him for some time, a tribute to the esteem in which he is still held by his admirers."[39] The cheers for anything Melbourne were short-lived: Collingwood won by 44 points.

The Australasian praised the Magpies' first month, saying it was "one of the smartest teams that ever wore their colours. They have enough big men to furnish the necessary weight in the ranks and in addition to being big, they are clever enough."[40]

Collingwood's rucks were doing a good job, following on from a tradition of the past few years, but other clubs were catching on to the Magpies' tactics. "Not that long ago, the Collingwood team initiated a system of frequent changes in the ruck, and like any other innovation, it has been copied by other teams. Each of the rucks open their respective quarter, but after 10 minutes they are changed so that followers are always fresh and never allow the ball to get away from them."[41]

Again, the first loss of the 1921 season came to Minogue's Richmond, by one point at Punt Road. It was "a hair-raising finish". Late in the game, Seddon levelled the scores at 52-all, but a late

---

38 ibid
39 *The Australasian*, May 14, 1921
40 *The Australasian*, May 28, 1921
41 *The Australasian*, June 4, 1921

behind to Bob Weatherill "kicked over his shoulder" gave the Tigers the win. Then, in the middle of the season, a series of four consecutive losses not only cost Collingwood top spot, it even put in jeopardy the club's run of appearances in finals. The losses were to Carlton, Fitzroy, Melbourne and Geelong.

A win over Essendon, with Lee kicking eight of the club's 10 goals, broke the run of outs, but Richmond's recent dominance over Collingwood continued a week later, and this time the margin was a clear-cut 26-points. There were no arguments. The Tigers were too good, and McHale must have been worried about Collingwood's patchy form.

Incredibly, a worse loss was to come, though it would never be included amongst McHale's defeats as a coach. In September 1921, just a fortnight out from the finals series, and in the middle of a bye weekend, Collingwood travelled to Wonthaggi on a trip away, and lost a match against the local side. While it was an enjoyable trip for the party of 40, the loss did come as a surprise to everyone concerned, though an excuse was offered, albeit several months later. In the Annual Report, members were told: "Although a fairly strong team represented your club, a gale wind blowing across the exposed ground made concerted play impossible and your team suffered defeat by a narrow margin. The local team are to be congratulated on their excellent display, and the opinion was freely expressed by the visitors that they would hold their own with any country team in the state."[42]

It is doubtful, given the result, and the form slump, that McHale would have enjoyed the dance on the Saturday night or the motor drive to Anderson's Inlet the following afternoon. As it turned out, it would be a fortuitous loss. Over the next few years Collingwood would recruit several players from the Wonthaggi area, including the three Baker brothers—Ted (later a Geelong premiership captain), Reg and Selwyn. And the Bakers would tell Collingwood about a young kid

---

42   Collingwood Annual Report, 1922

from the nearby hamlet of Woodleigh, Bob Makeham, in 1923. He would become an important player in McHale's most famous team.

Successive losses to Carlton—in the final round and in the first semi-final—ended Collingwood's season. In the first match, *The Herald* explained the Magpies' shortcomings: "Carlton were the best side all the way, playing their long game at times perfectly, while in contrast, Collingwood were fumbling a good deal over that short play which has been their specialty for years."[43] The margin was 27 points.

The final was a fair bit closer, with the Blues keeping Collingwood to only one goal in the first half. But five goals to the Magpies in the third term cut the margin back to only four points at the last change. As McHale made his speech to the team at three-quarter time, a small boy "with a Brownie camera trotted onto the field. Naturally the footballers gave the youngster every assistance and for a few minutes he had the time of his life and was the envy of every small boy around the ground."[44] Among his long forgotten photographs there is a snap of the umpire, Jack Elder. As the young boy took the photo of the umpire, one of the wags in the crowd screamed out: "Put it in the Chambers of Horrors."[45] The Magpies put up a struggle in the last term, but went down by 13 points.

If 1921 was deemed a wasted year, the decision by the Collingwood District team to appoint Hugh Thomas to coach the reserves would be a good one. The relationship between Thomas and McHale would, on occasions, be sorely tested, but for almost 20 years, they formed a unique, if distant combination. Some of the club's greatest players would controversially cite Thomas as just an important an influence on a generation of Collingwood players as the more feted McHale. Perhaps that would fuel the rivalry between these two characters, who would take their respective teams at either ends of Victoria Park on training nights—Thomas, who developed the skills of those young

---

43   *The Herald,* September 24, 1921
44   *The Herald,* October 1, 1921
45   ibid

Magpies heading through the ranks, and McHale, who managed the seniors as an elite team, and gave little private tuition.

As always, there were strong numbers of young hopefuls at Victoria Park before the 1922 season. McHale liked to have plenty of new players to choose from, and the Pies needed a host of new faces. Doc Seddon had retired, Alec Mutch, Charlie Laxton and Bert Colechin had left, and Con McCarthy (Footscray) and Gus Dobrigh (Port Melbourne) had transferred to the VFA. Les Hughes had effectively retired, too, and would play only two games in 1922 to earn his 15-year certificate. The drain on the senior Magpies would put a strain on the club's fortunes, but would also force McHale to go for youth. He blooded eight new faces in the opening round, a 17-point loss to Richmond. A week later, in a loss to South Melbourne by a goal, 14 of the 18 players who represented the Magpies had played fewer than 20 games, with Harry Saunders (85) and Tom Drummond (84) the only men to play over 50 games. Among the new faces was Leo Wescott, who would become a dual premiership player with Collingwood.

The Magpies lost the first two games of 1922, to Richmond and South Melbourne. One of the other "greenhorns", as his famous brother would later describe him, was Syd Coventry. Originally signed to St Kilda, he immediately changed his mind and resolved to play with his brother Gordon, and was forced to play under Thomas's tutelage in the District side in 1921, after protests from the Saints. In time, he would become the most successful captain in the club's history, and one of the best footballers the game has seen. Reflecting on this time some years later, he would tell *The Adelaide Advertiser* he had come into a great learning environment—"I owe a lot of my success to our coach, Jim McHale, who taught me the essential points

... I found that the Collingwood fellows were really good sports. They wanted to see a young fellow coming along."[46]

The omens were not good in the lead-up to the Round 3 match against Carlton, at Victoria Park. Ted Baker was a late arrival at the ground and was without his uniform after his bag was stolen in a city restaurant on the morning of the game. Worse still, as McHale was stalking the rooms and talking to his players in preparation for the game, a most unusual and perhaps even unsettling occurrence took place. *The Australasian* reported: "Collingwood might have been expected by the superstitious to have regarded it as an evil omen that, as a team was stripping, a dead man (a supporter whose heart had given way) was carried into the dressing room. But if there was any such feeling on the part of the players, they gave no sign of it."[47]

Dick Lee was back for his first performance of a year that would be his last for Collingwood. Charlie Pannam Jr. had returned from injury, and experienced players Saunders, Drummond, Harry Curtis and Maurie Sheehy were also giving the young team some assistance. At three-quarter time, the Blues led the inaccurate Magpies by five points. But in a finish that set the tone for the season, Collingwood kept Carlton without a goal, kicked two of their own (through Lee, who had only started training a week earlier) and went on to win by seven points.

It was the start of a month of wins for McHale's team. At the end of Round 2 it was only percentage off the bottom. By the end of Round 7, it was in second spot behind Essendon.

The win over Fitzroy in Round 7 had been comprehensive. Lee and Gordon Coventry—a dynamic forward duo in any era—kicked seven goals between them as Collingwood secured a 32-point win. *The Australasian* summed up the win by suggesting: "Never in the history of these two teams has one been so immeasurably superior. In their best days Collingwood never played better, while no one can recall a Fitzroy side so ineffective and full of mistakes."[48] It went further to show that in the past three games, "49 goals and 30 behinds ... tells a tale of excellence, of accuracy, of prolific scoring, which opponents have been unable to check and in each case the Magpies' swoop has been of the flock—not the individual, with all sharing equally in the success."[49]

A loss to Melbourne followed, but significant wins against Essendon, who were previously undefeated, and Richmond once more saw Collingwood elevated to premiership favourites. The 19-point win over the Tigers at Victoria Park was the first time the Magpies had beaten them since the 1919 Grand Final. *The Argus* declared: "Collingwood was always in the lead and they exhibited greater dash and better judgment. They were helped by serviceable handballing and the unselfishness of their forwards was very helpful to the team. Their teamwork was always well directed."[50]

But, as always, it seemed, Carlton at Princes Park proved a stumbling block. Collingwood had not won there since 1916, and the Blues brought about the Magpies' last home and away loss for the 1922 season with a five-point deficit in Round 12. *The Argus* noted it was "football history repeating itself ... for the match was won by Carlton only at the last minute because in that particular minute they were uppermost on the see-saw."[51]

It was a spiteful clash, with *The Argus* scribe suggesting: "My impression is that a Collingwood back confused the game of football and the one they play in stadiums, but whether (Carlton's Alex) Duncan had 'asked for it' was not so readily decided."[52] Collingwood's Harry Saunders and Eric Cock would receive hefty suspensions.

The outcome of the minor premiership came down to the last round match between Collingwood and Essendon at Victoria Park.

---

48 *The Australasian*, June 17, 1922
49 ibid
50 *The Argus*, July 17, 1922
51 *The Argus*, July 31, 1922
52 ibid

Just before the start of the contest, a heavy rainstorm "reduced the park to mud and the match largely to a matter of luck."[53] The Magpies were without Lee due to injury, but importantly Bill Twomey had returned a few weeks earlier after ending his season with Stawell. Twomey had finished second in the Stawell Gift in 1919 and moved to Stawell at the end of the 1921 season, for athletic and football purposes. But after the season had finished up the bush, he returned for the last four weeks of the VFL season and the finals—his last games in black and white.[54]

Essendon led by five points during the last term and, for a time, looked like securing the result. But Collingwood had an unlikely hero, and McHale had chosen him for the role. With Lee out, the Collingwood coach gave fifth-game player Harry Chesswas—known to his teammates as 'Bottles', for his collection of bottles as a supplement to his family's income as a kid—the chance to fill-in at full-forward. Before a full house of 32,000, Chesswas kicked four of the club's six goals on a wet and windy afternoon, with the last coming just seconds before the final bell, a moment that brought about "tremendous cheering" from the crowd, and no doubt, some satisfaction from the coach. Collingwood had locked in top spot, and secured a second chance in the finals.

But that satisfaction did not last long. In the next game, a fortnight later, in the semi-final against Fitzroy, Chesswas had the chance to secure the win, but inaccuracy cost him. As *The Machine*, a book on Collingwood's famous team from 1927-1930, said: "Chesswas had a horror day (in the 1922 semi-final). It started when he unintentionally got in the way of a low, goal-bound kick from Ernie Wilson and deprived his side of six valuable points—and it progressively got worse. He recalled later that he kicked about eight or nine points that day—the last of which, if converted, would have won the game for

---

53   *The Argus*, September 18, 1922
54   Bill Twomey would win the Stawell Gift in 1924

his side."[55] Chesswas would go on to a grand career with the Magpies, winning four premierships in his 154 games before his retirement in 1931. Collingwood had kicked 3.0 in the first term but finished with 5.12—four points behind the Maroons; this loss necessitated a Grand Final after Collingwood utilised its right to challenge. It would be against Fitzroy again, after the Roys proved too strong for Essendon in the preliminary final.

McHale could at least bring back three players for the season decider, with Lee proving his fitness for what would be his 230th and final match, and Saunders and Cock resuming from their suspensions. There was a quiet confidence in the camp, with captain Tom Drummond telling *The Herald* on the eve of the match: "We stand a good chance and after a hard game, we should just about win. Our side has plenty of pace and they should more than hold their own in the air."[56] And the Collingwood District side, coached by Hugh Thomas, had played in—and won—the curtain-raiser before the main game, beating Essendon juniors.

Despite the closeness of the semi-final, *The Herald* said: "Collingwood's chances were favoured by the majority who follow the game and they argued that the Magpies would have a distinct advantage seeing that Fitzroy had been through two severe engagements in the two previous Saturdays, while Collingwood had had a rest."[57] But there was very little in the game in the opening half. Fitzroy had led by two points at the first change of ends, and Collingwood carried a five-point lead into half-time.

But Fitzroy did most of the attacking on the resumption. *The Herald* said: "In a meteoric few minutes at the opening of the third term, Fitzroy swept everything before them and then scored three goals with a run while Collingwood appeared to be momentarily paralysed."[58]

---

55   *The Machine, the inside story of football's greatest team*, Glenn McFarlane and Michael Roberts, Collingwood Football Club, 2005
56   *The Herald*, October 13, 1922
57   *The Herald*, October 14, 1922
58   ibid

By quarter's end, Fitzroy had added six goals to Collingwood's three. The difference at the last change was 15 points, and a wasteful 2.7 in the last term did not help the Magpies' cause. They lost the match— and the flag that could have been theirs—by 11 points. Lee, who would be named as a forward in Collingwood's Team of the Century in 1997, kicked two goals in his final game to take his tally to 707 goals from his 230 games. He led the League goal-kicking table eight times, a remarkable achievement for a player standing at just 175 centimetres.

One of the Magpies' goals that day was a family affair, with Syd Coventry passing to Gordon. The Coventry brothers would miss out on a flag that day, yet would look back on it years later as a great learning point. In a discussion with *The Herald* at the end of his career, Gordon said: "We were a pair of greenhorns those days—just a pair of duds that didn't really know or really care what a Grand Final meant." Syd responded: "That was Dick Lee's last match. Remember the ground was so hard he could not scratch a hole in it to place the ball. That Fitzroy bunch were a real premiership team. They could hit you, and keep on hitting you, till you felt like nobody's darling. As I look back, I reckon we were so green. We were lucky to be in the side that day, especially you, 'Nuts' (Gordon's nickname since childhood)."[59]

1923 was a tough year for Jock McHale on a personal front. He lost both of his parents in the space of 321 days. His mother, Mary, passed away, on January 7, after suffering a cerebral haemorrhage and subsequent respiratory failure. She was 65. Jock registered her death and carefully noted Mary's 11 children—James (40), John (38), Mary (dead), Sarah (34), Eileen (32), Michael (dead), Lillian (dead), George (26), Dorothy (24), Alice (21), and Edward (dead) on the death certificate. He didn't mention the stillborn child that Mary had

59   Interview with Syd and Gordon Coventry, *The Herald*, 1938

mourned decades earlier. Perhaps he hadn't even been aware that the child had existed. The long list of names summed up Mary's hard life in Australia, where she struggled to raise her children against a backdrop of appalling infant mortality rates. On November 24, John McHale succumbed to heart failure at the age of 67. The family's links to Ireland, where John and Mary had been born and raised, were gone.

It was also a tough period on the football stage, too. Collingwood missed the finals in 1923 and 1924—the first time in the club's history that it had missed out in consecutive seasons. There were a number of reasons for these failures. Clearly, the loss of Lee was always going to be sorely felt. But McHale pinned his hopes on Gordon Coventry as being the man who could become the focal point for years to come. But it was the loss of other players at that time, long before they had reached their best, which frustrated the club, and McHale.

McHale still had the support of the committee after the 1923 season. In the 1924 Annual Report the club said: "The success which attended his efforts is written in the history of this club ... his energy is still unabated and his enthusiasm is as keen as ever for the continuance of his work."[60]

But, as the Annual Report attested, McHale's success as a coach was the very thing impacting on his player resources. Having already lost a number of senior players in the previous few years, Collingwood lost more at the end of the 1922 season. The toughest one to deal with was that of Charlie Pannam jnr, who had switched to South Melbourne. Pannam, whose father had played with McHale two decades earlier, accepted a well-paid position as coach of South Melbourne for 1923. This prompted a hard-line stance from the club, and a warning to its players—and football clubs around the state—to stay away from its players. Under the draconian rules of the era, Pannam, who was just 26 at the start of the 1923 season, had to stand out of football for three years to gain a clearance, even though he still operated as South

---

60   Collingwood Annual Report, 1924

Melbourne's non-playing coach. He would not play again until Round 4 of the 1926 season, at the age of 29.

To a lesser extent, the club was disappointed to lose the previous year's captain Tom 'Chick' Drummond to coach Benalla, and Maurie Sheehy to coach Northcote; at least they were transferring to clubs that would never play against Collingwood.

Collingwood was emphatic that enough was enough. The Annual Report stated: "Last year in the Metropolis and Country associations there were 12 former pupils instilling in others the precepts learned at Victoria Park. The actions of a League club in enticing a leading player (referring to Pannam) away from his own club last year (1923) to act as coach, and pretend to live in the new district in the hope of getting a clearance is 'the straw that broke the camel's back'. Your committee has, in consequence, decided that no clearances will be granted to players as coach except for legitimate reasons."[61]

Part of this was because clubs were intrigued by the Collingwood system and style of play. Undoubtedly, the mystique of McHale was a part of it. He was considered one of the most astute coaches in the game, and clubs across the state clambered to recruit men who had played under his direction. A profile on McHale in a Collingwood newsletter from 1964, 11 years after his death, stated: "Players were besieged with coaching offers on retirement (and often before), and ex-Collingwood players were the first choice wherever possible. It was a well-known fact that to appoint a 'McHale-coached' applicant as coach, the country team was assured of success on the field."[62]

Before the start of the 1923 season there were suggestions that all was not well within the Collingwood ranks, a suggestion denied by a reporter from *The Argus* in mid-April: "Despite the rumours regarding Collingwood's players, all is well in the Magpie nest, where Jim McHale has been appointed coach for about the 10th year in

---

61   ibid
62   Collingwood Football Club, newsletter, 1964

succession (sic)."[63] There had been talk that Percy Rowe and Harry Saunders were considering offers to leave. Both preferred to remain at Collingwood. Rowe was appointed captain, but resigned after three games because it was affecting his form. Harry Curtis took over the on-field leadership.

In 1923 Collingwood narrowly missed the finals in an extremely even season. Losses to Geelong (without Ernie Wilson and the Coventry brothers) and Richmond late in the season did not help the cause. It was hoped a trip to Tasmania might lift the spirits of the young group. But, on their return, the Magpies fought out a thrilling draw with Carlton, with Bob Makeham, in his 12th game in his debut season, kicking a goal late to square the ledger.

Despite the fact that Collingwood won its last two games of the home and away season, it could not edge its way into the final four. The 51-point win over Melbourne in the final round left Collingwood two points adrift of making the finals, given other results did not go the club's way. The committee told its members: "Your team, for the first time in the past 12 years, fell a step too low on the premiership ladder, and failed to win a place in the first four. It will be generally admitted you had a fine combination of players, and on return from the trip to Tasmania, they were at their best. The match at Carlton was the stumbling block, the drawn game proving responsible for their omission for the finals."[64]

The 1924 season was just as frustrating for McHale, and for Collingwood. According to Percy Taylor's history of the club, "the payment to players was increased to £2/10/- a match each", but it still wasn't enough to stop the departure of a number of key players with offers to join other clubs. This time Rowe decided to leave, and

63   *The Argus*, April 16, 1923
64   Collingwood Annual Report, 1924

head to Albury. Ted Baker went to Horsham (he would return to the League in 1927 at Geelong). Curtis retired, and would soon become Collingwood's president. Charlie Tyson took over as captain.

Despite winning its first four games of the season, six straight losses would follow in a topsy-turvy season that saw the club end up in sixth position, two games out of the finals. The club was not happy, telling its members: "The constant drain of your leading players to provide coaches for the football world has at least had its effect and your team failed to maintain the Collingwood tradition of winning a place in the final four."[65]

McHale tried to unearth new talent, and build a team that might again challenge for a premiership. Incredibly, he would blood 14 players in 1924. Three made their debut on the same day, in Round 3 against Melbourne. Two—George Clayden and Charlie Dibbs—would play key roles in future flags. Dibbs had been recruited as a rover or forward, but McHale cannily deduced that his prodigious kicks could be effective in defence. Those well-directed and long kicks would play a big role in the club's future success. In the absence of regular full-back Saunders, the coach started the 174cm Dibbs in the defensive zone; he would go on to become one of the club's great full-backs.

The other Magpie debutant that day, Roy Allen, would live until he was 100 (his life's longevity was far beyond his longevity in the game! He played just one more game for Collingwood). Years later, he would recall that McHale had tossed up whether to use Dibbs or him at full-back. The coach went with Dibbs, who would go on to play the vast majority of his 216 games with the club at full-back. Allen would play just two. But he would always recall what McHale would say to the players at training. Allen, who died in 2001, said: "You never called him Jock. He was always Mr McHale. Mr McHale didn't really give you any advice. At training he used to say two things: 'Keep on your toes' and 'When you get the ball, run 10 yards and kick it to a man.'"[66]

---

65   Collingwood Annual Report, 1925
66   Interviews with Glenn McFarlane, 1990 and 2001

To many football fans of the time, McHale was somewhat of a mystery. He was the rather stern man in the hat and overcoat sitting around the boundary line, watching grimly, or the man in the baggy shorts showing off his knock-knees standing in the middle of Victoria Park barking orders to his men each Tuesday and Thursday nights. Rarely did they get an insight into what made the man tick. Even with the increased media attention that the game was now attracting, McHale rarely gave much away, and preferred to keep many of his coaching philosophies within the group.

An article in *The Sporting Globe* (then only a year old) in 1923 did give a wonderful insight into McHale, the coach. The most incredible aspect of it was that the writer was Wallace 'Jumbo' Sharland, who was not only a journalist for the paper, but also a Geelong footballer (from 1920-1925). Incredibly, four days after Sharland's feature story on McHale appeared, he was back at Victoria Park playing against the Magpies.

Sharland, then only 20, described McHale, 40, as having a "grave and intelligent-looking countenance". The Collingwood coach explained the four pillars of what he expected in a player: "keenness, determination, combination and anticipation". (These) are the qualities McHale tried to make every Collingwood footballer gain."[67] Harmony was essential, especially for new players. McHale said: "When a junior player comes to a senior team ... it is the job of the committee and the coach to make him feel happy. If you have that happy spirit prevailing in the dressingroom, the players will have a better understanding."[68]

McHale was already looking at the psychology of players, and how best to deliver his message to the many different personalities he had on his playing list. He told Sharland: "Every coach must study the temperament of every player he has to deal with otherwise he cannot hope for the best results. If a player is moody and has a decided objection to any heckling, it may be unwise to disturb his peace of

---

67   ibid
68   ibid

mind, for he will not play at his best. (He) advises coaches to speak quietly to players of such disposition and they will respond well. By building up their hopes, they will gain confidence and consequently a rapid improvement is made to their play. It is useless for any coach to call out at the top of his voice on the field to any player. For he will resent it and dislike him."

McHale emphasised to Sharland the importance of training. "I believe in making the players take as keen an interest in their practice as they do in a match, for indifference when at practice will probably be responsible for a careless action in a game. On the Tuesday night the players should have a little match practice, and to be kept moving solidly for half an hour or more. Twenty minutes' practice at marking and a little work in stab kicking and the marking of short passes should keep the men up to scratch."

He emphasised the importance of a solid match practice on the Thursday night before games. But he had no issue in "spelling the small men on a Thursday evening if they are fit, for they have tough work to perform on a Saturday."

The Collingwood coach attributed the club's success to the interstate and country trips that the team took during breaks in the season. He said: "The players get to know each other better on the trip and they form friendships which may be difficult to form on the playing field or the dressing room. The players enjoy the relaxation, put on condition, and return to the city for the final battles with the zest of colts."[69]

In contrast to Worrall, who had famously declared "booze and football don't mix ... players who prefer beer to eucalyptus will be struck off the list",[70] McHale believed in beer in moderation. Although he may have felt obliged to say this given he was a cellarman at the Carlton Brewery, McHale believed in the value of a glass or two. He declared: "There is no need for a man to wash himself in it, but a taste

69   ibid
70   *Footy's greatest coaches*, Stephanie Holt and Garrie Hutchinson, Coulomb Communications, 2002

now and again is the best thing going." But he was not such a fan of spirits, and claimed whiskey "is as bad a drink possible for any player, and he should leave the spirit well alone. With plenty of rest and plain food, every footballer who trains well should be in the best of fettle."[71]

There were plenty of changes ahead of the 1925 season. The VFL decided to admit three new teams from the VFA—Footscray (coached by former Magpie Con McCarthy), Hawthorn and North Melbourne. In addition to that, there was a rule change that Collingwood would quickly learn to exploit and would form part of the McHale game plan in the coming years. A free kick was to be paid against the team that had last touched the ball around the boundary line. It would last until 1939, and in that time Collingwood would win six more premierships. And the McHale legend would be made.

But no one knew that at the time and the Magpies' task early in 1925 was to restore its lost standing. Collingwood almost lost one of its best players on the eve of the 1925 season when Syd Coventry accepted a job to coach Horsham. Fortunately for the Magpies, Coventry's wife, Gladys, found she didn't like the environment when she arrived up there, and the pair turned around and returned home. Gladys's misgivings may not have made any difference as Collingwood was prepared to inform Coventry that his clearance would be denied, as McHale didn't want to lose one of his best players.

Collingwood played nine new players in 1925. One almost got his start by accident. The story goes that 15-year-old Albert Collier was playing cricket for Collingwood and asked to have a run with the football team. Secretary George Connor introduced him to the coach. Collier, according to Lionel Frost's *The Immortals*, "remembered McHale pointed a finger, which had a pronounced bend in it, and

---

asking him, 'How old are you, laddie?'"[72] The rest of the conversation went like this:

Collier: 'I'm 15, Mr McHale.'

McHale: 'Oh, you're too young to be playing here. I only started (playing football) when I was 16.'

Connor: 'Well, he's brought his togs tonight, Jim. Let him go out on the ground and have a run.'

McHale: 'All right, sonny, you can go out on the ground, but keep away from those big fellows. You'll get killed out there."

Years later, in an interview with Richard Stremski, Collier recalled thinking that McHale was "a bloody old fool ... (once on the ground) I mowed into every big and small bloke as much as I could."[73]

Collier clearly made an impression. He played his first game in Round 1, 1925 when he was still 68 days short of his 16th birthday. He kicked a goal against Essendon at Windy Hill. And although he played only four games in the seniors that season, he showed real promise of things to come. Collier's brother, Harry, almost two years older, was one of five more debutants the following year. Whether it was by good luck or good management, Collingwood was building a strong side. In Albert Collier's first year, Frank Murphy, Bill Libbis and Jack 'Jiggy' Harris played their first games. In Harry Collier's first year, other debutants included Jack Beveridge and Bert Lauder.

Collingwood had a few financial issues during the 1925 season, so much so that McHale took the unusual step of writing to the committee to inform them that he would be content to take a pay cut until the situation rectified itself. The committee refused McHale's offer, but the coach would not take no for answer. The club obviously meant more to him than the cash did. He was a highly principled man when it came to money.

---

72 *The Immortals, Football people and the evolution of Australian Rules*, Lionel Frost, Wiley, 2005
73 ibid

Collingwood had a slow start to the 1925 season, and was not in the top four for the first eight weeks after a 4-4 start. From then on, it held a spot in the top four until Fitzroy displaced it with a 14-point win at Victoria Park in Round 16. There were excuses, however. Percy Taylor's book explained: "The losers (had) four cripples." Laurie Murphy and Harry Saunders were hurt in the first quarter, and Charlie Tyson and Ernie Wilson were hurt in the second. The equation was simple. In the last round Collingwood had to beat South Melbourne well to make up for the 5.5 percentage points that separated it and Fitzroy. The Magpies did that, with a 65-point win, while the Maroons kicked a woefully inaccurate 7.24 (68) to scrape over the line against Carlton. Collingwood had made the finals for the first time since 1922, by the small matter of 1.4 per cent.

McHale's team continued its good form, with a semi-final win over Essendon, by 10 points, and then a thrashing of Melbourne in the preliminary final, by 37 points. (Melbourne had beaten minor premier Geelong, which had lost only two games through the season, in the previous week's semi-final.) There was much criticism of Collingwood's aggressive approach in the Melbourne game, particularly from Ernie 'Sugar' Wilson, which prompted letters of protest to the newspapers.

In a post-career interview with *The Herald* Gordon Coventry would recall: "He (Wilson) was carried off the field on the trainers' shoulders after the game. I can see him sitting up there like Jacky, laughing at the crowd in the old stand with the wooden front—what did they call it?—Yes, the smokers' stand. He waved a towel at them. Gee, that gang could hoot for old men."[74]

The Collingwood team was treated to a day at Yarra Glen the day after the win over Melbourne, and *The Argus* reported the players "were like a lot of schoolboys out for a holiday."[75] It was back to business the next week. though. The club was to meet Geelong, which was exerting its right to challenge in an attempt to win its first premiership.

---

74   Interview with Syd and Gordon Coventry, *The Herald*, 1938
75   *The Argus*, October 9, 1925

The Argus said that, despite having lost its two games to the Cats during the year, the Magpies will "not hear of defeat ... the committee and the players are in complete accord and there is not a discordant note at Victoria Park."[76]

That wasn't entirely correct. There was an undercurrent of rivalry between the senior team and the district side, which reflected the ongoing tension between their respective coaches, McHale and Thomas. Some of the players who had been under Thomas's tutelage for most of the 1925 season bristled when asked to move up to the senior ranks leading up to the finals.

Albert Collier and George Clayden defied McHale when he sought to play them in the seniors late in the season. They wanted to win the premiership in the reserves in a team that also comprised future stars Harry Collier and Jack Beveridge. Clayden is alleged to have said to McHale: "I'm not going to bloody well play for you, Jim".[77] This dispute, bizarre on reflection, would have only increased the tension between the two Collingwood coaches.

In the end, Collingwood won the District final, but lost the senior Grand Final a few hours later. In the first Grand Final to attract more than 60,000 fans—it was 64,288—Geelong proved too strong for their opponents, but only after a desperately close struggle. The Magpies had trailed all afternoon, and were 25 points in arrears at the last change. The Cats could not manage a goal in the last term, kicking six behinds, while McHale's men added three goals. For a time, it looked as if they would make up the difference. With almost 20 minutes elapsed, the difference was back to eight points. But Geelong managed to hold on to win by 10 points.

There were celebrations at the MCG for long-suffering Geelong supporters, who had not seen a VFL flag before, and for those who had listened to this game on the radio on 3LO. But for McHale, there was nothing but disappointment. Never a good loser, he was not among

---

76   ibid
77   *Kill For Collingwood*, Richard Stremski, Allen and Unwin, 1986

the Collingwood deputation of its captain Charlie Tyson, its president Harry Curtis and its secretary George Connor that made its way into the victorious Geelong rooms immediately after the game. The Magpie trio, reported *The Argus*, "offered unstinted congratulations … and acknowledged Geelong superiority".[78] McHale wasn't ready for such a concession.

Given the tensions going into the finals series, the coach would not have been pleased with part of the assessment of the season in the Annual Report, released just before the start of the next season. It read: "The highest commendation is due to our coach, Jim McHale. His untiring efforts were greatly appreciated by all of the players. Your second XVIII was even more successful than your first, by winning the premiership."[79]

There was to be more frustration the following year. Collingwood had won 13 of its first 15 games in 1926, and for much of the season had loomed as the team most likely to win the premiership. That belief was shaken when it lost to Geelong in Round 16 by 33 points. It brought the Magpies and the Cats level on points, and they remained that way to the end of the home and away season. Collingwood secured the minor premiership—and the double chance—on percentage, a margin of 4.1 per cent, setting up a clash with Melbourne in a semi-final.

The Australasian stated that Melbourne was "a breezy and dashing lot, with such an aversion to molestation that other teams lay their plans accordingly. It required no particular football knowledge to know that Collingwood, where they study all phases of play, as it is common in all industrial centres, for it is their game, would stick close to their opponents and hamper them on every possible occasion."[80] But if the

---

78   *The Argus*, October 12, 1925
79   Collingwood Annual Report, 1926
80   *The Australasian*, October 12, 1926

Magpies—and Wilson—had stunned Melbourne with aggression 12 months earlier, it would not be so effective this time around.

Melbourne beat Collingwood in the semi-final by 11 points, and then defeated Essendon to set up a Grand Final with Collingwood, using its right of challenge. 'Old Boy' of *The Argus* stated: "In the last few weeks, the Melbourne players have ... developed an ability to withstand the bumps of a vigorous game."[81]

Despite McHale's firm belief that the Magpies would win their first flag since 1919, there were a few cards stacked against them. The defence was weakened by the loss of Charlie Dibbs to injury, and George Clayden to suspension. Such was the club's desire to win, that there had even been a suggestion that Dick Lee could be brought into the side, despite the fact that he hadn't played since the 1922 Grand Final.

The Argus claimed that "some enthusiasts wanted to include Lee in the team"[82] after the former champion forward booted seven of eight goals in a kicking competition on the club's picnic to Mornington and Hastings, on the Sunday after the Melbourne-Essendon final. It never happened, as Gordon Coventry had reeled off his most productive season, kicking 83 goals for the year, to win the VFL goal-kicking award.

In a game debated and dissected for weeks and months and even years afterwards, Melbourne kicked 4.5 to 1.1 to the Punt Road end with the assistance of the wind in the first term. *The Argus* would document that it came from a "slight breeze ... (with Melbourne captain Bert) Chadwick, winning the toss, decided to have first use of the breeze."[83]

Twelve years later, Syd Coventry would suggest the Magpies had won the toss. He told *The Herald:* "We could not do anything right. Charlie Tyson, our skipper, won the toss and kicked against the wind.

---

81   *The Argus*, October 11, 1926
82   *The Argus*, October 8, 1926
83   *The Argus*, October 11, 1926

That was the start. We were on the wrong leg all day and Melbourne kept us there."[84]

According to Richard Stremski, Albert Collier was given conflicting advice when matched on Bob Johnson snr, who was 11cm taller. McHale, who generally believed in fair play, told the 17-year-old to keep his mind on the ball. Chairman of selectors Doc Seddon said to Collier: "Get into him; knock him over a few times."[85] Johnson kicked four of his six goals on Collier before Tyson moved himself on to him.

There were two other positional changes that bewildered supporters after half-time, when the Magpies trailed by only nine points. Jack Beveridge, a star in his first season, was shifted out of the centre where he had been doing an excellent job on Ivor Warne-Smith, and moved to the half-forward line. Warne-Smith relished the move, and Beveridge's replacement, 'Bottles' Chesswas was no match for him. The other came about when Syd Coventry was switched out of the ruck to try to quell Johnson in the second half. But his absence in the middle of the ground was sorely felt.

There has been much conjecture about who made the changes. Was it the captain Tyson, or the coach McHale? Perhaps it was a combination of both. Regardless, Tyson's form in the game was not of his usual standard, and this would become an issue early in the following year. He was unusually aggressive on a few occasions, which was not in his normal on-field demeanour. The fact that he had been concussed in the previous game might have had an impact on his form in the Grand Final, though few people knew that it had occurred.

The game was all but over in the space of half an hour in the third term; Melbourne kicked seven goals to Collingwood's one for the quarter, and it left the Magpies 45 points in deficit at the last change McHale must have known that only a miracle could save his club's premiership dreams. The miracle would not come as Melbourne

---

84   Interview with Syd and Gordon Coventry, *The Herald*, 1938
85   *Kill For Collingwood*, Richard Stremski, Allen and Unwin, 1986

outscored Collingwood again in the final term, to win by 57 points—the highest winning margin in a Grand Final to that time.

As Melbourne rejoiced—including the "father of the game" the former Melbourne champion, Colden Harrison, who got an early 90th birthday present with the result and was seen in the rooms after the game—Collingwood mourned a pitiful end to a season that had promised so much. As they had a year earlier, Tyson, Curtis and Connor went into the opposition rooms. *The Argus* reported that they "were received most cordially when they visited the Melbourne team to offer their congratulations. They said they were disappointed, but could take off their hats to a superior team."[86] *The Argus* noted the disappointment at Collingwood as the club had "set their hearts on the premiership".[87]

86   *The Argus*, October 11, 1926
87   ibid

CHAPTER 8

The McHale Manifesto

1925

I f the cult of celebrity was a phenomenon crafted out of the 20th century proliferation of the media, the most likely starting point in terms of Australian football can be traced back to the early- to mid-1920s.

There were numerous leading footballers and administrators responsible for the game's development and growth during its first 60 years, but rarely did the public garner any significant insight into what made those men tick. The supporters flocked to the suburban grounds to watch them on the weekends. Some of the heartier souls even took to attending training sessions during the week. But rarely were they engaged with the philosophies, personalities or driving influences of the stars of the competition.

The post-war landscape would change this, to a certain degree, and over the many decades that would follow, this link between the sportsman and the spectator would transform into what we have today.

In the 1920s, the leading metropolitan newspapers began to provide a more detailed analysis of the evolving tactics and trends in a competition whose reach was extending far beyond the clubs' suburban boundaries. Game day photographs and feature shots became more prevalent, especially following the birth of Melbourne's morning daily *The Sun News-Pictorial* and its bi-weekly stablemate, *The Sporting Globe* in 1922. The use of cartoons and caricatures depicting some of the sport's most familiar faces became regulars in all the newspapers.

The gradual growth of radio played its part; from the middle of the 1920s, radio broadcasts of some games brought coverage to those who that could not make it to the football on Saturdays.

Importantly, too, interest was again on the rise, after the draining years of the First World War had sapped the collective spirit of the community, with attendances dropping through the war years, and afterwards.

McHale was now well established as a cellarman and supervisor at the Carlton Brewery in Bouverie Street. He would never gain his driver's licence, and would either use public transport from his home in Brunswick to work, and would often walk from the heart of the city to football training at Victoria Park on Tuesday and Thursday nights. Even as he was fast becoming a figure of renown—a public figure—this was a routine that would not change.

At the start of the 1925 season, he had been associated with Collingwood for 22 years—more than half his life. He had been coach for 13 years and had led Collingwood to two premierships from six Grand Final appearances; three other coaches—Dan Minogue (1920 and 1921 at Richmond), Norman Clark (1914 and 1915 at Carlton) and Syd Barker (1923 and 1924 at Essendon had won two flags. Only one man had coached more VFL premierships to that stage than this quartet, and that was the father of coaching, Jack Worrall.

Worrall, almost 21 years McHale's senior, had won five premierships (1906, 1907 and 1908 at Carlton, and 1911 and 1912 at Essendon) but had not coached since his last game with Essendon in 1920, preferring to pursue his lifetime career as a newspaper columnist. He had been working in newspapers since he had first arrived in Melbourne in the 1880s from country Victoria, and would continue to be one of the most acclaimed sports writers in the country, most notably with *The Australasian*.

McHale was one of 12 coaches (six non-playing and six playing coaches) in the expanded VFL competition that year, but his record as a player and a coach gave him a presence beyond the rest. He had coached three of his rivals (Richmond's Dan Minogue, South Melbourne's Charlie Pannam jnr and Footscray's Con McCarthy), though he had little time for Minogue and Pannam as they had left Collingwood in controversial circumstances.

It was no surprise that McHale's reputation as a coach of the highest merit saw his wisdom being sought from newspapers anxious to record the thoughts of the maestro of the Magpies.

Twice in 1925, he sat down to pen two extraordinary documents, detailing his football philosophies giving a rare glimpse into the methods and motivation he used on his players.

The first was a list of commandments and hints for schoolboys intent on getting the most out of their football lives, a well-used list of points he would outline in his many visits to schools—often well beyond Collingwood's borders—detailing what was required to reach the highest levels.

This would range from advice on diet and discipline; from health issues to how many hours sleep is required for a schoolboy footballer; but more than that it described McHale's personal values, values that would never diminish. His summary included words that defined McHale, and the players he would seek to perform for Collingwood: "All this may be summed up in one word—character—and if that is not worth developing, nothing is".

The second, dictated to 'Jumbo' Sharland and published in *The Sporting Globe's* May 2 edition of 1925—was just as assertive and personal. The mere fact that this article was commissioned, and afforded such prominence, is an indication that not only the star of McHale was rising, but so, too, the reputation of coaches as leaders of clubs.

He wrote of the Collingwood tradition—already well-defined although the club was only just more than 30 years old—and of the pillars that he "insisted upon"—keenness, determination, anticipation and unselfishness. Not surprisingly, he defined the importance of the coach: "Coaching is the most important thing for a footballer and his team. If a coach has natural talent at his disposal he will be a poor mentor if he cannot get his team into a high place. A good coach should also be able to bring along a weak side, and to improve the form of his players." He described his training methods and how to manage the many and varied temperaments of his players; and of the obligations of the players to the coach, and coach to his players.

Almost 90 years on, these two documents provide a window into McHale's world, and what was happening at Collingwood at the time. He was certain that if he could gather around him a collection of like-minded footballers willing to subscribe to his plans then success would follow.

McHALE'S COMMANDMENTS TO SCHOOLBOY FOOTBALLERS

TRAINING

1. Attend to your training and to your practices. Don't let other engagements interfere with your regular attendances. 'Practice makes perfect'.
2. To train hard means denying yourself certain luxuries. But it is worth it. To be included in your school XVIII is a great honour and something to be proud of and something to look back on with satisfaction in after years.
3. Don't eat more food than you can reasonably digest and be careful not to eat too quickly.

4. Don't eat food that is too rich—the plainer the better. Avoid soft drinks, heavy suet puddings, sweets, except chocolates—in short, any doughy food which takes a long time to digest.

5. Immediately after rising in the morning, and just before going to bed at night, it is advisable to drink a glass of cold water. In this way the intestines receive a good cleansing.

6. A boy in training requires nine hours' sleep. If possible, never go to bed later than 10.30pm.

7. Take a cold bath every morning unless you are feeling unwell, but take your bath while you are feeling warm. Then a good rub down with a hard towel will put you in good fettle for the rest of the day.

8. A hot bath once a week is necessary, and, for preference, Saturday nights after the practice games. This should remove all the stiffness.

9. Avoid sprinting for trams and trains immediately after breakfast. This will undo all the beneficial results of your training. Get up in time to avoid injurious exercise.

10. It is suicidal to produce a violent perspiration by kicking a ball about, etc, in your ordinary clothes and then to sit in a classroom and gradually cool off. Therefore it is not advisable to play in your ordinary clothes.

11. Don't let your keenness slacken for one moment. A boy who is not keen is not worth inclusion in any team. Keep your enthusiasm and your game must improve accordingly.

12. Remember what you are undertaking to do and nothing is worth undertaking unless it is worth doing properly. The school expects from you your best. You can't do more.

SUMMARY

There is more in football than merely kicking a ball about. You will discover this as your training progresses. If played in the proper spirit, this game brings out the very best that is in a boy. It develops him morally and physically. It teaches him that to flinch spells cowardice. It teaches him, perhaps more than any other game does, the art of self-control. To be cool, with a level head, is absolutely essential. It teaches him to be unselfish and manly. All this may be summed up in the one word—character and if that is not worth developing, nothing is.

A FEW HINTS

1. Never let your man get in front of you. If you do he will meet the ball first and you will be chasing him all through the match.
2. Get off the mark quickly. Don't wait until the ball comes to you, you have to meet the ball. Remember it is the pace that staggers your opponent, but come through with the ball, not without it.
3. Don't kick wildly. Always try to kick it to a man. Remember the lower you kick the less time it takes for the ball to go where you want it.
4. Don't think of bouncing the ball as soon as you get it. Think of kicking it.
5. Never turn your back to the field and never hug the ball when you get a mark. Passing must be quick and accurate to be effective.
6. If you get a mark or a free within shooting distance of goal take plenty of time and have a deliberate shot. Many goals are lost through unnecessary hurrying or through trying to pass to a man in a worse position.
7. Don't try to play the other side yourself. Seventeen men are there to help you. If in difficulties, handball to men in a better position. Do not be selfish.
8. Don't stop when you miss a mark. A quick recovery may put you in a better position than the mark may have done. If you find that your man is marking over you, go up with one hand in an endeavour to spoil him.

9. Don't be discouraged when your man beats you. It must happen sometimes, no matter however good you are. Follow him as hard as you can when he gets away with the ball. He may drop it, then your turn comes, apart from that there is always a next time to get even.

10. Note—if you are near one of your own men when he gets the ball, there are two things you must do (a) SHEPHERD if your man is in a better position than you, and (b) RUN ON and in the right direction and give him a chance to pass the ball either by handballing or kicking. This is the essence of systematic play.

11. Never call for the ball if you are in a worse position than the man who has it.

12. Don't kick into the man at the mark. This is an unpardonable mistake and often leads to disastrous results.

13. Don't take defeat too badly and don't crow over a victory. A team should be modest in victory and undaunted by defeat.

14. Always take the field in a confident manner, but at the same time never underestimate your opponent's ability. Always go your hardest. Remember the game is never won until the final bell is rung.

15. Brains play a more important part in football than in any other game. THEREFORE, USE THEM

THE McHALE COACHING MANTRA

Jim McHale tells *The Sporting Globe* his methods of coaching Collingwood, May 2, 1925:

It is an easy task for me to put my methods of coaching into operations when the players are on the field. It is a different matter altogether to endeavour to write an article explaining the coaching business.

Coaching is the most important thing for a footballer and his team, providing the coach is a good one. He should be an experienced man, with mature judgment and plenty of tact. A coach should be a man who has played the game and knows exactly what is required of a player. Always he should be on the lookout to note weaknesses.

The success of a coach depends greatly on the material at his disposal. It may be good or weak. If a coach has natural talent at his disposal he will be a poor mentor if he cannot get his team into a high place. A good coach should also be able to bring along a weak side, and to improve the form of his players. Coaching has many aspects, and it is only considerable experience that teaches what is mostly required.

I had the good fortune to learn football in a particularly good school. By playing and mingling with some of the best known figures that the game has produced I have gleaned many useful points which other young players probably would not be able to pick up. I was particularly lucky to be under the charge of Dick Condon. He was a master mind as far as football was concerned, and it can be said of him that what he did not know about the game was not worth knowing. Condon was a man who believed in the players practising and training assiduously. He realised that fitness was the first equipment a footballer should possess.

QUALITIES INSISTED UPON

Fifteen years' coaching of the Magpies has convinced me that a young player who wants to make good must have keenness, determination, anticipation and he must not be selfish. Any player who is careless or slovenly in his methods is not of much use in a team, and should not be in demand. A player must be keen to razor-sharpness.

Determination is also wanted. Determination generally means success in any sphere or walk of life, for if a fellow makes up his mind that he cannot be beaten in a certain thing, it is seldom that he fails. Unselfishness or combination comes in when a player has to be an assistant to his teammates. Football is all combination work, and a player has to fit into his team's work and style.

Anticipation is necessary for the footballer. You cannot go hot-headed after the ball. One must be cool, watchful, and be able to gauge the flight of the ball. Keep your eyes on the ball, and you begin to study its peculiarities, and note how it will travel faster and lower with a drop kick, and higher and slower with a punt kick.

Any player, particularly a youngster, who enters into a senior club's rooms for the first time must be made at home. It is the object of the committee at Collingwood to make the players happy, and any new member is accorded a warm welcome. Collingwood has become renowned for its hospitality, because the officials have treated the players well—not like a lot of schoolboys, or persons who are paid just for their services as players. A little kindness will work wonders anywhere, and if a player is made happy in a club room he soon wants to make his neighbour happy.

On the other hand, if a player is ignored, he soon commences to growl to the other players. Thus dissension is created and it is not long before certain players and officials are at loggerheads. While they are unfriendly a club cannot hope to compete successfully against other teams on the field. A happy spirit, fostered in the dressing room from the start of the season, goes a long way towards the winning of the premiership.

This happiness I attribute in a big way to the past successes of the Collingwood teams. The players have been taught to pull together, and they have done so with a will. One can point to a few other clubs, and reveal how their sides have failed, though gifted with excellent material.

At Collingwood we have also encouraged the old players to come round and have a talk with the present players. It is a common sight to see a young player benefiting by the hints of an old player. Those old players will not refer disparagingly to the game nowadays, and laud the heroes of the past. One will always strike a few cranks in this respect, but the men desired are those who will have a friendly chat with a player. A player never likes to talk to anyone who knows nothing about the game.

PRACTICE MAKES PERFECT

I try to induce every player to take as keen an interest in practice as he does in a match. Probably an indifferent action in practice will be responsible for a careless action in a match.

On a Tuesday evening the players should have some match practice, and be kept moving for a solid half an hour or more. About twenty minutes should be devoted to marking, practice and stab kicking. The marking of stab kicks is also important, and plenty of this work will get the players in good fettle.

A good man playing in the centre wants plenty of twisting about, and short, nippy work. The half-back wants dash, and should be taught to come through a pack fearlessly. A half-forward needs to be a man who marks well, and can turn quickly on either foot. By practising a player can become fairly proficient in quick turning. It is excellent practice for a big man. Ruck men need plenty of work that will improve their stamina.

Of the forwards I have had anything to do with; I consider that there is none to Dick Lee. He was a truly marvellous player. With all his wonderful ability as a kick and mark, his play was made of greater value by his pluck and coolness.

On a Thursday evening I consider that training should be lighter, but, while the players are on the field, they should put plenty of vim into their work, and have a good perspiration running from them. It must be remembered, however that a hard match is to be played on a Saturday. Therefore, too much energy should not be wasted by a player in practice.

STUDYING TEMPERAMENTS

Nearly every footballer has a different temperament. Some players are easily upset. Others do not worry over anything. A coach should make it his business to study the feelings of every man, and to learn his views on various things. It is wonderfully helpful to a coach, if he hopes to achieve the best results, if he knows exactly the temperament of each player.

I have studied the men under my charge at Collingwood, and know fairly well their good points, and any weaknesses that they may have. Some players are unduly anxious. Some are pessimistic and others too confident. Numerous other little faults are common.

I do not believe in too much bellowing at players. A quiet word spoken in place will generally do far more than a sharp, insolently delivered command. Sometimes the voice has to be raised when discipline is required, and some players are a little too fresh.

A moody man does not want bullying. He wants to be built up in hope, and quiet, well-spoken words of encouragement will often make him a force to be reckoned with.

Players should eat well and have plenty of rest. They should look after themselves. Very few players can last long if they dissipate. In regard to drinking, a teetotaller is not the only man who makes a good footballer. A player may have an occasional drink. Beer is the best drink in moderation. Spirits are no good at all. On a Friday, however, a player should leave the drink alone.[1]

---

1   As told to 'Jumbo' Sharland, The Sporting Globe, May 2, 1925

CHAPTER 9

Managing The Machine

1927-1930

J ock McHale coached Collingwood for more than half of his lifetime—a staggering 38 seasons stretched out over 714 games and 38 years. But if there was a time for which he was best remembered or with which he is most associated, it was a period of unparalleled excellence by Collingwood from 1927 to 1930. That bracket of 82 games played over a four-year window in charge of a team famously known as *The Machine* would be the pinnacle of his football life, and the stuff which much of his coaching legend was based on.

Collingwood teams had been described as "machine-like" on and off for decades, thanks to the club's systematic approach to the game. There had been similar references in newspaper match reports over the years suggesting the teamwork and slick operations of Collingwood— on and off the field—had been masterstrokes of good management. But the success of the Magpies from 1927 to 1930—shining like a beacon against a depressing backdrop of financial gloom—would see this team forever enshrined as *The Machine*. As Bruce Andrew, one of the members of that famous team would say with pride: "We were

The Machine ... we were one very strong unit. Everyone only had two thoughts. One was black and one was white. We were nothing else— just Collingwood."[1]

What is less widely known is that McHale didn't particularly like the "Machine" moniker. As he told leading sports writer Hugh Buggy just a month before his death, he thought it sounded inflexible and not reactive to change when it was required. Buggy did not file these musings until after until McHale had died, preferring to use it in his warm obituary for "the dean of coaches", as *The Argus* sub-editors used in the headline accompanying the story. More popularly, and increasingly, McHale would become known as the 'Prince of Coaches', or the 'King of Coaches'.

McHale had told Buggy in September 1953, revealing much about himself, the way he coached, and his expectations of his players: "The funny thing is that, as a non-playing coach, I did not set out with any specific intention of building a football 'machine'. Football writers of the day began to call the Collingwood side a 'machine'. I never liked the term, because it suggested the side was a combination which worked to a rigid plan, and could not think. And if there is one quality we demand at Collingwood, it is the quick-thinking player with a dash of imagination."[2]

He continued: "The main idea in 40 years of coaching was to field 18 players who were fit, and who were in form at the moment. On that foundation I aimed to develop good teamwork, not on this line or that, but all over the field. I had no time for a side built up around three or four star players. Give me a fit bunch of players with a good general level of ability."[3]

Those eight sentences summed up the core of McHale's approach to football. Egalitarianism was the crux of it. He wanted—no, demanded—that his players be paid the same amount—£3 per

---

1   Interview with Bruce Andrew, courtesy of Tom Wanliss from the Collingwood archives committee
2   *The Argus*, October 6, 1953
3   ibid

game, as it was in those glorious years. He was happy to be paid almost the same, even if he could have made much more at rival clubs. Those clubs never came knocking, for they understood that McHale was Collingwood and Collingwood alone. But throughout his career it didn't stop country and metropolitan clubs seeking McHale-trained players to be their coaches, often to the detriment of the man whose methods they were seeking.

The other thing that shines through in McHale's analysis was the importance of choosing fit and in-form men. Reputations counted for little. If a man wasn't fit and ready to physically give of his best, he would not play. McHale would only fall for this trap a few times in his coaching career, once famously before a Grand Final. He watched his men intently and with such a watchful eye that he could glean any injury concerns his players might conceal in an endeavour to stay in the team. One time Leo Wescott was nursing a sore shoulder and did not tell the coach because he desperately wanted to play. Instinctively, McHale knew. As they were in the dressing rooms after training, he threw a ball to the unsuspecting Wescott, who flinched. He did not play that weekend.

As 'Jumbo' Sharland recounted in *The Sporting Globe*, in an analysis of the club, and coach, in 1931: "On the track the Magpies go through practically every phase of training that makes them fit. Jim watches every man closely to see that he is fit. If a player informs him that he feels 'in the pink', McHale soon puts him to the test by making him do some short, snappy work that quickly puts to rest any doubts about a player's stamina."[4] He added: "Collingwood know only too well that no man could fill the job better than McHale. Therefore, they leave him alone, strong in the faith that he will mould footballers and blend them together into a match-winning combination."[5]

That's precisely what McHale was aiming to do on the eve of the 1927 season, having had little choice but promote young talent after

4   *The Sporting Globe*, July 13, 1931
5   ibid

so many of his senior players had left to seek greater remuneration. In the past three seasons he had added youngsters, such as Harry and Albert Collier, Frank Murphy, Charlie Dibbs, George Clayden, John 'Jiggy' Harris, Jack Beveridge, Bill Libbis, among others. Many came from the football production line that was the Collingwood district team, coached by Hughie Thomas, who continued to be more willing than McHale to give personal tuition and training, particularly in the development and refining of skills. McHale was more concerned about the collective than the individual. When Thomas sent up players to senior team, they were expected to have skills at a sufficient standard to satisfy the senior coach. Two of the new players in 1927 were Harold Rumney, who would make Carlton pay for a decade for letting him go, and Norm MacLeod. Percy Rowe was also back from Wangaratta.

McHale had already started to take advantage of the new "out of bounds" rule, where the last team to touch the ball before it went over the line would be penalised, and the coach intended to exploit it some more. As *The Machine*, a book on the famous team and its era, explained: "(The rule) made the game quicker and forced teams into a much more direct approach in which 'corridor football' ruled. McHale and his brains trust were among the first to react and change their style of play accordingly, and with a dominant full-forward (Gordon Coventry) about to emerge, the Pies were ideally placed to capitalise."[6]

His philosophy was a simple one. Get the ball from point to point with as little deviation as possible. That meant full-back Charlie Dibbs booting in as long as he could, and he was a prodigious kick. Six decades later Harry Collier told *The Sun*: "We were told that if you had to handball to get out of trouble, then to do it, but otherwise, kick the bloody ball because you can't beat a 50-yard roost."[7] It also meant players sticking to their positions, and not switching from the plan.

---

6   *The Machine, the inside story of football's greatest team*, Glenn McFarlane and Michael Roberts, Collingwood Football Club, 2005
7   *The Sun*, October 2, 1990

Players who did were given a quiet talking to at one of the breaks. One of his players, Len Murphy, said in the *Herald Sun* in 1992: "He (McHale) never missed anything on the ground."[8] During the later stages of his time with *The Machine*, and into the 1930s, the coach would even have white lines marked out on the Victoria Park ground for training sessions, and he would forbid players to go outside their zones.

But, for all his great strengths, McHale, and Collingwood for that matter, were under extreme pressure heading into the 1927 season. The Magpies had lost successive Grand Finals, the last one by a record margin, and they had not won a premiership since 1919. Four Grand Finals losses had followed (1920, 1922, 1925 and 1926) and for a football club that prided itself on performance, this was not good enough. There was a sense of dissatisfaction in the community—and within a section of the club—that suggested change was not too far away. In what shape or form, no one knew. It wasn't as if McHale faced the sack, as other coaches from rival VFL clubs habitually feared on a year-to-year basis. But it is fair to suggest that he was feeling the heat to perform as he headed into his 16th season as coach.

Collingwood, the suburb, was feeling as much heat as Collingwood, the football club. The first signs of economic deterioration were starting to bite. It would only get worse. As historian Gillian Hibbins concluded in a history of the suburb: "(The Depression) seems to have come early for the industrialised suburbs, hit them the hardest and left them last."[9] Already there was an estimated 10,000 Victorians were out of work in 1927. Fortunately for McHale, and his family, he would retain his position with Carlton Brewery. In fact, he would even do his best to secure positions for some of the young footballers he coached.

It was said: "The club and its successes had been the axis on which many Collingwood residents had existed for more than three decades.

---

8   *The Sun*, March 12, 1992
9   *A Short History of Collingwood*, G.M. Hibbins, Collingwood Historical Society, 1997

What happened on the stretch of land bordered by Lulie, Bath, Turner and Abbot Streets deeply affected the majority of those in the municipality. That feeling permeated the suburb—from the crowded footpaths along bustling Johnston Street, to the sweat-filled boot factories that employed so many locals (and more than their fair share of Collingwood footballers), to the sports-obsessed playgrounds of the state schools, from which the football club derived so many of its players. Even John Wren, the one-time Collingwood resident, former tote owner and regular club benefactor, now safely ensconced across the Yarra River in Kew, shared the same frustration as the barrackers."[10]

The building impatience at failing to win a premiership since 1919 resulted in a heated annual meeting at the Collingwood Town Hall in March 1927. It was meant to be a bit of a milestone night for McHale. It happened to be his 25th straight annual meeting since joining the club as a 20-year-old with the hope to stay for as long as he possibly could. Instead, it turned out to an evening when the pent-up emotions of the past two Grand Final losses would spill over into near hostility.

When club president Harry Curtis rose to his feet to speak, a wave of criticism came from the floor. Some angry supporters "tore up their (membership) tickets ... in rage." Veteran *Herald* journalist 'Kickero' (Tom Kelynack, who had covered the VFL since its beginning), reported he had never seen such angst at a Collingwood gathering. On the eve of the 1927 season, he wrote: "Knowing the Collingwood club ever since it was formed in 1892 ... I have never seen such disappointment at the loss of the (1926) Premiership as was shown by their barrackers when Melbourne whipped them in the fight for last year's flag. There were many who had not recovered from the shock."[11]

There had been rumblings for several weeks that there would be changes. 'Kickero' had already forecast that there was the prospect

---

10   *The Machine, the inside story of football's greatest team,* Glenn McFarlane and Michael Roberts, Collingwood Football Club, 2005
11   *The Herald,* April 29, 1930

of replacing Charlie Tyson as captain. But when the practice games took place in early April, he was in charge of the likely team, while Ernie Wilson took charge of the other team of hopefuls. Syd Coventry, the logical replacement, if there was indeed going to be one needed, missed one of those early games, as he was playing with his brother Gordon for Diamond Creek in the local cricket finals.

But on the day of the 12th anniversary of the Gallipoli landings—just five days out from Collingwood's first game against Geelong—Tyson was sacked without warning. Not just as captain, he was deleted not just from the captaincy but from the club's playing list. Three other players were also dumped. Tyson believed his sacking followed a conspiracy at committee level. According to *The Machine*, he transferred to North Melbourne but contended that: "A man is only an individual and it does not pay to have a body of officials against you."[12] He also claimed that his sacking stemmed from a players' meeting in December he had been involved with to discuss the possibility of bonus payments. Instead, the committee promised the players a trip to Western Australia the following year. Collingwood's secretary George Connor dismissed the suggestions, saying the selectors (of which McHale would have had a major say) "considered we have young and nippier men."[13] Tyson was 29, and had played 106 matches in his seven seasons with the Magpies.

The timing of the decision to replace Tyson with Syd Coventry as captain gave rise to speculation—almost certainly unfounded— that Tyson had "played dead" in the 1926 Grand Final. He had been criticised for a few positional changes in the second half of the game (which may well have been McHale's doing) and his play was described as "peculiar" with the normally unflappable Tyson cautioned on at least two occasions for rough play. An examination by Richard Stremski, *in Kill For Collingwood*, found that this was hardly the sort of behaviour

---

12   *The Machine, the inside story of football's greatest team*, Glenn McFarlane and
      Michael Roberts, Collingwood Football Club, 2005
13   ibid

that would have been expected of a player said to have "taken a dive." He revealed that Tyson was still carrying the effects of a concussion, and that he remained friends with some former teammates, many of whom were certain the allegations were untrue.

Tyson was forced to defend himself a few months later when he wrote to *The Herald*, insisting on his innocence and threatening legal action against anyone who might wish to repeat it. Tyson wrote: "Allegations, which it is unnecessary for me to say are quite without foundation, are now being widely circulated that I have received sums of money to induce me not to do my best for Collingwood in last year's final. I have only two courses of action to adopt, one of which is to ask you to publish this letter, and the other to take proceedings against those foolish and credulous people who are responsible for this injury being done."

What seems certain in this messy incident is that there was no conspiracy, but that Tyson had likely outlived his usefulness. The belief from sections of the committee, from the president and almost certainly McHale, was that he was too much of a "gentleman" and that they had a man in the wings who would be a better captain— Syd Coventry. The fact that it took so long to orchestrate the change meant there must have been some dissent. If not, Tyson could have— and probably would have—been sacked earlier. Stremski claimed vice-president Charlie 'Torchy' Laxton, a former player, was one who had serious misgivings.

Those who made the decision must surely have felt vindication after Syd Coventry was best afield in the Round 1 clash with Geelong, a 23-point win to the Magpies. *The Herald* reported that he "led like a tiger"[14] while *The Sporting Globe's* 'Jumbo' Sharland claimed: "Never have I seen a man display such indomitable spirit as Syd Coventry did."[15] Sharland also made the first reference to Collingwood's machine-like qualities, noting the extraordinary teamwork that McHale's men

---

14   *The Herald,* April 30, 1927
15   *The Sporting Globe,* April 30, 1927

displayed. He wrote that the team's "machine-like movements were an eye-opener ... (you) could not be but astounded and delighted with the magnificent football of Collingwood."[16]

The club's secretary, George Connor, no doubt with the approval of the coach, would write a weekly message on the bulletin board in the Collingwood dressing room throughout the 1927 season. It was meant to entertain and inspire the players. The first instalment, accompanied by a photograph of Melbourne unfurling the 1926 premiership flag, said much about how much residual damage resulted from failing so badly in the previous year's Grand Final. The message was simple: "The flag that you could not win in 1926 ... What about the one we can win in 1927? Players—it is now left up to you."[17]

A reality check came just a fortnight later—only days after the Duke of York officially opened the Federal Parliament house in Canberra—when Richmond brought about Collingwood's first defeat of the season by just six points. There was a sense of frustration in the camp at the conclusion of the game. One Collingwood official who chose to remain nameless told *The Argus:* "Brains won the game for Richmond. The wind destroyed judgment, and there was usually a Richmond man scouting around the edge of the pack ready to get the ball away."[18]

Five wins in a row would follow, proving the Magpies were clearly one of the teams to beat. McHale's strict adherence to 'corridor football' had provided Gordon Coventry with the best chance to kick goals, and he was starting to take his game to a higher plane. In two of those early games he kicked 11 goals—both in the Round 5 game against Fitzroy and the Round 7 game against St Kilda.[19] Clean-living Coventry would hardly have had cause to have any issues with the

---

16   ibid
17   *The Machine*, the inside story of football's greatest team, Glenn McFarlane and
       Michael Roberts, Collingwood Football Club, 2005
18   *The Argus*, May 16, 1927
19   The score-line of 25.19 (169) against St Kilda in Round 7 was the second highest club
       tally to that stage, behind only the 28.16 (184) kicked against Footscray in Round 8,
       1926. They would the two highest scores of McHale's time at Collingwood.

bulletin board message in the midst of that winning streak. It advised players to "keep fit by being regular with meals ... (players) should not indulge in eating, drinking, or smoking, and if they go jazzing, the early part of the week was the time for it." The words had the coach's philosophy all over them.

Carlton, or more was the point, Alec Duncan, stopped the run of consecutive wins in the Round 9 match at Victoria Park. He turned in one of the great individual performances, taking 33 marks in a match that would become known as "Duncan's match". The 12-point loss cost Collingwood top spot for a week. 'Onlooker', from *The Argus*, penned: "Many former footballer and legislators described the match as the best since pre-war days and referred to the play of Duncan, of Carlton, as the finest individual effort in the same time."[20]

McHale feared Melbourne, of all teams, no doubt with the memory of the previous year's rout deep set in his mind. So he was pleased when Collingwood overcame their conquerors from the previous year, by seven points at Victoria Park in Round 11. The *Argus* said: "Collingwood delighted its supporters ... when it avenged the defeats in the semi-final and final matches last year."[21] The barrackers might have felt the urge to crow, but the coach didn't. After the game he confessed: "To tell you the truth, I am most afraid of Melbourne. Should the Red Legs get into the four, they will cause no end of trouble on the Melbourne ground. I greatly fear the pace of their men, and the lightning manner in which they attack."[22]

His experience of travelling to Sydney with the team in his first year (1903) instilled in McHale belief that a trip away in the middle of a season was the best thing to bond a team. So it was that Collingwood left Victoria bound for Perth in early August, after six successive wins

---

20   *The Argus*, June 27, 1927
21   *The Argus*, July 11, 1927
22   *The Machine*, the inside story of football's greatest team, Glenn McFarlane and Michael Roberts, Collingwood Football Club, 2005

that followed the loss to the Blues. They left without their captain, Syd Coventry, and their prolific full-forward Gordon Coventry, who were both required for the state match.

The party left on a good note. An eight-goal last term against South Melbourne, who failed to score a goal, set up a 79-point win in Round 15 at Victoria Park. Three days after the victory, the Magpies boarded the train and headed across the country, with McHale convinced it would bond the team into a premiership unit. They stopping at a few locations on the way to mix with local Aborigines, who seemed a little bemused with these young men in their black and white blazers. In a photograph for the newspapers taken at Perth central station, McHale wore a beaming grin, something he didn't always feel comfortable in showing off in public.

The club's trip to Perth gives a glimpse of how Collingwood—and McHale—were looked upon on a national front. *The West Australian* reported on the morning of Collingwood's arrival that: "As a club, they stand supreme. There has always been that fraternal feeling between players and commitment that spells success and there have been few discordant notes."[23] Remarkably there had been no residual damage arising out of the Tyson affair. "Jim McHale ... has mainly been instrumental in inculcating in their players the need for team work. The clock-like work of the Collingwood team has been its outstanding feature at all times. Their half-distance passing is a revelation, while their dash is generally superb. In brief, any footballer who wins his way into a Collingwood team can be labelled with the hall mark of efficiency."[24]

In the *West Australian*, the Collingwood coach was asked about the young team he had brought west. McHale described them as such: "A very even side, each man pulling his weight, and fighters all. The absence of the Coventry brothers will be sorely felt, for I am of the opinion that Syd is the best footballer in Melbourne today, while

---

23   *The West Australian*, August 12, 1927
24   ibid

Gordon is a leading forward. However, we have a nicely balanced team, and I expect them to do well."[25]

Two matches were played, and the Magpies won one and narrowly lost the other. But the off-field experiences over the eight days would have a lasting effect, as McHale had hoped for. The social activities included a motor launch down the Swan River, dinner and smoke nights, a night at the Theatre Royal, a night at the Gloucester Park trots and a motor trip into the Perth Hills. At the end of the visit, the weary Magpies boarded a steamship home and on arrival, McHale espoused the values of the trip: "I had heard it was the golden west and I was not disappointed ... it was the finest trip I have been on in my long experience."[26]

There were few worrying signs for McHale at half-time of the return match against Fitzroy, at Brunswick Street. Collingwood led by 33 points, but the events of the next hour would have troubled the coach. Fitzroy kicked eight of the following 11 goals, to cause one of the upsets of the season. *The Argus* said Collingwood admitted it had been beaten by a better team, but "excused its performance by the fact that the players had not yet recovered from the effects of the journey from Western Australia, from where they returned on Wednesday."[27] One of the players returned a stone (6.3 kilograms) heavier and another admitted after the game that he would have "given a quid for a sleep at three-quarter time."[28]

But many of the men who went on the trip would say later that it would forge the fire of future premierships. Still, Connor's handwritten

25   *The West Australian*, August 13, 1927

26   *The Machine*, the inside story of football's greatest team, Glenn McFarlane and Michael Roberts, Collingwood Football Club, 2005

27   *The Argus*, August 29, 1927

28   *The Machine*, the inside story of football's greatest team, Glenn McFarlane and Michael Roberts, Collingwood Football Club, 2005

assessment of the Maroons' loss was not thinking long-term. It read: "Do you realise the seriousness of that defeat? Are you going to allow the history of the past two seasons to be repeated by failure at the critical time? Loss of the 1927 Premiership would be the greatest blow which could be given the club and a repetition of Saturday's performance means Premiership suicide. Buck up. Pull yourselves together."[29]

There were signs that Collingwood had lost its spark. In the next game the Magpies failed to score a goal in the first half of the Round 17 match against Essendon, and trailed by 18 points at half-time. Somehow, though, they fell over the line by a point, kicking 3.13 to 4.6, keeping their opponents scoreless in the last term. An easy win over North Melbourne at Arden Street in the final round confirmed the minor premiership over Richmond, who entered the finals after a 66-point win over Hawthorn at Punt Road.

The Argus made a detailed assessment of Collingwood on the eve of the finals, and was dubious as to the value of the mid-season break: "Since the team returned from Western Australia ... there has been a little staleness in its play, and as a consequence, there was a slight feeling of uncertainty in the minds of their admirers. It was contended that the premierships of the last two seasons ... were lost because the team had become 'stale', and when the tour of the West was arranged, it was with the hope that the team would return refreshed and with the will to win strongly developed. The committee was confident that, when the effects of the journey had worn off, the team would play with renewed vigour."[30]

That's precisely what happened in the first final against Geelong. McHale had not tasted success in a final since the 1925 preliminary final against Melbourne, but there were no issues in this game. Collingwood kicked nine goals to one in the first half, and powered away to win by 66 points. "The virility and eagerness of the team" were as good as they had been all season, according to *The Argus*.

---

29   ibid
30   *The Argus*, September 26, 1927

CHAMPION PLAYER: By 1910, when this portrait of McHale was taken, he was a star for the Magpies and was considered to have been their best player through the finals series, which ended with a bitterly-fought Grand Final win over Carlton.

BIRTH CERTIFICATE : James 'Jock' McHale was born in the inner-Sydney suburb of Alexandria on December 12, 1882. A clerical error meant it was spelled as 'McKale'.

Photo: Glenn McFarlane.

FOOTY CARD: Jock McHale featured in a number of cigarette cards throughout his VFL career, including this one from 1907.

NEWSPAPER: The date of this player postcard, released through *The Weekly Times*, is not known, but is thought to be around 1910, in the middle of McHale's playing career.

FOOTY TRIP: A team photo from an exhibition game played around 1915. McHale is the first player on the left in the second back row. Dan Minogue is in the second front row, between two committeemen. Like everyone at Collingwood, McHale never forgave Minogue for his defection to Richmond at the end of World War I.

Photo: Collingwood Football Club.

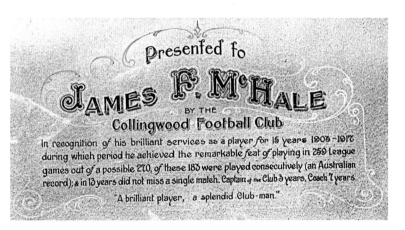

Presented to

JAMES F. McHALE

BY THE

Collingwood Football Club

In recognition of his brilliant services as a player for 15 years 1903-1917 during which period he achieved the remarkable feat of playing in 259 League games out of a possible 270, of these 183 were played consecutively (an Australian record); & in 13 years did not miss a single match. Captain of the Club 3 years, Coach 7 years.

"A brilliant player, a splendid Club-man."

LONG HAUL: McHale was honoured by the Magpies in 1917, a premiership year, for his brilliance as a player, his success as a coach and his staunch loyalty to the club.

Photo: Collingwood Football Club.

FLAG UNFURLING: Collingwood's 1910 premiership flag is unfurled before the first game of 1911 at Victoria Park. McHale, wearing a long-sleeved jumper, is in the middle of the players, with his hand resting on the railing.

Photo: Michael Roberts collection.

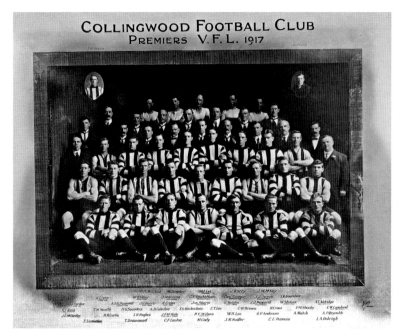

PREMIERS: The 1917 team was the first premiership team to be coached by McHale, who is in the second row from the front, fourth from the left. To the immediate right is Percy Wilson, while next to Wilson is star full-forward Dick Lee.

Source: Collingwood Football Club.

RARITY: McHale lent his name to a table-top football game during the 1930s. The National Sports Museum at the Melbourne Cricket Ground is believed to possess one of the few remaining examples of this game in existence.

Photo: Michael Roberts collection.

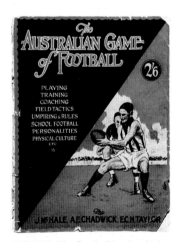

AUTHOR: This football book, which McHale co-authored with Melbourne champion Bert Chadwick and journalist E.C.H. Taylor, was a huge hit when published in 1931 because there were so few football books at the time.

Photo: Collingwood Football Club.

MASTERMIND: By the late 1920s, when this portrait was taken, McHale was in his coaching prime and would lead the Magpies to a record four straight flags between 1927 and 1930. His team became known as *The Machine*.

Photo: Newspix.

WARM WELCOME: The Magpies are welcomed to Perth during a mid-season trip in August 1927. A smiling McHale is at left, while stand-in skipper Ernie Wilson (right) shakes the hand of the West Australian captain, Harold 'Nugget' Gepp (centre). (Syd Coventry stayed at home to play for Victoria.) Albert Collier (obscured) is at the back left of Gepp, while long-time Magpie treasurer Bob Rush is at the right of the picture.

Source: Collingwood Football Club.

PLOTTING VICTORY: McHale is deep in thought during a game some time in the 1930s. This is considered an iconic image of the Collingwood coaching legend as it captured the pose he is best remembered for holding during a match, irrespective of the score. The image is recreated on the McHale Medal (pictured inset) which is now awarded every year to the AFL premiership coach.

IN MODERATION: Perhaps due to his long service at the Carlton Brewery, McHale believed that consuming moderate amounts of beer posed no health problems for footballers. In 1930 he lent his name to an anti-prohibition movement.

Source: Glenn McFarlane.

FATHER AND SON: This team photo from 1944 at Victoria Park is rare because it features two generations of the McHale family in a football context. Jock jnr is the fourth player from the right in the back row. Jock snr is at the end of the row wearing his trademark hat and tie. Lou Richards is third from the right in the front row.

FAMILIAR POSE: Deep in concentration from his usual position immediately behind the boundary line, McHale watches the Magpies in the late 1940s. Bob Rush (right) and Syd Coventry (behind) formed part of the Collingwood brains trust.

Source: Newspix.

THE GOSPEL ACCORDING TO JOCK: Phonse Kyne (at the back), Jack Green (black jumper) and Bernie Shannon listen intently at Victoria Park to Collingwood coach Jock McHale in 1949, his last season at the helm.

Source: Newspix.

KING OF THE KIDS: This is one of the last images of McHale as coach. It is from the pre-season of 1950, just weeks before he announced his retirement.

Source: Newspix.

OUT OF THE ORDINARY: Neil Town, a photographer for *The Argus*, captures Jock McHale kicking during training at Victoria Park in the pre-season of 1950, after his retirement as coach. Town would say later it was the first time he had seen McHale kick a football in 13 years covering Collingwood training sessions.

SOURCE: Newspix.

GUEST OF HONOUR: McHale was honoured by the Magpies with a gala dinner at the Collingwood Town Hall in August 1950, several months after he stepped down as coach. His magnificent contribution to the club was a feature of the souvenir menu.

Source: Glenn McFarlane

KEEPING TIME: McHale liked to time the quarters with a fob watch. This one was presented to him by the Collingwood Football Club after his coaching career had ended, to mark his 50-year association with the club.

LOYAL: The four pillars of Jock McHale's life were family, faith, Collingwood and the Carlton Brewery, where he worked for half a century. So loyal was McHale to his employer that he chose to drink there after matches rather than at the football club. This photo captures McHale in one of the few instances where he didn't wear a black tie, a practice he adopted following the death of his teenage daughter Jean in 1934.

Source: Newspix.

IN RETIREMENT: McHale remained a powerful figure at Collingwood in the period between his retirement as coach in 1950 and his death in 1953. His final act at the club was to convince coach Phonse Kyne to play Ron Richards on the wing—where he starred—in the 1953 Grand Final.

Source: Newspix.

FAMILY MAN: Jock McHale's final resting place at Coburg Cemetery where he lies with his wife Violet and two of his children who died before he did, Frankie and Jean.

As the minor premier, Collingwood had the safety of the right of challenge in the finals, but McHale and his team fervently believed they did not need it. The only thing that stood between them and the premiership was Richmond ... and the weather. In the week leading up to the 1927 Grand Final, fears had been expressed that Victoria's dry winter and early spring would result in a drought. Then, on the night before the game, the heavens opened. The VFA preliminary final, scheduled for the same day, was cancelled. For a time, it looked as if the VFL Grand Final would have to follow suit.

Harry Collier recalled: "They (VFL) thought about abandoning the game. It really wasn't too bad underfoot ... it was just that the water was over the top of the grass."[31] The VFL had to make a decision by midday, and the rain had eased a little by that stage. They chose to play the match, and from the moment this decision was made, the rain belted down and would continue for the entire game, played before 34,551 doughty fans, 25,000 fewer than had attended the 1926 decider.

In the cramped change rooms McHale was about to make one of the most important speeches of his coaching tenure to date. After losing consecutive Grand Finals, he knew what losing a third would do to the club, and perhaps to himself. Sometimes he would not even speak to the team as a group before games, allowing the president Harry Curtis to do the talking. Sometimes he preferred to speak individually to his players before the game, saving up his main speech for half-time. But on this wet and wild afternoon, he spoke to his young team about his demands. They included "marking on the chest, not out in front" and "kicking the ball off the ground wherever possible."[32] It was simple stuff, but exactly what was required as the torrential rain continued to sweep across the MCG.

Richmond started the game strongly, but could not put their early ascendancy onto the scoreboard. Four behinds came from the Tigers;

---

31   Interview, Harry Collier, courtesy of Tom Wanliss

32   *The Machine, the inside story of football's greatest team*, Glenn McFarlane and Michael Roberts, Collingwood Football Club, 2005

one for the Magpies as the waterlogged arm-wrestle made it difficult for the players, and for coach McHale who was being saturated on the sidelines. The rain eased in the first term, but fell with greater intensity in the second. Fortunately, for Collingwood, Gordon Coventry kicked two goals for the quarter—one of them early on and the other just before the half-time interval. It gave Collingwood a 14-point lead on a day when scores were going to be at a premium.

There were "complete changes in uniform" from both sides, while the showers in the rooms, rubdowns from the trainers and coats of oil all over their bodies, made it an exceedingly long break. Incredibly, many fans, drenched almost to the skin, sought the exit, unable to deal with the conditions any longer. The fans who stayed to brave the conditions listened to the piping of bagpipes through most of the break. And when the Collingwood team re-emerged from the room, there was an omen that fans of the black and white could not dismiss. *The Argus* documented: "There were loud Collingwood cheers when a magpie—club emblem—was seen to fly across the ground. 'Now, we cannot lose,' said one man."[33]

The players threw themselves into the contest in the second half. Three key players—Syd Coventry, Jack Beveridge and Harold Rumney—were knocked over in the opening minutes of the term, as the Tigers tried to gain a physical advantage. But each side could manage only three behinds for the term and the margin at the last change was the same as it had been at half-time. Within a minute of the last term Richmond finally scored its first goal, via Jack Fincher, but it would be its sole major on a doubly bleak afternoon.

Collingwood held on grimly to win by 12 points. Its 2.13 (25) might have been the club's lowest score in a match since another premiership year—1910—and it would stick in history as the lowest winning Grand Final score. But that didn't matter to Collingwood or McHale.

---

33   *The Argus*, October 3, 1927

The *Argus* credited McHale's tactics, particularly given the weather, as a key reason for the club's first premiership in eight years, saying: "Collingwood fully deserved its victory. It displayed better tactics, particularly in regard to long-kicking whenever the ball was picked up. It showed greater pertinacity and also handled the ball better while the players were content to stand down and allow Richmond to fly for and miss the ball."[34] Given the anger that had followed back-to-back Grand Final losses, it was no surprise that, "after many disappointments the victory ... was hailed with unbridled joy by Collingwood officials and players."[35]

Some of the players and trainers tried to hoist captain Syd Coventry onto their shoulders, but modesty prevented him from accepting the offer. Later, in the rooms he would say it was the proudest moment of his life. He would need to revisit that in time. *The Argus* reported: "A pipe band played the players off the ground. It was an exceedingly difficult task for the players to reach the dressing room, for they were swamped by hundreds of enthusiastic supporters, and wet and cold, they were nearly exhausted by the time they struggled through. Collingwood had the small dressing room, and this was filled to overflowing, while a strong doorkeeper kept hundreds more from forcing their way inside."[36] There were 21 speeches made. One came from Richmond secretary Percy Page, who spoke of the "friendly feelings" that existed between the suburban neighbours. Things had clearly changed since the frosty years in the early twenties, after the defection of Dan Minogue to Richmond.

There was little mention of McHale in the celebrations. The only quote offered in the rooms from the now three-time premiership coach was this: "They are a modest band and most of them are quiet living fellows. In fact some of the players are real silent men."[37]

---

34   ibid
35   ibid
36   ibid
37   *The Machine, the inside story of football's greatest team*, Glenn McFarlane and Michael Roberts, Collingwood Football Club, 2005

Then he added that he regarded this team—with an average age of only 24—as one of the best he had seen at Collingwood, with the prospect of more success in the coming years.

Losing another Grand Final was not an option. To win it against Richmond would have been an added bonus given it was that club which had deprived Collingwood of the 1920 pennant.

The Annual Report, which was released early the next year, "had no hesitation in saying that the trip to the West was one of the main factors in winning the premiership ... it was proclaimed by all those who were fortunate enough to be in the party as "the trip of all trips."[38] The harmony amongst the group was praised: "Never in the club's history have we had a more pleasant and meritorious season."[39] Gordon Coventry's feat of kicking a record 97 goals was celebrated, as was the effort of Syd Coventry winning the fourth Brownlow Medal, and the club's first. The captain was described as "a most brilliant and fearless and fair leader."[40] He would also win the inaugural "Copeland Medal" (Trophy), named after the club's former long-serving secretary. The decision to replace Tyson—however harsh—was justified. Gordon Coventry's goal spree set new marks. His 88 goals in the home and away season had beaten his own record, set the previous season, by ten; his season tally topped his 1926 mark by 14 goals. He was now the undisputed champion full-forward of the era.

McHale ended the 1927 season as the most feted current coach in the game. His committee called him "the King of Coaches", and wrote: "We are extremely fortunate in having the services of such a capable sportsman as 'Jock'. His loyalty to the club is without parallel. His club record stands alone."[41]

Incredibly, Jock McHale took on a new coaching position at the start of 1928, and he would hold the role for two seasons. That didn't

---

38   Collingwood Annual Report, 1928
39   ibid
40   ibid
41   ibid

mean he was leaving Collingwood. In fact, he was more entrenched than ever at Victoria Park. But in what surely must rank as one of the greatest—and most unusual—coaching coups in Australian football history, McHale agreed to "coach" Old Xaverians. He would not be paid for the role, and he wouldn't be coaching the team on Saturdays, but he would train the players one night during the week.

This was done as a personal favour to his good friend, John Wren, whose sons attended Xavier College. It was an extraordinary appointment that even Wren's grandson, John, was unaware of when told years later. "I'm not surprised," Wren's grandson said. "They were close, grandfather and Jock. You would think that he would have gone to see Jock and put it this way—'Old Xavs aren't going that well, so can you help them out?' I suppose he would have thought, let's just get the old icon down there, and things might improve."[42]

Who knows what sort of strain this extra commitment would have placed on McHale's relationship with his wife, Violet, or his role in the upbringing of his two living children, John (sometimes called Jack) and Jean? McHale would work his long days at the Carlton Brewery. On Wednesday, he would tutor Old Xaverians. On Tuesdays and Thursday, he would be at Victoria Park, putting the Collingwood players through their pace. On Saturdays, he took charge of *The Machine* in matches, as it sought further glories. And he would often be at the Collingwood ground on Sundays, after mass at St Ambrose's in Brunswick—where he often acted as the collector when the plate went around.

In the first year at Old Xaverians the young club reached the finals for the first time, in B grade. But in 1929, as Collingwood was compiling its greatest season, Old Xaverians struggled and was relegated to C Grade. McHale could not keep up the extra-curricular role, and sought a replacement in Bert Laxton, a man with Collingwood links, to take over the amateur club.

---

42   Interview with John Wren III

It's a wonder that McHale was able to devote any time at all to Old Xaverians in 1928, as Collingwood was forced to overcome a few pitfalls in their quest for more success. The coach had a favourite expression that he would use whenever the teams he coached were confronted with adversity. McHale would urge his men to "stoke the stove." And it was something that the coach would have to say on many occasions during the 1928 season. It would become a McHale catch-cry at Collingwood for generations. While it might have been a little well-worn at times, it would rarely fail to stir the emotions. Percy Bowyer, one of the new players to make his debut in 1928 along with his soon-to-be mates Bruce Andrew and Len Murphy, said he would never tire of McHale's famous mantra. "He would almost use it on a daily basis," Bowyer would recall. "They were inspiring words, and quite a number of the regular supporters coming into the rooms would often say 'Stir up the stove, boys' to get us going."[43]

The hurdles Collingwood faced in defending that 1927 flag were many and varied. Firstly, there was a controversial pay-cut delivered to the players, a move that took them to the brink of strike action. There were allegations that two players took money to play below par. There was an injury crisis that threatened to derail the premiership hopes. Finally, there was a late-season form slump.

Bowyer and Murphy would play in the opening match against Geelong at Corio Oval. Two things stood out to the former. One was the fact that McHale was "very definite that we should walk from the Geelong Station to the football ground ... it would have been about a mile, but he walked with us, and he kept an eye on every player."[44] The other was how the young players in the team were protected by the senior men. "I was playing in the back pocket and the first words

---

43   Interview with Percy Bowyer, courtesy of Tom Wanliss
44   ibid

I heard were 'Come through kid'. Here was Ernie Wilson—'Sugar' Wilson—shepherding an opponent so that I got my first kick."[45] Wilson was in his tenth and final season at Collingwood.

The Magpies won that first match, and then celebrated the unfurling of the previous year's pennant in front of a joyous Victoria Park, disposing of Fitzroy in a game in which Gordon Coventry kicked as many goals as the Maroons—nine. His brother, Syd, told *The Sporting Globe* after the game: "I think we are going to be harder to beat for the Premiership this season."[46] But Richmond soon made the Magpies appear more than a little mortal with a come-from-behind two-point win at Punt Road. If some were speaking of a possible decline, Sharland, writing in *The Sporting Globe*, had too much faith in McHale's systems, saying: "They may not be as good as last year, but their defeat proves nothing in regard to deterioration. No, there is no indication of Collingwood cracking up."[47]

This was shown when McHale's men were able to get on an eight-game winning streak that stretched from May to the end of June. On the same day as Collingwood's 12-point win over Melbourne on June 9, Charles Kingsford-Smith and Charles Ulm safely landed the *Southern Cross* on Australian soil, in Brisbane, after becoming the first airmen to cross the Pacific Ocean.

But the club officials produced a shock just ahead of the Round 12 game against Geelong. They had decided to cut the players' wages from £3 per game to £2/10/- —a 16 per cent cut—claiming that the looming economic downturn justified the move. On the day the news was relayed to the players, Collingwood lost to Geelong by 11 points. The blame for the loss could not be placed solely on the dispute, as Percy Rowe and Ernie Wilson had been injured in the game. But it didn't help morale.

45   ibid
46   *The Machine*, the inside story of football's greatest team, Glenn McFarlane and Michael Roberts, Collingwood Football Club, 2005
47   *The Sporting Globe*, May 9, 1928

What followed next threatened to disengage the harmony that had long existed between the committee and the players, putting McHale delicately in the middle of the debate. Stremski revealed a 30-minute meeting took place between the players on the following Tuesday night. Wilson put forward a motion—seconded by Albert Collier a day after his 19th birthday—that the team should refuse to play for the sum of £2/10/-. George Clayden said the majority of the team had agreed with "the tenor of the motion."[48] Bowyer recalled: "To go back to £2/10/- didn't worry me nor most of the younger boys. Yes, (the senior players) were upset; particularly Ernie (Wilson)."[49]

McHale was compromised, as he was not only the coach, but he was also a member of the general committee, as well as of the match committee. It came down to the club's captain, Syd Coventry, to emerge and take hold of a situation that was sliding out of control. He told the players that the ramifications of taking strike action would tarnish what they had achieved, and what they wanted to achieve in the future. Bowyer explained: "He was our captain, and after all was said and done; you have to be sensible about things."[50] The players went back to the football, with lighter pockets but a lesson in leadership.

The Geelong defeat had McHale searching for some more speed. So he had a word to district coach Hughie Thomas to seek his fastest player. The District full-forward, Bruce Andrew, was the player chosen. He recalled almost 70 years later the night that changed his football life. "Hughie wasn't very happy with Jock at the time. I said to him 'I don't want to go up there (to the seniors.) He said: 'You better go, otherwise they will blame me.' I went up the other end of the ground and took part in their practice match and circle work. McHale came up to me at the end and said: 'Are you Andrew?' I said: 'Yes, sir.' He said: 'Have you ever played on the wing?' I said 'No, sir.' He went

48   *Kill For Collingwood*, Richard Stremski, Allen and Unwin, 1986
49   Interview with Percy Bowyer
50   ibid

'Huh!' and that was the end of it. They went off to the rooms and I went back and finished my training with Hughie Thomas."[51]

Andrew was in the side for the game on the weekend after that one training session, and in a position he had never played. McHale wanted a fast man to serve his purpose, and that is exactly what Andrew provided in the game against Fitzroy at Brunswick Street, and for the remainder of the season.

Despite a run of four straight wins after the Fitzroy match in Round 13, Collingwood appeared a little vulnerable because of injuries to senior players. They were to meet Carlton in the last round, and there was no incentive other than pride on offer as the club had already secured top spot. Incredibly, on the day before the game, *The Herald* gave an insight into the lead-up. 'Kickero' recorded: "No match for years has been the subject of as much rumour and talk. Ordinarily one pays no heed to loose-tongued, ill-informed gossips ... but for weeks the rumour that Collingwood would be easily defeated has been so common that the management and players of each club has been stirred to indignation. What has been said is that Collingwood are safe with two chances of the premiership, there is not the necessity for them to work as hard tomorrow. However, the assurance has been given that Collingwood will go their hardest."[52]

Collingwood lost by 20 points after trailing all day. The club put the performance down to staleness. Sharland, who had a reasonable relationship with the Collingwood coach, wrote in *The Sporting Globe:* "Had a stranger from another state casually visited the Collingwood ground on Saturday, he would have been entitled to the opinion that Collingwood was not taking the game seriously ... My faith in the integrity of the Collingwood Football Club was severely shaken."[53]

Such an assertion would have shaken McHale. He was a principled man who loved nothing more than to win. Losing, or not trying,

---

51 Interview with Bruce Andrew
52 *The Herald,* August 31, 1928
53 *The Sporting Globe,* September 5, 1928

would have been incongruous to him. Still, there were allegations that day—never proven, it must be said—that two Collingwood players accepted £50 to play poorly. Syd Coventry was not one of them, but he revealed that he had been approached with a bribe before the game, and instantly knocked it back. He later joked that he might as well have accepted it, as his form in the game was poor.

That form had turned around in the first three quarters of the semi-final against Melbourne. Collingwood had opened up a 30-point lead by three-quarter time. On a windy afternoon, Melbourne had the assistance of a strong breeze in the final term and few people thought it could reel in the difference. But the "Red Legs" did—just. They stormed home in near-darkness, kicking 5.0 to nil, with a goal to Tommy McConville near the end of the game levelling the scores and resulting in the first finals draw in history. The game finished at 5.27pm, in darkening gloom, a mood that was matched in the Collingwood rooms. Collingwood had squandered a chance, and the coach knew there was no other option but to respond.

The Magpies did that, but again, only just. Playing in similar crosswinds, the replay final was not a lot different from the previous week's game, although the Magpies had some injury concerns. It was said Syd Coventry should not have played in the drawn game with a serious bout of influenza, and brother Gordon (whose recent form slump was concerning) should not have played in the replay. After kicking eight goals against Hawthorn in Round 15, he missed the following week with injury; in the next three three games he managed a total of just four goals, and was goalless in the replay. Collingwood took a lead of 11 points into the last quarter, and Melbourne again finished strongly. This time, however, Collingwood matched the Melbourne push, kicking 5.1 to Melbourne's 6.2, and hanging on to win by four points. "It was a hard, at times desperate game," according to *The Argus*, "in which the fortunes varied throughout, and it was so even that it was anybody's game until the last two minutes of play."[54]

---

54   *The Argus*, September 24, 1928

Collingwood had led at every change, and still held a four-point buffer at the end.

There was much enthusiasm in the Collingwood camp. McHale had always feared Melbourne, particularly after the thrashing in the 1926 Grand Final, and to survive two close calls was a relief to all at Victoria Park. The Redlegs captain, Ivor Warne-Smith, recently announced as a Brownlow Medal winner for a second time, went to the visitors' rooms and said: "I am a rotten speaker, but I simply had to come and congratulate you. Melbourne and Collingwood have played some great games, but I think the last two games have stood out."[55]

Now the Magpies had two shots at the Tigers—if required—under the challenge system, but there were many within the camp, McHale included, who suspected they wouldn't need the double chance. In fact, the club's secretary George Connor had a message for sports fans worried that the draw meant football would encroach on the cricket season. He told *The Argus*: "We have got through our bad patch. Our men are back to their form again. The public need not be alarmed about the Melbourne ground (MCG) being delayed for cricket. There will be no Grand Final. We will win on Saturday."[56]

McHale had some plans to make that a certainty, and it revolved around a special team meeting that he and Syd Coventry presided over on the Thursday night before the game. The coach sensed after the battles of the past fortnight that his players were exhausted. He gave them an easy night on the track, and then brought them in for a think-tank session—as such meetings would be called later—that was seemingly ahead of its time by years. It was time to "stoke the stove" again.

Coventry revealed later the extent to which Collingwood dissected their opponents that night. They went through the Richmond side line-by-line, and player-by-player, talking about their strengths and

---

55   ibid
56   ibid

how to stop them, and about their weaknesses and how to exploit them. Over-confidence was something that was raised. As detailed by *The Machine*, the captain said: "Richmond was brimming with confidence. That is a great thing for a side, but it seemed to us that they were a little too sure of their own ability to dominate the whole field."[57]

It was decided to sledge their opponents, to throw them off their game. Coventry said: "Richmond had some fine players, but some of them are very easily annoyed and thrown out of their natural stride, even by jokes made at their expense on the field."[58] The Magpies even resorted to a bit of name-calling, but McHale was adamant about one thing: "At every minute of the game, and regardless of what might occur, every man should make the ball his first objective."[59]

There was an instruction to punch the ball away unless players were certain they could mark it, to shake Richmond's strong aerial capabilities. There was also a decision to change the club's followers on a regular basis, especially in the first half, to keep them fresh. Syd Coventry revealed: "We decided to run plenty of men into the ruck. We put them on the ball for two or three minutes—resting our other men, and bring these useful fellows into the fray with extra dash and pace that left the Richmond big men behind all the time. We had the Richmond followers puzzled all day, and by three-quarter time our big men were still fresh."[60] Gordon Coventry recalled it was one of the first games that Albert Collier would spend some time in the middle of the ground, as well as starring on the backline.

McHale and his selection committee included Percy Rowe for his first game since Round 16, with a specific plan for him to block and clear a path for Gordon Coventry—and assist his return to form. Rowe drove the Tigers' defenders red with rage by abusing them, even

---

57　*The Machine*, the inside story of football's greatest team, Glenn McFarlane and Michael Roberts, Collingwood Football Club, 2005
58　ibid
59　ibid
60　ibid

resorting to making faces to put them off their game, while using his bulky frame to assist Collingwood's gun forward. Gordon Coventry told *The Sporting Globe* later: "No one thought it possible for one man to shoulder such a burden, but Rowe thought lightly of it."[61] Syd Coventry added: "Percy saved Gordon from any interference in going for marks, and to a man who relies so much on his marking ability, it meant the difference between the nine goals he (Gordon) got and the two or three he might have got without protection."[62]

Coventry's nine goals (of 13)—an individual performance which would not be equalled in a Grand Final game for another 61 years when Gary Ablett kicked the same tally for Geelong in a losing side in 1989—played a massive role in Collingwood's 33-point win. So, too, did Rowe's selfless acts. But the thing that truly secured the club's first back-to-back premierships since 1902-03 was the pre-game preparation that showed just how advanced Collingwood was in its planning. Other clubs wouldn't catch up for some time. The Annual Report released the next year said: "The result of last year's final (1928) was certainly a surprise to most football tipsters, but not so to your famous coach and captain, Jock McHale and Syd Coventry, who worked so hard in bringing into execution the wonderful combined teamwork that won the premiership in such a decisive manner."[63]

Collingwood was fortunate enough to have a committed team prepared to make sacrifices to win. It also had an inspirational and far-thinking captain not prepared to ask his men to do things that he wasn't prepared to do himself. And, it had a coach who believed in the traditions of the club—and the game—but was not afraid to challenge the status quo when it was needed.

---

61   Interview with Syd and Gordon Coventry, The Herald, 1938
62   ibid
63   Collingwood Annual Report, 1929

If anyone thought Collingwood and McHale, were satisfied by successive flags, they were to be sorely mistaken because the Magpies produced a season unmatched in the history of the game in 1929. They won all 18 home and away games, by an average of 43 points. No other team in the history of the game has won all regular season games before the finals. The domination was much more than that, though. Collingwood became the first team to win 20 consecutive games—adding in the two finals of 1928. Twenty-year-old Albert Collier—whose bullocking work through packs then and later once prompted McHale to exclaim "God! Nobody could stop that, could they?"[64]—won the Brownlow Medal with six votes, from a group on four votes, including Warne-Smith, and the 1930 winner Allan Hopkins. Gordon Coventry won the VFL goalkicking award with the first century of goals record (124), and Collingwood became the first team to score 2000 points in a season.

All of this came without veterans Percy Rowe and Ernie Wilson, who had left the club, but McHale had a cast of hopefuls hoping to win a spot on the club's list. *The Herald* recorded: "The prince of coaches ... has the knack of bringing out all that is best of a young player for the benefit of the old club. He has schooled thousands in his time."[65] The reality is, much of this tuition would have come from Hughie Thomas, a process that is hard to understand, but was clearly effective. Two of the likely new recruits—Horrie 'Tubby' Edmonds (from Coventry-country in Diamond Creek) and Charlie Ahern, would play key roles in the 1929 premiership.

The season started in remarkable fashion, too. Collingwood unfurled its 1928 pennant in front of their old protagonists, Richmond, and opened its new grandstand—built almost on the side of the old 'Cowsheds' from McHale's early days at the club—in front of a packed crowd. The players put on a show, too. By three-quarter time, the

---

64 *Kill For Collingwood*, Richard Stremski, Allen and Unwin, 1986
65 *The Machine*, the inside story of football's greatest team, Glenn McFarlane and Michael Roberts, Collingwood Football Club, 2005

Magpies had kicked 13 goals without a blemish. It was only when 'Bottles' Chesswas sprayed a ball early in the last term that the first behind was registered. Collingwood won 15.2 to 11.9.

The grandstand—shared with the Collingwood Cricket Club—would be named after the other 'King of Collingwood', Jack Ryder, the suburb's cricket colossus, who was Australia's cricket captain. It could so easily have named after McHale, who, by then, had been a part of the Collingwood Football Club for 26 years.

McHale may have had issues with *The Machine* name—which was gaining currency and popularity with each win and each laurel that fell his team's way—but his captain was not worried about using it. After the 96-point win over South Melbourne in Round 3, Syd Coventry said: "The team seemed to work like a machine, and there was dash and complete understanding throughout the organisation."[66] That win was the start of a six-week period in which there would be no changes to the 18 players of the team. One of the club's recruits, Bob Ross, would be the emergency for the duration.

As the wins piled up, players began to conceal ailments and injuries. As the economy tightened, life outside the football world was tough, and finances were tight. The difference between playing and getting paid, and not playing and missing out, was often the difference between a good week and a bad one. Jobs were hard to come by, and hard to keep. McHale did not believe in professional footballers. He wanted his men to have a job, and sometimes helped them achieve work. His son would recall almost 50 years after his dad's death: "My father believed that you couldn't be an out of work footballer."[67] In 1929, and in the early 1930s, there was often not much choice for players.

The closest Collingwood came to defeat in that supreme home and away season was against St Kilda on a wild afternoon at the Junction Oval in Round 8. The Magpies fell in, by four points. Big wins followed, including an 86-point win over Hawthorn in Round 13, a game in

---

66   ibid
67   *The Sunday Herald Sun*, March 8, 1992

which Gordon Coventry kicked a VFL record of 16 goals. The record would not last long. He would break it himself the following season (against Fitzroy in Round 12, he kicked 17 goals). Coventry had been called 'Nuts' since growing up on the family orchard in Diamond Creek, but his performance that day gave him a new nickname within the group that never really caught on—'Hungry'.

Bowyer recalled the origins: "I remember seeing Harry Collier running into goal, and then I heard a voice saying 'Punch it behind, punch it behind'. Harry did, and Gordon got another goal. (John) Wren gave him £50, and that didn't worry us. We thought we would all get £1 each, and 'Nuts' would be left with 33. But I can tell you that we didn't get a zac. After that, a couple of the players began to tease him, and call him 'Hungry'. It was a nickname that he had for a while after that."[68]

But McHale didn't care. His view was that the full-forward was meant to be the man who got the goals. The coach sometimes chastised wingmen or other non-forwards who sneaked down to score goals.

McHale always maintained that he was fortunate to have played with, and coached, the great Dick Lee. Through the childhood eyes of a kid who worshipped Lee, Harry Collier would always recall just how good he was: "Jesus Christ, I don't know if you ever saw Dick Lee kick goals ... he would do place kicks off the boundary 40 yards, with people throwing cigarette boxes and orange peels (at him). He would just put the ball and put it through."[69] To have the more prolific, if less spectacular Gordon Coventry follow Lee, was Collingwood's—and McHale's—good fortune.

But there were no celebrations—other than a few backslaps—when Coventry became the first man in VFL history to score 100 goals in the Round 16 game against Fitzroy, when he booted seven goals. There was no clear response from McHale. As much as he respected the achievement, he "wasn't the sort of bloke to encourage individual

---

68   Interview with Percy Bowyer
69   Interview with Harry Collier

players. His whole idea of coaching was to develop teamwork and discipline, with every man working together."[70]

All the indications were that the Magpies were unbeatable. But Richmond, and in particular 'Checker' Hughes, had a plan to cut down the Magpies. They had to beat Collingwood in successive weeks to win the flag. Before the semi-final match, which most football supporters naturally assumed would be another cakewalk for Collingwood, Hughes told his players that they needed to work over the Magpies physically, with a battle cry of "Give them all you have got, and they will crack."[71] And that's what happened from the outset when Syd Coventry and George Clayden were flattened. Jack Worrall writing in *The Australasian* said that both were hit "in a manner that displayed a reprehensible spirit that marred play all day".

Richmond's dominance was such that the game was effectively over at half-time. They led by 41-points. The margin had stretched out to 62 by the end of the game, with *The Herald* calling it "the most extraordinary upset in the history of football ... Eighteen spanners were thrown into works, and the Machine was smashed to smithereens."[72]

More than 60 years later, Harry Collier was still at a loss to explain the defeat. "They hit us pretty hard. It was an amazing day. Maybe we were a little overconfident. I can tell you it is still very hard to how work out how we got beaten in that one."[73] Bruce Andrew, who was on the other side of the fence that day, due to injury, was certain that it was because Richmond had "tried to take out the Coventrys and the Colliers. But it only happened in that match. There was no chance they could do it second time around."[74] Bowyer added: "Richmond annihilated us. We had a few too many injuries. Everything went right for them and nothing went right for us."[75] There was an added

---

70   *The Machine*, the inside story of football's greatest team, Glenn McFarlane and Michael Roberts, Collingwood Football Club, 2005
71   ibid
72   *The Herald*, September 16, 1929
73   Interview with Harry Collier 1993
74   Interview with Bruce Andrew
75   Interview with Percy Bowyer

difficulty for Richmond. It had to face Carlton in the preliminary final, with Collingwood, with the right to challenge, having a week off to gather their spirits, and ease any lingering pains.

McHale demanded that his players attend the Richmond-Carlton contest. What they saw was a draining, brutal encounter that must have been precisely what the Collingwood folk would have wanted to see. Then he gave the team a light week leading into the Grand Final—much to the chagrin of the Magpie supporters who had attended training that week. Syd Coventry recalled: "That week Jim McHale would not let us handle a ball. We did nothing at all. Some of the ardent crowd were wringing their hands and they were hostile on McHale."[76]

In the week leading up to the game, the coach had a none-too-subtle dig at his counterpart, Hughes, and his tactics of the previous week. McHale said: "We will be holding a meeting of our players after training on Thursday night and my instructions will be for our men to play the ball at all times—Collingwood want to win the Premiership by fair means only."[77]

The coach and the match committee had to make a few tough calls at selection. Gibbs was harshly dropped for not taking the chance to square up against the player who felled Syd Coventry. McHale asked Hughie Thomas for a player who could "protect" Coventry, and it was agreed that Charlie Ahern was the perfect man. Ahern, who had made his debut in Round 9, at the age of 24, was about to play his third VFL game—and his last—and would win the endless admiration of his teammates for his performance. There were other casualties from the team that lost the semi-final, with regulars Norm MacLeod and 'Jiggy' Harris dropped. In an interview with *Sporting Life* in 1951 it was said: "Thomas agreed to nominate a big recruit from the seconds named Charlie Ahern, and the selection received wide publicity and criticism. 'Why play a

---

76   Interview with Syd and Gordon Coventry, The Herald, 1938
77   *The Machine*, the inside story of football's greatest team, Glenn McFarlane and
       Michael Roberts, Collingwood Football Club, 2005

raw recruit in such a match,' was the comment of the Collingwood district. (But) Collingwood beat Richmond, and as Thomas puts it, it should be called 'Ahern's final'."[78] Ahern would be dead from bowel cancer within 18 months of that grand performance, but his feat in protecting his captain on the most important football day of his life would never be forgotten by his grateful teammates.

Importantly, there was another ploy that Collingwood would use in the 1929 Grand Final that worked a treat, though it remains unclear whose idea it was. It was supposedly decided to use Gordon Coventry as a decoy for the first-year Magpie 'Tubby' Edmonds, who happened to come from the same town as the game's great goal-kicker. The plan was to use Edmonds wide out near the boundary line in the belief that he could get loose and kick a few goals. He did better than that. He kicked five, while Coventry managed just two.

Andrew claimed it was a deliberate tactic from McHale and the selection committee. "They used a decoy that day," he said. "I think it was worked out collectively. Whether Jock was the originator, I don't know. But Jock had some very experienced (past) players on the committee back then. Edmonds couldn't have worked it out for himself."[79] Harry Collier disagreed with his teammate's assertion, claiming: "It wasn't McHale's move. 'Tubby' Edmonds had a brain. He didn't look like a footballer because he wasn't built the right way— he was tubby and short. But he had a very good football brain and I'm sure it may have been just worked out in the forward line."[80]

Whatever the case, Collingwood dominated the game, with Ahern (who received a greenstick fracture to his arm but kept playing) copping punishment in trying to protect Syd Coventry, and Edmonds almost unstoppable. The two unlikely heroes would not have been the subject of the death threats that arrived in the MCG dressing room— in the form of 11 handwritten letters—but by game's end, those two

---

78   *Sporting Life*, July, 1951
79   Interview with Bruce Andrew
80   Interview with Harry Collier

players were as vital as anyone. Nothing came of the threats with the club's officials not telling the players until long after the game.

The Magpies kicked six goals to two in the first term, and never looked back. The final margin was 29 points, and Collingwood's third successive premiership was achieved. In the rooms after the game, Coventry acknowledged the role that the coach had played in the game, and the season. He said simply: "It was a great win for Jock."[81]

McHale had now won five premierships (as many as Worrall) and his team had equalled Carlton's record three flags in a row. The team had lost but one of its 20 matches. Not surprisingly, that night there was talk of the prospect of a fourth flag, as early as in the rooms after the game and at a concert at the Collingwood Town Hall the following day. McHale was pictured, with his arms affectionately around one of Syd Coventry's sons on the steps of the Town Hall, while the Collingwood captain was shaking hands with the Collingwood mayor.

However, that fourth premiership of Collingwood's remarkable quadrella would prove to be the hardest to attain, and incredibly, on the day when it would come to be decided, McHale would be almost helpless.

It was a struggle throughout much of 1930, but it could hardly be compared to the struggles of the community—and the country—as the tentacles of a worldwide depression wrapped relentlessly around individuals and institutions. Only 26 days after the Pies had won that 1929 flag, there was a meltdown on the US stock market that pushed a panic around the world. *The Argus* described it as "the most terrifying selling since the war days of 1914 ... City financial circles received the news yesterday of the collapse of the Wall Street gambling boom. It is hoped that the break that has now occurred will cause a rapid

---

81   *The Machine*, the inside story of football's greatest team, Glenn McFarlane and Michael Roberts, Collingwood Football Club, 2005

return to financial stability."[82] It wouldn't. The struggle in suburban Collingwood, which had been bad enough for the previous few years, was about to get a whole lot worse.

In 1929 Australia's unemployment rate was 12.1 per cent. By the end of the 1930 VFL season, it had reached 20.5 per cent, and would continue to creep upwards. In the inner suburbs, the figures were considerably higher. More than 31 per cent of the labour force would be out of work in Collingwood in the last year of *The Machine's* reign. Those who didn't have a job did everything they could to secure the few on offer, and those lucky enough to possess one fought with tenacity to keep their employment.

In that bleak year of 1930, Australian sport was lucky enough to have a few rare shining lights, some small antidote to the anguish. Such trivialities could not change the circumstances of people struggling to survive, but they could at least offer a diversion. 22-year-old Don Bradman would smash a world record 452 not out for New South Wales six days into the New Year and would so comprehensively dominate Australia's tour of England later in the year that he would change the game of cricket. A four-year-old chestnut gelding called Phar Lap was dominating the Australian turf scene and would become the only horse in history to run in the Melbourne Cup—and win—at odds-on. And in the inner-city, industrialised suburb of Collingwood, a football team about to be the most successful side the VFL had seen was on its way to another premiership. *The Machine* would become so ingrained in the popular culture, with 'Kickero' of *The Herald* once claiming the Magpies were "the Bradmans of football."[83]

A pre-season hurdle came in the form of a job offer to Syd Coventry to coach Footscray for the sum of £10 per week. But the Magpies were not going to let him go without a fight, and they successfully challenged the move. When interviewed in 1993, Harry Collier reflected: "Without

---

82   *The Argus*, October 26, 1929
83   *The Machine*, the inside story of football's greatest team, Glenn McFarlane and
      Michael Roberts, Collingwood Football Club, 2005

being disrespectful to old Jock, you could have called Syd a captain and coach really. When you put on the black and white guernsey, you had to follow him and do what he told you to do."[84]

But the Magpies did lose their secretary George Connor before the 1930 season after some financial irregularities were uncovered, undoing much of the good and feisty work that he had done around the club. His replacement, Frank Wraith, would be one of the most significant appointments in the club's history. Wraith would remain with the club for the next 20 years, and his influence would be enormous.

The VFL introduced the Coulter Law, named after retiring Melbourne delegate Gordon Coulter, in March 1930 to keep a rein on the expenditure of club payments to players. Clubs were restricted to paying a maximum of £3 per game with a series of penalties put in place to ensure that they stuck to the agreement. There was also the scope to add a further £3 for unemployed men, though few of the clubs could afford to pay even the full level of the first payment.

The Coulter Law would become ingrained in the competition for many years, but another rule change in 1930 did not. The VFL altered the holding-the-ball rule. *This Football Century* explained: "Coaches were critical of the new rule which required a player to punch or kick the ball as soon as the ball was held. Collingwood's Jock McHale said unless the VFL re-introduces the 'flick pass', the VFA would replace the league in the public's favour."[85] The rule was repealed with two months. What was more successful was the introduction of the 19th man. Collingwood, and McHale, had been pushing for the introduction of a substitute for injured players for several years.

Jack Regan, who would go on to become one of the greatest defenders in the history of the game, got his start on the bench against South Melbourne in Round 3. He never made it on the ground. He didn't need to. Collingwood won the game by 31 points, a third successive win to start the season. It wasn't a great start to what would

---

84   Interview with Harry Collier
85   *This Football Century*, Russell Holmesby and Jim Main, Wilkinson Books, 1996

be a great career. In Round 8 Regan would fill in for regular full-back Charlie Dibbs, who missed a game to get married to his sweetheart Pearl, and Regan would have 10 goals kicked on him by the great St Kilda forward Bill Mohr.

After winning their opening three matches the Magpies lost successive games to Geelong and Fitzroy. That fact alone was cause for alarm. It was the only time during *The Machine's* 82-game run through 1927-1930 that it would lose consecutive games. Worrall wrote in *The Australasian* after the 18-point loss to the Cats: "While the defeat will prove a blessing in disguise for Collingwood, it is also the best thing possible that could happen to the game. There have been unmistakable signs that the Magpies have felt the strain of many years' exertion ... the team needs new blood."[86]

A month of wins put McHale in better spirits, but a loss to the top-of-the-table Blues in Round 10—by only four points—once more exposed form issues after their opponents had outscored them seven goals to four in the last term. That was the last real sign of vulnerability for the home and away season. Collingwood won the re-match against Carlton at Victoria Park in Round 17, taking top spot off the Blues and claiming the top of the table position for the first time of the season.

There were some memorable moments in that clutch of eight wins leading up the finals, particularly in Round 12 when Gordon Coventry managed to kick 17 goals against Fitzroy. The race towards a possible fourth consecutive premiership, which 'Kickero' said would never be achieved again if attained by the club in 1930, was on in earnest. And, there, in the first week of the finals, was the team that Collingwood had teased and taunted in three consecutive premiership playoffs—Richmond.

Incredibly, the Tigers had the better of the first half, shooting out to a 22-point lead at the long interval. But somehow Collingwood

---

86   *The Machine*, the inside story of football's greatest team, Glenn McFarlane and
Michael Roberts, Collingwood Football Club, 2005

responded to the challenge, perhaps after one of McHale's trademark, stirring half-time speeches. Years later, Bruce Andrew spoke of the power of those half-time McHale addresses. "He was remarkable. He could tell you what you had done and what you hadn't done. He used to speak to some of the players individually, he didn't speak to everyone. He was a bit aloof. Then he would talk collectively to the team. I think (as a result) Collingwood played a lot of inspired third quarters."[87] Percy Bowyer agreed: "At half-time he would get you in the corner, and it would be like there wasn't another soul in the house. He could give you a bit of a tongue lashing, and not another member of the side knew that I had had a roasting. Jock was very careful to speak to the team *as* a team."

Whatever McHale said that day, *The Machine* responded in the third term. After half-time, there was "a complete Collingwood recovery and in that period the Magpies' flight transcended the wonderful leap of the Tigers in the second quarter."[88] Collingwood kicked eight goals to one for the quarter, and looked certainties to go on and win. But Checker Hughes's team had one last crack at the Magpies in a frantic last term. With just minutes left the Tigers trailed by only a point, but Collingwood held on to win by three points. Harry Collier, who had controversially been denied the Brownlow Medal after a controversial count back presented the medal to Richmond's Stan Judkins, was the best man on the ground. He would have to wait another 59 years to gain what was rightfully his, after the League removed the countback provision, and made that ruling retrospective. Collier would be 82 when presented with the 1930 Brownlow.

With Collingwood having the right of challenge—this was to be the last season in which the challenge would apply—Geelong had to win in successive weeks to stop Collingwood's run of flags. They had little trouble pushing past the Magpies in the first game, starting with a four-goal to nil first term, before going on to win by 26 points in the

---

87   Interview with Bruce Andrew
88   *The Argus,* September 29, 1930

Final. About the only positive that came from the game was the fact that Gordon Coventry took his tally of goals past Dick Lee's League record of 707 goals.

If the club's extraordinary run had provided countless triumphs over adversity, another significant hurdle would be placed in its path to becoming the first VFL team to win four successive premierships. Collingwood was under serious duress in the week leading up to the Grand Final. While the club was preparing for its date with destiny, the man who had been in charge since 1912 was seriously ill and confined to bed, at his Brunswick home. He had contracted pleurisy and a serious dose of influenza. His doctor had advised him to stay away from the club, and later in the week he would be ruled out of attending the game. Jock's daughter-in-law, June, who didn't meet him until the 1940s, said the illness must have been exceedingly serious for him to miss a Grand Final, a crowning glory of the Machine success.[89]

The question was: how was Australian football's most successful team going to operate without its famous coach? How could they deal without his stirring half-time speeches that were the cornerstone of Collingwood's remarkable record in third terms during that four-year period? How would it "stoke the stove" without him?

Even from his sick bed, McHale was sending instructions back to Victoria Park, putting in countless hours' preparation in his convalescence. As part of an obituary for McHale 23 years later, Bruce Andrew recalled the extent to which the coach went to orchestrating plans. "On the Sunday he sent for some members of his selection committee to talk over the game," Andrew wrote. "Then, on the Tuesday, he sent for the secretary, Mr. Frank Wraith. He gave Mr. Wrath specific instructions that the team was not to use a ball at training on the Tuesday and Thursday nights. He said, 'I'm satisfied from what I've heard the players have had too much football and are

---

89   Interview with June McHale

leg weary.' Everyone was loudly critical. McHale, a sick man though he was, took full responsibility."[90]

The Sun News-Pictorial declared on the morning of the 1930 Grand Final: "It is today or never (for Collingwood) to pull off the greatest record in league history, for it will probably be many years, if at all, before another team gets close to four premierships on end."[91] It was a perfectly fine day, and that was expected to play into Geelong's hand. They were seen to be young and sharper. The Magpies gamble on the fitness of injured pair Len Murphy and George Clayden. Had McHale taken another risk from his sick bed, or did his selection committee make the call?

McHale's only link to the game was via the radio. With a wireless placed by his bed, he would have listened to the ABC (3LO) coverage of the game, with Jumbo Sharland, former Carlton champion Rod McGregor (one of McHale's great centre rivals of a generation earlier) and former Tiger Mel Morris providing the call. Radio coverage of the game was in its infancy. The first game covered had been the Geelong-Melbourne semi-final in 1925, by 3AR (the ABC's second station in Melbourne), and the rest of the finals were also covered. This was only the sixth Grand Final to be broadcast.

The first half was not pleasant listening for McHale. As had been feared by some within the club, Collingwood was under pressure in the opening half. It had led by three points at the first change of ends, but Geelong turned on a big second term. By half-time, Geelong led 21 points, with many in the crowd thinking it was going to be tough for the Magpies to win their way back.

It was left to long-time Collingwood administrator Bob Rush, whose links to McHale went back to school at CBC Parade, to stand in for the Collingwood coach at half-time. A gifted speaker, and a passionate believer in the black and white, Rush implored the

---

90   *The Machine,* the inside story of football's greatest team, Glenn McFarlane and
      Michael Roberts, Collingwood Football Club, 2005
91   *The Sun,* October 11, 1930

tired players to lift for their coach, and for themselves. He told them McHale would be listening, and as sick as he was, the coach would be aware of the players who were letting him, and the club, down. In many ways, it was the tonic that the whole team required, and a hush came over the Collingwood dressingroom.

It was one of the most "inspirational" speeches Harry Collier had heard. "That was the year that Jock was crook. Old Bob Rush was a great man for Collingwood. He got up and I remember him addressing the players, especially at half-time. You know we respected him as much as anyone. Everyone loved old Jock, too."[92] *The Argus* noted the calm in the Magpies' rooms at half-time, saying it was "a very serious place ... there was no repining, no blaming the other fellow."[93] There was no panic, only inspiring words and a belief that the momentum that the club had carried though four years had an hour left in it.

Eight goals six behinds for the quarter was the astonishing result of that half-time reflection. Geelong could only manage 0.1 in response. The Magpies had conjured up a 53-point turnaround. After trailing by 21 points at the long break, they took a 32-point lead into the last change. How McHale must have listened proudly as his team produced what *The Sun News-Pictorial* termed "one of the finest performances ever seen in football ... it was an object lesson to every term in rising to the occasion after being apparently beaten, and by sheer grit and magnificent teamwork, sweeping down every obstacle in the way of finals success."[94]

Collingwood and Geelong both kicked three goals when the steam was out of the game in the last term. When the final bell sounded, the margin had edged out to 30 points. *The Sun News-Pictorial* painted a picture of the celebrations on the Monday morning, proclaiming: "The crush to reach the dressing room after the game was tremendous."[95]

---

92 Interview with Harry Collier
93 *The Argus*, October 13, 1930
94 *The Sun*, October 13, 1930
95 ibid

Syd Coventry, such a pivotal player and personality, summed up the feeling in the rooms: "We were up against the greatest odds a team could face at half-time, and I thank the boys for the way they rose to the occasion. It was a wonderful effort from the whole team."[96]

It was, as it turned out, a fitting end to four years of sheer dominance. But no one knew that at the time. There were many celebrations to come, and when he recovered from his illness, McHale was pleased to be a part of it.

In fact, the club held a premiership celebration in his honour at the Collingwood Town Hall on October 22—11 days after the victory. The Annual Report stated: "To celebrate the winning of the premiership and to record our appreciation of the almost life-long service of our esteemed coach, Jim McHale, your committee tendered a complimentary smoke social, and in the presence of his Excellency Sir William Irvine KCMG, and a large representation gathering presented him with a silver tea and coffee service. A fine musical programme and speeches and compliments and congratulations crowned a wonderful night in honour of our coach."[97]

Better still, in the packed, victorious MCG rooms in the moments after the 1930 triumph, Collingwood launched a testimonial fund for McHale. Fans were tipping in money as he lay in his bed in Brunswick. The club declared in its Annual Report: "We hope this testimonial will receive the support it richly deserves."[98]

But for a man who had never been motivated by money, and who was content to receive the same pay as the players, the fund that was coming his way would not mean as much as the four consecutive flags that had enshrined him and his team in football history. McHale was now a six-time premiership coach—one more than Jack Worrall. He was rising 48 and was at the peak of his powers. And he was determined that it wasn't going to end there.

---

96   ibid
97   Collingwood Annual Report, 1931
98   ibid

CHAPTER 10

Disappointment and Despair

1931-1934

Could there have been a better time than the early 1930s to be associated with the brand that had become Jock McHale—doyen of coaching, winner of four successive premierships, moulder of boys into men and one of the most famous names in what had become the most publicised game in the country?

While the Great Depression tested many of the social and economic institutions as never before, McHale's personal stocks had never been higher. He was not yet 50, he held a vice-like grip on the coaching position at all-conquering Collingwood for seemingly as long as his health allowed, and he retained his position at the Carlton Brewery at a time when any employment had a tenuous tenure. McHale was doing everything in his power to ensure some of the men he coached gained employment with the brewery.

Meanwhile, the Magpies were well placed to keep on winning. The average age of the 1930 Grand Final team was still only 25 years and 74 days, with many of the club's best players still in the prime of their football lives. Only a drifting of the motivation that had driven the club through an extraordinary period of success, and perhaps the competitive counterpunches from rival clubs, now also well coached, might stand between Collingwood and an almost inconceivable fifth successive premiership.

McHale had fully recovered from the health scare that kept him from the MCG in 1930. He was well enough to be back at work soon after the Grand Final and to be the centre of attention at a special premiership celebration in his honour at the Collingwood Town Hall less than a fortnight after the victory. His family would say that he rarely had a day off work in his time with Carlton Breweries.[1] The company even used McHale in a series of anti-prohibition newspaper advertisements in 1930 extolling the virtues of brewery employees who worked hard, kept themselves in a good condition yet who still didn't mind a glass or two of Carlton Draught.

The sad irony was that one of those featured in some of the ads was Harry Saunders. Saunders, nicknamed 'Sammy' after a prominent boxer of the time, had not played at Victoria Park since 1926, but he was well respected and liked by all. In late 1930 he took ill with pancreatitis, and died on December 9, aged 32. The Carlton Brewery closed down as a "mark of respect"[2] as the funeral procession passed the Bouverie Street factory. McHale was there, and the Magpies paid tribute to Saunders in their Annual Report, which came out the following March, saying: "His sudden death in the prime of his manhood was particularly felt by his comrades."[3]

McHale enjoyed a busy start to 1931. He was working to an unfamiliar deadline. He had been approached to assist with a new book. McHale, former Melbourne champion Albert Chadwick and leading Melbourne Grammar school teacher E.C.H. Taylor (not to be confused with leading sports journalist Percy Taylor) came together to

---

1   Interview with June McHale, 2009
2   *A Century of the Best*, Michael Roberts, Collingwood Football Club, 1991
3   Collingwood Annual Report, 1931

produce a book on football. The book, *The Australian Game of Football*, was released for the start for the 1931 season.

The timing was perfect. After all, two of the co-authors on this collaborative work had been associated with the previous five VFL premierships. As Taylor the educator would tell the sports writer Taylor 21 years later in *The Argus:* "We pooled ideas and learnt from each other. It was successful. Chadwick led the 1926 Melbourne team. Collingwood, under Jock, won the next four flags straight. Jock explained his training methods, with blind turns, kicking to position and so on. [He explained] The (Victoria Park) ground was marked in squares, and no player was supposed to get away from his area. They had to kick to a man."

The rationale behind the publication had nothing to do with money. This was stated in the editor's note, signed by Taylor, but it had McHale's stamp all over it. It said: "The margin between the cost of product and distribution and the price asked of the general public is so infinitesimal that we have waived any thought of money consideration. We are seeking no reward. All we ask is that you will share with us our love and enthusiasm for our great Australian Game; and that you who are players and you who are enthusiastic supporters will by your activities, your expressions and your influence, help to put the game beyond the prize and keep it wholesome."[4]

The book claimed: "So far as can be ascertained, no attempt has been made to publish a text book on the Australian Game of Football. It has long been felt that such a treatise would be welcomed by many adherents of the Australian code. We took courage and here we are."[5] That wasn't entirely correct. St Kilda's Dave McNamara had written a book, *Football*, in 1914 outlining his beliefs on the game, and in 1923, H.C.A.(Colden) Harrison, at the age of 86, had written his

---

4 *The Australian Game of Football*, J.F. McHale, A.E. Chadwick and E.C.H. Taylor, C.G. Hartley, 1931

5 ibid

memoirs, *The Story Of An Athlete*. As fate would have it, there was a fine photograph of a young Jock McHale in McNamara's publication.

Eighty years on, the book from McHale, Chadwick and Taylor remains a fine examination of Australian football at the start of the 1930s. On the cover was a sketch of Bruce Andrew ready to baulk and there were numerous photos and diagrams used throughout the text. Many of them were Collingwood players, clearly used on McHale's advice, even if one caption has labelled Harry Collier incorrectly as Albert.

McHale seems to have had more than just a responsibility for helping Taylor, who oversaw the "literary" side of the book. On the inside front there was a full-page advertisement for Victoria Bitter, with the catchphrase 'Radiant Health'. On the inside back there is one for T.W. Sherrin, "wholesale manufacturers of high-class sporting goods", which could well have been pre-arranged with Syd Sherrin, vice-president of the Collingwood Football Club. Inside, too, there was a half-page advertisement for 'Rosie' Dummett men's football boots, a business established by McHale's former Collingwood teammate, Alf Dummett. Dick Lee had worn Dummett boots, as did Gordon Coventry. In the advertisement McHale described them as "the best football boot ever made".[6] And there was also a small advertisement for Curtis Accessories—"Importers of Motor Accessories and Spare Parts"— which was the company of Collingwood president Harry Curtis.

But the content was more important than the consumer products on offer. Many future VFL footballers would gain some of their first lessons about the game through the 128 pages of this book; and it wasn't just the juniors who found benefits. In 1931, Charlie Dibbs was one of the best full-backs in the competition, and had played in four premierships. But he, and other members of *The Machine*, organised themselves to grab copies of the book, and he would treasure it for the rest of his life.

---

6   ibid

On the cover it promised to look at all aspects of the game: "Playing, training, coaching, field tactics, umpiring and rules, school football, personalities, physical culture, etc.". The president of the Victorian Football League, Dr W.C. (William) McClelland, wrote the foreword in which he commended the book to young players, "believing it will aid them to avoid the acquirements of bad habits and failing methods, and to Senior Players in the hope that it will help them to recognise their failings and adopt the indicated remedy".[7]

There were countless bits of advice and more than a few aphorisms, one-liners that seemed to be dotted around footy clubs in these years. The emphasis on physical preparation—the essence of McHale's playing career and the catalyst on which he based his coaching—was apparent from the start of the book. Early on, it stated: "An athletic career is the foundation of health, and if properly controlled will help to develop self reliance, self control, poise, and above all, character. And no other game can develop those qualities more than football."[8]

In the section marked 'Training', it shows that McHale believed that a five-week pre-season was essential for footballers. It stated: "You should allow yourself a period of five weeks consisting of two evenings a week, if possible, with an occasional run on a Saturday afternoon in a practice match, before the first premiership game. At the beginning of the season's training, a coach will no doubt find that he has 50 or 60 recruits to try out, as well as the old players to train."[9] McHale and Hughie Thomas (at opposite ends of Victoria Park) managed to turn some of them into key players.

McHale's parochial passion for recruiting locals from the heart of Collingwood shines. "As far as the players are concerned," he wrote, "we would always prefer them to be local men. You may, no doubt, secure a most accomplished footballer from another district, or even another State, but that importation cannot possibly be imbued with

---

7   ibid
8   ibid
9   ibid

the same love of the club, with the same desire to serve it through thick and thin, as the recruit who has born and bred in the district, and who has grown up with the club."[10] All this from a man born in Sydney, who spent most of his years living in Coburg and Brunswick, and who never lived in Collingwood at any stage of his life. In truth, McHale's district was confined to wherever Collingwood needed to be, his family home, and his workplace.

McHale preached that eight hours' sleep was critical for players, saying: "Remember an hour after midnight is worth two after that time" and "regular habits produce regular players." The coach was a creature of habit. In terms of advice on diet, it was stated that "well cooked plain food should hurt nobody" and "beer in moderation produces no harmful results, but spirits unless taken medicinally are injurious." The advice was to drink a glass of cold water on rising in the morning and before going to bed to clean the intestines. A cold bath each morning and one hot bath once a week was also offered up.

Not surprisingly, McHale's coaching thesis was replete in the chapter entitled "The Coach". It starts out with something that had become personal: "The position of the coach should be the most important office in any football organisation and yet how often it is abused? At the commencement of each season, one reads scores of advertisements in the daily newspapers—'Wanted, playing coach', and the fabulous sums that have been offered to induce good players to apply for the posts. It is perfectly obvious that many men accept these positions who have not had sufficient coaching experience, and it is also obvious that many clubs who engage these men are desirous of securing a reputed champion player than a football instructor."[11] McHale added, no doubt to stress the point: "Bear in mind, that the best footballers are not necessarily the most accomplished coaches."[12]

---

10   ibid
11   ibid
12   ibid

There was no false modesty when he described his ideal coach. It makes extraordinary reading all these years later, when the role of the coach as king has morphed into coach as leader of coaches. Whatever the time and place, the essence of the McHale message remains permanent. "In the first place he should be a man of strong personality, one who naturally takes the lead the moment he enters the team's dressingrooms, one whom everybody respects, and almost reveres, one who is able to extract the very best that is in his men, without apparent effort. Secondly, the coach must have a sound knowledge of the game ... a long experience on the playing field. Your pupil must be shown how to play' not merely 'told how to play'. Field tactics, the knowledge of which is only gained after years of practical experience, must be instilled into the team ... a hundred and one little matters crop up, which only experience can solve."

"Thirdly, a coach must be a trainer as well as a demonstrator and instructor. His object is to have his men fit on match days ... the most anxious time for a coach is when a player is 'at his top'. That is the period when his training should be lessened. Otherwise, staleness will appear, and appear very quickly ... the watchful eye of the coach should never miss little signs. Fourthly, a coach should exercise firmness. He must let it be clearly understood that he is the 'master of ceremonies' and that those under him must obey his instructions. He must direct practices and map out the plan of action for the Saturday matches, and what is most important; the players must abide by his decisions."

"Next, a coach should be tactful in his dealings with the players. Study the temperament of each man, for nearly everyone you meet is differently constituted. A good-natured slack lump can be driven and 'cursed', while a highly strung 'thoroughbred' can only be coached by persuasive means. To treat both men in the same way would be disastrous.

"Select honest men and stick to them; do not be too hasty in rejecting an enthusiastic recruit. It is remarkable that many of our best players at the present time have been rejects from other clubs. A young player who possesses that determination and 'devil', the type that will not shrink in the hottest attacks, who possesses the willpower to go through an almost impenetrable barrier, is the man worth teaching the finer points of the game. That is the kind of man you require in your side and is worth twenty 'fair weather champions'."

"And lastly, believe in yourself. You would never discourage your men, but at the same time you would never lie to them ... Believe that what you are doing is correct and convince your team, both by precept and example, that your methods are sound and common sense. If you can do this, you will succeed. Then you can turn a deaf ear to the ridicule hurled at you and the opposition to the path you have laid down for yourself. You will be criticised. One must expect that, but (do) not let it deter you."

The chapter finishes with the opening four lines from Rudyard Kipling's *If*

If you can keep your head when all about you
Are losing theirs and blaming it on you,
If you can trust yourself when all men doubt you,
But make allowance for their doubting, too

McHale's standing in the game also saw the makers of a football board game use his image and name. It is not known what year the game was first made, or how widespread its reach was. But it is likely to have been marketed in the 1930s. One of the 'Jock McHale Table Football' games is housed in the MCG's National Sports Museum alongside typed notes of McHale's commandments and his Collingwood hat-bands.

The Melbourne Cricket Club library's journal, *The Yorker*, described the McHale game as "Perhaps the most attractive Aussie footy board game ... it is housed in a box with an illustration of a footballer in kicking action. On the breast of a greenish guernsey is a large map of Australia, with the words 'Australian football'. The player is super-imposed over a yellow backdrop, which features a playing field with a set of goalposts, a grandstand, a scoreboard, and a crowded outer.

In an oval at the top right-hand corner of the box lid is a head and shoulders photograph of Jock McHale in his Collingwood guernsey. According to the blurb on the box this is "an interesting, thrilling, simple game for 1, 2, 4 or 6 players".[13]

The other thing that was happening for McHale in 1931, as he gathered his *Machine* and the usual array of fresh faces around him for another tilt at a title, was the testimonial that had first been started in the rooms after the previous year's Grand Final. In June *The Argus* reported that the "president and the committee of the Collingwood Football Club were anxious that the testimonial fund for the champion coach J. McHale, initiated last year, should now be closed. There are many lists out and it is hoped that these may soon be returned. A sum of £120 has already been subscribed and it is hoped that this will be doubled before the fund closes."[14] It would be. By year's end he had been presented with a cheque for £250 (including £100 donated by the club) with the president Harry Curtis saying: "The services rendered by Jock McHale to the Collingwood club eclipse those of any man who has ever been connected with any league club."[15] The following year's Annual Report would say: "His long connection with our great game has won him affection and fame that will never die."[16] A special gift was arranged for his wife, Violet.

To put this figure of £250 into the context of the time, it would almost been enough for McHale to buy a new Vauxhall car, if he had been so inclined. McHale never sought his licence. It was more than double the gatetakings for all but one of Collingwood's home games for the year. The average weekly wage at the time was only 4/9/-.[17]

They say in depressions that the best place to work is in a brewery, and McHale would retain his long-held position with the brewery, as would the rest of the crew—just—after union intervention.

---

13   *The Yorker*, Journal of the Melbourne Cricket Club library, Issue 39, 2009
14   *The Argus*, June 31, 1931
15   *Western Mail*, September 3, 1931
16   Collingwood Annual Report, 1932
17   *Australia Through Time*, Random House, 1999

In *The Amber Nectar*, a history of Australian Brewing by Keith Dunstan, it was stated: "Carlton and United was proud that not one member of the staff lost their job because of the depression, but they went close. CUB warned the unions that with reduced output it was not possible to run the brewery at a profit. Ten per cent of the staff would have to go. There was a mass meeting of the employees of the Liquor Trade Union. They agreed to accept an eight per cent reduction in salary and so the crisis was averted. Employees who earned 5/10/- or under took a salary drop of eight per cent. Those earning more dropped 10 per cent."[18] In 1929 there were 3,439,912 dozens of bottles produced. By 1932 it was down to 2,649,166.[19]

This agreement was more the exception than the rule. The heartache of unemployment was everywhere, but manifestly worse in the highly industrialised inner-city suburbs, with Collingwood one of the worst affected. There was struggle and strain, and often angst to go with it. In one instance in 1931 the eviction of a woman and her eight children from Alexandra Parade was followed by the attempted demolition of the house by a "militant organisation of unemployment".[20] It was reported that, "all the doors, except the front door, were torn from their hinges and broken ... all the windows in the house were smashed ... and later the wreckers returned and continued to knock down the interior brick walls with a crowbar until warned of the approach of a constable."[21] Collingwood's town clerk, Mr W. R. Butcher, tried to find new accommodation for the evicted family while trying to pacify the mob.

Mob rule prevailed, with Butcher saying later: "The crowd told me that my place will be the next to be wrecked."[22] It was against this backdrop that Collingwood lost one of its most important players

---

18   *The Amber Nectar, a celebration of beer and brewing in Australia,* Keith Dunstan, Viking O'Neil, 1987
19   ibid
20   *The Argus,* July 21, 1931
21   *Morning Bulletin,* Rockhampton, July 21, 1931
22   ibid

before the 1931 season. Albert Collier was already a champion. The 1930 Grand Final had been his 101st game; it had been his brother Harry's 100th. By the start of 1931 Albert was still only 21, and he had the 1929 Brownlow Medal, four premierships and a Copeland Trophy to his name. But he was out of work, along with 28 per cent of the population that year,[23] and, as Richard Stremski's *Kill For Collingwood* documented, the club and its secretary Frank Wraith had opted not to pay the sustenance payment of up to £3 per week for unemployed footballers (on top of the £3 per game). Collier was unhappy with this. When Tasmanian club Cananore offered him £9 per week as a playing-coach and an extra £7 per week as a labourer, he had little option but to take up the offer. (A five-room house in inner Melbourne cost about £550 at this time; he could have bought such a house after two seasons.) McHale had lost one of his best players, but the loss was in accordance with the club's philosophy that no player deserved more payment than any other player.

Collingwood stood firm on its decision to pay each of the players the same for games, but the loss of Collier meant new ways had to be sought to retain players. One was a greater commitment to obtain jobs for out-of-work players. McHale, Wraith and John Wren would assist in this regard in the future. Wraith also instituted a provident fund for players in 1931, which would provide "a fixed sum to every qualified player on his retirement, according to the number of years he had had with the club".[24]

For all the stresses besetting the community, football continued to drive passion, and Melburnians kept asking, as noted in a headline in *The Sporting Globe* on the eve of the 1931 season: "Will Collingwood keep

23   *Up Where Cazaly?*, Leonie Sandercock and Ian Turner, Granada, 1981
24   Collingwood Annual Report, 1932

it going this season?"[25] 'Jumbo' Sharland, the paper's leading football writer, was content to wonder, "that none of the other clubs have been able to break down the system that has made the Collingwood side famous. Surely if one plays against an opponent often enough he must learn sufficient about his play to be able at length to checkmate!"

Sharland showed that, even in that era, sportswriters liked to have two bob each way with their opinions. He added: "There is no doubt that Collingwood are fortunate in having the two Coventrys, and while coach Jim McHale is able to make his influence felt, they will always be a great side."[26] And then some more: "Who can take the steam out of Collingwood? Their organisation and team management are peerless. And what teamwork! Every man pulls his weight and assists his teammate. So do other sides do this? Of course, they don't. That is why Collingwood is always formidable. (But) I do not think the Collingwood team of 1930 was up to the standard of the Collingwood teams of 1927, 1928 and 1929. Syd Coventry, Gordon Coventry, Bob Makeham and Chesswas are not getting any younger and must slip up sooner or later. Will it be this season? I fancy it may be."

In the same article, Syd Coventry said: "Our fellows have had an extraordinary run of success. Our teamwork and determination have pulled us out of the fire often (perhaps a reference to McHale's "stoke the stove" expression) and the players have rallied around me magnificently at critical periods. But I am not optimistic as to believe that we can sit on top of the world all the time, though we'll try to stay there at all costs." Asked about Albert Collier's loss, he said: "Players of Collier's ability are rare, but while (Bob) Makeham, (Charlie) Dibbs, (Bill) Libbis, Harry Collier, (Harold) Rumney, George Clayden, Frank and Len Murphy, (Jack) Beveridge and (Harold) Chesswas are available, Collingwood will be all right."[27]

---

25 *The Sporting Globe*, April 29, 1931
26 ibid
27 ibid

The ongoing Richmond-Collingwood rivalry meant the Tigers had led a campaign to change the finals system. The Challenge system, which had helped Collingwood in its quests for past premierships, including 1929 and 1930 triumphs, was replaced in 1931 by the Page system, named after Richmond's League delegate Percy Page, who worked with a rising 21-year-old mathematician, Ken McIntyre, to introduce a new finals make-up that was mathematically sound, gave double chances to the top two teams on the table, and gave the League and the game's supporters comfort that whichever team won the premiership would have to earn it, by winning at least two finals. At the time *The Argus* noted: "The alteration in the system of deciding the premiership was due to Richmond delegates, who realised that Collingwood with its double chance as winners of the first round had had an advantage in recent years. It may be that before the semi-finals are reached, Richmond will realise that in grasping at the shadow, it has lost the substance."[28]

The new system guaranteed four weeks of finals, a boost for the finances of the League and the clubs. And it as argued that the system would maintain interest in the home and away season because of the battle for the first two places on the ladder and the accompanying double chance. First would play second for a place in the Grand Final, with the loser going to the preliminary final, against the winner of the first semi-final. For the first time, a team *had* to win two matches to win the flag, as against a possible one under the old system.

Season 1931 started in a familiar fashion, with few signs of trouble for Collingwood in the first three rounds. It was a tight clash with Geelong to start with, won by a late goal to Gordon Coventry sealing a five-point victory, but the next two victories over Hawthorn and

---

28   *The Argus*, May 23, 1931

South Melbourne were solid enough. Richmond, the team that had so often had to play second fiddle to Collingwood, narrowly edged out the Magpies by four points to bring about their first defeat of the season. Then, Carlton made it two losses in a row with a 16-point win. Four wins in a row followed for the Magpies.

Sharland gave another insight into McHale in July 1931, two days after Collingwood had lost to Essendon at Windy Hill by 24 points (a game in which president Harry Curtis—who always spoke to the players before the game—missed his first game in years due to influenza). Sharland said: "(McHale was) almost childlike in his enthusiasm. It cannot be said he is an enthusiastic loser. Few of us are, but Jim takes defeat very seriously, though he is not slow to give credit to the play of the other side, and to condemn the weaknesses in the play of his own men. Let it not be imagined that McHale is mild-mannered with his own team. His addresses at half-time are renowned."

By this time Sharland, a keen observer and a fine writer, had been watching McHale for many years, both during matches and during the week. "Much of the training is brought as near as possible to actual match play and McHale often umpires these sharp practice runs and remedies fault on the spot. Any weakness in the work of a player, such as poor marking and slow turning, are patched up. Blind turns, or in other words, turning the wrong way to get out of trouble, is an art that has made Collingwood players famous. McHale is a great believer in the long distance kick to position, and that is one of the reasons why Collingwood, when they get a run on, often paralyse opponents. He also believes in a player working hard for a short time at training, instead of allowing a man to take his time over his work spread out over an hour or more."[29]

"The coaching methods are so good and the general club organisation so excellent and the spirit of the players so fine that

---

29   *The Sporting Globe*, July 13, 1931

continuous failures are practically impossible. While McHale retains his health one can state he has a life-time job at Collingwood."[30] No one scanning *The Sporting Globe* that evening could have possibly understood just how close to the mark Sharland would be in the years to come; although keen football fans would no doubt have had the same mind, as McHale's record was so outstanding, and his connection to Collingwood untouchable.

McHale was realistic enough to know that Collingwood could not go on winning premierships year after year. He told Sharland: "I am not such a fool as to believe that we can always be at the top, but Collingwood have a loyal band of players and I fancy we will be knocking at the door. I realise the form of the teams is evening up, and continual success is harder to obtain, but we should have our share of it."[31]

Sharland wrote "(McHale always chose) a team of fighters ... players who are not only good winning footballers, but (who) know how to stick like 'glue' and fight every inch of the way when they are behind. And it is this 'never-say-die' spirit that has changed many matches from near certain defeats to brilliant victories. Too many stars of other teams crack up when they see they cannot get a run on, and instead of trying to remedy faults and fight to the bitter end, they throw the sponge and the play in their side goes to pieces."[32]

But for all this praise, Collingwood just seemed to be a bit more vulnerable throughout 1931. Syd Coventry missed a stretch of five games in the middle of the year with a "fractured jaw" before returning late. Bill Libbis had a lengthy suspension and suffered appendicitis, while Jack Beveridge fought injury issues. Coventry returned for the Round 15 match against Richmond, but Collingwood's vulnerability was on show again, as the Tigers wrested top spot off Geelong, leaving Collingwood vulnerable in fourth spot.

---

30   ibid
31   ibid
32   *The Sporting Globe*, June 10, 1931

Those doubting the Magpies had to do a rapid re-think when McHale's men thrashed a serious challenger in Carlton a week later. The margin was 61 points. *The Machine* that had spluttered for a part of the season suddenly seemed to find its gear. Collingwood kicked 20.15. Carlton could manage only 10.14. So comprehensive was the win that few walking away from Victoria Park that night would have given Carlton any chance of beating Collingwood should the two teams met again in the finals.

Incredibly, Collingwood scored 20.8 the following week only to lose, with St Kilda kicking 21.16. Gordon Coventry and Bill Mohr kicked 11 goals each in a classic display by two great forwards. Former Saints forward Dave McNamara said the shootout showed how it was almost too easy to score. McNamara told *The Sporting Globe*: "Just fancy, 41 goals in a match, it is ludicrous. The game may have been fine to watch, but the high scoring makes it look rather foolish. I wish I was in my prime today. I guarantee that if Gordon Coventry and other forwards can kick 10, 11, or 12 goals in a match, well I think Dick Lee, (Ernie) Sellars (St Kilda), Vin Gardiner (Carlton), myself and other forwards would score just as easily as they do."[33]

It was the first time the Saints had beaten the Magpies since 1925, and with one game left before the finals, the reigning premier was sitting uneasily in fourth position on percentage only, with a seventh straight finals series hinging on a big win over Melbourne. That much was never in doubt. Collingwood's 70-point win over Melbourne at a rain-swept Victoria Park saw the club hold onto fourth position (with a 12-6 winning record) by 13.8 per cent, finishing just one rung lower than Carlton, the Magpies' scheduled opponents in the first semi-final. It was 1-1 between the two sides for 1931, but Collingwood's most recent dominant win appeared to tilt the scales in its favour.

The Sporting Globe was equivocal: "Carlton or Collingwood? It will be a knockout affair. On recent form Collingwood must be strongly

---

33   *The Sporting Globe*, September 12, 1931

favoured. Wet or fine, the majority of opinion favours Collingwood, but we shall not see a Carlton debacle. Rather am I inclined to think that Carlton will play one of the best games of the season. Always a force to be reckoned with, Collingwood generally play at their best in finals. But they are not the side of previous years. A fine day should see a fine player in H. (Harry) Vallence (Carlton's full-forward) at his top."[34]

It was a remarkably prescient observation. As a coach, McHale would have been concerned with Carlton's capabilities and the form of Vallence, who was the VFL's leading goalkicker that year. Even in the four-year dominance of *The Machine*, the Blues had always been tough opponents. Bruce Andrew recalled: "We could beat Richmond. They could beat Carlton. But we always seemed to have trouble with Carlton."[35]

What McHale didn't know was that the Carlton players at the previous meeting of the teams had taken umbrage at some of things said to them on the field. Nineteen years later, Hugh Buggy revealed in *The Argus* that taunts from some Collingwood players during the Round 16 game had fired up the Carlton players. Buggy described the feelings: "There were hints, taunts, and asides, which suggested that some Carlton players had not fought out the game with the traditional Carlton tenacity. Rightly, or wrongly ... they got the idea that those disparaging comments had come first from Collingwood."[36]

At the heart of it was a man whom McHale had known for 20 years. Dan Minogue had first been a teammate and later a captain under McHale's coaching. But any sense of closeness was severed when Minogue had returned from the war and announced he wanted to join Richmond in 1919. His picture was still facing the wall inside a dusty cupboard somewhere inside the Collingwood rooms at Victoria Park. The pair had squared off as coaches in the 1920 Grand Final. They

---

34   ibid
35   Interview, Bruce Andrew, 1995
36   *The Argus*, May 6, 1950

were about to do it again in the 1931 first-semi-final, with Minogue now in his third season as Carlton's coach.

Buggy recalled: "For forceful and dynamic last-minute addresses to his teams, Minogue had no superior. And on that day he faced an audience more receptive perhaps than usual. They had to avenge their previous humiliating defeat, he said. They had to stop and smash the Magpie *Machine*. There was to be no flinching or fumbling. They had to stick to their Collingwood opponent like a shadow. They had to shatter that system by fearless, virile football. The Blues set out not to stop, but to tear to pieces, the Magpie *Machine* as if the life of every player depended upon success."[37]

Bruce Andrew would not have disagreed with Buggy's assessment, particularly the use of the words "tear to pieces". His recollection of the 1931 semi-final might have come 64 years later, but time had not healed the wounds suffered by the Collingwood players that day. He recalled: "That was a slaughter from the first bounce. At the first bounce every Collingwood player within range got flattened. That was the pattern for the day. We had at least three injuries from the first bounce, and two Collingwood players were unable to stay on the ground. It was tough."[38] Syd Coventry, one of the players who copped plenty of punishment, said at the end of his career: "We were on the wane ... and beginning to lose some of our toe. Carlton sailed in. We got a few men knocked. After that, we did everything wrong."[39]

'Old Boy', of *The Argus*, acknowledged Carlton's superiority on a day that it "smashed" *The Machine*, but he was left in no doubt that some of the tactics that Minogue's men adopted were questionable, saying they "went beyond the spirit of the laws of the game".[40] Carlton attacked the man and the ball with ferocity that left Collingwood in its wake, and there was little McHale or his men could do about it.

---

37   ibid
38   Interview with Bruce Andrew, 1995
39   Interview with Coventry brothers, The Herald, 1938
40   *The Argus*, September 21, 1931

After the initial barrage, the Blues put a score on the board when kicking against the wind in the first term, 3.1 to 1.7. But five goals to nil with the breeze in the second quarter effectively buried the match. "Could Collingwood produce their famous third quarter burst was the chief topic (of conversation in the crowd) at half-time?"[41] was the question from *The Sporting Globe*, but not even another trademark, fired-up McHale speech could combat what had taken place in the first hour. Collingwood had been battered almost into submission. Carlton was motivated not to just beat the Magpies, but to bury them.

The Sporting Globe reported that Minogue wanted to reduce "the Collingwood machine to a mere conglomeration of ineffective parts ... (and) make the mighty 'magpies' look like 'sparrows'." That's the way it was, too. Three goals each for the teams came in the third term, but the Blues kicked nine goals to one in the final quarter. In one of the best individual performances in a final, 'Soapy' Vallence kicked 11 goals for the game, taking advantage of an injury to Collingwood full-back Charlie Dibbs, who had to play on, despite being lame since the first term. McHale earned post-game criticism for leaving Dibbs too long in defence given his predicament, with *The Sporting Globe* declaring: "It was folly for Collingwood to leave Charlie Dibbs in goal. He was crippled and could hardly move but he pluckily stood to his job."[42] Carlton won the match by 88 points. Minogue described himself as "the proudest man in Melbourne"[43].

McHale hated excuses. But anyone who caught a glimpse inside the Collingwood dressing room that night would have seen part of the reason for the blowout, if not the defeat. It was described as "like a casualty clearing station" and a "pitiable" sight to see Dibbs (strained knee), Syd Coventry (thigh), Harry Collier (bruised thigh), Gordon Coventry (back), Frank Murphy (sprained groin), Harold Rumney (bruised thigh), Fred Froude (bruised thigh/sprained ankle), 'Tubby'

---

41   *The Sporting Globe*, September 19, 1931
42   ibid
43   *The Argus*, May 6, 1950

Edmonds (twisted ankle), Don Harris (torn thigh muscle) and George Tatham (sprained ankle) struggling about in the rooms. Bob Makeham finished the game "covered in bruises"[44].

Collingwood's great run was over; something it thought might last forever had come to an end. McHale knew he still had a strong side but others thought the club's playing list was in need of a make-over. *The Sporting Globe* commented: "Though Collingwood fought it out, the match proved conclusively that they have slipped, and will have to look to younger men to replace some of the old champions."[45] Albert Collier had been sorely missed. As fate would have it, on the day that Collingwood was being feasted on by Carlton, 22-year-old Collier had led Cananore to a premiership in the Tasmanian Football League. Carlton would be knocked out in a tight match in the preliminary final, with Richmond having won the first second semi-final in the game's history to play off for the fourth time in five seasons. The result was the same again for Richmond, with Geelong, the minor premier, winning by 20 points. Percy Page had driven the new system, which apparently favoured Richmond after that semi-final win, but the Tigers would have to wait another year to break through.

The objective at Victoria Park for 1932 was clear, as described in *The Argus*. It was, "the premiership regained".[46] As Collingwood prepared itself with a series of practice matches in early April—just a few weeks after the Sydney Harbour Bridge had been opened in the city of McHale's birth and around the time that Phar Lap's death in the United States had shocked a nation—*The Argus* observed of Collingwood: "The veterans are as keen as the juniors to rehabilitate

44   *The Argus*, September 21, 1931
45   *The Sporting Globe*, September 19, 1931
46   *The Argus*, April 4, 1932

themselves, but the committee is not prepared to stick to old men if there are juniors who warrant inclusion."[47]

There was a push to change the out-of-bounds rule, in place since 1925, provided that a free kick against the team which touched it last before it went out of play. Collingwood, and in particular McHale, were "hostile",[48] and little wonder. The Magpies had exploited the rule for their own benefit, and it formed part of McHale's game plan of direct, long football up the middle of the ground. Before the start of the season, the Collingwood coach said: "I am definitely opposed to a return to the old rule. The unsightly jostling of the old rucks was an eyesore, and many players who in the past were selected to do what was mildly called shepherding were in fact included for the sole purpose of stopping a star player of the other side. Let us encourage the clean, fast and skilled player by obliterating the undesirable. The old play encouraged 'neutral play' that is the wilful wasting of time and opportunities by forcing the ball out of bounds."[49]

He said: "Within recent years we have seen some wonderful and thrilling recoveries by losing teams that have been as many as eight goals down at the three-quarter time bell. This could not have happened had the old law been in force, as the leading team would concentrate on boundary play and prevent that spectacular up and down play. Listen to the cheers of the crowd and you will hear the deep-throated roar when the ball is moving quickly, an unconscious expression of opinion that the present rule is the better.

"In my experiences at Collingwood ... I have made a close study of our great game and its players in all conditions, and my desire is to see the game kept fast and open, and unduly rough play eliminated. Let us teach players to turn both ways, kick with either foot, and handball with either hand. My advice to all players, young and old, of this wonderful game of ours is to study all the finer points of play,

---

47   ibid
48   ibid
49   *The Mercury*, March 31, 1932

kicking, running, passing and baulking. Then when you have finished your playing career, let it be said that you were a footballer, and not a shepherder or a bullocker.

"The Collingwood committee, consisting of men who total, combined, 103 years' playing under the old rule, and several experienced players of the present rule, are unanimously against the proposed change. To the men who are privileged to control our great game, we at Collingwood say, 'Improve a rule where possible, but do not take a backward step. Let the grounds be of standard size; introduce the flick pass, and reduce the teams to 15 men (on the field). We shall then see what I imagine is ideal football'."[50] Collingwood won the battle—for now. The rule would be modified, which gave the umpires the chance to call for a throw-in in certain circumstances, particularly when doubt existed over who was the last to touch the ball but not changed outright just yet.

For a time, it looked as if *The Machine* was clicking back into gear. As the Annual Report would say of 1932: "When the season opened a general consensus of opinion predicted a very lean period for the Magpies, the chief reason given, being that some of the regular players had passed the stage of practical football, but to the astonishment of these critics your team gave a convincing answer by refusing to be displaced from the coveted position among the leaders."[51] The club won three of its first five games—losing to reigning premiers Geelong, and its 1931 conquerors, Carlton.

Collingwood—the club and the community—was still hurting financially in 1932. Nationally, unemployment was sitting around the 30 per cent mark, and things had not improved since ousted Prime Minister Jim Scullin—who had lost at the December 1931 election to Joe Lyons—had stated the previous year: "Australia is facing the gravest financial crisis in its history."[52] In such times, community

---

50   ibid
51   Collingwood Annual Report, 1933
52   *Australia Through Time*, Random House, 1999

was important to Collingwood, the football club. In 1932 the Magpies introduced a system whereby sustenance workers—or 'sussos' as they were called—were permitted to gain admittance to the games for free. Such was the popularity of the gesture that for a time it was restricted to Collingwood locals only. The VFL would follow suit the following year with an across-the-board benefit. And, in 1934, the Magpies would institute school football as curtain-raisers at Victoria Park, where a number of star recruits would get their run on the famous ground.

There was a testing time for the Collingwood players leading into the Round 5 clash with Carlton at Princes Park. Due to the worsening economic situation, the club's secretary, Frank Wraith, deemed it necessary to review the finances, and rumours had reached the players before the game that they were about to have their wages cut.

There was a "heavy argument"[53] in the rooms before Bruce Andrew was dispatched as a players' representative to speak with Wraith and the treasurer Bob Rush. He reported back to the players that the club had no choice but to cut wages. In the end, the Magpies decided that they had to play—even though they were to be late out on the field— and, as *Kill For Collingwood* documented, they ran out with captain Syd Coventry's words ringing in their ears: "Let's go out and kill the bastards."[54] Unfortunately, the Magpies couldn't manage to do that. They lost by 20 points.

It became a seminal moment for McHale. When he was a playing-coach, he would receive double pay for the two roles. When he retired from the game, and remained on as coach, he took home a wage of approximately 10 shillings more than his players. But when the players agreed to accept the cut wages in 1932, McHale also took a 10 shillings cut. When the players' wages went back to £3 midway

---

53 *Frank Wraith, A Magpie Misjudged*, Gordon Carlyon, Collingwood Football Club, 2003

54 *Kill For Collingwood*, Richard Stremski, Allen and Unwin, 1986

through the next season, the coach personally decided he wanted to receive the same. *Kill For Collingwood* described it as "a remarkable sacrifice for a frugal man who could have written his own ticket at any other club in Australia."[55]

Seven successive wins after the loss to the Blues showed there was little lingering issue in the playing group in regard to the cut in wages. The run saw the club in third position, just behind South Melbourne (who had recruited a number of quality players from interstate) and Carlton. But two losses in the second half of the season to the same teams that had beaten then in the first half, Geelong and Carlton, had a few people dismissing the Magpies as premiership contenders. Still, McHale had guided the club to yet another finals series, setting up a first semi-final clash with South Melbourne at the MCG.

Eight goals to one in the first term set the scene for Collingwood's 26-point win over South Melbourne. It was a comprehensive performance, but some still pointed out that South had outscored Collingwood by 11 goals to nine in the remaining three quarters. *The Argus* noted: "Collingwood must be congratulated on a very fine performance, and one which gave satisfaction to its supporters, and caused many to change their opinions regarding their premiership prospects. The pennant does not seem still a certainly for Richmond or Carlton."[56] Clearly when South Melbourne went to the Collingwood rooms to congratulate the players after the game, they commended that "the combined experience and skill of J. McHale (as coach) and Syd Coventry (as captain) had been too much for South".[57]

Carlton, the minor premier, had lost the second-semi to Richmond in a high scoring game at the MCG, setting up a preliminary final against Collingwood. On the last training night before the preliminary final against Carlton—and Minogue—it was said of Collingwood:

---

55   ibid. In early 1933 the club sought to reduce wages again by 10 shillings. One player, four-time premiership player Bill Libbis, refused to accept the demand, and was soon cleared to Melbourne
56   *The Argus*, September 10, 1932
57   ibid

"Officials of the club, while appreciating the fact that Carlton was likely to provide them with stern opposition on Saturday, were confident of victory. Some of the leading players were experienced in the fight for the premiership, but still had youth on their side."[58] Sadly, the optimism reported by *The Argus* would be misplaced.

In a match that mirrored the final of 12 months earlier, Carlton produced yet another "rout" of Collingwood, winning by 75 points. This time the damage was done in a devastating third term. At half-time the Magpies trailed by just 14 points, with Collingwood's renowned third quarter burst to come. Instead, it was the Blues who dominated, kicking 10.7 to 3.1 in the third term to change the game. Again, it was Vallence who did the damage, matching his performance from a year earlier to kick another 11 goals in a final, an amazing individual effort. The Magpies were non-plussed at the extent of the loss, as noted in the club's Annual Report: "During the season, your team produced some wonderful exhibitions of football, and by their decisive win in the semi-final against South Melbourne, gave supporters every encouragement to anticipate yet another pennant; but practically the same side gave a very different display against Carlton, and we had to once again acknowledge defeat at the hands of our old rivals."[59]

McHale's sense of fairness and fair play—and that of all Australians—was about to be tested in a different sporting sphere. On the last day of 1932, he and more than 36,000 Melburnians attended the MCG for the second day of the Second Test between Australia and England. The tour would remembered infamously as the 'Bodyline' series where English captain Douglas Jardine came up with a controversial plan to counter the world's best batsman, 24-year-old Don Bradman, instructing his fast bowlers to bowl repeatedly at the body with a close-in leg side field in support. If McHale had come a day earlier he would have seen Bradman fall for a duck first ball to

---

58   *The Argus*, September 23, 1932
59   Collingwood Annual Report, 1933

Bill Bowes in one of the greatest shocks encountered by a crowd at the MCG. As it was, on day two, McHale got to see the Australians resume at 7-193 before Harold Larwood sent off the Australian tail for an innings total of 224, and then watched Bill O'Reilly stun the English batsmen by taking 5-63 with some fine leg-spin as the visitors collapsed for 169. Australia would go on to win, its only victory of a summer that would boil over in extraordinary circumstances in the Third Test in Adelaide a fortnight later.

The Sun News-Pictorial recorded McHale's visit to the cricket: "It seems incongruous to meet Mr Jock McHale, veteran coach of Collingwood, in the outer ground at the Test match on Saturday. But Mr McHale is by no means a one-sport man. In fact, until 1905, he played with a junior (cricket) team at Coburg, and took a respectable number of wickets in addition to building up a comely batting average. But football was always his chief love and when he found himself a permanent member of the Collingwood league team, he decided to abandon his ambitions of test selection."[60]

In 1933 there were six new coaches appointed to the 12 VFL clubs. Arthur Coghlan took over at Geelong, Arthur Rademacher at Hawthorn, 'Checker' Hughes at Melbourne, Billy Schmidt at Richmond, Colin Deane at St Kilda, and Jack Bisset at South Melbourne. The redoubtable McHale was fronting up for his 22nd season, and was intent on Collingwood rebuilding itself to a position of prominence again. *The Herald* commented in late March: "An indication of the keen scouting by Collingwood this season is furnished by the fact that there are 80 recruits from all parts of Victoria at the moment (trying out). They are discarding smaller and lighter players and have a number of promising big players around. Collingwood's

---

gradual decline during the last two seasons is causing the committee some concern. The selectors realise that those stalwarts of other days cannot go on forever and must be replaced. The chief weakness has been the lack of big men and the partial return to the old 'throw-in' rule has made this more manifest."[61]

The best "recruit" was not among the 80, but was Albert Collier, who had returned to Melbourne to much goodwill from the faithful. *The Herald* said of his return: "Some of the old Collingwood enthusiasm prevailed at training during the week. Jock McHale was in charge ... the return of Albert Collier has given a delight to the club's big army of supporters and the old players welcome him with open arms. A big, heavy man, he is very active for his weight and his movements on the field compelled the admiration of his former mates. Collingwood feel invigorated by the return of Albert, who is a jovial fellow in the training room, while on the field he is black and white to the backbone."[62]

Importantly, Collingwood was not going to lose Collier again. He was appointed as a painter at the Carlton Brewery. This time it is believed that it was not Jock McHale who got him the job, but John Wren who approached the general manager of the brewery after Frank Wraith asked him to intervene, and a position was found for the Collingwood champion.

The career of Jack Regan was about to take great strides. He had first played in 1930, and was classified as a forward for the first few years of his career. His one game at full-back in 1930 saw him have 10 goals kicked on him. But after being selected to play for Victoria as a forward in 1933, he actually played in defence in the state game. His form was so good in that match that McHale put him to the backline permanently in late 1933. As a forward he had struggled, and on one occasion early in his career when he missed a late goal that cost Collingwood victory, he apologised to "Mr McHale". Football folklore

---

61   *The Herald,* March 29, 1933
62   *The Herald,* March 18, 1933

has it that the coach told him: "Go and throw yourself in the bloody Yarra."[63] Regan would develop into a full-back of extraordinary ability.

Over the next few years Collingwood would bring through a number of recruits who would be the cornerstone of the efforts to rebuild a team to resemble *The Machine*. In 1933 Marcus Whelan, Alby Pannam, Jack Carmody, Keith Fraser, and Leo Morgan would play their first games; in 1934 it would Phonse Kyne, Vin Doherty, Jack Knight and Lou Riley; in 1935 it would be a kid called Ron Todd, as well as Bervin Woods, Keith Stackpole, Pat Fricker and Marcus Boyall.

Another player to represent Collingwood for the first time in 1933 was Norm Le Brun. Having already played with South Melbourne and Essendon, and to play with Carlton in the future, Le Brun played 19 games in a two-year period at Victoria Park. Of all the Collingwood players to have represented the club in Jock McHale's time, Le Brun is believed to have been the only one of indigenous background. The indigenous hero, Doug Nicholls, a star with Fitzroy (from 1932-37) and later to become Governor of South Australia, is said to have trained briefly with Collingwood in 1929 before returning to Northcote.

Gordon Carlyon, who would later become a leading and long-serving administrator with Collingwood, would recall: "Jock used to say to me not to try and recruit young Aboriginal boys. He felt it would not do anyone any good to take them away from their homes in the Northern Territory and places like that where they had a lot of freedom and then bring them to Melbourne. It made a lot of sense because in those days there weren't (many) aeroplanes. They couldn't just go home for the weekend if they got homesick. That's one of the reasons why for so long Collingwood didn't have any Aboriginal footballers, though not a lot of clubs did in those days."[64] McHale can hardly be condemned

---

63   A Century of the Best, Michael Roberts, Collingwood Football Club, 1991
64   *The 500 Club, Footy's Greatest Coaches*, Kevin Sheedy with Warwick Hadfield, News Custom Publishing, 2004

for this by applying late 20th and early 21st century morality to what took place in the first 50 years of the competition. The sad reality was that there are only six known indigenous players to represent VFL clubs before the start of the Second World War, a conflict in which Le Brun would tragically be killed.

If the team was changing, then McHale's methods weren't. A letter to *The Herald* by a reader highlighted the extent to which McHale insisted his players—however old or young they may be—stick to their positions during games and training. The epistle came from *Enthusiast, from East Malvern*. It read: "Sir, whenever a League match is played at the Collingwood Football Ground, it is noticed that a broad white line is drawn down the middle of the ground connecting each goal base. Perhaps this line forms part of the Collingwood's team's system or tactics directing the play to goal by the shortest method. On no other ground is such a line drawn. I have frequently heard people comment on this matter and no doubt an explanation through your columns will be of interest to the fans."[65]

The answer came: "The idea originated in the mind of the club coach (Mr J. McHale) and was adopted some years ago as a means of defining the positions of certain players. Altogether there are three white lines painted on the ground—one down the centre from goal to goal, and one at each end of the field running across the half-back and half-forward lines. The centre line serves a useful purpose in keeping the wingmen on the flanks and they are instructed not to come within five yards of it. Similarly, the flank men in other positions know that when they are on or close to the line they are out of position. The cross line is put down for the purpose of conveying to the full and pocket players that once they are outside of it, they have run too far from their base. There is no doubt the system has enabled Collingwood to play the open style of game and has assisted them in finding the shortest way to goal."[66]

---

65   *The Herald*, June 20, 1933
66   ibid

But a football match that didn't involve Collingwood impacted heavily on McHale and his family around this time. His son, John (often known as Jack in those days) had been showing a bit of ability with a team connected to North Melbourne Christian Brothers' College, where he had gone to school. His mother, Violet, attended most of his matches because his father was coaching Collingwood. John, who would later become known as Jock jnr, recalled many years later: "I (first) went to a school in Brunswick and I was nicknamed 'Macca' McHale. When I went to North Melbourne College, I was called 'Young Jock'. He (Jock Sr.) took a bit of an interest in my football at the time, but it was more my mother who went to every game. When it sort of looked like I would be a footballer, he (Jock snr) virtually insisted that I go to the amateurs. North Christian Brothers had started an amateur team in D Grade, and that's where I had my bad luck."[67]

McHale's bad luck came in the form of a horrific football injury. An incident in a game ended with John McHale receiving a ruptured bowel and other internal injuries. He recalled: "A fellow ran in and kicked me in the tummy, and I got a ruptured bowel. I was hospitalised for quite a long while."[68] His future wife, June, whose brother was one of his best mates, would say: "My Jock was only 17 or 18 when he had that. He was at a private hospital out in Brunswick for nearly 12 months. He copped a knock to his spleen and got a ruptured bowel. I can always remember that a Dr Roach, who was an eminent surgeon in Melbourne, did some 'first-ever' surgery on him. My Jock was very precious to his parents, especially after what had happened. He didn't go to the war (the Second World War) as a result of that."[69]

The 1933 season was an inconsistent one for Collingwood. The first six weeks went win-loss, win-loss, win-loss, and three consecutive losses late in the season made a finals appearance out of the question.

---

67   Interview with Jock McHale jnr, 1999
68   ibid
69   Interview with June McHale, 2009

The Magpies used 39 players that year as they searched for long-term replacements to the champions of the past. The 1934 Annual Report described change thus: "The all-important policy of re-organisation and rebuilding had to be carefully and systematically handled."[70] But for the first time since 1924, Collingwood and McHale were watching on in the finals. They finished sixth in 1933, a game and percentage out of the four, despite winning the last three games.

The result that hurt the most was the six-point loss to South Melbourne in Round 14. After leading at one stage by 42 points, Collingwood could muster only four goals after half-time. The finish was not without some controversy. *The Herald* said: "Once again the match was won and lost through a field umpire not having heard the first sounds of the bell denoting the end of the game. The scores were level and the ball was coming into the air to (Terry) Brain (South Melbourne) when the first sound of the timekeeper's bell, which is in the grandstand at the other end of the ground, was heard in the press box. P. Ellingsen, the field umpire, apparently did not hear the bell until after Brain had marked. Brain ... scored the winning goal. Clearly, Collingwood was deprived the honour of sharing the points."[71] One letter writer to *The Herald*, J. Keating, of Brunswick (where McHale lived) made a call for an "electric bell or some shrill sounding device" to alert umpires of the end of the game.[72]

Syd Coventry intended to retire at the end of the 1933 season, but was convinced to play on to chase "the Centenary premiership" in 1934 (to mark the first 100 years of permanent settlement in Victoria) and to be there when his brother Gordon reached 1000 goals. Gordon reached the four figures with four goals in the drawn game against

---

70   Collingwood Annual Report, 1934
71   *The Herald*, July 29, 1933
72   ibid

Geelong in Round 5 at Corio Oval, saying, in something of an understatement: "Well, I don't feel any different, but it is a grand thing to have done it." Only Richmond's Jack Titus, who kicked 970 goals from 1926 to 1943, came anywhere close to Coventry's numbers in this era. The milestone was but one high point of Collingwood's year; after losing to South Melbourne in Round 1, the Magpies did not lose another game until they met South the next time around in Round 12.

The most controversial game of the season came in Round 10 when the already inflamed relationship with Carlton went from bad, to much, much worse. It would bring about one of the most violent matches ever played at Victoria Park, with both sides blaming each other for the fracas. Perhaps the seeds of the trouble had been late sprouting after the 1931 first-semi-final when the Blues gave the Magpies a physical battering. The first half was full of vim and vigour, some of it fair, most of it not. It was only going to deteriorate.

In the third quarter Syd Coventry gave Gordon Mackie a whack on the neck. Mackie's response was brutal. He belted the Collingwood captain to the point of unconsciousness, inflicting serious facial injuries, with Coventry saying the following day: "It's all a blank to me. I got a knock, but where and how I got it, I cannot say."[73] Mackie's attack on Coventry—whose injury was later confirmed as a fractured skull—incensed the Collingwood players, including his normally taciturn brother Gordon, who ran from one end of the ground to the other to remonstrate with the perpetrator. Almost all of the players on the field were involved. Carlton blamed Collingwood for the brawl, and the Magpies blamed the Blues. As it turned out, three charges came out of the match—all Carlton players (all of them suspended)—and this infuriated the Blues, who sought to gain a VFL investigation into certain Collingwood players. It didn't help, as all that the VFL's only action did was to suspend the umpires who had provided a clean sheet for Collingwood.

---

73   *The Argus*, July 16, 1934

Bruce Andrew claimed on radio that week that Carlton had tried to counter the Collingwood *Machine* in that famous 1931 final by using "shock tactics". A letter in *The Herald*, from a clearly committed reader, letter-writer and Collingwood observer, John Keating, from Brunswick denounced Andrew's comments, saying the Magpies weren't as innocent as had been made out. He wrote: "It is absurd for Mr Andrew to claim that Carlton's robust play beat Collingwood in 1931. Collingwood were on the wane that season and finished in fourth place. It is interesting to note that a book on football, one of the authors of which was the Collingwood coach (Mr J. McHale), made mention of the grand final between Collingwood and Geelong in 1930. Mr McHale's book stated that Geelong never recovered from Collingwood's "shock tactics. Evidently Collingwood knew something about "shock tactics" before they met Carlton in 1931."[74]

Away from football, few people knew of the very private battle that the McHale family was enduring through much of 1934. It would change all of their lives—forever. In keeping with their fiercely private natures, and with their deep religious faith, they didn't want to talk about it to anyone either. This was a battle they would go through alone. The McHales were living at 112 Victoria Street, West Brunswick at the time. Three days after Collingwood's win over Essendon at Windy Hill in Round 13, Jock and Violet's beloved 17-year-old daughter Jean passed away at St Elmo's Private Hospital in Moreland Road, West Brunswick. Nothing would ever be the same for Jock again.

Jean had been fighting cerebrospinal meningitis for two months. She also had internal hydrocephalus (a build-up of fluid on the brain), which was described on her death certificate as "indefinite". The heart failure that followed was "sudden". Dr E.W. Sutcliffe had attended

---

74   *The Herald*, July 18, 1934

her that day, but there was nothing he could do. Like her brother before her (Frankie) and another child, who was perhaps stillborn as no records exist (possibly known as Michael),[75] Jean had lived an inadequately brief life, and her passing had devastated Jock, Violet and Jock jnr, who was only 19 years of age, and had survived a close call himself. A service was held for her at St Ambrose's—where she, Frankie and Jock jnr had been christened—the following day, and she was buried with the brother she had barely known in a single grave at Coburg Cemetery.

The death notice on the front page of *The Argus* could not adequately express the pain that Jock and Violet were going through again. It read: "On August 7, at a private hospital, Moreland, Mary Jean, beloved only daughter of James and Violet McHale, of 112 Victoria Street, West Brunswick, most affectionate sister of Frankie (deceased) and Jack. Aged 17. (Interred privately on 8th August. R.I.P.)"

Jean McHale died on a Tuesday. McHale had been expected at training that night, but he never arrived, and when the news of her passing came through to Victoria Park, the club decided to abandon the session as a mark of respect. It's not known whether Jock made it to training on the Thursday night, but there was a gap in the season for a state match on the weekend, so McHale was not required on a match day until August 18, when the Magpies were scheduled to meet Hawthorn.

But what has been uncovered in the research for this book is the first page of a letter of condolence typed by Bob Rush to Jock McHale a day after Jean's death. It reads:

"Dear Jim,

Needless to write there was quite a gloom over the room last night, when the President announced the sad news of the great trouble which had stricken your home, and after the members stood in silence for a few minutes, I was directed to convey to you and your poor wife the very sincere sympathy of all your Clubmates.

---

75   Interview with June McHale, 2009

We all know the love and affection you have for your family and our hearts go out to you in your grief.

God has bestowed on the Irish race such soft affectionate natures that the loss of those nearest and dearest would simply be unbearable had He not blessed them with a religion which brings such comfort in the hour of trial, and which teaches that Death should have no terrors but is merely the passing of the soul from the Church Militant to the Church Triumphant. Your little saint has surely passed into the care of our holy Mother, and it could be almost selfish to wish her back to face the trials and temptations of this world."

That is all that remains of the letter. It ends abruptly, just as Jean's life did, and the second part to it has been lost over time. But what it does show is how the club must have rallied around their coach in the most distressing time of his life. To lose a son, perhaps two of them, must have terrible. To go through it again a number of years later, and to lose a daughter he doted on, must surely have been unbearable.

Carlyon would say: "You could always get a tear in his eye if you mentioned his daughter. He was loyal. Very loyal."[76]

June McHale tells of a heartbreaking ritual that McHale would follow assiduously, to almost the time of his death 19 years later. She recalled: "He was tremendously fond of her (Jean). Old Jock wore a black tie to Jean's funeral. He never wore any other tie but a black one after that. And every Sunday—without fail—he and Violet would go to the cemetery to visit the grave. My Jock—young Jock—would have to drive them there because old Jock never had his licence."[77]

Football must have seemed more than a little superfluous to McHale in those first few weeks after his daughter's death. A minor relief would come 11 days after Jean's death, in Collingwood's next home and away match: The Magpies kicked their highest score of the year (23.22) on August 18 to thrash Hawthorn by 87 points at Victoria Park. Gordon Coventry kicked 14 goals in that game, and 20-year-old

---

76   *The 500 Club, Footy's Greatest Coaches*, Kevin Sheedy with Warwick Hadfield, News Custom Publishing, 2004
77   Interview with June McHale, 2009

Marcus Whelan, in only his 21st game, kicked five. It was the game in which Syd Coventry returned from his fractured skull, with the captain perhaps playing a little earlier than expected to honour his coach. He would cop another concussion and end up in hospital. That win kept Collingwood equal top with Geelong.

But successive losses to Richmond and Geelong followed, which left the team vulnerable again. A five-point win over Fitzroy and an 88-point victory over North Melbourne closed out the season, and left Collingwood set to meet South Melbourne in the cutthroat first semi-final. Collingwood dominated the opening term, kicking five goals to one, to open a four goal lead. But South Melbourne hit back to cut the deficit to only four points at the half-time break. Then, scores were locked level at the last change.

With five minutes until the final bell, it appeared as if Collingwood was safe. Syd Coventry would tell *The Herald* on the Monday following the game: "I thought we were safe. I had that feeling all through the second half. But our run of behinds in the third quarter was one of those things that no one could control. It would not happen again in perhaps 100 matches."[78] His brother Gordon was one of the worst culprits, kicking 5.8, plus out of bounds once and shots which fell short on two occasions. Gordon told *The Herald*: "On Saturday, I was so disappointed that I was in bed by 7pm. It seems that I had struck one of those periods for which there is no remedy."[79]

Collingwood had 30 scoring shots to 23—and scored 9.21 (75) to 11.12 (78). In this 227th and last game Syd Coventry had the ball in his hands when the bell rang, but his shot after full-time did not make the distance. Collingwood's season was over.

For McHale, with the season over six weeks after the death of his daughter, it was a time for reflection. There were two ways he could have gone after the death of his daughter. It could well have signalled the end of his coaching career, and, given his record and his years of

---

78   *The Herald*, September 21, 1934
79   ibid

service, no one would have blamed him for doing so. If he had resigned there and then, he would still have gone down in the history books as one of the most remarkable and successful coaches of all time. That he didn't shows how much the club meant to him. Instead, he did what he had always done: immersed himself in his job, and coached to the best of his ability. He was determined to finish what he and the selectors had started out trying to do a few years earlier: the time had come to remodel the *The Machine*.

CHAPTER 11

Remodelling The Machine

1935-1939

J
ock McHale's well-worn and oft-expressed belief was that the team was infinitely more important than any individual. In many ways, it was hard to argue with this philosophy in the context of Collingwood's history. Time and again, the Magpies, under McHale's firm hand, had been able to re-shape their team and their on-field leadership while more often than not challenging for the flag. But, in the lead-up to the 1935 VFL season, this capacity of Collingwood to reinvent itself was about to be seriously tested by a departure as critical as any other in the history of the football club.

It wasn't McHale who was thinking of leaving, though no one would have blamed him if he had, as he and Violet tried to rebuild their lives after the death of their daughter, Jean. During these difficult times, Jock jnr would often take his mother to the movies on training nights to keep her mind busy on the nights when her husband would be out. Despite the serious injury suffered two years earlier, Jock jnr harboured an ambition to play football again—but he didn't tell his father, at least for the moment.

The thing that was going to sorely test Collingwood heading into 1935 was the retirement of Syd Coventry, one of the club's greatest players and perhaps its best captain. There were many people sceptical about whether the Magpies could challenge for the premiership without their champion skipper. Four flags came under his on-field stewardship, and he helped the team ride through some inordinately tough moments, including two potential strikes, in 1928 and 1932, that he almost single-handedly averted.

Coventry could not go on forever as a player. He had originally decided to retire after the 1933 season, but was coaxed back by a club desperate to retain his leadership and his labour in the heat of battle. The 1934 season had been difficult for Coventry. He had twice been affected by serious head knocks; the result of one of those knocks was a fractured skull, which he suffered in the infamous brawl with Carlton. He was rising 36 heading into 1935, and he knew his playing years were at an end.

McHale was in no doubt the club could still find a way without Coventry, while others around the club were fatalistic about it. Some of those who loathed the club—a feeling that was not uncommon even in these early years—rejoiced in it.

Reflecting on this time, McHale told *The Sporting Globe* on the eve of the 1936 season: "When Syd Coventry, champion that he was, and a great personal friend of mine, retired as a Collingwood footballer after the 1934 season, quite a wail went up from the pessimists. 'Without Coventry, Collingwood will no longer be a force', they chanted in a dirge; 'they'll go to pieces—it's the end of them'. These cheerful folk even showered us with letters, many anonymous, gloating or lamenting, according to their club sympathies, that the proud Magpies would soon be humbled in the dust—or the mud."[1]

It wasn't just Coventry who had reached the end. A few other members of *The Machine* moved on either during 1934 or at the end

---

1   *The Sporting Globe*, April 18, 1936

of that season. Frank Murphy and Jack Beveridge took coaching job offers in Perth. 'Tubby' Edmonds had a run-in with secretary Frank Wraith during the 1934 season in which he took issue with Wraith's questioning of how hard some players had worked in a game. Edmonds left for Richmond almost immediately and ended up being the reserve in its 1934 premiership side. Bruce Andrew, vice-president of the club, had played a handful of games in 1934, including the semi-final against South Melbourne, but he retired in 1935 at the age of 27.

McHale and his selection committee had started their policy of renewal and regeneration in 1933. In hindsight, the coach would refer to that season as the tipping point for the successes that were to come.[2] The members of *The Machine* were getting older. Some were in the process of retiring or moving elsewhere to capitalise on their experiences with the most famous club in Australia, and its legendary coach. New players were tried. Some of them suited the coach's requirements; others were moved on. There was no shortage of teenagers willing to try out.

By 1935 some of these young players had gained a foothold in the senior team. Players such as Jack Ross (first game in 1931), Marcus Whelan, Alby Pannam, Jack Carmody, Keith Fraser, Leo Morgan (1933), Phonse Kyne, Vin Doherty, Jack Knight and Lou Riley (1934) began to make serious impressions. Others who had been only bit players during *The Machine* years became important players by the mid-1930s. Those included the great Jack Regan, who took time to find his feet as a young forward but would do so spectacularly in defence, and Fred Froude.

McHale would continue to foster first-year players in 1935. *The Sporting Globe* explained in April 1935: "The type of recruit on offer is so fine that (Collingwood) officials are finding it difficult to make up their minds. Frank Wraith said: 'Even players of some experience are being hard-pressed by the new blood."[3] Five players

2   ibid
3   *The Sporting Globe*, April 22, 1935

of the club's nine debutants in 1935 would go on to become key players in the coming years: Ron Todd, Bervin Woods, Keith Stackpole, Marcus Boyall and Pat Fricker.

The first imperative was to find a replacement captain. Fortunately, just as was the case in 1927 when Syd Coventry replaced Charlie Tyson, McHale was sure there was a man waiting in the wings who embodied the same traditions as did Coventry. Harry Collier, who had been born just a stab-pass from Victoria Park, and who had sold *Football Records* there as a kid, was the logical choice. He might have been about nine centimetres shorter than Coventry, but lacked nothing in toughness or leadership. His brother, Albert, even tougher and just as talented, was chosen as vice-captain, and the pair set about providing the inspiration and protection for a core of young Collingwood players coming through the ranks.

To help consolidate Collier's new role, and to satisfy McHale's long-held belief that a mid-season interstate trip was the stuff that builds premierships (as it had in his first year at the club), Collingwood agreed to a trip to Brisbane, Newcastle and Sydney in late July and early August. This time they would visit those cities with South Melbourne, the team that had narrowly denied Collingwood during the previous year's finals series, and had loomed large as the team to beat for the 1935 pennant.

As luck would have it, the Magpies met South at home in the opening match of the 1935 season. It was to be a watershed day as 27-year-old Harry Collier, in his 169th game, took over from where Coventry had left off. These were interesting times, with former Melbourne champion Ivor Warne-Smith claiming in *The Argus* that it would be "strange to see the Collingwood team go on to the field without the famous leader, Sid (sic) Coventry."[4]

The season's opener saw a Collingwood win, though it could so easily have gone the other way. Having led by as much as 20 points

---

4   *The Argus*, April 26, 1935

at the first change of ends, the Magpies allowed South Melbourne back into the contest. Deep into the last term, with less than five minutes remaining, South led by nine points. As McHale and the rest of the 30,000-strong Victoria Park crowd watched on with a feeling of helplessness, a dramatic transformation came over the contest. A slick pass from Whelan—whom McHale had earmarked as Beveridge's replacement in the centre—to Phonse Kyne resulted in a goal to reduce the margin, and give the Magpies a glimmer of hope. *The Argus* described the last act of a tense afternoon: "(Keith) Fraser coolly passed the ball onto (Vin) Doherty. He sent it calmly to (Lou) Riley, alone in front of goal. Riley's deliberate kick sailed through the centre of the goalposts as the bell rang."[5] For Riley, it was his fifth goal, and "sweet revenge"[6], as he described it in *The Argus*, as he had been one of the players to miss a late shot in the tight 1934 final. Each of the players involved had been a part of McHale's rebuilding program.

Another of those players brought into the club in 1934, Alan 'Ginger' Ryan (from Melbourne), was responsible for another thrilling conclusion on the public holiday that was granted to celebrate King George V's 25th anniversary as monarch. Fitzroy led by a goal as the final siren approached. Then, in the last few seconds, Ryan was awarded a free kick. *The Argus* described the chaotic scenes: "Surrounded by an admiring throng of youths who had rushed the ground, and with a trooper's horse a few feet away, Ryan drop kicked a goal to make the scores level."[7]

Collingwood did not lose a match in the first two months of the 1935 season. Aside from the draw, and the close call with South on the opening day, those victories included some significant performances. The club won its first game in Geelong since 1929, on the occasion of Charlie Dibbs' 200th game, and on the train on the way home

---

5   *The Argus*, April 29, 1935
6   *The Argus*, May 4, 1935
7   *The Argus*, May 7, 1935

McHale made a special presentation to the grand defender, referring to his great service to the game and the club.

Importantly, there was also a win over Footscray, which had finally gained the services of Syd Coventry as coach after several previous attempts. Coventry took over in late May (relinquishing the coaching job at suburban club Alphington) and, according to *The Argus*, even told the Magpies after they had granted permission for him to coach: "Don't be surprised if we beat you."[8] The Pies won by 51 points.

There had been no hard feelings about Coventry's return visit to Victoria Park. He had assured McHale, and Collingwood, that he would never play against them; only coach against them. *The Argus* reported that Coventry was "warmly applauded when he walked off the ground after he had given advice to Footscray's team at three-quarter time."[9] His brother, Gordon, was not so charitable. He kicked nine goals for the game, with one of them being his 1100th career goal. But the Collingwood players gave Syd a glimpse of what he had left behind. It was, according to *The Argus*, "a dazzling display of scientific football ... Dazzling chains of accurate passing, spectacular marking and perfect position play were seen in Collingwood's systematic moves and speed; vigour and relentless determination were consistently displayed by every one of its men."[10]

Collingwood almost had to forfeit its Round 7 game against St Kilda at the Junction Oval in unusual circumstances. A dispute had arisen between the operators of the ground and the Liquor Trades Union over the employment of non-union labour in the beer booths around the oval. The complicating factor for Collingwood was that

---

8   *The Argus*, May 22, 1935
9   *The Argus*, June 3, 1935
10   ibid

many of its players—and its coach—were union members through their employment with the Carlton Brewery. If Trades Hall had declared the Junction Oval a "black" venue, as appeared likely in the lead-up to the clash, it could have placed the players and the coach in an invidious position.

Many VFL footballers worked in the breweries during the Depression years, but perhaps half of them happened to play for Collingwood.[11] A number of them could thank their positions to three pro-Collingwood people: McHale, John Wren and Carlton Brewery general manager Thomas Millea, a Magpie supporter.

Percy Bowyer, a Collingwood player from 1928 to 1938 had secured a brewery job much earlier, independent of the club influences. He said in an interview in 1996: "They (the club) might say to him (Millea), 'We have a player we are anxious to help', and there would be a job at the (Carlton or) Abbotsford Brewery. If you got a job at the brewery, you had a job for life."[12] Some Collingwood people who worked for the breweries included McHale, Bowyer, Harry and Albert Collier, Jack Ross, Vin Doherty, Marcus Whelan, Fred Froude and Jack Carmody.

On the eve of the St Kilda game, *The Argus* revealed: "It was ascertained last night that there are 15 players of the Collingwood team who are members of unions. Many of them are members of the Liquor Trades Union and are employed in breweries, where the principle of preference to unionists prevails. Should the St Kilda ground be declared "black" by the Trades Hall, those players would not be allowed to take part in the match or they would lose their employment."[13] This led to a Collingwood delegation—made up of president Harry Curtis, secretary Frank Wraith and treasurer Bob Rush—visiting Trades Hall to seek a quick resolution.

11 *Kill For Collingwood*, Richard Stremski, Allen and Unwin, 1986
12 Interview with Percy Bowyer, 1996
13 *The Argus*, June 7, 1935

A meeting of the Collingwood committee, of which McHale was a member, resolved to ask the VFL to consider moving the game to a neutral venue, such as Princes Park. Ominously, the committee warned: "If the request had been refused, Collingwood would have forfeited the match to St Kilda."[14] That had never happened in the history of the club, so the fact that it had even been discussed highlighted the gravity of the situation. Fortunately, a deal was thrashed out between the operators of the Junction Oval and the union, and the brewery workers were able to take part in the match.

Bowyer liked to think that it was about this time that McHale began taking a select few players back to the Carlton Brewery after games to have a few beers. The coach may well have been doing it earlier, but Bowyer was first invited back to the brewery (where he worked) in about 1935 or 1936. He recalled: "In those days some of the players had been going to the Oxford Hotel after the games. Jock McHale got to know about it, and he managed to get us to go down there (the brewery). It was very nice. We got free beer. It cemented the bonds of friendship."[15] The tradition would last—for a select few—for the rest of McHale's coaching days.

Collingwood's unbeaten run in 1935 came to an end in Round 9 against Carlton, but there were excuses. Albert Collier and Jack Regan were on state duties in Perth, and skipper Harry Collier and Bowyer were last-minute withdrawals. After a promising start, the Magpies were swamped by the Blues in the second half, going down by 29 points. It was an even worse day for umpire Blackburn, who suffered an unusual injury during the course of the game, as was detailed in the press: "A stray dog joined in the play ... (it) hindered play so much that the umpire (Mr Blackburn) stopped play. He chased and caught the

14   *The Argus*, June 8, 1935
15   Interview with Percy Bowyer, 1996

dog and was carrying it to the fence when it turned on him and bit his hand. Mr Blackburn got rid of it quickly by throwing the dog among the spectators."[16]

Another close game followed at Punt Road when a late goal brought about the third dramatic finish for Collingwood in that season. *The Argus* explained: "Few players could see who had kicked the winning goal, for the bell rang immediately afterwards. When enquiries were made in the Collingwood rooms one or two players were given credit for the final goal, but finally it was established that the appropriately named (Jack) Knight was the hero in the nightmare finish". It was a fitting end to Harold Rumney's 150th game in black and white. (He had played 15 for Carlton in 1925 and 1926 but was sacked for supposedly being "too old (19), too slow and too gutless—a no-hoper in fact".[17] Rumney showed none of these traits at Collingwood. In time, he would be selected in Collingwood's Team of the Century.)

It was at this time that Ivor Warne-Smith raised the issue of whether non-playing coaches should be permitted on the field to instruct players during the course of a game; it was in the days before runners were introduced. Warne-Smith told *The Argus*: "Not long ago a League club secretary suggested (it) ... this would be an agreeable move to the coaches. If a written copy of the coaches' speeches were taken from week to week, it would be found that every phase of the game is thoroughly explained. Unfortunately for the coach, his advice, so ably and forcibly spoken, is like a stone thrown into the water. It sinks—to the players' boots."[18]

The dual Brownlow Medal-winner, who coached Melbourne for five seasons from 1928 to 1932 (but only one season, 1932, as a non-playing coach), continued: "On the field the coach would have the satisfaction of immediately correcting errors instead of muttering to himself, as he does now, on a seat alongside the boundary line.

---

16   *The Morning Bulletin*, Rockhampton, June 24, 1935
17   Correspondence with Harold Rumney, 1985
18   *The Argus*, July 12, 1935

Even the spectators might obtain a little fun from a tense struggle if they saw the burly form of Dan Minogue, (now) St Kilda's coach, attempt to dodge, with an agile sidestep, a lightning stab pass."[19] He acknowledged though that the "League would never grant the boon to coaches."[20]

It is an interesting insight as to how McHale, sitting on the wooden bench on the sidelines, managed to communicate with his players during matches. There was no interchange at the time; the lone reserve (instituted in 1930) sitting beside him could only replace an injured player for the rest of the game. It has long been accepted that McHale relied on several trainers to deliver messages, which undoubtedly happened at times, but this practice was rarely used to effect positional changes. If changes were to happen in the course of a quarter, it would generally be on the advice of the captain.

Syd Coventry told *The Herald* in 1938: "No, sir, I remember receiving a message only once (from a trainer). We were in a bit of a jam, and Harold Rumney and Len Murphy—two fresh men—were pulling it out for us. Jim McHale sent a message telling me to leave them in the ruck and stay out myself. I told the trainer to tell Jim that he need have no fear, for I couldn't run another yard, let alone take a turn on the ball. There's this to it: Jim McHale and the match committee at Collingwood hit straight from the shoulder. They have the happy knack of pointing the finger in the right direction."[21]

Coventry revealed that McHale would not burden his players with instructions or intricate plans that could be forgotten once on the ground. In the same discussion with *The Herald*, he said: "This is the good oil I am giving you. We never had a (specific) plan. We believed that if you loaded players with plans you cramped their natural game. Football can't be played to a plan. We encouraged players to think for themselves and to help each other. The first ten minutes of a final can

---

19   ibid
20   ibid
21   Interview with *The Herald*, with the Coventry brothers, 1938

blast any plan you've made. No, we tried to play football, to help each other, and to meet every emergency as it came along."[22]

South Melbourne delivered a blow to Collingwood in Round 12, defeating the Magpies by 53 points. Bob Pratt, who had kicked a record 150 goals the previous season, kicked as many goals in the game as Collingwood did (10). Unlike the events of Round 1, he had Jack Regan's measure. It was said in *The Argus* that Regan "at least had the satisfaction of knowing that no one else could have held Pratt",[23] but the pair did manage to share a few "friendly" glasses in the dressingroom after the game. Talk in both teams centred on the forthcoming tour of the northern states by Collingwood and South Melbourne.

But before that, Collingwood had to meet Fitzroy, and it provided Jock McHale with the chance to grant the wish of a young Collingwood supporter. Twelve-year-old Magpie barracker Kevin Brophy, who was suffering from paralysis in the Austin Hospital, lived out a childhood dream of coming to Victoria Park and meeting his heroes. *The Argus* reported that: "He (Brophy) was taken to the match by two nurses in a moveable cot. After the game he achieved the height of ambition when he chatted with Jock McHale, Harry Collier, Jack Regan and a few more of his footballing heroes."[24] McHale could be hard and unrelenting, gruff and to the point. But he always took the time to speak with the many young black and white fans who crossed his path.

The three "friendly" matches to be played against South Melbourne on the tour would at least allow McHale and the players to cast a critical eye over their likely finals opponents before September action. Although these games were generally played on the day after some serious drinking the previous night, the Magpies managed to win two of the three matches contested. The first game, in Brisbane, resulted in a 32-point win to Collingwood, and the second, in Newcastle, was

22   ibid
23   *The Argus*, July 15, 1935
24   *The Argus*, July 22, 1935

won by three points. South Melbourne reversed the result when the teams played in Sydney, winning by four goals.

Boywer did an interview with Tom Wanliss, from the Collingwood archives committee, in 1996. Bowyer gave a fascinating insight into the propensity to have a good time while on tour. "We beat them (in Brisbane)," he said. "Len Murphy did all the damage. He ran into half a dozen of them. The night before we had been to a dance ... I had to help him up the stairs (on their return to the hotel). Then we came down to Newcastle and 'Leeter' (Albert Collier) had a night out. He didn't feel too good and McHale gave me his spot in the ruck. From then on, I was a ruck-rover. Then we went to Sydney and that was the only game where there was a prize for the (winning) players. It was an Akubra hat, a prized possession. They got their Akubras and we were not happy."[25]

McHale's use of smaller, more mobile back-up followers at times during the late 1920s and more frequently in the 1930s has sometimes been seen as a predecessor for the ruck-rover, as defined by the tactics of Melbourne in the 1950s. As *Footy's Greatest Coaches*, a compendium on football coaches and tactics, explained: "He (McHale) assigned only a single ruckman near the boundary and rotated marginally smaller players as crumb gatherers. This was the advent of the ruck-rover, a quarter of a century ahead of Ron Barassi's incarnation of the role for Norm Smith at Melbourne."[26] Albert Collier (180cm) and Percy Bowyer (179cm) were the followers in the 1935 and 1936 Grand Finals.

Collingwood responded well on its return from the interstate trip; it did not lose another game in the home and away season, albeit scrounging a draw with Melbourne in Round 16—their second for the season. McHale continued to try out new players. A kid called Ron Todd made his debut against Essendon in Round 14. The 18-year-old, whose family had been close friends with Dick Lee, had worn

---

25   Interview with Percy Bowyer, 1996
26   *Footy's Greatest Coaches*, Stephanie Holt and Garrie Hutchinson, Coulomb
     Communications, 2002

Lee's No.13 on his back as a child. He did not score a goal in his first match. He was dropped a week later, and managed just four games in his first season. Bowyer remembered in his 1996 interview that district coach Hughie Thomas had the belief that Todd would be a star, saying: "I was not able to get to training too early (in 1935) and finished with the seconds. Hughie said to me, 'Help me teach this kid to kick. He holds it like this, and he kicks it out of sight. We want him to hold it like this.'"[27]

Collingwood finished second on the table, four points adrift of South Melbourne, but McHale was clearly confident of beating South in the second semi-final. At training during the week, he was asked by *The Argus* about his team's chances of causing an upset. He looked back at the team as it made its way off Victoria Park, and said: "There is our team, what do you think?" Then, later, he said: "We have a well-balanced side of young players who will be all out for Collingwood. Their form is as good as it has been at any stage of the season."[28] Such confidence was not fulfilled. With six goals to Pratt, South Melbourne won by 21 points to move into the Grand Final.

Collingwood found better form in the preliminary final against Richmond. After trailing by three points at half-time, the Magpies won by 28 points. *The Argus* reported: "In the Collingwood room the players heard their final war cry in the form of the following verse:

Tradition is your key word and tradition never dies,

And win or lose, you'll always put the game before the prize.

Sustain that fighting spirit, lads, uphold the club's good name,

And honour those immortal words, 'Play up, and play the game'

It's not known who spoke the words. It's likely they may have come from club president Harry Curtis rather than McHale. The coach did not always speak to the group before the games, while the president almost always did. McHale would often go around quietly

---

27   Interview with Percy Bowyer, 1996
28   *The Argus*, September 20, 1935

and have a few individual chats to players he felt needed a few words of encouragement before reserving his main speech for half-time.

The win over Richmond set the scene for the seventh clash between Collingwood and South Melbourne for 1935, including the three matches played on tour, two from the regular season and the second-semi-final. Fittingly, it came 39 years to the day after the two clubs' meeting in the 1896 VFA Grand Final; Collingwood won its first pennant that day.

There was a belief internally that Collingwood could turn the tables from the result achieved a fortnight earlier. McHale had often expressed a belief that a champion team would always be preferred to a team of champions, and there was a feeling within the Magpies group that individuality formed too much of South Melbourne's approach to the game.

But a sensation on the Thursday afternoon before the 1935 Grand Final would not only deprive South Melbourne of its most important player, it would tilt the premiership scales heavily in Collingwood's favour. Bob Pratt had just stepped off a tram along congested High Street, Prahran, when he was knocked to the ground by a truck loaded with bricks. He was taken home and later the club doctor had diagnosed a number of ailments, including a sprained right ankle, a lacerated leg, an injured left foot and a badly bruised finger.

Magpie captain Harry Collier was unaware of the dramatic turn of events as he walked along Collingwood's bustling Johnston Street later that day. In an interview in 1993, Collier recalled: "I remember coming home from work and going up along Hoddle Street, and someone said to me, 'How are you going, Harry?' I said, 'We will win it if there is no Pratt', and (I didn't know) bloody 'Pratty' got knocked down."[29]

Pratt's injuries would lead to unsubstantiated rumours that a football betting syndicate might have been responsible. There were also

---

29   Interview with Harry Collier, 1993

theories that a Collingwood supporter might have been trying to give the Magpies an unfair advantage. In an interview for a documentary to celebrate the AFL's centenary, *100 Years of Australian Football*, in 1996, Pratt suggested that there were allegations that notorious Melbourne gangster 'Squizzy' Taylor had been somehow connected. Taylor had died in a gun shootout with 'Snowy' Cutmore in October 1927.

The man who had accidentally run Pratt down was, in fact, a South Melbourne supporter, C.T. Peters, who was so affected by the incident that he went to the champion goalkicker's house that night to give him a packet of cigarettes to say sorry.

McHale was not without his own injury concerns. Four players could not be considered: Len Murphy, Jack Knight, George Carter and Jack Power. But the club was still confident that the grooming of the young players over the previous few years, the outstanding leadership of the Collier brothers and the strong remnants of *The Machine* would stand the team in good stead.

In a typically hard and aggressive Grand Final, South Melbourne took first advantage of the wind to open up a 15-point lead by the end of the first term. There was no Pratt, but had it not been for South's inaccurate kicking (3.6), the margin could well have been more sizeable. Collingwood, largely through some fine work from centre half-forward Phonse Kyne (who had attended CBC Parade in East Melbourne, just as McHale had done much earlier), played its way back into the match with a solid second term with the breeze. As the players headed in for their half-time rev-up, the MCG scoreboard showed a 10-point buffer for the Magpies after they had kicked five goals to one in the second quarter.

A stalemate existed for much of the third quarter as both sides worked hard to gain an advantage. Neither could manage it, although Collingwood increased its lead marginally, to 12 points, at the last change. In the last quarter, it appeared as if South Melbourne had the upper hand in terms of general play, but fittingly it was Harry

Collier who pulled the game out of the fire. The first-year skipper took advantage of a free kick to score a late goal that increased the lead to 19 points.

South Melbourne would not give in. But Collingwood was up to the challenge. The loss of South captain Jack Bisset, who had left the field with a serious concussion at three-quarter time, was a blow to the Southerners. The absence of Pratt also proved too great a hurdle to overcome. Collingwood also lost Charlie Dibbs in the last term after he suffered concussion, but Dibbs' replacement, the diminutive Keith Stackpole, came onto the field and kicked a late goal.

The Herald summed up the difference between the two teams: "The Magpies were a far more versatile team, adapting themselves to all emergencies, winning in the heavy clashes and taking the straight route to goal [typically of McHale's game-plan] whenever possible. South foolishly tried to show Collingwood a few points about hard bumping, but they came off second best, and declined into a ragged and uncertain team."[30]

The final bell saw Collingwood 20 points clear and gave rise to the sort of celebrations that could well be mistaken for a club that had not won a flag for some considerable time. For Collingwood, it had been only five years. But that was long enough. Harry Collier was carried from the field; Jock McHale was congratulated by all and sundry. The last time Collingwood had won a premiership he had been at home—seriously ill—in bed. This time he was able to enjoy it in full. In a famous photograph of the team posing out on the ground (minus Dibbs who was unconscious on a rubdown table in the rooms), McHale wears the smile of a winner. He is dressed in his customary suit, vest and black tie, with his hat still firmly on his head. In a sign of the unity that had seen the club through the rebuilding process, his captain Harry Collier, who was Collingwood's best player, is reaching out to shake McHale's hand.

---

30   *The Herald,* October 5, 1935

It was no easy task for the team to get back into the rooms. *The Herald* reported that: "Players had to run the gauntlet of officials and supporters who insisted on a round of handshaking. Club songs were revived and sung with tremendous applause. For more than a quarter of an hour, the majority of the players were still in their uniform, endeavouring to make their way to the showers." *The Argus* reported that Collingwood's president, Harry Curtis, declared it "the greatest premiership the club has yet won ... We had a young team to be remodelled for this and other premierships in the future, and our plans have so far been successful." Wraith said the premiership could be attributed to McHale's capacity to rebuild teams, and delicately weld old machinery with new parts, saying: "Collingwood had done the right thing in choosing its coach early and sticking with him. To Jock McHale, we owe most of this year's success."[31]

The celebrations carried on that night and for many subsequent nights. As Richard Stremski's *Kill For Collingwood* documented, a piano in the middle of Victoria Park played a part in the celebrations. On the following night Harry Collier and Harold Rumney and their wives—as well as Collier's twin brothers 'Pinky' and 'Bluey'—were involved in an accident when Collier crashed his car into the front gate of Catholic Archbishop Daniel Mannix's house in nearby Kew. The team and the coach were presented with £5 each, presented to them by committeeman, councillor and businessman Jim Ryan, who even opened up his Brighton home for a soiree.

McHale was justifiably proud of his remodelling of *The Machine*. In an extraordinarily frank column that he wrote in *The Sporting Globe* in April 1936 ("as told to P.J. Millard"), he wrote: "Think of it, a great player and captain, and one of the most outstanding footballers of his time (Syd Coventry), retires and, despite this severe loss, the (1935) team gallantly rises to the occasion, and jumps from fourth to first in a season."[32]

---

31   *The Argus*, October 7, 1935
32   *The Sporting Globe*, April 18, 1936

He described a philosophy that may be eternal in the development of successful football teams: "There's a lesson in that—the lesson that a football team functions as a complete machine; its success dependant on the cooperation of its whole 18 players on the field, and the soundness and vision of its administrators. Those who predicted Collingwood's sudden downfall, following the loss of Syd Coventry, forgot those things. They forgot we have, as we always have done, been developing young players to take the places of veterans dropping out."[33]

The Sporting Globe sensed it had a scoop with the coach who had always preferred to let others, particularly the secretary or the president, do the talking for him. He preferred to concentrate on the pigskin more than the press. The precede (a journalistic term for the teaser below the heading) to McHale's feature story read: "This article is all the more interesting because hitherto, McHale, a coach of the shrewd, taciturn type, has almost invariably refused to speak for publication."[34]

In the article, he spoke about the famous but difficult-to-define Collingwood spirit that was almost as old as the club itself, and how it gave players a kind of "mental telepathy". He wrote: "The basis of the Collingwood system is, broadly, short stab-passing ... to a comrade leading out and making position. We aim to keep the game moving so fast that we are a couple of 'thinks' ahead of opponents. That calls for football sense ... a kind of mental telepathy that enables players swiftly to anticipate moves. Our chaps seem to acquire that priceless asset."[35]

He insisted that only team players were wanted at Collingwood— "We never tolerate slackness ... Players must train strictly. We have no time for the flash player intent on individual glory. His place is not in the Magpie 18." And he re-emphasised the fact that he needed to treat all players differently, and had no interest in belittling them in front of

33   ibid
34   ibid
35   ibid

their teammates if they made a mistake: "If a player has to be spoken about his play, say at half-time, I do it quietly and privately." Then he added with emphasis: "Nobody else is allowed to do it."[36]

Perhaps the most candid statement came from his stated belief that Collingwood would back up its 1935 flag with another in 1936. He said: "True, we have lost those fine footballers, (Harold) Rumney and (Charlie) Dibbs, but there are keen, bright young players eager to fill the gaps, and fill them just as efficiently as happened after we lost Syd Coventry. For those reasons, I cannot help feeling optimistic over our prospects. It is not in my nature to boast bombastically 'We'll be premiers'. I've been brought up in too hard a football school for that. Nevertheless, I honestly expect the Magpies to fly off with another pennant, or go very close to it."[37]

Few would have disagreed after the first nine matches of the 1936 season. Collingwood won all of those contests, with the closest being a six-point win over Carlton in Round 6. By the end of Round 9 the Magpies were a game clear of South Melbourne on top of the ladder, with the clash between these two sides eagerly anticipated. Ahead of it, though, the aftermath of the win over North Melbourne saw Albert Collier suspended for six weeks for striking North's Jack Smith. It was a big loss for the Magpies, but there were even more telling tribunal penalties to come later.

The fans had to be patient in waiting for the pairing of the previous year's Grand Finalists. It didn't come until Round 10. And when the day came, they were forced to wait another week. Incessant rain caused the postponement of all games that afternoon—for the first time since 1923—with the decision to call off the games made at 11am.

---

36   ibid
37   ibid

The Victoria Park surface was described by the League's Adverse Weather Committee as "unfit for play ... In shocking condition".[38]

When the two teams did square off for the first time since the 1935 Grand Final, South Melbourne prevailed by 11 points. It was, as *The Argus* termed it, "a nerve-tingling and remarkably good match".[39] The visitors shot out to a five-goal first term lead before the Magpies stormed back in the second quarter, heading into the dressingroom only three points behind. Despite keeping Bob Pratt in reasonable check (he would kick only two goals) South edged out to a lead of 11 points at three-quarter time and held that margin at the end of the game.

It was a described as a surprising result by *The Argus:* "South Melbourne made many friends by its forceful, fast and clever display, for it missed (Brighton) Diggins, (Jim) Reid, (Len) Thomas, (Ron) Hillis, (Syd) Dineen, (Reg) Humphries and (Alan) Welch."[40]

What followed was a bigger surprise for Collingwood. It lost again to Geelong—at Corio Oval—making it two successive losses for McHale's team for the first time since early 1934. *The Argus* acknowledged this, saying: "Collingwood had the unusual experience of being defeated twice in succession. Officials admitted that Geelong played excellently, its finish being admirable, and its pace and team work (was) better. Collingwood feels the absence of such players as A. Collier, (Jack) Knight, (Lou) Riley, (Leo) Morgan, and (Fred) Froude."[41] The frustration for the coach would have been that Collingwood had led by 21 points at half-time, but was overpowered in the second half, kicking only three goals after the long interval to the Cats' nine.

But if that was a shock to the system, imagine what the aftermath of Round 13 would have meant for McHale and his team. The Magpies scored a 16-point win over the Tigers at Punt Road, but it was a

---

38   *The Argus*, July 6, 1936
39   *The Argus*, July 13, 1936
40   ibid
41   *The Argus*, July 20, 1936

spiteful contest. Collingwood's normally unruffled forward Gordon Coventry clashed with his Richmond opponent, 'Joe' Murdoch. What happened next took Collingwood to the point of fury. At a tribunal hearing, Coventry was suspended for eight weeks—which ruled him out for the remainder of the season. It was his first offence. Sixteen years without a blemish had counted for little inside the tribunal room.

There had been mitigating circumstances, though Coventry chose not to elaborate on them on the night of the tribunal. *The Argus* reported: "Halfway through the third quarter, I went up for a mark and got a blow to the head," Coventry told the tribunal. "I do not remember what happened after that."[42] What he would privately allege was that Murdoch, who would be handed a four-game suspension, had been hitting the back of his neck, in the knowledge that Coventry had been suffering with boils. This might have prompted the anger from Coventry. He threw a punch and copped a massive penalty as a result. As Bowyer recalled: "'Nuts' (Coventry) was suffering from boils. He would have (had cause to strike back) if he got a whack on the boils."[43]

It was a sleepless night in Collingwood on the evening that the VFL tribunal sat. That night was one of the most sensational hearings of the 1930s. *The Argus* described the atmosphere: "Great interest was taken in the case which was not heard until 10pm, and about 100 persons including a number of young women and youths gathered outside the building awaiting news. During the night scores of telephone calls were received at the League rooms. These included inquiries from Collingwood picture theatres, at which it was intended to project (the result of the verdict) on the screens."[44]

Murdoch claimed years later that, on the morning after the match, he had been approached to go and see John Wren, or one of Wren's associates, who asked him to insist that Coventry had done nothing

---

42   *The Argus*, August 5, 1936
43   Interview with Percy Bowyer, 1996
44   *The Argus*, August 5, 1936

wrong.[45] He would also deny the story about deliberately trying to hit Coventry's boils. After the passing of 75 years, it is impossible to verify Wren's role in the drama, or Murdoch's claims about intervention. But when Coventry retired briefly after his penalty was handed down, the long-time Collingwood benefactor handed over a cheque of £50 with a letter congratulating him on his career and the manly way in which he had accepted the tribunal verdict. Wren had never made any secret that the Magpie forward was his favourite player, once employing him for a time at one of his companies, Effront Yeast.

McHale, who had never been suspended in his long, illustrious playing career, must have felt for Coventry. He had seen all but one of his 287 games to that stage and all but seven of his 1287 goals. Coventry had been the man who had passed McHale's long-time games record at Collingwood. The coach knew he was a scrupulously fair player who had retaliated under provocation. Former Collingwood administrator and authority on the club's history, Gordon Carlyon, would say many years later in a newspaper interview: "It nearly provoked a suburban war ... Wren was furious ... McHale thought it was a set-up. The boils issue wasn't mentioned. He (Coventry) didn't believe in squealing."[46] Carlyon added: "Murdoch knew he (Coventry) had the boils. They belted him until he exploded, and he got eight weeks—for retaliating."[47]

South Melbourne had been without Pratt in the Grand Final the previous year; this year Collingwood would have to make do without Coventry. It left the coach and his selection panel, including chairman of selectors, 'Doc' Seddon, with a dilemma about whom to choose as the full-forward in Coventry's absence. *The Argus* believed: "The choice will probably come down to Kyne, Todd and perhaps Riley."[48]

---

45   *Richmond Football Club, The Tigers, A Century of League football*, Rhett Bartlett, GSP Books, 2007
46   *Herald Sun*, May 8, 1999
47   Interview with Gordon Carlyon, 1999
48   *The Argus*, August 10, 1936

It meant for plenty of debate at the selection table, with Harry Collier recalling in 1993: "I was on the selection committee and Jock said, 'We have got to get a full-forward'. I said, 'We have got a bloody full-forward. He (Jock) knew, he knew. That was young 'Toddy' and he should have been in the side a few years earlier."[49] Todd would kick five goals in the next match, against Fitzroy (his 12th game overall), but would be left out of the final home and away game, and the second semi-final against South Melbourne. But he would be recalled for the Grand Final, and the rest is history.

Collingwood won the second semi-final against South Melbourne. The Magpies had led by 25 points at half-time before a sustained third term (usually reserved for Collingwood) went in South's favour as they stole the lead back with a six-goal to nil burst. Still, the Magpies stormed home with six of their own in the last term to hold out their opponents by 13 points, playing, said *The Argus*, "steadier and displaying more cooperation and stamina".[50]

But the critics were not convinced. Percy Taylor, of *The Argus*, insisted that South Melbourne would still win the flag, by defeating Melbourne in the preliminary final (which it did) and then Collingwood in the Grand Final. His rationale was that Len Murphy had been reported for striking Brighton Diggins (breaking his jaw in the process) in the second semi. Having missed the 1935 Grand Final with a shoulder injury, Murphy would miss the 1936 one, too, after being handed an eight-week ban. Taylor also pointed to the injury concerns that Collingwood had—Harry Collier and Jack Regan both had suffered jarred shoulders, while Jack Carmody's ankle was troubling him.

The Magpies had no players over 30 (Harry Collier was the oldest at 29 years and two days—he had actually made a birthday wish at the last training session of another premiership). The youngest Magpie was Todd, who was recalled for his 16th game, just 20 days shy of his

49   Interview with Harry Collier, 1993
50   *The Argus*, September 21, 1936

20th birthday. McHale was 70 days short of his 54th birthday. To that time, no premiership coach had ever been older.

Most of the young Magpies were locals, brought up on the success stories of the club's past. Only three "country" players were in the side that took its place at the MCG against South Melbourne on October 3—Marcus Whelan, from Bacchus Marsh; Jack Knight, from Bendigo; and Bervin Woods, from Mortlake before joining Brunswick in the VFA. Other "outsiders" included Jim Crowe, from Carlton, and Lou Riley, from Melbourne.

The anticipation for the game was such that a crowd of 74,091—just a tick under 20,000 more than the previous year's playoff—crowded the MCG on Grand Final day, 1936, with people clambering for every vantage point, desperate to find the best viewing locations. This led to several accidents and falls from the stands. Seventy-two people were treated on the day, with three missing the match after being rushed to hospital.

Each team was hoping for an omen in its favour. South Melbourne won the toss for the colour of the shorts to be worn, choosing white. Each team that had won a final that season had worn white shorts. McHale didn't care about that, saying that "black shorts will do us". He said it was even better that Collingwood had been allocated the Melbourne dressing rooms, which he had always felt were the club's lucky rooms for games at the MCG.

But it wasn't just luck he was counting on. He believed he had a strategy to beat South Melbourne. Part of it rested on his choice of an opponent for Laurie Nash, whose own father Bob had once been McHale's teammate at Collingwood. He planned the unusual move of playing Jack Ross at centre half-back on Nash. Ross might have been conceding 6cm and 13kg, but it would be one of the best moves of the entire match.

There had been surprise expressed in *The Argus* by Percy Taylor when Collingwood had released its team on the Thursday night.

Taylor said there had been a "long deliberation" on Todd's inclusion, while "the most interesting move, however, was the shifting of Ross from the half-back flank to centre half-back. He will endeavour to check Nash, whose form is feared by Collingwood. It is certain Ross will have difficulty in holding Nash in the air."[51]

If Harry Collier had doubted McHale's part in the "decoy" tactic from the 1929 Grand Final success over Richmond (which saw Gordon Coventry used as a decoy for 'Tubby' Edmonds) he would have no hesitation in suggesting that the coach was the man behind this move. He would recall in 1993: "He (Ross) won the Grand Final for us, against 'Nashy' in '36. That was a move of Jock's as far as I knew. He worked that out. He (Ross) never gave 'Nashy' the ball once. Nash would be in your top half dozen players and 'Rossy' (142 games from 1931-40) had hardly ever been heard of. He was one of the best clubmen Collingwood had."[52]

Sixty years after the event, Percy Bowyer recalled one of the very first moments of that 1936 Grand Final: "The umpire put the ball up in the air, and these were the words 'Keep it clean, boys'. Then (Laurie) Nash screamed. Jack Ross stood on his foot. Nash couldn't move, and that didn't suit Laurie. I don't know who told him (Ross) to do it. The unusual thing was that Jack Ross wasn't big enough for a centre half-back (he was 173cm). But Nash wasn't tall either (179cm). Jack was a great spoiler."[53]

The other unusual move that McHale made was to play Keith Fraser (who was 183cm) on the South Melbourne resting rovers, and it was successful, with Fraser continually out-marking them. In attack, Alby Pannam was outstanding, having 32 touches and kicking five goals. He had played in a second VFL premiership, replicating the performances of his father, Charlie Pannam snr (1902 and 1903), and his older brother, Charlie Pannam jnr (1917 and 1919). His nephew,

---

51   *The Argus*, October 3, 1936
52   Interview with Harry Collier, 1993
53   Interview with Percy Bowyer, 1996

Lou Richards would captain a Collingwood premiership 17 years later, and another nephew, Ron, would be one of the best players in that game.

Next to Pannam, Todd kicked 4.10 from 16 shots at goal. Clearly, he still had some work to do on his kicking—as Hughie Thomas had forecast the previous year—but he was showing signs that he would be the natural successor to Coventry in the coming years. Gordon Coventry would say two years later: "We put Ron Todd up forward, and he did wonderfully well. He showed us that day what was in store for full-backs in a season or two."[54] Whelan was among the best players. Kyne kicked a critical goal in the last term that guaranteed the success, and Carmody was also a strong contributor.

Collingwood had led at every change of the game, but inaccurate kicking had cost it dearly, particularly in the second term when it managed 4.10. That left the Magpies with a lead of 21 points at the main change, but South Melbourne had cut that back to seven at three-quarter time. In the end, the Magpies held out to win by 11 points, with Taylor suggesting: "Collingwood demonstrated again the value of team work against spasmodic efforts."[55]

The Collier brothers typically were prominent. But Bowyer recalled Harry being a little frustrated when the final bell sounded: "I was near Harry Collier when it (the bell) went. I said, 'Well done, 'Skip', and he looked around at me. I said, 'What's happened? Are you hurt? He said to me, 'We should have won by more'. To win a premiership is the best you can do in Australian Rules. But that was the attitude of the Colliers."[56] His mood improved when it was announced that an "anonymous supporter" (John Wren) gave him and McHale £25 each, as well as another £100 that the committee reserved for the rest of the team.[57]

---

54   Interview with the Coventry brothers, *The Herald*, 1938
55   *The Argus*, October 5, 1936
56   Interview with Percy Bowyer, 1996
57   *The Argus*, October 5, 1936

McHale, who had brought out an updated version of *Our Australian Game of Football (1936)* along with Bob Pratt and Haydn Bunton, had just coached his eighth premiership success. The next morning, in the Collingwood rooms, as the celebrations continued, in front of more than 200 people, it was said in *The Argus* that McHale was "besieged for the recipe for winning premierships."[58] No one in the room at the time, least of all the man who was being feted, could have imagined that there would be no more. He would coach for another 13 seasons without a flag.

As the 1937 football year dawned, the Collingwood Annual Report summation of the 1936 season forecast more success: "We can look forward to the future with confidence, and hope that we may yet defeat our record of four successive premierships."[59] The club thanked McHale: "His indomitable spirit and well known skill, imparted to the players in his care (showed) all the essential characteristics so well displayed in the winning of the 1936 premiership, an achievement which adds further lustre to his brilliant career."[60] Congratulations were also reserved for McHale and his chairman of selectors, 'Doc' Seddon on "completing 25 or 30 years respectively as selectors ... and an important part of the answer to that oft-repeated query: 'What is the secret of Collingwood's success"?[61]

The Annual Report, released in March 1937, also revealed that the committee had convinced Gordon Coventry to have one final season. It said: "Under very regrettable circumstances, (Coventry) announced his retirement from the game (last year). He took all the punishment and buffeting, to which a notable forward is subjected, with a smile, till

---

58   ibid
59   Collingwood Annual Report, 1937
60   ibid
61   ibid

the 13th game of last season, the 'Devil's Day'. Your committee do not feel satisfied to allow this great player to sever his connection with the game under such repelling circumstances, therefore, in prevailing him upon him to play again, we will be performing a popular service that will meet with applause and approbation of every Collingwood member and thousands of football followers."[62] Coventry would work in tandem with Todd (who shifted out for a year to centre half-forward), and the pair would kick 134 goals between them for the season.

1937 would also see the arrival of one of the best young footballers to play for the Magpies. Des Fothergill would be a revelation in his debut season, winning the Copeland Trophy in his first—and second—seasons. He was 16 years and 318 days when he made his debut against Carlton in Round 6, kicking a goal, and showing "great form", after having already played for the reserves. Incredibly, he was almost 19 years younger than his teammate Coventry, having been born 30 days (on July 15, 1920) before the champion Collingwood forward played his first game in Round 15, 1920.

Another new player to start his career that season had a closer link to McHale. He was Jack Murphy, from Fairfield, and he happened to be a nephew of the coach, the son of McHale's sister Sarah. He would, in time, win a Copeland Trophy as well.

There had been another tribunal sensation that season. A complaint from North Melbourne that Albert Collier had spat on a female supporter resulted in another hefty suspension. Collier, who had apologised to the woman after the game, was later summoned to an investigations committee on a charge of "unseemly conduct". But acting on legal advice, he appeared briefly before walking out. In the end, that earned him an eight-week suspension—a "holiday with pay" (£5 a week) from Wren[63]—and he came back, ironically, in the club's next clash with North Melbourne in Round 14—the week before Coventry became the first man to reach 300 VFL games.

---

62   ibid
63   *Kill For Collingwood*, Richard Stremski, Allen and Unwin, 1986

Collingwood dropped from top spot when it lost to Melbourne—for a second time that year—in a high-scoring encounter at Victoria Park in Round 16. Forty-three goals were kicked, but the most worrying aspect for McHale had been the last half hour. After leading by 35 points at three-quarter time, the Magpies were overwhelmed in the last term with two goals to the visitors' nine. These were the first wins Melbourne had over Collingwood since the 1926 Grand Final.

The tonic seemed to come a week later when McHale and his men left for Tasmania for a trip during the state representative break. This time they would be accompanied by Geelong, the team that had displaced them at the top of the ladder. McHale gained a good look at the Geelong side that had beaten Collingwood in their Round 12 encounter. In the match at Devonport, the Magpies prevailed by 11 points. Reviewing the trip, the club said: "Contested with all the earnestness of a premiership match, the contest resulted in a victory for Collingwood. There was a record crowd and hotel accommodation could not be obtained within 50 miles of the ground."[64] Prime Minister Joe Lyons attended the match, having just returned from England, where he attended the coronation of King George VI.

McHale had always enjoyed these moments away. This was no exception. On a trip to a wallaby farm, he gave his players a strange training session. *The Argus* said: "Here the coach (Jock McHale) offered a prize of 2/- to each player who could catch a wallaby. The offer cost him 4/- but he said it was worth it, as the footballers were completely outclassed in nippiness. Teamwork alone was responsible for the success of the two prize-winners (not named). They linked hands and cornered their wallabies."[65] Earlier, the Collingwood coach had won "first prize for old-time waltzing at a dance in Burnie ... no one in the Collingwood Football Club ever suspected that the veteran coach was

---

64   Collingwood Annual Report, 1938
65   The Argus, September 4, 1937

an exponent of the old-time waltz."[66] He also won three bottles of whiskey when "playing in a four-ball match at Risdon golf links, he holed out in one".[67] The club president, Harry Curtis, informed that, "Jock, who works in a brewery, never drinks."[68] What Curtis should have said is that McHale never liked spirits (as documented in his manifesto from 1925)—but he certainly enjoyed a beer.

Harry Collier recalled having quite a few drinks with the Geelong players on that trip. The teams had a good rapport. But in less than two months, he would come to regret some of the things he told them over a few beers. He said: "We went away to Tassie and we were all boozing out one night, and having a feed. I was with the Geelong blokes, and I said, 'Do you know what's wrong with your bloody mob? You have got them all placed in the wrong positions'. We were down in Devonport. And, you know, Jesus Christ, they swung them all around on us (in the Grand Final). I would say that was caused by myself, in a way."[69]

Collier was referring to the game which has long been acknowledged as one of the greatest Grand Finals, the 1937 clash between Collingwood and Geelong, and specifically the stunning moves by Cats captain-coach Reg Hickey that caught the Magpies by surprise. Collingwood had finished third on the ladder at the end of the home and away season, behind Geelong and Melbourne, but the hopes of becoming only the third team to win three consecutive premierships remained alive with powerful wins over Richmond in the first semi-final (51 points) and Melbourne in the preliminary final (55 points).

Collingwood remained confident that it could send off the retiring Gordon Coventry with one last premiership on the day of his 36th birthday—to make up for the one he had missed through suspension the previous year. McHale and the Magpies were confident they could

66   The Argus, August 28, 1937
67   ibid
68   ibid
69   Interview with Harry Collier, 1993

achieve this, with *The Argus* saying: "The greatest possible enthusiasm was manifested at Collingwood ... Premierships are no novelty, but for some reason or another, there is a great keenness among the players to complete the 'hat-trick'."[70]

There was great anticipation of the contest with Percy Taylor declaring in *The Argus* on the eve of the match: "The game should be one of the best and most spectacular contests of the year—a fitting end of the season."[71] He could not have known how right he would be. *The Football Record* forecast: "The sides appear evenly matched, both being well equipped with powerful rucks, aerialists of ability, and nippy small men who excel in ground play."[72] Incredibly, an Australian record of 88,540 fans attended the game, smashing previous records, and ensuring some close-to-the-action access, with spectators spilling onto the ground at times.

Perhaps it was the fact these two teams played exciting, sometimes aesthetic football. Perhaps it was the fact that Geelong's Reg Hickey had trained the Cats along Collingwood lines. Perhaps it was a diversion from some of the other things happening around the world at the time. On the weekend of the 1937 VFL Grand Final, "Herr Hitler" was meeting with "Signor Mussolini" in Munich, and the Japanese were conducting remorseless raids on China. The world was to soon change in a way that few could comprehend. But for now, in Melbourne, the only thing that mattered was the quality of play in the Grand Final had been.

Ivor Warne-Smith, in *The Argus,* called it: "Perhaps the greatest Grand Final in the history of the league ... This Grand Final will never be forgotten." The official Collingwood review of the game would say that it "unquestionably takes its place in the history of football as one of the greatest exhibitions of the game ever seen".[73]

---

70   *The Argus*, September 24, 1937
71   *The Argus*, September 24, 1937
72   The Football Record, Grand Final, 1937
73   Collingwood Annual Report, 1938

Collingwood started brilliantly, kicking 6.3 to 3.3 in the first term, with Ron Todd causing all sorts of headaches for the Cats defenders. It would prove the catalyst for a change that would transform the game, and leave the Magpie coach unable to respond. Twelve months earlier, McHale had made the stunning moves—albeit before the game and forecast when the teams were announced—but this time Hickey made them in the course of the match. Some of them would help Geelong win its way back into the contest, as the Cats outscored Collingwood in the second term, to set up a tied score-line at the last break.

Such was the good spirit and good will that existed between these two teams that many players actually shook hands before the start of a last quarter that Geelong would win.

The Hickey changes were "courageous", according to Warne-Smith, the exact same word that had been used to describe McHale's use of Ross on Nash in 1936. The biggest was to move Geelong full-forward Les Hardiman onto centre half-forward Todd to try and quell his influence. Warne-Smith continued: "This unusual alteration in the team's disposition turned the game."[74] There were more. According to *We Are Geelong*, a book published to commemorate 150 years of the Geelong Football Club, Hickey "moved Les Hardiman from full-forward to centre half-back, forward pocket George Dougherty replaced him at full-forward, and (Joe) Sellwood went into the forward pocket (from centre half-back) to alternate with Peter Hardiman in the ruck."[75]

The last quarter was all Geelong's, and Collier was left to lament the fact that he had told his opponents on that trip to Tasmania that they needed to make some positional changes to achieve some success. It was a stunning spectacle of a game, with "grand high marks, fine long distant and accurate passing, cleverness and team work of the highest order, and never has there been such a sustained pace".[76]

---

74   ibid
75   *We Are Geelong, The Story of the Geelong Football Club*, edited by John Murray, Slattery Media Group, 2009
76   *The Argus*, September 27, 1937

The final margin was 32 points; the win a comprehensive triumph for Hickey. Six goals to one in the last term snuffed out Collingwood's hopes, and also the three goals kicked by Coventry left him forever on a career tally of 1299 goals. It would be a record that would last for another 62 years. Coventry would say the following year: "(It) was the greatest game I've played in. I thought we had the game won at half-time, but just as we tossed them in 1930, they tricked us. We finished in a walk."[77] While Curtis, Collier and Wraith went in to congratulate Geelong on the extraordinary spirit shown in the game, once more McHale stayed away from the winner's rooms. As a pure lover of football, he would have appreciated the special nature of the contest. As a pure lover of Collingwood, it is likely that he took defeat badly.

Collingwood faced another hurdle with the tribunal in 1938, and Harry Collier maintained to his dying day that it cost the Magpies a premiership that year. And for all the goodwill that existed between the friendly rivals of Geelong and Collingwood in 1937, there would be none of that between the protagonists in the 1938 Grand Final— Collingwood and Carlton.

Collier had been moved to the point of frustration after the Magpies had given up a lead of 39 points at half-time, and 23 points at three-quarter time, to go down to the Blues by 16 points in their Round 5 game at Victoria Park. Carlton had kicked nine goals in the last term.

Percy Taylor, of *The Argus*, said the Blues had been "resentful" over an incident after the final bell when, he wrote: "(Jack) Carney, the smallest player on the field, had rushed up to shake hands with his leader (captain-coach Brighton Diggins). As he was doing so, Carney was struck on the face by a Collingwood player and fell to the

---

77   Interview with the Coventry brothers, *The Herald*, 1938

ground."[78] Collingwood captain Harry Collier had been the culprit, but he believed no one had seen him, and he remained confident that he would escape, even when Carlton made an official complaint and the matter went before the investigations committee, as had his brother Albert's case had a year earlier.

In 1990, Harry Collier told *The Sun News-Pictorial*: "At the end of the day I went down to shake Brighton Diggins' hand (the pair worked at the brewery together) because they'd just knocked us off. Anyhow, I stood with him, and the next minute (Jack) Carney comes up alongside of me, and passed a remark. I couldn't tell you what he said—you couldn't put it in (the newspaper). But I wasn't happy, so all I did was turn around—I didn't punch him—I sort of pushed him and said, 'Don't argue'."[79] Later (at the investigations hearing) they said, 'Mr Collier, have you anything to say?' I said I have played 231 games, and have never been rubbed out."[80] Collingwood hoped that Collier's previous good record might sway the committee to give him a light sentence. It did anything but. Collier was suspended for rest of the season, leaving the club to compete without its inspirational skipper.

The Argus reported that a petition was later signed by more than 2500 "Collingwood members and other fair-minded football followers of the game"[81] and presented to the VFL delegates. The North Melbourne delegate, Mr. J.F. Meere, said: "If letters of this kind can be accepted from every Tom, Dick and Harry, there would be an unending stream of them." In response, Collingwood's delegate, Bob Rush, replied: "I must remind you that Tom, Dick and Harrys to the number of 2500 supporters of our game have asked for its consideration."[82] The proposal to accept the petition was defeated 11 votes to 10.

As Stremski explained: "Everyone associated with the club felt that jealousy was instrumental in precipitating three major suspensions

---

78   *The Argus*, May 23, 1938
79   *The Sun News-Pictorial*, October 2, 1990
80   Interview with Harry Collier, 1993
81   *The Argus*, August 6, 1938
82   ibid

(Gordon Coventry, Albert Collier and Harry Collier) in three years."[83] McHale never expressed his views publicly on this, preferring to keep his frustration within the walls of Victoria Park, but it is believed he was as angry as anyone at the club that his star players had received at the hands of what was hardly an independent tribunal or investigations system. What compounded the loss of Harry Collier even more was the absence of his brother Albert in 1938, due to a serious knee injury.

This led to McHale abandoning one of the pillars of his coaching career—never play injured players in matches. He had stuck with the policy with almost an iron will for a generation. He had rarely succumbed to the temptation of going against it. And the men who played under him—whether they liked him or not—would describe him almost to a man as the best judge of the fitness of a player that they had ever seen. But McHale sensed something was missing in the make-up of the team without a Collier in it. He had desperately wanted to be able to consider Albert Collier for the finals.

Collingwood finished fourth in the home and away season, with Carlton on top of the ladder. But the Magpies produced two big finals—beating Footscray by 41 points in the first semi-final and their 1937 conquerors Geelong by 37 points in the preliminary final to set up a Grand Final against Carlton—the first time the teams had met in a premiership playoff since 1915. In that preliminary final, Todd had produced one of the most remarkable finals performances on record, kicking 11 goals for the game—equalling the figure kicked by Harry Vallence in the two finals against Collingwood in 1931 and 1932.

Albert Collier had returned to play in the preliminary final after missing a month of football, and kicked a goal, but had clearly not been fit for the contest. *The Argus* reported: "He (Collier) seemed to falter early in the game and it was evident his injured knee was worrying him ... The selectors have had some criticism levelled at them since

---

the team was announced. Supporters said it was an unforgivable act to select a man who was not perfectly fit."[84]

The question mark on Collier's fitness would last all week, and his light training at the final session on the Thursday night before the Grand Final was watched by thousands. Percy Taylor wrote: "Collingwood enthusiasts were present in their thousands last night ... and most of them went away convinced that Albert Collier, their captain, would not be chosen to play."[85] But when the teams were announced, he was selected. Harry Collier would say in 1993 that his brother did not want to play in the game, but was given no choice. He said: "That's right, Jock talked him into playing. He didn't normally do that (play injured players), but he (Jock) was desperate."[86]

Collier's injury through 1938 had been "so serious that he was absent from work for much of the season",[87] and he would play just six home and away games. And it was the fact that he was rostered off from work on the morning of the 1938 Grand Final that led some Carlton footballers, Brighton Diggins included, to suggest that McHale had somehow fixed the Carlton Brewery rosters to ensure Collier was off and Diggins was on. Diggins was said to have been dispatched to work in the steam rooms at the Carlton Brewery on the morning of the match where he had to clean the barrels, while Collier was able to put his wounded knee up for a few extra hours at home. Many Carlton players alleged it at the time and later, while Collingwood officials have always strongly denied that McHale had any part in it.

The prospect of the story being apocryphal seems most likely, even though the Carlton captain-coach had suspected that McHale was somehow involved. McHale was a supervisor at the brewery, but he did not have any roster duties related to Diggins. Carlton's Jim Francis said Diggins had arrived at the football on Grand Final day "swearing

---

84   *The Argus*, September 19, 1938
85   *The Argus*, September 23, 1938
86   Interview with Harry Collier, 1993
87   *Kill For Collingwood*, Richard Stremski, Allen and Unwin, 1986

vengeance" and was "bloody ropeable". He added: "We all knew why it happened."[88] Francis suggested that Diggins should not get mad—he should get even. Francis said in 1993: "He (Diggins) was going to flatten 'Leeter' Collier at the first bounce. I said to him (Diggins) 'Wait a minute, we know Collier has a bad knee. He can't kick and he can't run. If you deck him, they will bring on a fit player (reserve Jack Carmody). We decided nobody was allowed to knock over Collier. We left him alone all day. Every time he got the ball, the only thing he could do was to handball. It cost them dearly."[89] Albert Collier would end up playing in attack, barely moving from the goal-square because of the state of his knee.

The Collingwood selectors' plan to play Collier as inspiration to the players proved disastrous. In front of a record crowd of 96,834 fans, Collier was ineffectual. As Ivor Warne-Smith wrote in *The Argus*: "(Collingwood) had practically only 17 men—Albert Collier was not fit to play. Collingwood carried on and on against a superior side. Every moment of the game teemed with incident, the fierceness and fearlessness of the players gripped the imagination of the vast audience."[90]

Jock's son, Jock jnr, would claim in 1999 that the decision to push for Collier to play had not been his father's, but the selection committee's choice. He said: "He was a great one with players' injuries and making sure everyone was fit. Footballers had to be 100 per cent fit, that was his great belief. He didn't care who you were. Albert (Collier) had a knee injury (in 1938) and my father didn't want him to play in the Grand Final, but the others (on the selection committee) overrode him. Albert went onto the ground as if he was going to frighten them, but it proved unsuccessful."[91]

Whatever the case, the Grand Final had been a tense, tough and tight contest all day, and the fact that Collier could barely run, let

---

88   *Herald Sun*, August 21, 1993, and the *Sunday Herald Sun*, May 25, 1997
89   *Herald Sun*, August 21, 1993
90   *The Argus*, September 26, 1938
91   Interview with Jock McHale Jr, 1999

alone kick, was a decided disadvantage. The Magpies trailed by a point at the first change, by 20 points at half-time, by 22 points at the last change. To their credit, Collingwood kept coming. At one stage of the final term, the difference was back to four points after a Todd goal. But Carlton rallied again to win by 15 points, securing the Blues' first premiership in 23 years.

Jock jnr recalled an unnamed Collingwood official had said after the game that the club had "no regrets" about the match, or the decision to play Collier. He said: "We were beaten by a stronger side on the day and they won a well-fought game."[92] But *The Argus* added: "Answering criticism of the wisdom of playing A. Collier, who was obviously feeling the effects of a leg-injury, Collingwood said his leadership was needed."[93]

While McHale and—or—the Collingwood selectors took a rare risk, and blundered in doing so, Diggins made a few telling moves of his own. He had Jack Hale and 'Mick' Price shadow the dangerous Des Fothergill (four goals) and Alby Pannam (two goals); he moved Jim Park onto Ron Todd (who kicked three goals); he had Ken Baxter keep the attacking Jack Regan deep in the defensive zones, stopping any run he might have; and he instructed his flankers to play wide and allow Jack Wrout to have a clear path at centre half-forward.

Years later, Todd would be highly critical of McHale for his coaching leading into and during the 1938 Grand Final. He would say: "Old Jock McHale really blundered that day. He had this thing about Albert Collier being imperative to the team if we were to win. (But) 'Leeter' was so badly injured (that) he was worse than useless, yet Jock demanded he be selected and then wouldn't take him off. It was embarrassing because Carlton's playing coach Brighton Diggins could be heard telling his players to go easy on 'Leeter'. He didn't want him to be knocked around in case Jock took him off. We were effectively a player short all day."[94]

---

92   ibid
93   The Argus, September 26, 1938
94   *The Blue Boys, the history of the Carlton Football Club from 1864*, Brian Hansen, Brian Hansen Nominees

Within a week of Collingwood's Grand Final loss, England Prime Minister Neville Chamberlain returned from Munich where he had met Adolf Hitler and signed a pact that he said meant "peace in our time." *The Argus* reported Chamberlain's speech, saying: "The agreement signed last night was symbolic of the desire of both of our peoples never to resort to war against each other."[95] It would not be worth the paper it was printed on. Within a year, the world would be back to where it had been before—25 years earlier—and where it had hoped it would never go again. As 1939 rolled on, war was seemingly inevitable, and the *war to end all wars* tag that had described the Great War was shelved forever.

Collingwood had long prided itself as a stable club where every part of its operation ran smoothly. But some serious issues had arisen in late 1938 and early 1939 in regard to disputes between the senior committee and that of the reserves committee. In some ways, it mirrored the competitive professional rivalry that existed between their respective coaches, Jock McHale and Hughie Thomas. The fact that some of McHale's *Machine* team members had been lavish in their praise of Thomas as a skills teacher over the years, and most notably, Gordon Coventry, in an article in *The Sporting Globe* in 1938, had frustrated McHale. And in an interview for *Kill For Collingwood,* long after McHale had died, Percy Taylor, author of the first history of the club, had believed Thomas "was a better coach than Jock ever was".[96]

But when "irregularities" were discovered by the senior committee in the reserves' financial affairs, it set the scene for an all-out war between the two parties. As Stremski documented in detail, the senior committee overruled £10 allocated for a testimonial for Thomas. It revealed: "The committee overrode the objections of ('Doc') Seddon, who was a close mate of Thomas, and deducted £10 from its regular fortnightly contributions. The seconds' committee found other ways to

---

95   *The Argus,* October 1, 1938
96   *Kill For Collingwood,* Richard Stremski, Allen and Unwin, 1986

raise money for the testimonial. One way was a picnic. Another was to take advantage of the club subsidy for each senior player attending the end of season trip sponsored by the seconds. The seconds' committee overstated the number of senior list players who accompanied them to Kyabram that year, where Thomas was presented with a £20 gift."[97]

The senior committee instituted a look into the "irregularities" and put forward a petition to members criticising the running of the seconds. It brought a bitter rivalry to a head. Seddon, furious with how the senior committee was treating the reserves committee, was a part of a ticket, as was Thomas, to challenge. Part of the challenge was based on the mistake of playing Albert Collier as an injured player in the previous year's Grand Final. In the Annual Report of early 1939, the committee said: "It is undoubtedly true that the present opposition has risen because the committee, as guardians of the club's financial stability, insisted upon the investigation and adjustment of the unsatisfactory state of affairs that developed with the finances of the Collingwood District Football Club, the controllers of the second eighteen."[98]

Then, the committee made its points under the headline 'How to Avoid Friction and Discord'. It read: "You are on a roll. It lies with you to say whether you are satisfied with what the committee and those proved and tested officials have done or whether you will expose the club to the danger of internal friction and discord. We have no doubt as to what your reply will be, but we want it to be so emphatic that it will be an overwhelming expression of your confidence in our management."

It was. The challengers, including Seddon, who had been McHale's chairman of selectors since the early 1920s, were dismissed. Wraith and Curtis had their way, and got what they had sought all along, control of the seconds. Seddon was ousted and Thomas replaced as seconds coach by former *Machine* member 'Tubby' Edmonds.

---

97   ibid
98   Collingwood Annual Report, 1939

Thomas's son, Harold, would say that Hughie was "devastated" by what happened in early 1939 after he had given a lifetime's service to the Collingwood district team, as well as the development of the junior schoolboys program that had been such a big part of the club in the 1930s.

He said Thomas's relationship with McHale had never especially been strong, but they had always tried to make it work for the sake of success at the club. That he was pushed out of the club after failing at the election was something he would never forget.

"I think there must have been a bit of personal jealousy between the two of them (Thomas and McHale)," Harold Thomas would say. "He was very upset with what happened then."[99]

Harold Thomas said his father vowed to put a "curse" on Collingwood—and perhaps even McHale—after being dumped in early 1939, and said he would never return until McHale had finished as the senior coach.

"He definitely cursed them. He didn't want them to win another premiership," he said.

Call it a curse or not, Collingwood, and McHale, would lose a third successive Grand Final—the club's fifth premiership playoff in as many seasons—in 1939, this time to Melbourne, and to 'Checker' Hughes, who had finally beaten McHale in a Grand Final as the opposing coach. Collingwood had enjoyed a strong year on the field to finish in second spot behind Melbourne on percentage only. The Magpies had lost the second semi-final to the Demons by 14 points, with Whelan (who would win the Brownlow Medal and the Copeland Trophy that season) best for his team. But a 29-point win over St Kilda in the preliminary final, with Todd once more kicking 11 goals in a final, pushed Collingwood into a Grand Final once again.

Collingwood had kicked six goals to three to open up a three-goal lead in the game. But Melbourne played the better football after that

---

99   Interview with Harold Thomas, 2010

period, kicking seven goals to four to hold a narrow four-point lead at half-time. The Demons ran away with the contest in the second half, with Hughes finally getting one up on his old sparring partner, McHale. The final margin was 53 points after the Demons had kicked the highest Grand Final score to that time, 21.22 (148) to 14.11 (95).

Harry Collier could sense leading into the game that Melbourne had Collingwood's edge. He said years later: "I could see Melbourne were going to win that flag. They were just a better side than we were."[100]

Todd would take his season tally to 121—one more than his 120 from the previous year—with his sixth goal kicked in the Grand Final. The club praised him for his efforts: "His success, he regards, as the success of the side. The football public saw in the preliminary final against St Kilda how his teammates unselfishly plied him with the ball, not merely because they desired to win, but because they eagerly wanted him to better his own record of 11 goals in a final, and one which he jointly shares with Vallence, formerly of Carlton. Ron equalled his record and possibly the hardest things said about him when he struck the post from what looked like the easiest of positions were said by himself."[101] Todd looked as if he had been pre-ordained to become one of the game's greatest forwards, possibly better than Lee and Coventry.

The Grand Final had been played 27 days after Prime Minister Robert Menzies declared that it was his "melancholy duty" to announce that Australia was at war—just after Germany invaded Poland. Everything was about to change at home, and abroad.

In time, the ramifications of the Second World War on the Collingwood Football Club would be far more significant than those of the First World War. And there were separate series of other events that would push Collingwood—and McHale—to the brink, and would leave Hughie Thomas wondering if his curse had been the cause of at least some of the misfortunes.

100   Interview with Harry Collier, 1993
101   Collingwood Annual Report, 1940

CHAPTER 12

Defections and the Dark Years

1940-1944

Leaving Collingwood was something that Jock McHale had never seriously considered. Leaving for sake of money was anathema to him. He could never come to terms with, let alone understand, why a handful of players sought better financial deals at other VFL clubs, in the VFA or in cashed-up country leagues. Some famous names in the club's history—Dick Condon, Dan Minogue and Charlie Pannam jnr, to name a few—had left in the past, and had been all but excommunicated. To that end, McHale and the Magpies' administration grumbled about losing players and the decline in loyalty, but in many ways they just got on with the job, and seemingly had a knack of bringing a wave of younger, hungrier players happy enough to wear the black and white, and content to receive the same pay as their teammates.

McHale's intrinsic belief that all footballers *must* be paid the same has been expressed in other sections of this book. It was something that he had believed in since he first became involved in the VFL players' push for professionalism in early 1911. Almost 30 years later, on the eve of the 1940 season, few clubs had maintained the rigid Collingwood model of egalitarianism. Through the 1930s the Magpies had held firm, while a host of rival clubs, including South Melbourne, had chased recruits from across all the football states, with the promise of a nice return for those willing to take the lure. Was it any wonder that McHale took particular delight in the fact that his remodelled *Machine* had defeated South, considered a great team of individuals, to win the 1935 and 1936 Grand Finals? But those jealously guarded beliefs would be sorely tested by the defections that would rock the club, and the coach.

The two main stories on the front page of *The Argus* on January 1, 1940, said much about the dichotomy of circumstances confronting Australians at the time. Yes, there was a war on. But that all seemed so far away four months into the so-called "Phoney War", a phase of relative inactivity that would stretch into the early months of 1940 before being shattered menacingly by mid-year. There were few changes experienced by most Australians in those first few months of the conflict, where the theatres of war had seemed distant—as they had for those who had not joined up in the First World War—but all of this would change, and dramatically, in time.

The lead story had sinister undertones. It reported a speech from Germany's Adolf Hitler to mark the New Year, and to call for the destruction of the British Empire, which meant Australia as well. The article read: "Hitler violently attacked Britain and 'the Jewish capitalistic world' today in a New Year proclamation to the Nazi Party, and the German Army. He stated that Germany and all Europe 'must be liberated from the coercion and incessant emanating from the former and present-day England.' Hitler forecast a Nazi victory 'probably next year'."[1]

Accompanying this sombre story was a series of photographs of Melburnians celebrating the ringing in of 1940 with women dancing

---

1   *The Argus*, January 1, 1940

and a man jazzing away on a saxophone, as well as a spectacular fireworks display. *The Argus* observed: "Troubles of 1939—even the war—were forgotten last night, when, at St Kilda, at the bayside resorts, and at hundreds of private parties, Melbourne gaily welcomed the New Year. Men in tails and dinner jackets and women in evening gowns, mingled in the street, and on the beach and lawns with less formal revellers in sports clothes and bath suits. In the city ... crowds amused themselves, window-shopping while they waited for clocks to strike midnight. The revelry continued until dawn."[2]

McHale could hardly have known—as the 1939 calendar flipped over to 1940—that it would also herald the start of the most unsuccessful decade of his career and the start of an unprecedented five successive years without a finals appearance. In some ways, it might have been an opportune time for the Collingwood coach to call it a day. He had led his team into five consecutive Grand Finals (albeit losing the past three), but he was now 57 and was not as active at training as he had previously been. What had he left to prove? His record as a coach meant that, by the end of 1939, McHale had coached Collingwood teams into 17 of the past 25 Grand Finals contested. But the thought of retiring never crossed his mind.

With the luxury of hindsight, it is easy to see how a number of factors contributed to Collingwood's free-fall in the first half of the 1940s. The changing nature of the Second World War, as the conflict crept closer and closer to Australian shores, meant that the enlistment numbers of past and present Magpie footballers would be significant, as they matched—if not exceeded—most of the rival VFL clubs. That put pressure on the numbers at training and on the coach, as he was often forced to select a patched up group of players, made of up those who for one reason or another could not or would not enlist, or those on leave from their military secondments. Through the 1930s, Collingwood would have up to 100 men training in pre-seasons,

---

2   ibid

but through the early 1940s it was a battle simply to have enough men on the track.

Two massive defections of star players at the start of the decade, and the questionable, enforced retirement of two of the club's champions pretty much before a ball had been kicked in anger would also play key parts. The first defection came just before the start of the 1940 season; the second a year later. The fact that the players concerned were 23 and 20 (yes, 20!) when they vacated Victoria Park was enough to tear the heart of out of Collingwood supporters. So, too, was the decision by the committee, including club secretary Frank Wraith and coach Jock McHale (who was on both the selection committee and the general committee) to end the careers of siblings who had long been the heart and soul of the place, and were reluctant to leave because they felt they had much more to give.

In truth, there had been an earlier defection at the end of the 1938 season that had set the scene for what was to come. Marcus Boyall had finished equal third in the 1938 Brownlow Medal (with 15 votes, behind the winner Dick Reynolds [18 votes] of Essendon, and Stan Spinks [17], of Hawthorn) when he left the club and the job it had secured for him; he left just months after being adjudged as one of Collingwood's best players in the losing Grand Final. By November, he had been announced as the new assistant curator at the Glenelg Oval (Test cricketer Mervyn Waite was the curator), where he was expected to play cricket and football. Collingwood heard about his move from the newspapers. An unsuspecting Frank Wraith told *The Argus*: "Perhaps he thought he would like a summer in Adelaide."[3] *The Argus* reported: "As Boyall has come to Adelaide to improve his employment position, it is not expected that he will have any difficulty in obtaining his clearance."[4] Nothing could be further from the truth.

Collingwood not only rejected Boyall's request for a clearance, it gave him a dressing down in the Annual Report as it summed up its

---

3   *The Argus*, November 9, 1938
4   ibid

1939 season—a year in which the star centre half-back was forced to stand out of the game. The club said: "Your committee and your coach worked on Boyall with patience and perseverance in an effort to make him a first-class player in his fourth season (he had made his debut in 1935)—we doubt very much if any other club would have observed such patience—he suddenly demonstrated that ability which we had sensed was latent in him. He became an integral and important cog in the Collingwood organisation. Just when we were looking forward to having his services for years, and so securing a return for all our labour, he left us without the slightest notice. It was only through the press that we learnt of his movements and intentions. We feel sure that you (the members) recognise the cavalier treatment meted out to your club by this player is not exactly that which would predispose your committee to grant him a favour. In the interests of the club, and of discipline, we were left with no other alternative than to invite him to return or remain out of the game."[5]

Boyall belatedly got to play for Glenelg in 1940, and showed what Collingwood missed a year later when he won the Magarey Medal as the best player in the SANFL. He was 21 when he left Collingwood, and had played only 35 games. Time healed some of the wounds. The Magpies allowed Boyall to play a further 15 games in black and white (three games in 1942, six in 1944 and six in 1945) while on leave from the Navy. Incredibly, he was second in the club's goalkicker award in 1944, with 25 goals from his six games, behind 21-year-old Lou Richards. Richards' haul of 26 goals was the lowest tally of a Collingwood leading goalkicker since Ern Utting's 23 in 1920, the year Gordon Coventry had joined the club.

If Collingwood had been shaken by Boyall's departure, it was nothing like the next two defections. The first—the defection of Ron Todd—meant the Magpies were without a star full-forward for the first time in 35 years. The great champion Dick Lee started in 1906,

---

5   Collingwood Annual Report, 1940

kicking 707 goals before his retirement in 1922. He had overlapped three seasons with Gordon Coventry, who would go on to kick 1299 goals, himself having played three years with Todd. But when Todd—coming off successive tallies of 120 and 121 in the 1938 and 1939 seasons—shocked Collingwood by announcing he wanted a clearance to Williamstown—in the then powerful VFA—in early 1940, it looked as if it was going to rob the club of the man who, teammates say, had the potential to be the greatest of them all. By that stage, he had kicked 327 goals from his 76 games, and had the football world at his feet.

An *Argus* report from February 24, 1940, detailed offers that had been made to Todd, and also to Richmond's superstar Jack Dyer, to join the VFA. The offer came from Williamstown president Bill Dooley, who was also a prominent bookmaker. The £500 three-year deal, plus extra match payments, was an exorbitant amount of money in those days; it would comfortably have covered the price of a five-room house in inner Melbourne. Compare that with the £3 a game he could expect at Collingwood—or perhaps £60 for the year—and the choice was clear. The newspaper reported: "It is certain that Collingwood committee would refuse Todd a clearance because he is aged only 22 (sic, he was 23), and can look forward to many more seasons in League football. If Williamstown's offer is sufficiently attractive, his only alternative will be to leave Collingwood without a clearance. His transfer would create a stir in football."[6]

It certainly created a stir in Collingwood. McHale was furious. Todd formed a sizeable part of his plan for annexing another premiership. Never before as coach—other than a number of games here and there—had he been left without a champion forward. The committee was incensed. Harry Collier recalled in 1993: "He (Todd) was a confident bloke. But he was too anxious to get money too quick when he took off to Williamstown."[7] Five weeks before Collingwood's

---

6   *The Argus*, February 24, 1940
7   Interview with Harry Collier, 1993

first game of the 1940 season, Todd announced that he had decided to take up Williamstown's offer. It was assumed almost immediately that Collingwood would not buckle to the pressure, and would not even contemplate offering Todd money, with *The Argus* saying: "It has always been a policy of the club to place every player on a similar footing and even the veteran coach (Jock McHale) will not accept more than the £3 per week for his services ... most (other) League coaches receive at least £6."[8]

Principle had been at the core of McHale's stratagem at Collingwood. It meant as much to him as anything else, and was infinitely more valuable than any monetary gain. Even though he was likely to be the person on the Collingwood committee most affected by its decision to refuse to offer Todd more money to stay, he was adamant that the systems that the club had almost been weaned on needed to stay. Not everyone agreed. There was debate on the Collingwood committee, but not enough to change the philosophy.[9]

But the beliefs that many thought were antiquated and possibly an impediment to future Collingwood successes were to be maintained. A clearance was denied Todd at a committee meeting on March 26, and a few days later more than 1000 Williamstown fans flocked to the ground to see the champion forward train for the first time. The VFL considered blocking Todd's move with legal action. In early April *The Argus* reported that "Todd is said to have received £100 when he signed an agreement to play with Williamstown and will receive another £100 this season and £150 each for the next two years, in addition to a weekly payment."[10] In the story, Magpie officials insisted that the club had not given up on a kid who had Collingwood blood in his veins.

On April 13—two weeks before the VFL season's first game— came the news that Collingwood fans had prayed for. After a series

---

8   *The Argus*, March 25, 1940
9   *Kill For Collingwood*, Richard Stremski, Allen and Unwin, 1986
10   *The Argus*, April 12, 1940

of meetings with Frank Wraith, and a likely assurance from McHale that he would not hold the incident against him, Todd turned up for a practice match at Victoria Park and announced that he intended to remain a Magpie. *The Argus* described the moment: "To the great delight of Collingwood and the intense surprise of Williamstown, Ron Todd ... has decided to remain at Collingwood. He was at his old club on Saturday and was wildly cheered as he ran on to the ground in the second half of the practice match."[11]

There were, Todd said, a number of reasons for his about face. One of them was the uncertainty surrounding the VFA's future, given the war. He claimed another was the association he had with his coach McHale, and his words explaining the reasons surrounding his return may well have been aimed at smoothing over that relationship. Todd told *The Argus*: "My football was learned in Collingwood and the lure of the black and white uniform is too great for me. After all, there are other things in life than money. My past association with the Magpies—Jock McHale, my teammates, the committee and supporters, in fact all that Collingwood stands for—is too much for me."[12] The complicating factor was the fact that he had already accepted £100, and Williamstown refused to accept it back.

Todd was named in two teams for the last practice match of 1940— for Collingwood and Williamstown. He chose Williamstown; Percy Taylor of *The Argus* wrote: "This announcement followed a frantic effort by Collingwood supporters not officially connected with the club to retain him ... They pleaded with him late on Thursday until the early hours of yesterday (Sunday) morning."[13] Taylor said he had the feeling that Todd had little choice in the end as he had already signed a deal, and that it was likely to be binding. "From his demeanour one gathered the opinion that, although he would give Williamstown of his best, his heart was still at Collingwood."[14]

---

11   *The Argus*, April 15, 1940
12   ibid
13   *The Argus*, April 20, 1940
14   ibid

And so Collingwood, and McHale, lost one of its most exciting players. Todd would kick four goals in his first game with Williamstown (his teammate, the former champion Carlton sharpshooter Harry Vallence would kick 16), and he would end the season on 99 goals. More feats of goalkicking mastery were in store for Todd, but not in the famous black and white.

Collingwood addressed the matter in the 1941 Annual Report, defending its policies to its members. It was stated: "It has been suggested that those players might still be with the club had they been offered sufficient football inducement. All that need be said ... is that your committee made every effort to keep the players, short of financial discrimination as between player and player. Under no circumstances will your committee be induced to offer any player a monetary consideration above that which is enjoyed by all the other members of the team. It is our unshakeable belief that it is the team as a whole that counts. To depart from the principle of recognising the side as a whole would lead to internal jealousies and discontent would inevitably destroy the fine team spirit which has carried Collingwood through to many a memorable record-breaking triumph."[15]

There would be another massive defection to come a year later, but the club would stick to its "unshakeable belief" that the unity of the team was more critical than keeping a few individuals happy.

The other shock that ripped Collingwood at the time had people wondering whether the loyalty that had been demanded of Todd had been given to the long-serving Collier brothers. It was announced, at almost the same time as Todd finalised his decision to play with Williamstown, that Harry and Albert Collier were to "retire" from the game after spectacular careers. This had not been expected. In fact, retirement was not their choice, even though the club wanted it to appear that way. They intended to play on and chase that elusive

---

15   Collingwood Annual Report, 1941

seventh individual flag each. Albert had played in his first practice match a few weeks earlier after returning from holidays.

Harry was 32. Albert was 30. There had been some doubt about whether Albert's knee would hold up to another tough season. Certainly, Jock jnr would later highlight his father's propensity to dismiss players with long-term ailments, in a manner that bordered on ruthlessness. Jock jnr said in 1999: "In my father's day, if he knew you had a bad leg, he would virtually give you away there and then. He believed footballers had to be 100 per cent fit. That was his great belief. He didn't care if you were Harry Collier or Albert Collier."[16]

The decision rankled with both of them, even many years later, though Harry was not especially one for bitterness. More than 50 years later, he said: "They (the committee) told us the supporters didn't want us anymore. It wasn't the bloody supporters, it was the bloody committee. They blamed us when they should have been blaming themselves. I tell you, if there had been an election on, we would have been voted in by the supporters, not them."[17] Harry's assertion about the fans was spot on. When the club allowed him back for one final game—his 253th—against Essendon in Round 6 that year, to allow him to qualify for his 15-year certificate, the fans gave him a "special cheer ... remembering his brilliant deeds over the years."[18] He kicked two goals in the two-point win, which took him to 299 career goals—1000 behind the bloke he used to help feed, Gordon Coventry.

Collingwood did institute a testimonial for the Collier brothers, and they were presented with a collective return of £500—the same figure that one player (Todd) had been promised by Williamstown for three years—towards the end of the season. In the light of the debate on player transfers and payments, the club said: "We do not think that it can be said that Collingwood has ever failed to recognise and

---

16   Interview with Jock McHale Jr., 1999
17   Interview with Harry Collier, 1993
18   *The Argus*, June 3, 1940

reward outstanding service, and the pleasant function in which Harry and Albert Collier figured on the last day of the season demonstrated once again that the club knows how to look after its own."[19] Harry Collier went on to be captain-coach of the Essendon seconds in 1941, and they won the flag. Albert ended up playing 12 games with Fitzroy in 1941 and 1942. Both would express interest in McHale's job as coach when the position would finally become available. Other retirements before the 1940 season included Jack Ross, Jack Knight and Bervin Woods.

Jock McHale had a special reason for keeping a close eye on the Collingwood seconds at the tail end of the 1930s and into 1940. His son, Jock jnr (known to many of his teammates as Jack, a return to his earliest years), had somehow managed to convince his father to let him play football again after the horrific injury he had suffered in 1933. One time in the mid-1930s Jock jnr was having a kick of a ball in the park with some of his mates, and immediately he felt the presence of his father watching on. McHale snr did not want his remaining child to be put at risk in any way so he had actively discouraged him from playing football again, but finally he agreed to allow him to play. Jock jnr recalled his father saying: "If you've started up, then you may as well get it out of your blood."[20] It was his father's way of inviting his son to Victoria Park, to try out for the reserves, which he did in 1938, when he was 23.

June McHale said old Jock was fiercely protective of his son, particularly when it came to his football career. "Jock was really opposed to my Jock playing football (after the accident)," she said.[21] She added: "Old Jock was so overprotective. When young Jock announced that he was going to play for Collingwood, there were a lot of silent meals. They would pass each other in the hall and not talk to each other."[22]

---

19   Collingwood Annual Report, 1941
20   *Sunday Herald Sun*, March 8, 1992
21   Interview, June McHale, 2009
22   *The 500 Club, Footy's Greatest Coaches*, Kevin Sheedy, News Custom
      Publishing, 2004

By 1940, Jock jnr was captain of a reserves side that included a cheeky little rover with impeccable Collingwood bloodlines, Lewis Thomas Charles Richards. Everyone called him Lou. By 1941, Jock jnr was about to push himself beyond the reserves.

1940 was a difficult year for Collingwood. If losing Todd and the Colliers was not enough, Jack Regan (chosen captain as a replacement for Harry Collier) managed only nine games due to injury. Marcus Whelan, coming off a Brownlow Medal win in 1939, also played only 12 games. Four players managed to represent the club in all games that season—Phonse Kyne (who, as vice-captain, had to lead the club in Regan's absence, and whom McHale was increasingly using in the ruck in the late 1930s and early 1940s), Alby Pannam, Jack Murphy (Jock's nephew) and Des Fothergill, who was on the way towards a third Copeland Trophy.

Fothergill's form that year was exquisite. He took over the main roving role from Harry Collier and ended up kicking 56 goals in a stellar season. After the Round 7 game against St Kilda, which brought the club to 4-3 on the win-loss ledger, Fothergill was lauded for his extraordinary skills. Percy Taylor wrote in *The Argus*: "Rising splendidly to greater demands on his skill, Desmond Fothergill, Collingwood rover, is playing the best football of his career. The retirement of Harry Collier made Fothergill first rover and the departure of Ron Todd has left him with the feeling that he should kick as many goals as possible. His cleverness in extricating himself from difficult positions, his uncanny sense of positional play, and his ability to make openings for passes stamp him as a champion."[23]

Kyne was showing leadership qualities off the field, too. He led a meeting in late May, where, as reported by *The Argus*, the players "unanimously instructed the representatives of the general committee ... that in view of the serious war position, their payment should be reduced from £3 per game to £1".[24] Percy Taylor's history of the

23   *The Argus*, June 1, 1940
24   *The Argus*, May 31, 1940

club, published nine years later, said the committee agreed to the recommendation and "effected other economies."[25]

Almost at the same time as Collingwood was losing to Richmond (by 26 points) in Round 8, the Germans were rolling into Paris in a statement that brought about a dramatic escalation of the war. According to *The Argus*, Australian Prime Minister Robert Menzies pleaded for: "... everything we have, our savings, our property, our skills, the service of our hands, if necessary, the services of our lives for the country that we love."[26] The war position had progressively and rapidly become more difficult and dangerous. Australia had 20,000 soldiers abroad and more than 40,000 training in camps on home soil. There would be many more to come, and a number of the Collingwood team would soon swap a black and white jumper for a very different sort of uniform.

That loss to the Tigers saw McHale's team dip from fourth to seventh, and they never regained their momentum. *The Argus* concluded: "Collingwood is not the Magpie of old. It seems to have lost some of its feathers. That may give the side a slight bedraggled appearance, but the old spirit is still there."[27]

A break in the season came in early August when the VFL instituted a "Patriotic Premiership", a kind of lightning premiership played in the one afternoon before 30,407 fans at the MCG. It was the first time all 12 clubs had played in the same location and on the same day. All the players and umpires agreed to not only play for free, but also to pay for their own admission. In the end, it was St Kilda, the only one of the original VFL clubs not to have won a premiership, which took out the unusual event in the final against Richmond. There were more signs of Collingwood's decline, according to *The Argus*, which said: "A year or two ago a similar competition would have been easy for Collingwood, which has always specialised in lightning thrusts, as soon as the game

---

25   *The History of the Collingwood Football Club, 1892-1948*, Percy Taylor, 1949
26   *The Argus*, June 17, 1940
27   *The Argus*, June 19, 1940

begins. But Collingwood, on Saturday, was only a shadow of its former power and was well beaten in the first 10 minutes of its only game, against Footscray."[28]

Most of the problems affecting Collingwood came from their lack of a legitimate and powerful forward. How McHale must have yearned for the days in which he had three of the great full-forwards in his midst (sometimes with two of them at a time). But he continued to experiment and play new players, hoping to strike the same sort of formula that had worked so stunningly in the long years beforehand. The club acknowledged: "Due to the loss of his key players, from time to time, his (McHale's) duties were made heavy and his problem difficult, but for all that, he moulded a happy band of players around him, whose keenness to win a place in the final four never waned at any stage. His great work deserved better results."[29]

But towards the end of the season, after the 14-point Round 16 loss to eventual premier Melbourne knocked Collingwood out of the finals race for only the sixth time in the club's history, and the first time since 1933, the focus of all within the club switched to the reserves team, led by McHale's son. Jock jnr had been added to the senior list in the middle of the year, but had not yet played a senior game. In the 1920s and 1930s, the district side—under Hughie Thomas (who was now a reserves coach at St Kilda)—had at times made sacrifices to aid the senior team's quest for premierships. In late 1940, when the finals were out of reach, McHale, according to the Annual Report, made a "very sporting gesture"[30] to seconds coach 'Tubby' Edmonds by not choosing a few players—one of them his son—who could have been elevated in the last few games of the season. The senior Magpies finished with only eight wins from their 18 matches, and would end up in eighth position, the lowest rung in the club's history. Just like it was with the war, there would be worse to come before it would get better.

---

28   *The Argus*, August 2, 1940
29   Collingwood Annual Report, 1941
30   ibid

The 'gesture' paid dividends for the reserves. On Grand Final day, 1940, in the game before his old rival 'Checker' Hughes became a premiership coach for the third time, McHale got to watch his "precious" son lead Collingwood reserves to the premiership, beating Carlton 6.16 to 3.12.

Lou Richards, who played in that reserves Grand Final, described the event in his 1989 memoirs: "What a thrill it was. Melbourne and Richmond would play in the main match in front of nearly 70,000 (70,330) later in the afternoon but the MCG was just about packed to the rafters for our match. Collingwood beat Carlton and the media was as pleased with my roving performance as I had been myself. Later in the rooms ... we were joined by the senior coach Jock McHale. He walked over and stood in front of me, this legendary Collingwood figure. 'Young Richards', the great man said. 'Yes, Mr McHale?' 'Well played today, son. You'll be a Collingwood player.' Those few words, which were probably the most exciting I have ever heard, have stayed with until this day."[31]

The grandson of the great Charlie Pannam snr continued: "That night I couldn't get out of the ground quick enough to rush home and tell my mother and father that the famous Jock McHale had told me I would be playing for Collingwood. We always looked up to old Jock, particularly the younger fellows, because we were very scared of him, mainly because of his very gruff manner."[32] Richards was then 17.

Jock McHale jnr won the best and fairest in the reserves, a serious achievement for a player who only a few years earlier thought he would never play again. In the seniors, the 1940 Copeland Trophy was won by Des Fothergill, who also tied with South Melbourne's Herb Matthews for the Brownlow Medal. The pair were given replicas at the time (but presented with real ones 49 years later) because of the "unprecedented tie" that saw them poll not only the same number of votes (32), but also the same allotment—seven three votes, four

31   *The Kiss of Death*, Lou Richards with Steven Phillips, Hutchinson Australia, 1989
32   *Boots and All*, Lou Richards, Stanley Paul, 1963

two votes and three one votes. The performances of each player were sublime, and have hardly been equalled.

But only five months after he was feted as being one of the best, if not the best, player in the VFL, Fothergill dropped what Collingwood secretary Frank Wraith described as "a bombshell"[33] on the club.

The champion rover, who would not turn 21 until July, told the club he had signed a three-year deal to play Williamstown in the VFA, and for the third straight year, Collingwood was about to lose a star player to a more lucrative offer from another club.

When the news broke in February 1941, Wraith said much of the disappointment centred on the fact that Fothergill had been one of the first products of the club's curtain-raiser junior games. He stated: "Every effort will be made to retain Fothergill, the club would not depart from the policy of equal treatment for all players. The committee would not tolerate differential treatment to retain the services of even the most valuable player."[34] To rub salt into already sore wounds, on the night Fothergill fronted for his first training session with Williamstown (Todd was absent that night—having enlisted he was in camp) he did so in a Collingwood jumper, with CFC on one side of it, a photograph published in *The Argus* the next day.

The long-serving administrator Gordon Carlyon admitted: "Supporters were starting to resent the loss of such gifted players as Todd, Fothergill and Boyall, and began to question the dumping of the popular Collier brothers."[35] Much of the blame went on Wraith, even though the committee, which included McHale, was as steadfast as ever that if they changed the very premise on which Collingwood had paid its players from the start, it would create disharmony and ruin the team spirit that had driven the club to success in the past.

Those key losses and the increasing number of players joining up and heading off to camp, and then for overseas assignment,

---

33   *The Argus*, February 27, 1941
34   Ibid
35   *Frank Wraith, A Magpie misjudged*, Gordon Carlyon, Gordon Carlyon, 2003

almost crippled Collingwood in the early 1940s. Carlyon wrote: "It is considered probable that if Todd, Fothergill and Boyall had not left, Collingwood's success may have continued."[36] That was a fair assumption, given Todd's success in continuing to kick a swag of goals whenever he played for Williamstown and with Fothergill winning the VFA best and fairest award, as well as the Recorder Cup in 1941, and Boyall winning South Australia's Magarey Medal the same season. Collingwood had lost three great players.

McHale had used 14 debutants in 1941, including his own son, and Lou Richards. Twenty-six-year-old Jock jnr played the first of his 34 games under his father in the Round 1 loss to Richmond. He wore the No.17 jumper—the same number Jock snr did in three of his playing seasons (1915, 1916 and 1917). It was not the auspicious start that either of them had hoped. Jock jnr suffered an ankle injury during the third term, and had to be replaced by Gordon Hocking. It would be one of six games he played in 1941, but he would continue to improve in the coming years as Collingwood's depth dwindled. During these times Jock jnr would often drive his father to the game. He would recall: "He was enormously tense on football days. I had a car and I remember how I used to pick him up before a game. If I was five minutes late, he would be off on a cable tram."[37]

Richards would play the first of his 250 games for the club in Round 6 against Carlton at Princes Park. The Magpies lost by 17 points. But Richards would never forget his debut, in a sign of just how tough the game was back then: "I was playing in the forward pocket and this bloke came up to me, he looked like a tank and he said 'Congratulations on playing your first game, Lou, and I hope you

---

36   *Gordon Carlyon's Collingwood Football Club scrapbook*, Gordon Carlyon and
     Wayne Levy, Collingwood Football Club Library and Archives Committee, 1997
37   *Sunday Herald Sun*, March 8, 1992

have a good day, and good luck to you'. I thought, what a wonderful fellow. His name was Charlie McInnes, and I was standing there watching the ball get bounced and he's suddenly given me the best backhander I've had in my life."[38] Richards would not miss another game that year.

Norm Crewther, who played the first of his 14 games with the club on the same day, recalled how McHale would give a stirring message in the rooms to inspire his men. The coach may have been getting older, with a bit more paunch around his frame, and with hair that long since had headed off into greyness, but he could still give a rattling message to the team when it was required. It's just that the team didn't have the capabilities often during the early 1940s to act on such stirring rhetoric. In an interview in his 91st and final year of life, Crewther recalled: "Old Jock used to get up on the big long seats and walk along them in the change rooms, with his hat in his hands and he would be looking down on you, giving you his speech. And when he was on the boundary line, he would always have his hat and bloody coat."[39]

Collingwood fared a little better in 1941 (a year in which McHale's nephew Jack Murphy would win the Copeland) than it had the previous year, and missed the finals by only one game and percentage. The Magpies were outside the top four for the first 14 weeks of the season, and then gave McHale a glimmer of hope when they beat Footscray by 29 points in Round 15 to jump a game clear in fourth spot, ahead of Essendon.

But a loss to reigning premiers Melbourne by 23 points after kicking 11.21 to 17.8 saw the Magpies out of the top four for the remainder of the season. There was plenty of emotion in that game. The two teams lined up for a minute's silence to mourn the loss of Melbourne's 1940 premiership player, Ronald James Barassi, who had been killed at Tobruk a fortnight earlier. For once, the cold war between McHale and 'Checker' Hughes (Melbourne coach) was forgotten, as both men

---

38   *Herald Sun*, April 19, 1997
39   Interview with Norm Crewther, 2010

lined up with their respective teams (with hats off) as a mark of respect to the first VFL footballer killed in the Second World War. Sadly, he would not be the last.

One of the positives was the fact that McHale's men were able to win the "Patriotic Premiership" for 1941, the second time the 12 clubs had competed on the one day to raise money for the war effort. It came in May, and the Magpies won the lightning premiership by "playing purposeful and determined football."[40] The abbreviated games of two 10-minute halves saw Collingwood go through the miserably wet afternoon undefeated. It beat Richmond, Geelong, St Kilda and, eventually, Melbourne in the Grand Final with all matches held at the MCG.

The Argus reported: "Collingwood are delighted with its success and Jock McHale, coach, pointed out with pride that the team included 12 who helped the seconds win the premiership last season. Its only worry at the moment is at full-forward."[41] Crewther recalled: "It was a bloody wet day, that's what I remember about it. Once you finished one game, you took your jumper off and tried to get warm. Then you have to put it back on again. Jock had me at full-back that day on Norm Smith (in the final)."[42] (Crewther's uncle was former great Magpie full-back Bill Proudfoot).

A bigger positive amid the negatives surrounding the club was Collingwood becoming the first VFL club to possess a liquor licence. It had been a difficult process, but many people associated with the club had worked exceptionally hard to make it happen. Wraith had long wanted to secure a licence, which was extremely difficult to attain, and used the legal nous of former player Jack Galbally, to chase the licence that belonged to the Tivoli (German) club in Victoria Street, Abbotsford. The club initially tried to purchase the Tivoli's licence, but in the end it was handed back to the Liquor Commission. There

---

40   *The Argus*, May 26, 1941
41   ibid
42   Interview with Norm Crewther, 2010

was opposition on a number of fronts to the plan to acquire the licence, including from a group of irate residents.

But a lot of work by all those involved at the club, not the least John Wren, who, according to Stremski, had several of his political allies stress the legitimacy of the club's bid to the Licensing Court, saw Collingwood granted the precious licence. Wren's grandson would say many years later: "That licence was gained by my grandfather from the German club. He grabbed the licence and switched it over to Collingwood."[43] But it wasn't just Wren. Others such as Wraith, who put in extraordinary hours to make it happen, working himself to the point of exhaustion to achieve his goal. His son, Daryl, would later explain just what it meant to his father, and to the football club, saying it would be years before other VFL clubs could claim to have a liquor licence.

The social club, licence in hand, officially opened on April 23, 1941, three days before the club's first game that year. It was a gala opening, with the coach Jock McHale proposing the toast to the important guests among the 200 people who attended the inaugural dinner—including VFL secretary 'Like' McBrien, who admitted he was "playing the wag" from an important football meeting. *The Argus* reported the new clubrooms "comprise a bar, lounge, billiard and card rooms, while the players' dressing and training rooms are almost ornate."[44] It was a far cry from what McHale had told Carlyon about his early years: "Catching cable trams down Johnston Street (after leaving the brewery) to the Victoria Park ground and the primitive training room for the players ... it was merely a galvanised iron lined room with cold showers and no toilets. Players received their rubdown from trainers, (while) standing up."[45]

McHale, being the creature of habit that he was, preferred to drink at Bouverie Street, the home of his employer, than at Lulie Street's

---

43 Interview with John Wren III, 2010
44 *The Argus*, April 24, 1941
45 *Gordon Carlyon's Collingwood Football Club scrapbook*, Gordon Carlyon and Wayne Levy, Collingwood Football Club Library and Archives Committee, 1997

social club. Gordon Carlyon said Jock was a fan of Carlton Draught rather than the Victoria Bitter that was on offer at the Collingwood Social Club.

Carlyon said: "He was very loyal ... he wouldn't drink at Collingwood. We only had VB on tap, and after a game he couldn't wait to get out of the place and up to the brewery to have a beer. He'd take a few special blokes with him—Phonse Kyne, Gordon Hocking, those types of people."[46] His future daughter-in-law, June McHale, explained: "He had a key to the brewery and he would invite a few people back after a game. If you got an invitation, you knew you were in with old Jock."[47]

Lou Richards never forgot the times he was asked to join McHale. "He was a giant, a true legend of the game. He had three great loves— his family, the Collingwood Football Club and the brewery, where he was a foreman. If you played a good game, he would say 'Young Richards, you'd better come with me'. He'd take me down to the brewery near the City Baths and pour you a big pot. It was one of the biggest thrills of my life."[48] Richards added: "If we won, he'd take the players who he thought went well up to the brewery, where he would produce the keys to the brewery bar, and 'shout'. If we lost, he would often still take some of the boys up, but he refused to talk to anyone until after he had had about six pots, and then he became a little more expansive and even managed a friendly word or two."

Jack Pimm, whose 58 games from 1940, 1946-50, would be divided by the war, a conflict in which he would win a Military Cross, enjoyed the experience on a few occasions. He recalled in 2009: "The players regularly went down there, and we would all line up for a bottle of yeast. Some of the (younger) players used to get a bit pimply faced, and he would say 'this will clean your blood'."[49]

---

46   *The 500 Club, Footy's Greatest Coaches*, Kevin Sheedy, News Custom Publishing, 2004
47   ibid
48   *Herald Sun*, July 7, 2001
49   Interview, Jack Pimm, 2009

On the weekend that Collingwood won the "Patriotic Premiership", Prime Minister Robert Menzies had arrived home from a visit abroad, pleading for unity to fight the war effort. It would not come, at least from within his own party. Losing support, he was forced to resign, and to hand over to Arthur Fadden, who tried in vain to retain the minority government. But, by October, two independents crossed the floor, voting with Labor. Incredibly, it meant that the man who had been Jock McHale's cricket opponent and long-time friend, John Curtin, was now Prime Minister.

A few days before McHale's 59th birthday, in December 1941, the war took a devastating turn. The Japanese attacked Pearl Harbour—on a "day that will live in infamy", according to US President Franklin Roosevelt—and fears were held for the safety of Australia as Japanese troops swept south with menacing intent and capabilities. By February, the seemingly impregnable fortress of Singapore was over-run and Darwin had been bombed. By the middle of the year, midget Japanese submarines were in Sydney Harbour, and critically, the battle for Kokoda, in New Guinea, was essentially seen as the critical battle to save Australia.

These events changed the focus of the war irrevocably. Immediately, there were calls for more enlistments and more and more VFL footballers abandoned the game to join up. 1942 was the year in which Australia waited for—and fought against the prospect of—invasion from the Japanese.

It was against this backdrop that the Collingwood Football Club endured the worst statistical season of McHale's long and illustrious reign. In a year in which crowds decreased significantly, the VFA would go into recess, Geelong would not take part in the VFL, and the Brownlow Medal and Copeland Trophy would go into a hiatus, the Magpies won only two of its 14 games for the 1942 season. One of those wins, against bottom side Hawthorn, in the final round of the season saved Collingwood the ignominy of finishing on the bottom of the ladder for the first time.

For three rounds of 1942, Collingwood was bottom (Rounds 5, 6 and 7) and for much of the season it was only separated from last spot only by percentage. Hawthorn had led by 10 points at the first change of ends in that final game of the year at Victoria Park, before an inspired second term of nine goals had turned the scales in the Magpies' favour. The final margin was 14 points. One can only imagine the sense of relief that the coach would have sensed after the final-round win over Hawthorn prevented Collingwood grasping the wooden spoon. He had created enough history; he didn't want to be the first Collingwood coach leading a team to finish on the bottom of the ladder.

There were excuses though for the season's failure. Victoria Park had been seconded for the war effort in early 1942 and for a time the team had to train at Northcote. In the end, the club was allowed back to train and play, even though at stages there were "150 members of the (Southern Command) camped in a section of the concrete stand"[50] while several officers used the members' stand for their headquarters. Even the club's famous support dropped to critical levels, with only 942 members in 1942.

Collingwood had an embarrassing dearth of players and on some training nights McHale had such a small list of players on the track that it was hardly worth the bother. The shortage of numbers was so badly felt that the reserves were abandoned for a season and there was even some serious thought of joining up with Melbourne until the end of the war.

The club's players had been initially slow to take up the fight in the First World War, but it would be a different story this time around. According to Stremski: "Twenty-eight Magpies who had been on the senior list since 1939 were in military service in 1942. During the next three years 43, 46 and 48 current players, respectively, were in the armed forces."[51]

---

50 *Collingwood At Victoria Park*, Michael Robert and Glenn McFarlane, Lothian, 1999
51 *Kill For Collingwood*, Richard Stremski, Allen and Unwin, 1986

The Annual Report said of the 1942 season: "Almost to the last week of the opening of the season, we did not think that we would be able to field a side due to the many promising young players who were serving in the forces. Many of the games went against us by small margins, in fact with a small measure of luck the team could easily have won 10 games." The report said the team had played well considering many players were unable to get to training. The team had also played well considering McHale's view that serving in the armed forces unquestionably slows down speed.[52]

Jock McHale turned 60 a few months after his worst season as a coach. Collingwood too had turned 50 as a club that bleak season, and it also marked 30 years since McHale started coaching. He had been coaching for longer than any of the 19 players who represented the club in the Round 16 match against Hawthorn had been alive. But, despite the club's woeful performance in 1942, there were excuses in that the club was so severely drained of playing resources that some weeks it could only just field a side. The committee insisted that the coach could not be blamed for the team's poor performance.

The upshot of the lowest ebb in the club's on-field fortunes brought about a renewed effort to restore the seconds in 1943. Collingwood appointed two-time premiership player Bervin Woods as the reserves coach. What it also did was to start to look further afield—much further than McHale's usual narrow focus—for recruits and a total of 54 likely players were at training by mid-April. There were 12 debutants out of a total of 49 players who wore the black and white—a club record of players used in a single season that exists to this day. Another of McHale's records fell that year, when Richmond's Jack 'Skinny' Titus passed his consecutive games record of 191 (1906-17), on his way to 202 (which would in turn stand for more than 50 years before Melbourne's Jim Stynes would break it).

The season was another struggle, for numbers and for wins. The Magpies started with a victory—just, by four points—over North Melbourne at Victoria Park, with a scoreline of 6.22 to 7.12. But two successive losses followed, and then a mid-year bracket of six consecutive defeats pushed Collingwood to near the bottom of the ladder. Collingwood managed five wins for the season from its 15 games and finished 10th, behind only St Kilda, yet still three and a half wins off the bottom.

Jock McHale jnr managed 28 of his 34 games in the 1943 and 1944 seasons (after playing six in 1941). Taller than his father, he was used in the ruck on many occasions. It would prove an interesting dynamic having his father as coach. Jock jnr recalled: "I think it was tougher on him than it was on me because he knew I could never be the courageous footballer I might have been if I hadn't had the injury."[53] But the son of the famous coach learnt many lessons in his time at Victoria Park, some of which he would later apply in a highly successful business.

"I used to think he was getting a bit old (for coaching)," Jock jnr said in 1999. "But the more I got to know his methods in my time there, and in his last 10 years, the more I realised what a wonderful coach he was. In a different way from other people, he seemed to be able to make a footballer out of an ordinary player. He seemed to be able to select a player for a certain position. He had an absolutely uncanny ability to do that. He used to always say that nobody comes to a League club who is not a good footballer. You were a good footballer if someone had sent you to Collingwood, but it was a matter that some were made better than others."[54]

In an interview with the *AFL Record* not long before he died, Jock jnr gave a few more precious hints of what made his famous father

---

53   *Herald Sun*, March 8, 1992
54   Interview with Jock Jr. McHale, 1999

stand out from the rest. One of them was that the coach did not need say too much, just what was appropriate to suit the circumstance. "What he said, people listened to," Jock jnr said. "He would stand up on a little step and talk to them. He didn't go on with any nonsense—they'd be sitting and some standing, and he would speak. That was it." And McHale was firm that no one among the playing group would answer back to him. His son said: "There wasn't too much answering back, I can tell you that. The length of time that he was there (at the club) made the players slightly frightened."[55]

Richards agreed: "He was frightening, but he made the game simple. We used to call him Mr McHale. He would say: 'If you haven't got the ball, you can't kick it, so go and get it.'"[56]

Even in those dark years, when the players at his disposal were a shadow of those on the great lists of the past, he still believed that he could mould the group of young kids into a force to be reckoned with. In many ways the drive for success kept him going. Gordon Carlyon once wrote: "Jock McHale … had never entered a season without believing he could win a premiership. He had never entered a game that he did not believe he could win. Hype and fervour is a great asset, and can take a team a long way. He believed in man-on-man, grit and determination, and concentration every minute of the game. Of the teams that had all of these assets, any group of players can beat their opposition, McHale believed."[57]

The war had progressively turned in favour of the Allies in 1943 and 1944, but there was still a lot of work to be done. Tragically, for Collingwood, 1944 would be the year in which they would lose two former players five months apart—Norm Le Brun (19 games,

55   *AFL Record*
56   ibid
57   *Frank Wraith, A Magpie misjudged*, Gordon Carlyon, Gordon Carlyon, 2003

1933-34), who was killed in New Guinea, and Norm Oliver (13 games, 1940-41), who was killed while flying a Kittyhawk, also in New Guinea. The club was rightfully proud of the record of service of its players during the Second World War, including the achievements of Jack Pimm winning a Military Cross, and Hugh Coventry (8 games, 1941, the son of Syd Coventry), winning a Distinguished Flying Cross.

Collingwood struggled again in 1944, but the seven games it won during the season meant that it was never in danger of finishing on the bottom. It finished 10th with Hawthorn (two wins and a draw) and Geelong (one win in its first year back in the competition) trailing.

Three of those games (all in the space of five weeks and all losing matches) stood out for McHale, for very different reasons. The first came in Round 10 when Collingwood met St Kilda at the Junction Oval. It ended in a flogging, with the Saints winning by 68 points. That result came off the back of a pre-game burst from the St Kilda coach to his team. He implored them to come out and beat the Magpies, and to beat McHale. He reminded them that: "This is the team what (sic) gave me the arse!"[58] Hughie Thomas, McHale's old reserves coach and the man he had helped displace at the start of 1939, took great delight in watching his team run over the top of Collingwood that day. McHale would have hated it. Thomas's son Harold recalled: "It was a terrible blood match ... he (Thomas) stirred them up because he was still pretty hostile about what had happened to him. He wasn't going to forgive them."[59] The consolation for the Collingwood coach would come the following year with two big wins over the Saints in Thomas's last year as St Kilda coach.

The next match was more of a strain for McHale. He had to sit back and watch as his son became one of Richmond hard man Jack Dyer's victims. June McHale recalled: "My Jock defied his father by going to my brother's (Bob Skinner) wedding on the morning of the game. Old Jock was worried about him having a drink, which young Jock wouldn't have done, but there were a few angry words. I think that was the reason that my Jock went out and hit Jack (Dyer). There was no antipathy to Jack at all. He was just so fired up after arguing with his father that he hit Jack."[60]

Dyer was happy to admit that it was his fault many years later, but the reason for his decision to target Jock jnr was because he hated Jock snr with a passion. He told Brian Hansen: "My dream, and I dreamed it often, was to crush McHale (the coach). But it was an impossible dream (McHale had long been retired when Dyer made his debut in 1931). Then ... Lo and behold!! One day Jock McHale did line up against me ... in a Collingwood jumper and for four premiership points. At last ... So it wasn't the old boy ... so what?"[61]

Dyer added, with a typical touch of hyperbole: "It was Jock McHale jnr, his much loved son. The fruit of his loins and a worthy alternative. Better in some way. I got young Jock (he was 29 as opposed to Dyer's 30) good and proper and that really set the world on fire. I've got to give him credit. He came back at me nice and hard and I think I had to give him another one just to finish him off. Jock snr didn't like me ... he probably liked me even less after that."[62]

One of the boundary umpires of the day, Harold Smith, acknowledged Dyer had been the aggressor, though he said Jock jnr gave as good as he got. He said: "I can still picture that one; it was at the railway end (of Punt Road). They had a big fight, and we had to go and get in between them to stop it. In those days you were allowed to. We would run in and say 'cut it out, or you will have a holiday'."[63] The pair did. Dyer got four weeks—which would go down in history

---

60 *The 500 Club, Footy's Greatest Coaches*, Kevin Sheedy, News Custom Publishing, 2004

61 *The Magpies, the official Centenary History of the Collingwood Football Club*, Brian Hansen, 1992

62 ibid

63 Interview with Harold Smith, 2009

(incredibly) as the only suspension 'Captain Blood' would receive in his colourful 312-game career. McHale also got four weeks for retaliating.

The third game came in Round 14 when a special guest came to see the Collingwood-Footscray clash—McHale's old mate, John Curtin, Australia's war-time Prime Minister. McHale had admonished Curtin (in jest) when he attended a Magpies-Tigers match a year earlier and had failed to come into the rooms after the game. This time Curtin, the one-time Brunswick footballer, came into the Collingwood rooms at half-time with the Magpies five points down and desperately needing a lift.

The Argus said McHale had introduced the players to the Prime Minister. "The coach told them that when he was sitting with the Prime Minister, Mr Curtin said, 'What's wrong with you, Jock? [The Magpies were only five points down.] Those boys out there are playing well', and I replied 'Jack, 40 years ago, you and I played together and you then, as now, insisted on teamwork. You always contended that a team divided meant disaster.' Continuing, the coach said: 'And now, players, that's what is happening. Do as Mr Curtin advises. Pull together and you will win."[64] Unfortunately, the fairytale second half revival never eventuated. The Bulldogs won by 39 points.

Later that month, McHale was drawn into another family tragedy, with the bizarre death of his sister, Alice, aged 45, on August 14, 1944—two days after Collingwood had lost to South Melbourne. She had been found dazed and dying at the Fawkner Cemetery, with a bottle of Lysol—a disinfectant—beside her. She had died on the way to the Royal Melbourne Hospital. Jock had been called away from the Carlton Brewery to the city morgue to identify Alice's body, and had to appear at an inquest the following week where the coroner listed the cause of her death as "due to the effects of a poison known as Lysol ... The evidence available does not enable me to say under what circumstances such poison was administered."[65]

---

64   *The Argus*, August 7, 1944
65   Inquest, Alice McHale, 1944

Collingwood rounded out the 1944 season, and the dark early years of the 1940s, with a loss to Richmond in Round 18 at Victoria Park. Jock jnr was back in the team by that stage and up against Dyer again. But there were no repeat of what had occurred at Punt Road earlier in the year. It was to be Jock jnr's 34th and final game for Collingwood. He was on the list, but did not play another game as the motor accessories business he had started a number of years early was expanded.

But Jock McHale had no thoughts of joining him in retirement. Although there might have been a few rumblings around Collingwood that McHale was "past it" as a coach, given that he was starting to struggle to keep up with the modern trends of the game, no one expressed such thoughts publicly. They would not have dared. McHale still wielded enormous power within the club, and within the game. The coach just wanted to keep coaching.

CHAPTER 13

One Last Shot At It

1945-1949

There was a feeling of quiet anticipation at Collingwood on the eve of the 1945 VFL season. The war had finally taken an almighty turn for the better for Australia and for the Allied Forces. As the Magpies prepared for their first game, against North Melbourne on April 21, the Red Army was circling the outskirts of Berlin and Adolf Hitler had little more than a week to live. The battle of Okinawa, described by Winston Churchill as one of the most intense and famous in military history, was proving a bloody affair for both sides, but would signal the final throes of Japan's resistance. After five and a half years of sacrifice and suffering in most corners of the globe, it was hoped that a long-prayed-for peace would soon follow.

In pure football terms, Collingwood—and Jock McHale—were confident that they could similarly put to rest the frustrations of the past five seasons. It had been the darkest period in the club's history. The Magpies had not made the finals since 1939, the year in which the wretched conflict had started, and the long, bleak years in between had tested everyone's resolve and patience—even the coach's. In those years, it had seemed, the legendary catchment area for young Collingwood footballers had dried up, and the war service of senior players had seen them temporarily lost to the club—even though long-serving treasurer Bob Rush endeavoured to keep those enlisted men abreast of the club news through a Magpie newsletter sent to them at the front. The news Rush delivered was rarely positive.

But, as the world was emerging bleary-eyed from the darkness, it appeared as if the Collingwood Football Club too was about to get some illumination. Jock McHale, as industrious as ever at 62, if a fair degree less active on the training track than he had been in past years, would have been encouraged by some of the fresh faces who fronted Victoria Park in March for the start of the 1945 pre-season. By the time he had seen them go through their paces, those confidence levels must surely have been on the rise. The malaise that had blighted Collingwood for a number of years appeared to be over.

A cast of first-game stars and a few returning greats gave credence to this optimism in the club's opening game of the season—a 21-point win over an improving North Melbourne (on the way to its first finals appearance after 20 years in the VFL) at Victoria Park. Admittedly, it was only one game, against a team that had beaten Collingwood just three times in those two decades, but for many of the 13,000-strong crowd—most of them of a black and white persuasion—there was a feeling that the win was a portent. After a slow start, the Magpies kicked five goals in the third term to wrest control of the contest.

The club was eager to chase new talent, feeling that it would provide a chance for McHale to start remodelling the style he had managed through the 1930s, post-*Machine*. Just a year earlier, the Magpies had enticed former great Harry Collier back to the club—if he held a grudge over his enforced retirement in 1940, he had moved on from it—to act as an "agent" on the hunt for fresh blood. McHale introduced four new players for the opening game of the season. Three of them—Bill Twomey, Neil Mann and Len Fitzgerald— would become outstanding footballers.

The first of those three players carried a name that McHale was familiar with, although he hadn't recognised the teenager when he fronted to his first training session. The kid's name was Bill Twomey jnr, the eldest son of McHale's former star wingman of the same name; Bill Twomey snr had enjoyed a fleeting but famous career in black and white, playing 54 games from 1918-1922 (four Grand Finals, one flag) and 10 games with Hawthorn in 1933-1934. It would be the start of an intriguing, sometimes tempestuous relationship between the flamboyant, flashy player and the no-frills, no-nonsense coach.

Bill Twomey jnr would never forget his first night of training under McHale: "I don't know whether I had met Jock McHale or not, but he called me to the centre (of the ground) and he said: 'What's your name?' I said: 'Bill Twomey'. He said to me, 'Oh, you're Bill's son.' He even said to me, 'How do you reckon you will like playing in the first game?' I was already a Collingwood player ... in other words, no matter what I did down there, I had (already) been selected, and that's what I found very strange."[1]

Twomey was only 17 when he played his first game; Neil Mann was 20. Mann recalled his first meeting with the doyen of coaching: "I trained under Bervin Woods (in the seconds) and after training (on his first night in 1944) he said, 'You had better go up and see Mr McHale tomorrow night.' We all called him Mr McHale, never Jock."[2] Then McHale gave him a direction that had all the hallmarks of being an ultimatum: "Get your hair cut, son. Nobody can play football with hair as long as yours."[3]

Mann did, and made the senior list without playing a game in 1944. The big man would more than make his mark as a forward in 1945, and would then shift to the backline before becoming a top ruckman in the 1950s.

1   Interview with Bill Twomey , 1996
2   Interview with Neil Mann, 1996
3   A Century of the Best, Michael Roberts, Collingwood Football Club

Len Fitzgerald, the other debutant that day who would go on to become an important player, was six days short of his 16th birthday.[4] Fitzgerald (like Fothergill before him) had been a graduate of the club's junior curtain-raiser system, a system that had an uncanny knack of finding football prodigies. Frank Wraith, the man who had helped to start up the local schoolboy link to Collingwood, once told people that the club had found, in Fitzgerald, "another Albert Collier."[5] Like 'Leeter', he would leave Collingwood at his peak. Unlike 'Leeter', he would never return.

If those fresh new faces provided hope in early 1945, then the return of two familiar faces also warmed the hearts of Collingwood supporters. Alby Pannam had missed the entire 1944 season while serving in the RAAF. He was released to play for Collingwood in 1945, having enjoyed his 31st birthday two days before the first game. Phonse Kyne and Marcus Whelan were still in the services, so the veteran Pannam was elected captain (serving for only one year, as had his father, Charlie snr, in 1905, McHale's third season at Collingwood).

No one knew it at the time, but it would be Pannam's last year in black and white. Years later, he would tell the story of how he used to run a bit of an SP bookmaker's operation, and how on one afternoon in 1945 his coach—who was not renowned for gambling—scooped the pool, much to his captain's fears. Pannam said in 1988: "One day at half-time the coach ran up to me all smiles—I thought I had (finally) cracked it for some praise from Jock McHale. 'I think I have won your double, Pannam (he rarely used Christian names).' I said, 'Fair go, Mr McHale, how can I concentrate in the second half worrying about a big loss like that?'"[6]

Even Marcus Boyall, who had been the first of the big three defections of the late 1930s and early 1940s, was back for that

---

4   The fourth of the debutants to play for Collingwood in the Round 1 game against
     North Melbourne was Alan Brown. He played 16 games in 1945 and 1946.
5   *A Century of the Best*, Michael Roberts, Collingwood Football Club
6   *The Sun News-Pictorial*, April 21, 1988

North Melbourne game, one of six he played that season, while on service leave.

But perhaps the most interesting return was that of Des Fothergill, who had left Collingwood without a transfer for Williamstown at the end of 1940—aged 20—after winning the 1940 Brownlow and a third Copeland Trophy. He had left amidst much acrimony. The VFL had decided in March 1945 to lift the ban on those players who had transferred to the VFA without a permit, allowing Fothergill and others to return to their original clubs if they would have them. But, as *The Argus* predicted before the Round 1 game against North Melbourne (his first game with Collingwood since Round 18, 1940), he was to be met with a "warm welcome"[7] from the faithful.

Fothergill was not yet 25, but he had suffered a knee injury playing in a services match in Darwin, and he would modify his game to suit this. It dulled some of the brilliance he had displayed from an early age, although he showed in that first game back that he would be an important player for the club as it wound its way back up the ladder. The injury perhaps had seen him put on a little weight. Even so, *The Argus* preview of his return match was a little harsh: "He (Fothergill) is too solid for roving now and will be a wing/half-forward."[8] The one thing that 'Fother' had not lost was his uncanny goal sense. He kicked five goals in that return against North Melbourne, and would end as the club's leading goalkicker and third in the League, with 62 (only five behind Melbourne's Fred Fanning). He would go one better the following year, with 63 goals—again leading the Collingwood tally—while finishing second to Essendon's Bill Brittingham (66).

Potentially, that paved the way for the return of Ron Todd, the prodigious goalkicker who had preceded Fothergill's move to Williamstown by a year. For a time in the pre-season of 1945, it seemed as if the former favourite son would return to Victoria Park.

---

7   *The Argus*, April 20, 1945
8   ibid

In fact, *The Argus* reported on March 19 that Todd—still only 28—wanted to wear black and white again (he had made an application to the club to seek a return two years earlier, without success, as well as having written to Frank Wraith in 1944 saying he had regretted his "injudicious transfer."[9]). He informed the secretary of Williamstown of his intentions and it seemed as if the bad blood surrounding the defection from five years earlier might be spectacularly erased.

Gordon Carlyon claimed: "Rumours were circulating that Todd and Fothergill wanted to return. Frank Wraith immediately interviewed Fothergill and Des agreed if the VFL approved. Frank then had discussions with the VFL and eventually approval was granted for Fothergill to regain his place as a Collingwood player. Some of the VFL delegates wanted to charge Todd with an infringement of the Coulter Law by receiving a cheque for transferring to Williamstown. Wraith successfully defended Todd against this allegation and permission was granted for him to return to Collingwood. Todd met the players and agreed to play in the last practice match and attend the club's Tuesday night meeting."[10]

What Wraith also did was speak to Wren—who knew the value of a champion forward—and, according to Richard Stremski's *Kill For Collingwood*, the long-time club benefactor said: "You've got an open cheque."[11]

There was, however, Carlyon contended, some opposition at committee level in regard to Todd's return. Debate raged in the committee room over whether Todd deserved to be allowed back to a club he had deserted: "Should he be allowed back? Would he only come back for £3 per match? Was he truly repentant? Some wanted him back at any cost; others were adamant that all players must be treated equally."[12]

---

9   *Kill For Collingwood*, Richard Stremski, Allen and Unwin, 1986
10 *Frank Wraith, a Magpie misjudged*, Gordon Carlyon, 2003
11 *Kill For Collingwood*, Richard Stremski, Allen and Unwin, 1986
12 ibid

Sitting outside the room, waiting to address the committee, Todd heard most of the ruckus that was taking place inside, with raised voices and strong debate over the merits of allowing him back into the club. In the end, as Carlyon would later write: "They (the committee) did not have to make a decision. After hearing the debate, Todd left the passageway in disgust and signed up with Williamstown the next day."[13]

Jock jnr, who happened to be a close friend of Todd's, claimed to have played a role in the potential rapprochement. He had privately spoken to his father about Todd's desire to return to Collingwood, working overtime to get him on board for a possible return. But Jock jnr maintained that Todd failed to turn up at the pre-arranged time to deal with the issue.

Jock jnr said: "That disappointed me with 'Toddy'. He wanted to come back to Collingwood and my father wouldn't have a bar of it. Anyhow, I kept at my father, and at him, and at him, then he decided to tell him to turn up to training one night, and he would have a talk with him. 'Toddy' didn't turn up. He didn't get another chance."[14]

He added: "I think he was offered more money in the end (by Williamstown). We all know who gave him the money, that bookmaker bloke (Bill Dooley). Collingwood wouldn't pay Toddy any more than they were paying the ordinary blokes. It was a lot of money (he got), so you couldn't blame him in some ways. But we were trying to build a premiership side."[15]

With a sense of what might have been, Jock jnr declared: "He was a brilliant player. He was the best full-forward that I had ever seen. (If he had stayed at Collingwood) he would have been the best footballer of all time."[16] The two mates would stay friends for the remainder of their lives, but Jock snr's patience had well and truly run out.

---

13 *Frank Wraith, a Magpie misjudged*, Gordon Carlyon, 2003
14 Interview with Jock McHale Jr., 1999
15 ibid
16 ibid

Whatever the case, Collingwood reacted swiftly to Todd's decision to return to Williamstown, which came to light the day after that committee meeting that the forward had overheard from outside the room. *The Argus* announced on March 28, 1945, that: "Drastic action was taken against Ron Todd, former champion, last night, by the Collingwood committee. Todd, who by the decision of the VFL, was eligible to play again with Collingwood, and had said that he would play again with Collingwood, subsequently decided to rejoin Williamstown, to which club he went without a clearance (in 1940) and played with until he was transferred in the RAAF."[17]

The Argus report continued, saying that the Collingwood committee agreed that "Todd's request to rejoin Collingwood be refused, that he be expelled from the club, and be refused all the privileges of an ex-player and that he be advised accordingly; a copy of the letter to be sent to Williamstown."[18] It was swift, brutal and final. Some of those in positions of power at Collingwood believed that Todd had simply used them for bargaining power in a bid to rejoin Williamstown with a better deal. Others felt the bickering and debate simply made it too hard for Todd to re-appear in the black and white again.

Whatever the case may be, the shattering part about this messy footnote to Todd's association with Collingwood came in the context of the champion forward's season in the VFA that year, 1945, the year he should have been playing once more for the Magpies. His six goals in the Grand Final, which helped Williamstown to the premiership, took him to a phenomenal 188 goals for the season, taking him past the Australian record of 183, kicked by Bob Pratt at Coburg in 1941. Todd was a remarkable player, and one can only speculate on how many goals he might have kicked with Collingwood that year, and whether his presence might have been enough to bring about the ninth premiership as a coach for McHale.

---

17   *The Argus*, March 28, 1945
18   ibid

Two of those star first-year players for Collingwood in 1945 later expressed their disappointment that an agreement was not reached with Todd when a little more diplomacy on each side might have seen a different outcome.

Neil Mann said in 1996: "We thought our club should have matched that offer (from Williamstown). They barred him (Todd) from the club. He was a great player."[19]

Bill Twomey was even more emphatic, saying that the club sadly believed that it could own players back then. He said: "The thing that I was disappointed about (when he got picked to play with Collingwood) was that I thought Ron Todd was coming back. I (later) worked with Ron and I asked him why he didn't come back, and he said in those days you had to wait out there (while the committee met) and they would give you a call. He was waiting, and they kept him waiting. In the finish he just told them he was going back to Williamstown. At that stage they were all great administrators at Collingwood, but I think now in retrospect, they did think they had complete control of a person, and that is a hell of a mistake. It was a tragedy that he didn't come back because we would have probably won a couple of premierships. Although having the top full-forward doesn't guarantee you the premiership, we might have won that one in '45."[20]

Todd played 141 games for Williamstown from 1940-49 kicking 672 goals at an average of 4.77 goals per game. In his 76 games for Collingwood from 1935-39 he kicked 327 goals (average 4.30). His career tally in VFL and VFA matches totalled, amazingly, 999 goals at an average of 4.60. The leading average in the history of the game is Peter Hudson's 5.64 (129 games) in the 1960s and 1970s. Todd's predecessor at Collingwood, Gordon Coventry, averaged 4.25 goals per game in a 306-game career. On the all-time tally, Todd's career average (VFL and VFA) sits behind Hudson, Tony Lockett (4.84, 281 games) and Jason Dunstall (4.66, 269 games).

---

19   Interview with Neil Mann, 1996
20   Interview with Bill Twomey, 1996

Collingwood didn't win that 1945 premiership, but for a time, even without Todd, it looked like it was going to give the flag a real shake. The Magpies won seven of the first 10 games to set up their season, and put them on the path towards making the finals again. There was still a bit of inconsistency with what was a relatively young side, and that made for some fluctuating fortunes. In Round 8, McHale's men lost to Fitzroy by an incredible 95 points. A fortnight later, they beat Geelong by 97.

Without a dominant full-forward, it was left to Fothergill to kick most of Collingwood's goals. Twomey said: "He was pretty heavy then, but he was that beautiful in getting it (the ball) and getting out on his own. He was a beautiful kick, he could drop kick; he had a baulk that everyone loved to watch. I reckon he would have kicked 100 goals if we had kicked it to him better."[21]

Germany agreed to surrender on May 7, 1945 (two days after Collingwood's second win of the season, over Melbourne), with the banner headline of *The Argus* on May 8 simply declaring "Capitulation". The following day, the same newspaper's headline showed there was still some work to do, despite the rejoicing: "Nazis prostrate, Japs next."[22]

Prime Minister John Curtin was not well enough to appear in public for the end of the war in Europe. A year earlier he had been in the Collingwood rooms, at the behest of his old mate Jock McHale, but sadly he was now dying. It was left to acting Prime Minister Ben Chifley to state: "Let us all in this historic moment pause and remember those who have given or whose bodies and mind have been broken or scarred that we might live."[23] He could well have been talking about Curtin, whose own health had been sacrificed for the sake of leading Australia through the hours of its greatest need.

---

21   ibid
22   *The Argus*, May 8 and May 9, 1945
23   *The Argus*, May 9, 1945

The nation mourned Curtin when he died, six months after his 60th birthday, on July 5, 1945. Curtin, like United States President, Franklin D. Roosevelt (who had died on April 12), had come so close to seeing the end of the conflict that had more than likely brought a premature end to their lives.

The editorial in *The Argus* at the time of Curtin's death declared: "Like President Roosevelt, who died in harness and in the hour of victory, Mr Curtin, to whom also victory was clearly visible though still some distance off, is in the full technical sense of the term a casualty of war ... For John Curtin was in every respect a man of the people; a simple citizen who heard his country's call and forgot everything else in the terrible greatness of the moment ... (He) accepted without hesitation the responsibilities that war imposed on him. And in thus accepting them, he transcended politics, rising to greatness because he forsook smaller things for things immeasurably bigger."[24]

The end to the Pacific War would come swiftly, and with devastating effect, with the dropping of nuclear bombs on the Japanese cities of Hiroshima, on August 6, and Nagasaki, on August 9. It was to be the end of a long conflict, but the presentation of a new weapon of indescribable power and horrible strength that would change the thinking of the world. *The Argus* of August 8 chose to run some of the editorial from the *New York Times*, which pondered: "Can mankind grow up quickly enough to win the race between civilisation and disaster? Or will new would-be conquerors arise who will see in the atomic bomb merely certain means for instant realisation of their dreams."[25]

There was a delicate irony in the fact that, as Australians rejoiced in the peace that had long been sought, Australian football was about to go through one of its most violent finals series. And Collingwood, and McHale, were in the midst of it. The Magpies had finished second on the ladder to South Melbourne, by only a game, with North

24   ibid
25   *The Argus*, August 8, 1945

Melbourne and Carlton in third and fourth positions. It was the first time in VFL history that there had been four finalists who had not taken part in the previous year's finals. The Blues had been lucky to make it. They had been outside the top four in the penultimate round, and had to beat Footscray at the Western Oval in the last round to leap over them. They did that, winning by 53 points.

Alby Pannam had hurt his knee in the Round 19 win over Fitzroy. He missed the final-round win over Richmond (there were 20 rounds in 1945) as well as the second semi-final against South Melbourne, but there was still some hope that he would play in the later finals.

Collingwood had a 1-1 record with South Melbourne heading into that second semi-final. On the same day that his son, Jock jnr, was playing in the ruck for the Collingwood seconds in their preliminary final loss against Fitzroy at Victoria Park, Jock snr was back in the midst of what he loved most—finals—when the Magpies took on South at Princes Park. (The MCG had not been used since 1941). And the Magpie fans clearly loved being back in the finals for the first time since 1939, as evidenced by the turnout at training on Thursday night before the game. *The Argus* observed: "One of the largest crowds seen on the ground for years saw the final practice."[26]

At half-time Collingwood looked a good show of winning. It had established an eight-point lead after a tight and tense opening half. Perhaps another stirring McHale address could sweep them into another Grand Final. But it was the more experienced and more composed South Melbourne (with a team having an average age of 27 as opposed to Collingwood's 23) that would finish the harder. Kicking eight goals to five in the third term, the minor premier held on grimly in the last term to win by 11 points.

---

26   *The Argus*, September 15, 1945

Collingwood had hoped to have its captain Pannam back for the latter part of the finals, but he had injured his knee again, playing in an RAAF game leading up to the preliminary final against Carlton, which had overcome North Melbourne by 26 points in the first semi-final. McHale had given Pannam the permission to test himself in the services game, but it had not worked out as he would have hoped. Pannam was unable to play in the game against the Blues, and as it turned out, he had played his final match at Collingwood—his dodgy knee could no longer stand up to McHale's standards, and he would be forced to try his luck at Richmond the following year.

So, without its captain, Collingwood prepared itself to take on Carlton—in the first final these two teams had played since that 1938 Grand Final. Fothergill and ruckman Alan Williams were the two remaining Magpies of that most recent finals clash between the great rivals. It was a relatively good mix of the old and the new for Collingwood. Twomey, Fitzgerald and Phil Ryan were in the 20-and-under bracket; in the 21-25 bracket were Lou Richards, Des Fothergill, 'Mac' Holten, Charlie Utting, Ken Wade and Tom Wallis and the over 25s included Jack Murphy, Jack Burns, Alan Williams, Ron Carruthers and Herb Naismith.

The Argus reported that Collingwood believed its "young players, having played their first semi-final, will not find it so strange"[27] against Carlton, at the Blues' fortress, Princes Park.

Ray Riddell, in his first game of the season and only the third of his career, was selected as 19th man. He would sit next to McHale for the day, as the legendary coach rode every bump and grind (and there were plenty of them) throughout the afternoon. He recalled in 2009: "Jock wasn't a good loser. Anyway, this particular day we were up against Carlton and I was the 19th man. Well, I can tell you that Jock never took his head out of his hands. He was biting hard on his nails, I think. It was a big strain on him."[28]

---

27   *The Argus*, September 21, 1945
28   Interview with Ray Riddell, 2009

Collingwood had, for much of McHale's coaching career, struggled to beat Carlton at Princes Park—let alone in a final. But he told *The Argus* he believed the Magpies' "young players, having played their first semi-final, will not find it so strange"[29] this time. That's the way it appeared in the first term, as well, as Collingwood played superb football, kicking five goals to one to open a 26-point lead at the first change. But Carlton hit back, quite literally, in the second term, cutting the half-time margin to only nine points.

Fothergill had some close and almost certainly unfair attention from one of Carlton's fiercest players, Bob Chitty, who was lucky to be even playing that day. Chitty had sliced the joint off the top of one of his fingers in the days leading up to the game. But, against doctor's advice, and after getting the finger stitched and bandaged, he not only played, but he gave Fothergill an incredibly hard time of it.

Lou Richards, who booted three goals in the game, described the battering that Chitty gave Fothergill: "Chitty ... was doing everything but hit him with the grandstand and a goalpost. He was bumping him, pulling him by the hair and grabbing him by the athletic support, with the result that Fothergill was completely rattled and couldn't get a kick, and, to be perfectly honest, Des started to 'turn it up'. I suppose he had a reason for it ... Chitty was a tough customer."[30] Written almost 20 years after the event, at a time Richards was known for his media hyperbole, it was still a particularly harsh assessment of a teammate, particularly one as highly decorated as Fothergill. But it was what Richards said next in the book that caused even more controversy.

Richards claimed, in these 1963 'memoirs', that there had been a half-time incident between Fothergill and a clearly frustrated McHale. He wrote: "We were in a bad position at half-time (note: the team was actually in front), and when we went inside Jock McHale was sitting on a bench, looking very disgruntled. Fothergill went up to him and

---

29   *The Argus*, September 21, 1945
30   *Boots and All*, Lou Richards, Stanley Paul, 1963

asked: 'What will I do, Mr. McHale?' Jock looked up with despair, and quietly replied: 'You're a man ... aren't you?' and he let it go at that."[31]

Was it simply Lou Richards resorting to his burgeoning career as a story-teller? Or was any truth to it with McHale's frustration boiling over? Fothergill had no doubt: he angrily dismissed Richards's suggestion as "lies and rubbish."[32] Two of their teammates said they did not hear the alleged exchange, but found it difficult to believe given the two people involved. Twomey said: "Every ounce in my system would say no (it didn't happen). I don't think Jock McHale would have said something like that. Des probably knew more about football than probably anybody in the room."[33] Mann added: "I would back Bill (Twomey's version) on that one."[34]

Chitty's punishment of Fothergill didn't stop at half-time. *The Argus* said he "fell heavily" in the third term, and "six or seven of his teeth were loosened."[35] Twomey said it was "a mystery" as to why the umpire did not provide the Collingwood player with protection in the form of free kicks. He noted: "There was one instance that was terrible. He (Chitty) went straight into him and it was the old 'put your elbow in the face' type of thing. Des just took it. I don't think he lay down or anything. If it (the battering of Fothergill) hadn't happened, we might have won."[36]

Incredibly, only one player, Carlton's Fred Fitzgibbon, would be reported on the day (there would be 10 reports the following week, including Fitzgibbon, who didn't even play because of suspension but ran on to the field to take part in the fray). That Fothergill-Chitty clash was one of many in a game that was incredibly physical, and often well beyond the rules. *The Argus* called it: "One of the hardest and roughest games for some time ... there were many instances of rough and spiteful

31   ibid
32   *Kill For Collingwood*, Richard Stremski, Allen and Unwin, 1986
33   Interview with Bill Twomey, 1996
34   Interview with Neil Mann, 1996
35   *The Argus*, September 24, 1945
36   Interview with Bill Twomey, 1996

play and both sides can be condemned for their share in it. Elbow jabs, sly-kicks on the ankle, not-so-sly kicks in the packs, and a good deal of slinging and jostling occurred for most of the game."[37]

Collingwood dominated the third term, kicking five goals to two with the breeze to shoot out to a 28-point lead with only a quarter of football to decide which team would play South Melbourne in the Grand Final. For most of the 41,305 fans, it appeared to be the Magpies. It looked an even more secure bet when Collingwood scored the first goal of the last term, stretching the margin out to 34 points.

Then, suddenly, a dramatic transformation came over the game. In a withering burst, and aided by a strong wind, Carlton found a new lease of life and form, and Collingwood had no answer. The switch in fortunes was so sudden that fans were "dumbfounded,"[38] as the Blues kicked 7.3 to 1.1. In the end, the margin was 10 points in Carlton's favour; the home side somehow had orchestrated a 44-point turnaround in the space of less than half an hour.

In 1996, more than 50 years after the match, Twomey said: "I thought, 'it looks as though we are going to be in a Grand Final."[39] Mann thought the same: "I think we all thought we had the game won too soon. They (Collingwood) should have packed the backline."[40]

Carlton would go on to win a famous premiership. Some preferred to call it an infamous premiership, after the Grand Final degenerated into a series of brawls and beltings that led to the game being called "the Bloodbath". But there would be plenty among the crowd that day, and some of them who had been on the field, who insisted the

---

37   *The Argus*, September 24, 1945
38   ibid
39   Interview with Bill Twomey, 1996
40   Interview with Neil Mann, 1996

preliminary final was more vicious and more vociferously fought out than the premiership-deciding match a week later, which the Blues would win by 28 points.

Collingwood's Annual Report referred to the brutal nature of the game, and pondered just how the strong-arm tactics of Carlton may have impacted on the younger Magpies. It declared that after a first half of "outstanding football was produced, the game changed from a football spectacle to a hard, slogging, vigorous brand of play, quite foreign to our younger brigade."[41]

Ruckman Alan Williams was described in many newspapers as Collingwood's best player against Carlton in the preliminary final, with *The Argus* saying: "He had much of the ruck work to do, and was in the van all day."[42] But there was criticism of McHale for giving Williams such a monumental workload, while leaving a fresh man Len Hustler, chosen largely for his aggressive approach to the game, out of the play at full-forward. So was the rising 63-year-old coach—his birthday was two-and-a-half months away—too slow to react? Was he too cautious not to make a move?

With the benefit of hindsight, Twomey believed that to be the case. He said: "(Hustler) was capable of a good mark and he was a good kick. If they had put him in the centre, somewhere in the ruck duels, it might have livened things up."[43] Mann concurred: "Alan Williams had rucked all day, and had probably run out of gas."[44]

Running out of gas would become a theme for Collingwood during the remainder of the 1940s—for the rest of McHale's tenure. In the past, Magpie teams under McHale had been admired and feared for

---

41   Collingwood Annual Report, 1946
42   *The Argus*, September 24, 1996
43   Interview with Bill Twomey, 1996
44   Interview with Neil Mann, 1996

their withering bursts in games, particularly in what was viewed as the club's traditional third quarter onslaught. By the mid- to late-1940s, there were a number of examples of how Collingwood had been overrun in important matches, to the point where some people (including a few from inside Victoria Park) wondered if McHale had been training them hard enough. In a quest to make sure his men would not become "stale", as he had preached years earlier, the fear from some players was that he had not prepared them to be fit enough when it counted as the finals rolled around. Those who privately thought that McHale was behind the times in terms of his physical approach to the game would only have more ammunition in 1946.

In many ways, McHale had ruled with such control and with such success for so long that his long-held beliefs were rarely challenged. Even if there were times that a few eyebrows were raised, there were few people willing to challenge the coach or his policies. One time Mac Holten wanted to get a bit more practice out on the training track after McHale had already sent his team in, and he copped a rebuke from the coach who said that he knew when his players had had enough.

Lou Richards famously tells the story of how he, Holten and Jack Burns once tried to organise a players' meeting to "thrash out why we were playing poorly ... but Old Jock got to hear about it, and when we arrived on the Tuesday night to have the meeting, he was waiting there for us. He accused the three of us of being 'Commos' (Communists) trying to cause a revolution at the club, and told us that it had never happened in his 40 years with the club, and it wasn't likely to happen while he was still there. He polished us off by saying: 'Now buzz off', with which he kicked us out of the room, and said there was (to be) no meeting. He ruled the club with an iron hand, and stood over the players, yet behind it all was a very fair-minded chap."[45]

The club was rightfully proud of its achievements in rebuilding its list in 1945, and it had no hesitation praising the way in which

---

45   *Boots and All*, Lou Richards, Stanley Paul, 1963

McHale had reshaped the team. The Annual Report said McHale had once again "produced the goods ... for years he had to struggle with many and varied difficulties which seemed to conspire to keep his old club out of the coveted four, but in 1945 his efforts were crowned with success. His lifetime service and his phenomenal success as a coach stand as a monument to him. 'Like the brook, one expects him to go on forever'."[46]

The reasons for optimism in 1946 centred on the return of the likes of Phonse Kyne (who was elected captain), Marcus Whelan, Jack Regan, Gordon Hocking, Jack Pimm and Norm Campbell resuming with the club after absences. Regan, the 'prince of full-backs' had played just 13 games in 1943, since the 1941 season. Mann said: "Old Jock used to put a younger player on an older player (at training). Jock was the best coach to stir you up before the game. (But) I think we learnt more about football in those days from the older players who had come back from the war. They were teachers."[47]

But the emergence of a kid from Nyah West in the latter stages of the season also inspired plenty of hope. His name was Bob Rose. McHale had, early in his career, lauded Dick Condon—who incidentally died in the year Rose debuted for Collingwood—as the greatest player he had seen at Victoria Park and had later considered the Coventrys and the Colliers as almost peerless champions of the club. At the end of his life he would ponder whether this kid Rose, in the No.22 jumper, might just be the best.

So what did a young Bob Rose make of an old Jock McHale? Almost 46 years separated them, but Rose came to admire his coach, even if he didn't always agree with everything that he did. In 1999,

---

46   Collingwood Annual Report, 1946
47   Interview with Neil Mann, 1996

Rose gave an evocative description of McHale: "I remember him coming into the ground on Saturdays, wearing a suit, vest and a gold watch on a gold chain hanging across his chest. When we walked off at the end of the match, we had to walk past Jock. If we lost, his grey eyes would glare at you and you couldn't get into the rooms any other way than walking past him. I'm sure that look frightened us enough to find an extra goal or two."[48]

One night at training McHale said to him: "You'll be all right, Rose." Rose recalled one of their early encounters with McHale, walking along Johnston Street. The coach gave him two pieces of advice, with varying degrees of success. "He and I were walking from Johnston Street to the ground. He asked me: 'Do you keep a scrapbook?' I said: 'My mother does, of my boxing'. (Rose was a good boxer and fought in Melbourne on several occasions). He said: 'You should keep a scrapbook'. I'm grateful for that."[49] Rose would often say that the scrapbook of his career—a career that earned him four Copeland Trophies—would have been one of the first things he would save if his house was on fire.

The other hint that McHale gave him that long forgotten day in 1946 was not as fondly recalled. "On the same walk, he asked me what I ate before a game. 'Steak and eggs', I said. He said: 'You should eat tripe'. Well, I tried it once and I'm afraid I couldn't keep that advice. Never had it since'."[50]

Rose made his debut as an 18-year-old in round 17 against Footscray—two weeks after Jack Regan played his final game, just his sixth for the season. *The Argus* had said Rose "came to the club last year when he also had a few successes at the Stadium. This season he is concentrating on football."[51] His performance was such that he did not miss another game for the rest of the season, playing in all three

48 *The Herald Sun*, August 24, 1999
49 *The Sunday Age*, March 17, 1996
50 ibid
51 *The Argus*, August 16, 1946

finals the club played that year. But two other injuries from that strong 52-point win over the Bulldogs would have ramifications for McHale, and his team, that season.

One of them was the aggravation of Fothergill's old knee injury. He had been among the best players on the ground until he had to be replaced. He would not play again for the remainder of the year, and would be sorely missed in the finals. His 63 goals kicked would be the most by any Collingwood player since Todd's incredible 121 in 1939. Fothergill would play another four games the following year, but his troublesome knee would force him into retirement, with his last game coming just 10 days before his 27th birthday.

Twomey was considered the club's best player against Footscray that day. But he would cop an accidental knee into his thigh during the game that he insisted had done "a lot of damage."[52] He missed a game against Carlton with hamstring soreness a fortnight later, and didn't feel right to play in the second semi-final against Essendon, a matching that came about when Collingwood finished second to the Bombers at the end of the home and away season.

Twomey recalled of his first finals game on the MCG: "I didn't want to play, but they picked me. I rang up on the Saturday morning, I rang Frank Wraith and he said 'bring your boots'. I should never have taken them. They talked me into playing and I lasted 20 minutes. I had never been through so much pain in my life. You could hear it (hamstring) snap. I didn't play again (that year)."[53] In many ways, that was the first sign of the strain in the relationship between Twomey and McHale. McHale had been convinced he should play; Twomey was adamant he shouldn't have played.

Collingwood's task in the second semi-final against Essendon was always going to be tough without the injured Fothergill and Pimm, sidelined with flu, but losing Twomey in the first term made it all the more difficult. The Bombers held sway early in the clash, leading by

---

52   Interview with Bill Twomey, 1996
53   ibid

eight points at quarter-time. But a sustained effort in the second term saw the Magpies wrest the lead back. They increased the half-time lead of 13 points to 16 points by the last change, and it looked as though the Magpies would upset the minor premiers.

Described as "one of the most thrilling semi-finals in League history", Essendon kicked the opening three goals of the final term before Collingwood rallied to regain the lead by one-point heading into time-on. But the Bombers were not done with yet, and they managed to level the scores near the end of the game, bringing about the first finals draw since Collingwood and Melbourne had drawn their semi-final of 1928. It had been a thrilling conclusion, but Collingwood and McHale were left to lament a scoreline of 35 shots to 30—13.22 (100) to 14.16 (100); Richards kicked four goals in an outstanding display of roving. Most people believed that the Magpies had been the better side on the day with *The Argus* reporting: "Collingwood were faster, their relentless play-on style and spoiling tactics worried the opposition all day. (But) they missed easy shots and had they kicked accurately might have had an easy win."[54]

Adding to the confusion to the aftermath of the draw, it was reported a few days later that "a car belonging to Jock McHale, coach of Collingwood, was stolen from the car park at the MCG on Saturday afternoon. It was later recovered near Melbourne University. The car was damaged. Police believe it was involved in a collision with a tramways bus."[55] Clearly, it was not Jock's car because he never got his licence, and never drove. The probability is that the pinched vehicle was his son, Jock jnr's.

Collingwood led at quarter-time and half-time of the replay, and scores were tied at the end of the third. But Essendon proved too strong in the final term, to push away from the Magpies to win by 19 points in a low-scoring game. The Bombers were in a Grand Final for the first time since beating Richmond in 1942. Collingwood had

---

54 *The Argus*, September 16, 1946
55 *The Sun*, September 18, 1946

to beat Melbourne—and McHale's old foe 'Checker' Hughes—in the preliminary final on the day of the 1946 federal election—when Ben Chifley defeated Robert Menzies—to have another shot at Essendon. The consequences of the draw had meant that Wraith had to quickly reschedule the club's first planned tour of Western Australia since the famous 1927 season.

In the preliminary final, Collingwood led by 23 points at the last change. Mann had come off the bench after half-time to replace the injured Jack Green, and McHale instructed him to get into the forward line and to try and make a difference. He did just that, booting five goals for the game, including one in the last term. He would see that game as a turning point in his career. He would say: "I think that game stabilised me into becoming a (good) player for Collingwood."[56]

Surely a buffer of almost four goals would be enough to elevate the Magpies and McHale to another Grand Final, after a seven-year break. But, just as it had happened in the previous year's preliminary final, the Magpies blew a sizeable lead to bring an end to a 1946 season that had promised so much and had ended in two more disappointing finals losses, and a heartbreaking draw. It was all too much for the club's former great secretary, E.W. 'Bud' Copeland, who "collapsed after the game and was taken to the Royal Melbourne hospital."[57]

There were a few consolations to the pain of defeat. For one, John Wren, described as "one of Collingwood's staunchest supporters over the years,"[58] donated a cheque of £250 to the club, with the instructions to divvy up the tally to Fothergill (as the leading goalkicker) £50, McHale £30, and Kyne £20, with the other £150 to be split among the other players on the club's list.

The other consolation was the pre-organised trip to Western Australia soon after the club bowed out of the finals. The Argus reported a party of "nine officials, 27 players, a life member (McHale's old

---

56 Interview with Neil Mann, 1996
57 *The Argus*, September 30, 1946
58 *The Argus*, October 1, 1946

mate Ted Rowell), two trainers and three supporters"[59] started their journey across the country on the Tuesday after Essendon had beaten Melbourne in the Grand Final. The trip took in a brief stopover in Adelaide, time spent in Kalgoorlie where a match was played against a Goldfields side, a match against East Fremantle at Subiaco, and a game against a combined south-west team in Bunbury. The Magpies won all three contests, and had a wonderful experience in seeing the sights, including mine inspections at Boulder, watching a day's cricket involving the touring England side versus a Western Australia combined XI (including a couple of 'ring-ins' in Sid Barnes [NSW] and Ian Johnson [Victoria]), a night out at the Gloucester Park trots and a dance at the Subiaco Football Club.

The match report of the game against East Fremantle, run in *The Western Mail* referred to some of Collingwood's great players of the time, including "Lew (sic) Richards ... no finer display from a rover could be imagined."[60] At a function that night, McHale said: "The dinner was the best function and gesture of its kind to Collingwood by any other club during his 43 years' association with Collingwood."[61] The paper reported that "Jock McHale's compliment had the ring of sincerity about it."[62] On leaving Perth on the Westland Express, McHale told *The West Australian* it was one of the finest trips he had ever been on (which he had said also after the 1927 visit), adding: "We hope it won't be so long before we come to WA again."[63]

McHale must surely have cast his thoughts back what had happened in 1927, when he took a bunch of the young and the experienced ones to Perth, and returned home with a close and contented team that would win four successive premierships. But, as McHale, a few months short of his 64th birthday, planned for the short-term future, it was said that this trip to Western Australia gave

59   The History of the Collingwood Football Club, 1892-1948, Percy Taylor, 1949
60   *The Western Mail*, October 24, 1946
61   ibid
62   ibid
63   *The West Australian*, October 22, 1947

rise to the initial wondering about who would be the ultimate successor to the longest serving coach in history when he finally decided it was time to go.

When McHale did retire, in April 1950, veteran sports journalist Percy Taylor would pinpoint the club's tour to Perth as the first time it had been raised in certain circles that Bervin Woods—the club's reserves coach—was likely to be McHale's successor. Taylor wrote a month later, in May, 1950: "So far as can be gathered, the first signs were heard when the team was on tour to Western Australia several years ago. From something that was said on that tour, some of the older players felt that, when Jock McHale resigned, the job was cut and dried for Woods."[64]

Woods recalled many years later: "Nobody promised it to me when we were away on the trip to WA. There was a bit of talk about it then. I think it might have stirred a few of them up."[65] It is not known whether McHale had heard any of the speculation about who might be best served to lead the club into the future when he left the helm. Stremski stated in 1986: "During an end-of-season trip to Western Australia three years earlier (1946) the administrative triumvirate (Frank Wraith, Harry Curtis and Bob Rush) had promised Bervin Woods the coaching job when McHale had retired."[66] At that stage McHale was not yet ready to step down, and in the meantime another candidate, Phonse Kyne, who won the first of three successive Copeland Trophies in 1946, would famously step forward with some extraordinary performances on the field.

But instead of taking the next step in 1947, as McHale had envisaged after strong performances in the previous two seasons, Collingwood

---

64   *The Argus*, May 19, 1950
65   Interview with Bervin Woods
66   *Kill For Collingwood*, Richard Stremski, Allen and Unwin, 1986

missed the finals altogether. Its position in September had seemingly been secured for almost all of the home and away season, and it came down to the last few minutes of a long season to see it denied.

The Magpies won their first four games of the season, and sat a game clear on top of the ladder at that stage. But three successive losses followed. Critically, Collingwood only won one of its last five games, and that was enough to bury them. Lacking a powerful and high-scoring key forward, and other strong, big-boned young men, the Magpies struggled against the elite sides. When they beat Geelong in Round 14, to be third and two games clear of fourth spot, no one could have envisaged this would be their last win for the season.

A draw with South Melbourne hurt, so did losses to Melbourne and Richmond. In the final round the equation was simple. Beat second-placed Essendon, and retain fourth spot. Lose, and miss out. The signs were positive in that the Bombers had a poor record at Victoria Park, and the Magpies led by 23 points at three-quarter time. But once more Collingwood could not close out an important game. Even Dick Reynolds, Essendon's captain-coach, writing in *The Argus* said of Essendon's seven-goal to two last quarter burst: "It was only a remarkable recovery in the last quarter that gave us victory. Collingwood are unfortunate. I thought that they were certain to finish second, but they passed through a stale period which proved fatal."[67] Twomey said: "We were stiff not to make it that year. I thought we were going to win the (Essendon) game. Again, it was probably a fitness thing; we just weren't as fit as we could be."[68]

On that same day Melbourne's Fred Fanning kicked a VFL record of 18 goals, against St Kilda at the Junction Oval, to break Gordon Coventry's previous high of 17, from 1930; this astonishing performance must surely have re-emphasised to McHale, if he needed any, the importance of a prolific forward. Collingwood would have some solid goalkickers in this time, with Mann (48 in 1947), Richards

---

67   *The Argus*, September 1, 1947
68   Interview with Bill Twomey, 1996

(44 in 1948) and Pimm (34 in 1949), but no Collingwood player would push through the 50-goal mark again until 1958.

Two brothers of Collingwood stars started their careers at Victoria Park in 1947. Pat Twomey, who had just turned 18, was among the best players with his brother Bill in his debut game, against Essendon in Round 8, and 19-year-old Ron Richards joined sibling Lou in the Round 11 game against North Melbourne at Victoria Park. Pat played 10 senior games that season, but still managed to win the Gardiner Medal for the best and fairest in the reserves competition. Bill couldn't understand why Pat hadn't played more games that year. He recalled: "I remember saying to Jock, 'When are you going to give Pat a game?' Old Jock said, 'Don't worry, Bill, we have plenty of his type.' That was a bad phrase to use to the brother of a bloke."[69]

But not everyone had the same issues with McHale as Twomey. Ron Richards, who played five games that season, before going on to play 143, said: "I reckon he used to make some good decisions in matches. I worked with (Tom) Hafey and other coaches over the years, but they didn't have the flair that Old Jock used to have for making a move."[70] Richards, who would later serve as chairman of selectors under Hafey, recalls one testy night at training early in his career when: "I remember a bunch of young louts, about four or five of them. They were just going crook, and having a bit of a go. Well, Old Jock was in his 60s, but he had 40 players there, right behind him. They (the louts) shit themselves and they left the ground in a hurry. That was the power of Jock."[71]

69   ibid
70   Interview with Ron Richards, 2009
71   ibid

Recruit Geoff Brokenshire, who had been brought in from Sandringham, got a lesson in McHale's likes and dislikes early in the 1948 season. Gordon Carlyon, who had started full-time as assistant secretary at Collingwood in 1946, said: "Brokenshire came in and we had a talk about signing up. I said, 'That's the players' room over there and recruits strip off in this great big room.' Geoff went up (to speak with Jock) and he had a little moustache. He said, 'My name is Geoff Brokenshire'. Jock said, 'Yes, from Sandringham'. Geoff said, 'I have come up to throw my weight in with Collingwood, I thought I would introduce myself to you'. 'Well now, Brokenshire, are you coming back on Thursday? Well, get that bit of fluff off your upper lip, and get your gear—recruits train outside, only players come in here."[72] Brokenshire went on to play 13 games with Collingwood in 1948, before playing a further 21 at Carlton in 1949 and 1950.

There were a few other recruits to make their debut in 1948, and a number of them went on to achieve plenty, including Des Healey, Jack Hamilton and George Hams. Healey finally got a game after three years of trying without success. For some reason McHale was reluctant to give him a chance, despite the pleadings of reserves coach Bervin Woods, and it took until the 1948 season for him to be given the opportunity. "That was one of the great mysteries of all time," Twomey would later say.[73]

Jack Pimm would never forget what McHale said to him when he missed a shot at goal at Geelong right on the bell in 1948. He recalled: "I had the chance to kick it, but I missed it. I walked passed him that night, and he said to me, 'I thought you could do better, Pimmy'."[74]

Another interesting tale involving McHale and his steadfast approach to the things he believed in came at the end of the 1948 season. Hamilton had broken a collarbone in a match against Fitzroy that year and wanted to start training at a gymnasium by lifting weights

---

72   *Frank Wraith, A Magpie misjudged*, Gordon Carlyon, Gordon Carlyon, 2003
73   Interview with Bill Twomey, 1996
74   Interview with Jack Pimm, 2009

to rebuild his strength. Hamilton recalled later: "Stan Nicholes is my cousin and he mapped out a program for me. I think I was one of the first footballers to use weights as a part of pre-season training. Stan, at the time, was Australian weightlifting champion. He later became famous when he trained successful Australian Davis Cup players. But Collingwood coach Jock McHale didn't agree, and he told me not to do the training. I continued to do this without Jock knowing that I was paying for a course at the gym. I later found out that this was of enormous benefit."[75]

In 1948, Collingwood did something it had not done in nine years: win a final. For McHale, in the context of his football life, it must have seemed like an eternity. The season had started spectacularly with only two losses from the club's first 11 games, and the Magpies were sitting outright on top of the ladder from Essendon. But then, inexplicably, the staleness kicked in again, and the club lost three in a row late in the season, before dropping a couple of other late games. The fall away left Collingwood in third spot, with a clash against Footscray in the first semi-final.

Footscray led the game by 10 points at the main break, but it was an injury suffered by Bill Twomey that helped transform the game. Rather than take Twomey from the ground. McHale forced the brilliant centreman into attack. There has long been speculation that Twomey wanted to come off, instead of going forward. In an interview in 1996, Twomey denied this claim: "I had a bit of foot trouble, I felt as though I couldn't spring. It might have been a nerve or something. There have been a lot of things said that I asked to be replaced. I didn't ask to be replaced. All I can remember is someone said to just go down to the forward pocket."[76] He added: "I went down there and took a couple of marks, and kicked a few goals. After half-time, I think I kicked seven. You can do amazing things when you kick a few goals."[77]

---

75   *The Sun*, August 2, 1988
76   Interview with Bill Twomey, 1996
77   ibid

Dick Reynolds, Essendon's captain-coach, described the switch as the most decisive move in the match. He wrote in *The Argus*: "Why was Twomey placed at full-forward? This question was asked by more than 70,000 spectators. Twomey had been shaded by (Harry) Hickey in the centre for the first part of the game. When he sustained a foot injury late in the second term, he was not able to keep up with the elusive Hickey. He was shifted to a half-forward flank and on a couple of occasions I noticed that he was not able to run. With only five minutes left he was moved to the forward pocket. It looked to me as though he would be replaced. Then he suddenly made into the play. Whoever among Collingwood's officials saw Twomey's efforts in front of goal must have realised what a danger he would be at full-forward."[78]

In the end, Twomey kicked eight goals; the move had turned the match, enabling Collingwood to win its first finals win since the 1939 preliminary final. Reynolds even suggested that Collingwood "may have found its successor to Ron Todd."[79]

But the same ploy did not work the following week, in yet another preliminary final against Melbourne. Twomey managed three goals and Bob Rose kicked four. But it was not enough to stop a remorseless Melbourne from advancing to meet Essendon in what would ultimately be the first drawn Grand Final. Twomey said McHale and his match committee made a mistake in the lead-in to the game against Melbourne, although he was prepared to cop some of the blame. He said: "The big mistake was ... they were going to put me back in the centre the following week against Melbourne. 'Jock,' I said, 'Why don't you give me another go at full-forward,' and they did. That's where the selectors did make a mistake. What happened against Footscray definitely didn't happen against Melbourne."[80]

Mann blamed himself a bit. He reckons a case of "foot in mouth" might have contributed to the ease of Melbourne's win. He said in

---

78   *The Argus*, September 13, 1948
79   ibid
80   Interview with Bill Twomey, 1996

a 1996 interview: "On the Sunday morning I did an interview with 3AW, and they called us in. Shane McGrath (Melbourne) was also being interviewed. I made the fatal mistake of saying Bill had kicked his eight against Footscray the week before; I said to Shane, 'You will have to be on your best behaviour.' Well, Shane hardly gave him a look-in; he hardly gave him a kick."[81] At the other end, Jack Mueller, in only his third game for the season, kicked eight goals. Melbourne kicked 25 goals and won by 55 points, and went on to win the premiership after an initial draw with Essendon, the first Grand Final draw in VFL history.

Jock McHale was 66 as he saddled up for his 38th season of coaching in early 1949. He was reappointed on February 10. No one knew how long he could possibly continue, but his intention was as it had been in every one of the previous 37 seasons: to strive for the flag. It was the thing that still drove him, even if he was slowing up a little with his work on the track.

Carlyon said McHale remained an intriguing character, even as he headed into what would be his last season. He said: "Jock, to me, was a gruff old bloke, yet he had a twinkle in his eye. If you were a smart cookie, you would turn around and say this bloke is easy because he would talk to you, but if you rubbed him up the wrong way, you were in trouble. And if you took him to be a simple bloke, you were in trouble. He was very genuine and very loyal. You couldn't criticise any of his players (in front of him), he would get stuck into you (if you did)."[82]

Carlyon added: "On match day, I used to call the room to order. There would be 200 or 250 people in the back of the room, and they tried to clear them out one day, and he (McHale) said, 'No, let them hear what I have got to say.' Everyone would take their hats off. I used

---

81   Interview with Neil Mann, 1996
82   Interview with Gordon Carlyon, 1995

to get up on a seat and introduce the president Harry Curtis (who would speak) and then 'strict silence for our coach Jock McHale'. And he would get up and if there was a player just doing up his lace, Jock would stop there, and just look at him. Anyone in the back of the room, smoking or anything like that, he would just stare at them and someone would say 'shoosh'. And he would give the same instructions in front of those 200 people as what he gave the players. His famous saying was to 'go out there and stir up the stove', the old fighting call."[83]

The message was pretty much the same as it had always been, though the faces were different—so different—from when he first started making those speeches almost 40 years earlier. But the generation gap had started to widen between the ageing coach and some of his players.

Peter Lucas, whose first senior season at Collingwood was McHale's last as coach, said McHale was an exceptional speaker, but he had probably been passed it in terms of training the group. He said: "He was really passed it, I believed. He used to come out in his footy shorts, and just stand there in the centre of the ground, more or less. But he was a fantastic pre-match speaker."[84]

Bernie Shannon was another player to play his first game for Collingwood in 1949, having been signed as a tall forward by the great Dick Lee, originally as a 15-year-old, five years earlier. When he was finally selected for a senior game as a 20-year-old, Shannon recalled: "(Lee) came in to shake my hand and wish me good luck—which I thought was very nice of him—until Jock stormed in. Jock said to me, 'Hey, Shannon! You don't want these blokes blowing in your ear. You tell them to come and see me. All I want you to do is play like you trained on Thursday night ... (he would say) when you get the ball kick it as far as you can to the next position, and if they're not there, that's their fault."[85]

---

83   ibid
84   Interview with Peter Lucas, 2010
85   Interview with Bernie Shannon, 2010

One game Shannon won't ever forget was his sixth match, when Collingwood took on Richmond at Punt Road. The Magpies hadn't won at the ground in four years, and the pressure was on to turn around that record. At three-quarter time, the Magpies led by 20 points. As McHale went to address the huddle as he had done more than 700 times, his voice failed him and his emotion got the better of him. Tears came to his eyes. It was so unusual, but it showed a human side to McHale that few had seen.

Shannon said: "He wanted it so much that he cried at three-quarter time. He just went to talk and he couldn't. The words didn't come and he had tears in his eyes. That was when 'Phonsey' Kyne had to take over and speak on Jock's behalf. He said, 'You can see what it is doing to him, let's make sure we win it for him." The Magpies did, by three points.

Shannon said it was around the time of that win over Richmond that he was asked by McHale to be in a posed newspaper photo with him, Phonse Kyne and Jack Green. McHale is speaking to them about football, and they are watching almost with reverence. Shannon recalled: "They used to tell me about Jock, that if you played a good game he would talk to you and if you had a bad game he wouldn't speak to you until you'd put in a good one. Anyway, I was at training this particular night and the photographer came along and he wanted to photograph Jock and Phonse, and 'Jacky' Green. Now the photographer asked for someone else to be in the photo and I must have had a good one the previous Saturday, because as I was running around the track, Jock shouted out, 'Hey, young Shannon, over here! And I thought, 'Oh well, I must be going all right then'."[86]

McHale didn't especially like to show any emotion, other than the biting of nails, and gnashing of teeth throughout matches. In a special series of photos—following McHale through his fifth last game in charge as he sat alongside Syd Coventry that year—the coach's

---

86   ibid

expression hardly changed, while his former captain appeared to ride every bump on a rollercoaster of emotions.

In 1949 Collingwood won nine of its first 11 games. But losses to North Melbourne and Melbourne in the mid-season, and three defeats out of the last four games, were massive blows. The last-round loss to second-last St Kilda, by nine points at the Junction Oval, was a frightful blow. It left Collingwood vulnerable for the first semi-final against Essendon. The Bombers had unearthed what McHale could only dream for: a star forward in 20-year-old John Coleman.

Interestingly enough, he chose to play 20-year-old Shannon on Coleman, thinking that his height and pace could trouble the young Bomber who had taken the VFL by storm in his first year, kicking 85 goals to the end of the home and away season (he would finish with 100, the only player to kick 100 goals in a debut season).

"They say he could pick a footballer for his position even if he (the player) was walking down Johnston Street," Shannon said of McHale. "In the seniors, I had only ever played full-back in one other game. He never gave me any instructions or advice about it (playing on Coleman). It wasn't a gamble as far as he (McHale) was concerned; he just thought I was the right size to play on him. Coleman kicked six for the day, and Jack Hamilton came out and gave a free kick away, so I only count it as five (goals). He was a freak, Coleman!"[87]

The Magpies were the underdogs, having been beaten by Essendon by 46 points in the Round 17 clash. But McHale had never gone into a game before thinking his team couldn't win.

But there was to be no Collingwood fairytale to end the decade, or the coach's reign. The season ended with a flogging at the hands of an Essendon side that would go on and win the premiership. The Magpies lost by an embarrassing margin of 82 points. If it was any consolation for McHale his counterpart on the day, Essendon captain-coach Dick Reynolds (at 34, almost half McHale's age), wrote

---

87   ibid

in *The Argus*: "Essendon played so well in trouncing Collingwood on Saturday that I have no hesitation in saying that we would have annihilated any other League team on the day."[88] In time, the Bombers would do it to Carlton in the Grand Final, winning the flag (from fourth) by 73 points. Coleman kicked 15 goals in his three finals, including six in the Grand Final against the veteran Ollie Grieve.

For McHale, the decade ended as it began, with disappointment, and the 1940s remains the only decade of Collingwood's long and illustrious history in which it hasn't made a Grand Final. As McHale made his way off the MCG late that afternoon, he was carrying the hurt, but he was also carrying a secret he had told very few people. The man whose coaching career had spanned two world wars and a depression—and an extraordinary 714 games—was going to retire. But, for the moment, he kept his counsel.

---

88   *The Argus,* September 5, 1949

CHAPTER 14

The Painful Succession

1950

J ock McHale coached Collingwood for almost 14,000 days; his successor lasted only four days. What happened at the Collingwood Football Club during the months of April and May 1950 stand as one of the most remarkable and divisive transfers of power in the history of Australian sport. It was the antithesis of everything Collingwood had stood for almost 60 years— it pitted friend against friend; it gave rise to feelings of bitterness and betrayal; and it forever smashed the myth that the club was so secure as to make it immune from political upheaval.

The painful succession to McHale's long reign as the Magpies' coach would rock the club, and some of the people within it. The coach had been there for most of the life of the club and when he suddenly decided to retire from the position, the understudy that he had neither anointed nor wanted to replace him would hold his appointed position for less than a week. The decision to elevate the club's seconds coach Bervin Woods to replace McHale—instead of on-field hero Phonse Kyne, whom McHale, the players, and the overwhelming majority of the black and white supporters wanted—would set into motion a chain of events that would lead to the overthrow of some of the longest-serving and most respected men on the committee—men who had played significant roles in the success of the club.

Incredibly, not too many years earlier, McHale had chastised Lou Richards, Jack Burns and 'Mac' Holten for daring to try to organise a players' meeting in the midst of a form slump. McHale had stated emphatically—and with what he believed was absolute certainty—that there had never been a revolution at Victoria Park, and there never would be. There is no doubt the coach believed that at the time to be the case, and why wouldn't he? Aside from the schism with the seconds in early 1939, which brought about the departure of reserves coach Hughie Thomas, as well as chairman of selectors, 'Doc' Seddon, the Collingwood Football Club had been relatively seamless in its operations since its birth in 1892. But that would all change in 1950.

McHale had, on numerous occasions, extolled the virtues of stable administration as one of the cornerstones of Collingwood's extraordinary success in the Victorian Football League. In the section marked "Club Management" of McHale's collaborative book with Bert Chadwick and E.C.H. Taylor, *The Australian Game of Football*, published in 1931, the authors stated: "The success of the club depends to a great extent on the ability of the club's executive to manage its affairs in an orderly, tactful and business-like manner."[1] For the most part it worked, but there would be little that was orderly, tactful or business-like during the big Collingwood split of 1950. Also included in the "Club Management" section but referring mainly to players, there was a quote which read: "Remember that nobody is indispensible, and there is not a man living whose place cannot be filled."[2] 1950 would prove that, too.

There were two schools of thought on Jock McHale's coaching tenure among fans as Collingwood looked towards what it hoped

---

1   *The Australian Game of Football,* J.F. McHale, A.E. Chadwick and E.C.H. Taylor, Hartleys, 1931
2   ibid

would be a brighter 1950s compared to the dark 1940s. Many thought McHale was indispensible, having known no other coach in their lives. It was a coaching constant that seemed without end. Others feared the great leader might have gone beyond his coaching expiry date, citing his age, the manner in which the Magpies had capitulated to the Bombers by 82 points in the 1949 first semi-final, and the failure to recruit that next great full-forward to follow the line of Lee, Coventry and Todd that had been so important to the club's successful years. Essendon had shown the way with John Coleman playing such a key role in winning the 1949 premiership.

There had been rumblings almost immediately after that semi-final loss that McHale did not want to coach into the 1950s. But each time there was a noise made about it Collingwood would strenuously deny it, mainly through secretary Frank Wraith. When asked about the speculation that the club would soon be on the lookout for a new coach for the first time since the early months of 1912, Wraith repudiated those claims in October 1949, telling *The Sporting Globe* that the speculation that had been rife in the football world was "absolutely groundless."[3]

In an article written by leading writer Kevin Hogan in *The Sun* in February 1950 further doubt was raised on McHale continuing as coach. The article was a big talking point in the pubs and factories around Collingwood. Under the heading "Magpie Doubt", Hogan declared: "There is doubt about whether Jock McHale, who has coached Collingwood for 39 years (note: to that stage it was actually 38 seasons) will continue this season. After a committee meeting last night, the president H.R. Curtis said that the coaching appointment would probably not be determined until the club's annual meeting on March 1. Mr Curtis added that the position had not been discussed last night and, as far as he was aware, Mr McHale was available for re-appointment."[4]

---

3   *The Sporting Globe,* October 22, 1949
4   *The Sun,* February 22, 1950

Then Hogan added tellingly that he had asked McHale and not received a definitive answer. He wrote: "On Monday night Mr McHale told me that he had not yet decided whether he would carry on. He said he expected to be able to give the committee a decision by last night (February 21)."[5]

According to *Kill For Collingwood*, McHale had made his mind up not to coach again at the end of the previous year. Author Richard Stremski wrote: "McHale was ready to retire in October 1949, but Curtis and Wraith persuaded him to delay the decision so that they could clarify the appointment of a successor."[6] The reality was that the trio of Curtis, Wraith and club treasurer Bob Rush had already settled on McHale's successor, perhaps even as early as several years beforehand. That man was seconds coach, Bervin Woods. Woods was no dud: a solid dependable defender, without a lot of finesse but with a fine embodiment of team, he had played in five Grand Finals, for premierships in 1935 and 1936, in his 110 games (1935-1940). He had been reserves coach since 1943, and had put his playing characteristics into his coaching. He was a hard-working coach with the seconds, and had a good relationship with the players. Those who knew him, and played under him, thought he would have been serviceable as a senior coach. But there is little doubt that, at least among the playing group, that Kyne was valued higher in terms of his leadership capabilities and tactical nous.

Despite all the speculation surrounding the role, McHale was officially named as Collingwood coach for 1950 at the club's annual meeting on March 1. McHale would oversee a band of fresh recruits, and potential new full-forwards, as he took on the club's preparation from early March until the first few days of April. One of the recruits was a pint-sized kid who had been overlooked by Richmond's Jack Dyer, claiming that he was too little for the big league. The teenager had come to the city on the recommendation of former Magpie and

---

5   ibid
6   *Kill For Collingwood, Richard Stremski,* Allen and Unwin, 1986

now coach of Cobden Jack Murphy (Jock's nephew and the winner of the 1941 Copeland Trophy). The kid had also come to Melbourne to develop his cricket skills. His name was Thorold Merrett.

But the club was about to lose another young star in an episode all too reminiscent of the loss of Ron Todd and Des Fothergill a decade before. In February, utility Len Fitzgerald requested a clearance to South Australia. He ended up returning to Collingwood later in the season and played four more matches, but by the next season he was gone for good. He would go on to win three Magarey Medals with Sturt.

The Argus's Percy Taylor wrote in March that McHale was "the best-known football coach in Australia"[7] as he set out on yet another pre-season campaign for his team. Taylor wrote: "Last week I saw him in guernsey and knickers directing the work at Collingwood, and few would believe he is aged 68 years (note: he would not turn 68 until December 12, 1950). In football circles it is said that no one is a better judge of the condition of players."[8] Taylor had a long relationship with McHale, and in the midst this story, and almost certainly after he had gained direct knowledge from McHale, Taylor forecast: "This will be Jock's last season."[9] Then he added prophetically: "Who will be his successor? That is a difficult one to answer."[10] That would become an understatement of significant proportions.

But, just as preparations were cranking up for Collingwood's first game of the 1950 season (scheduled for April 22), the bombshell came. It was swift and sensational. On Tuesday, April 4, the man who had been coach of the Collingwood Football Club since the early months of 1912 decided to call it a day. In a decision that he always knew would have to come at some stage, yet secretly hoped wouldn't, McHale stood before the committee that night and told them he could no longer continue as coach.

---

7   *The Argus*, March 15, 1950
8   ibid
9   ibid
10   ibid

Gordon Carlyon recalled the night that Jock McHale resigned. He was at the committee meeting, making a requisition for some new gym equipment when the drama unfolded. He recalled: "I went to the committee meeting and Bill Angus (committeeman) said to me 'Do you know the news? The news about Jim?' Harry Curtis was in the chair and he said 'We have talked things over and Jock McHale would like to retire. He doesn't want to pick his successor.'"[11]

The push from the meeting was that the new coach had to be non-playing, a point emphasised strongly by Bob Rush. This view would become critical in the debate, as one of the most popular likely candidates was Kyne, technically still a player then, and training hard for the 1950 season. He had played in the semi-final thrashing of 1949, his 238th game since his debut in 1934.

When finally drawn to make a comment on his retirement, the typically taciturn McHale offered up thanks to the supporters as much as anyone. He said: "They have been wonderful to me. I've always been a good winner and a poor loser, and I know that many a time when I have been down in the dumps, the warmth and sympathy of the rank and file club supporters helped raise my spirit to look forward to something better next time."[12] He agreed to stay on as training supervisor until his successor was chosen, and even took to doing something he didn't normally do at training, kick the ball. *Argus* photographer Neil Town captured the look of intent on McHale's face as he kicked the ball in the middle of Victoria Park. Town would say that it would be the first time in his 13 years covering Collingwood sessions that he had ever seen McHale kick a ball at training.[13]

---

11   Interview with Gordon Carlyon, 1999
12   *The Herald,* April 12, 1950
13   *The Argus,* April 8, 1950

Retirement was one of the toughest moments of his sporting life, although he didn't rule out staying with the club. McHale told *The Sun:* "I would do anything for the club—I always would since I joined it in 1903. I am a sad man today, but I would be delighted if this grand side goes on to big things."[14]

Various reasons were cited for McHale's retirement—a seemingly strange decision 18 days out from the Magpies' opening game of the season against South Melbourne at the Lake Oval. The likelihood is that McHale never seriously intended to coach that season, and was only delaying an announcement to assist the committee to work out a process to procure a new coach, or smooth over the path for the replacement they already had in mind. Regardless, *The Argus* reported the news: "McHale said he had decided to retire because he was now living in Essendon, because of the illness of his wife (Violet), and because of the increasing pressures of his work (at the Carlton Brewery)."[15]

Jock and Violet moved out to Edward Street, Essendon (just a couple of streets from Windy Hill) to be closer to their son. It was a significant move for them, as they had lived in Brunswick for their entire marriage—41 years to that time. And it took them that bit further away from both the brewery and from Victoria Park, having in mind that McHale had never driven.

June McHale insists that the "illness" mentioned in relation to Violet at the time must have been a minor one, as she had always kept reasonable health. She doted on "her two Jocks" and if there were any health issues, they were quickly overcome.

Violet made a rare public statement when her husband retired. *The Sun* reported she considered her husband's retirement from coaching as the "best present" she has had for a long time. A lifetime of losing her husband for much of the week (with work and football) and every Saturday in winter must have been tough on the marriage, but the

---

14   *The Sun*, April 6, 1950
15   *The Argus*, April 5, 1950

ever-loving Violet summed it up simply: "He'll be able to enjoy the matches now."[16]

But June McHale says a more pertinent reason can be established for Jock McHale finally giving up his coaching—his son was about to go on an extended trip overseas, and he was worried that Violet would be on her own too often—given his enormous commitments to the brewery and the football club. She recalled: "It was more to do with the fact that my Jock was in business and was going overseas. They were both so mindful of Violet. It didn't take much to convince Jock (snr) to give it away. He had a very soft side to him. He didn't show it very often. When Jock (jnr) was away, he asked me to go and see his mum and dad. I used to take my mother out there, and we would all end up laughing about things."[17]

Incredibly, Jock jnr went away with one of his close friends, Ron Todd, the very man whose defection from Collingwood to Williamstown in 1940 had so incensed his father. Back in 1914, Jock snr had once prepared for an overseas with a football tour with players from various VFL clubs that was scuttled by the onset of World War I. In the end, he would never leave Australia, his travels confined to mid-season interstate and country football trips. A parochial man, he once said to his son: "What are you going to get over there that you can't get in Brunswick?" McHale was a shy man, but he had a sense of his place in Melbourne life. On one occasion, while at Melbourne's Princes Pier, farewelling friends about to embark on a cruise overseas, he was asked: "I'll send you a postcard from Suez, but should I send it to Collingwood or your home?" McHale replied: "Just send it to Jock McHale, Australia. It will reach me!"

Long-time administrator Gordon Carlyon offered up another alternative for McHale's apparently spontaneous decision—he wondered whether Jock McHale was coaxed into retirement by some members of the committee keen to see a new figure at the helm.

---

16   *The Sun*, April 6, 1950
17   Interview with June McHale, 2009

Although admitting his opinion was based only on an assumption, Carlyon said: "Jock never told me, but I think he was more or less pushed out, or told to retire. Every year the name of Jock McHale would come up, and whether he would be coaching again. He had been there 30-odd years. He felt like while he was still physically fit, and he had the respect and success, then why not (keep going)?"[18]

Carlyon added that the talk of a succession plan first surfaced on the club's end of season trip to Perth (mentioned earlier in the book): "It started off, I believe, when they went to WA in 1946. They started talking about his (possible) successors. There were the two Colliers (Harry and Albert). Syd Coventry wasn't interested. Who was it going to be? The name of Bervin Woods came up and he had done everything right in the seconds. I don't know whether it was promised to him, but that was the pact."[19]

Percy Taylor would later add in *The Argus*: "Inquiries show that there were rumblings of discontent long before the appointment of a successor to Jock McHale as coach was ever visualised. The appointment of Bervyn (sic) Woods, instead of Phonse Kyne, was the last straw. So far as can be gathered, the first signs were heard when the team was on tour to Western Australia several years ago (1946). From something that was said on that tour, some of the older players felt that, when Jock McHale resigned, the job was 'cut and dried' for Woods."[20]

Whatever the case, as much as Woods might have seemed a good option in 1946, things had changed internally by 1950. Kyne was seen by most as the most likely successor to McHale. He had won three successive Copeland Trophies (1946-1948),[21] had developed into one of the game's best ruckmen and was considered a great team man and leader, having taken over as captain from Alby Pannam from 1946.

---

18   Interview with Gordon Carlyon, 1999
19   ibid
20   *The Argus*, May 18, 1950
21   Kyne was also second in 1949 to Bob Rose

Kyne had also been captain in 1942, playing 10 games that year before war service intervened.

Carlyon said the likes of Harry and Albert Collier made inquiries about the position, as would Lou Riley (who had crossed to Collingwood from Melbourne in 1934, and would play in the 1935-36 premierships as a half-forward), but it was always going to come down to Woods or Kyne. Kyne made his intentions clear, when he agreed to resign as a player to meet the non-playing coach criterion. That scuttled the hopes of several key people who supported Woods, including the key administrators Wraith (who did not have a vote), Curtis and Rush.

McHale may not have named a successor, but there was little doubt in anyone's mind that he believed Kyne was the right man to take over from him, and to continue to coach the side with the same uncompromising values as he had preached over the long journey.

Again, Carlyon takes us to McHale's thoughts at that dramatic time, recalling almost 50 years later: "At the big committee meeting on the Tuesday night, the press were there and they said they wanted to get a photo of Bervin Woods. I said (to them) there was a committee meeting tonight. He (Woods) has gone home earlier. I went (over) to Jock and he said, 'You're wasting your time, Bervin Woods won't coach. (It will be) Phonse Kyne.' As we walked up the race, I said 'How do you work out (for) Phonse?' He said, 'We have got the numbers.' He said there was seven for Phonse and five for Bervin. I said to him, 'I hope you are right, but I can't see it.' He said, 'Why can't you see it?' I said, 'I can only count six for Phonse and that means six against. And that means Harry Curtis (would then have the casting vote) and he's dead against him (Kyne).' He (Jock) said, 'it won't come to that'."[22]

Indeed, it *would* come to that. In another sure sign that McHale's faith in the principles and people at Collingwood had been tested like never before, the vote on the replacement coach on Thursday April 14 was deadlocked, as Carlyon had forecast. As Stremski documented:

---

22   Interview with Gordon Carlyon, 1999

"After tallying the secret ballot ... Curtis informed the committee that Woods was elected coach."[23] Carlyon would say: "They had old dance tickets (as ballots), and they went out and put the names on the table. And Syd (Coventry) told me this later, as he went past a certain committeeman (whom he thought was pro-Kyne) it flung open and he saw a name there. And he was amazed. The voting was six for and six against. Harry Curtis, without any more ado just said 'Gentlemen, I have pleasure in announcing Bervin (Woods) as coach."[24]

Then, as Carlyon puts it, "all hell broke loose", with McHale in the thick of it. "Tom Sherrin stood up and said, 'Don't look at me like that, Jock McHale, I didn't swing my vote.' Jock said: 'I didn't say a bloody word.' He (Sherrin) said: 'You didn't have to, your looks are enough.' Then Jack Galbally got up and demanded to know what the voting was. Harry Curtis said if you want to know the voting was six for Kyne and six for Woods, and, as chairman, my casting vote went to Woods. He (Galbally) said: 'Mr President, for 25 years, you have brought honour and distinguished service to this club, and you have just torn it all down. You have done the wrong thing and the worst thing for Collingwood."[25]

Almost immediately *The Argus* reported a petition started doing the rounds calling for a special meeting to "lodge a protest at the passing over of Kyne."[26] Kyne's response initially was that he would play on but then he recanted, realising there was a movement afoot for serious change. Through it all, the man in the hot seat was Curtis, who pleaded for calm, in the wake of overwhelming bitterness. He told *The Argus*: "The Collingwood club is bigger than the individual. For that reason I am sure players and supporters alike will accept the appointment of Bervyn (sic) Woods and continue loyally to support the club. This is a club tradition."[27]

---

23   *Kill For Collingwood*, Richard Stremski, Allen and Unwin, 1986
24   Interview with Gordon Carlyon, 1999
25   ibid
26   *The Argus*, April 15, 1950
27   ibid

But if the atmosphere in the boardroom was hostile, it was nothing on what would happen at a practice match at Victoria Park on the following Saturday. From early that morning there had been rumours that the players would take action by withdrawing their services or quitting. It never got to that stage. The game went ahead, but *The Argus* reported: "Considerable feeling was displayed by many who had come to see the play. Chief figures in the selection of Woods were hooted and even Woods came in for some heckling."[28]

Bernie Shannon, who played in that practice match recalled the moment vividly: "It was a sad time. Frank Wraith had promised Bervin Woods the coaching job when Jock retired, and he really had no right to do it. It caused the biggest uproar of all time. I can remember turning up to training and seeing Woods walking the other way with the best black eye of all-time. I couldn't believe it! Bervin was a lovely guy, and it wasn't his fault that they picked him."[29]

Carlyon described that infamous practice match: "I was standing with the committee and they (supporters) were coming over and tearing up their tickets and tearing up paper, and abusing Frank Wraith and Curtis. Then, Jock McHale got up in the room and said, 'This is my last day as a coach. I will be handing over to my successor. I can only hope and trust that you give him the same support that I have had over the past 38 years'." He then noted that McHale told the crowd: "'The coach is not the man that I would have liked to have seen coaching, but ...' Then Phonse Kyne came through the gate at Lulie Street. They picked him up high and carried him. They drowned Jock McHale out."[30]

The day after the practice match, no doubt reflecting on how bitter and angry so many people had been, Woods offered his letter of resignation to the committee—four days after he had been handed a job that had not previously been available since the end of the 1911 season. Woods's letter said:

---

28   *The Argus*, April 17, 1950
29   Interview with Bernie Shannon, 2010
30   Interview with Gordon Carlyon, 1999

In my view of the situation which has arisen, I feel after careful consideration, that I cannot accept the position of non-playing coach of Collingwood. It is quite obvious that I cannot expect the united support of all, which is so necessary for the success of the club. I have taken this action in the hope of restoring the unity and good feeling which has always prevailed at Collingwood. Whatever decision that the committee may now make, the coach appointed is assured of my loyalty and support.

In the best interests of the club, I am, faithfully yours,

B. Woods, 41 Ryan St Northcote

The overwhelming majority of the players of the time supported Kyne winning the position, but they also felt for Woods, who was basically forced out of the job that he had long aspired to. Bill Twomey said: "What happened to old Bervin Woods was a tragedy. They should never have appointed him; they should have appointed Phonse Kyne"[31] ("Old Bervin Woods" was no doubt an overstatement based on the passing years. When appointed, Woods was just 40 years old.) Kyne got the support of the general populace and a £200 cheque from John Wren who suggested, as reported by *The Argus*: "You have, under the expert guidance of the incomparable Jock McHale, proved one of the greatest football tacticians produced in the last decade."[32]

When Woods quit, it was believed that McHale would continue to take training until his replacement could be found. In the end, it was the defender Gordon Hocking, about to embark on his 12th season at Collingwood, who would run the training. McHale could not do it, according to *The Argus*, for "domestic issues."[33]

---

31   Interview with Bill Twomey, 1996

32   *The Argus*, April 18, 1950

33   ibid

But if the angst was something new and unusual at Collingwood, then it would only get worse at the "special meeting" at the Collingwood Town Hall, a month into the season. The headline in *The Argus* of May 18 said it all: "Near fighting at meeting of the Magpies." The kicker to the story said: "The iron curtain comes to Collingwood!" shouted football club members who couldn't get into the meeting." The story said: "Collingwood almost staged a civil war last night. The stormiest meeting in the municipality's history overwhelmingly passed a vote of no confidence in the Collingwood Football Club social committee. A special squad of police had difficulty in controlling a rowdy mob which tried to enter the meeting place."[34]

There were allegations and cross-examinations as some of the most famous names in the club's history all but squared off in the meeting. Part of that, expressed by former player 'Jiggy' Harris, exposed some of the tensions that had more recently existed between the retiring coach McHale, secretary Wraith and president Curtis. Speaking to *The Argus*, Harris claimed firstly that Syd Coventry, Phone Kyne and Harry Collier had been "shunned" by Wraith. He then added: "Jock McHale will not allow the names of Wraith and Curtis, president, to be mentioned in his home. Those two men ran Jock's son out of the club."[35]

It was an extraordinary allegation. In his response later in the evening, McHale said that he "regretted" the fact that he had told 'Jiggy' Harris about his "expressed hatred of Mr Wraith and Mr Curtis". McHale also made a "passionate plea" that he should not be made the "stool pigeon" of the rebels. "He was given a mixed hearing when he appealed to the meeting "not to throw off the committee."[36]

Shannon recalled the night: "The town hall was packed, and Harry Curtis said: 'Righto, there's only one way out of this, and that's to split

---

34   *The Argus*, May 18, 1950
35   ibid
36   ibid

the camp on to both sides. Now 75 per cent went to one side and Harry said to a committeeman: 'Oh, we're home and hosed here," to which the committeeman said: 'They're supporting the other side, the bastards'."[37]

Jock jnr would reveal years later that losing Wraith and Curtis as friends in the skirmish was tough for his father, but the fact that his friendship with Bob Rush (whom he had played with at Collingwood from 1903-1908) was also badly damaged was a further sour point. "That was the way it had to go (trying to make Kyne coach), he stuck out for it, losing the friendship of Bob Rush and Frank Wraith," Jock jnr said. "They wanted Bervin Woods and he wanted Phonse Kyne to be the senior coach. Mr Rush got tempted into it, as Wraith was the one who really wanted to appoint Bervin. Frank was the chairman of the Tramways Board and he had employed Bervin Woods. 'Woodsy' had a job up the poles and he got electrocuted, so Mr Wraith was always interested in doing well for Bervin. Mr Rush stuck by him (Wraith) to out-vote my father. They didn't realise how tough that would be. Ninety-nine per cent of the Collingwood people wanted Phonse Kyne (as coach)."[38]

There were other amazing moments and repercussions. Jack Wren, son of John, named those who voted against Kyne for the coaching position as "betrayers". Kyne, who had won the senior coaching role when Woods resigned, asked the entire playing list to stand with him in support. Kyne told *The Argus*: "I was prepared to play under great old stars like Syd Coventry, or Harry Collier, or Albert Collier But I have no faith in Bervin Woods as coach—even though he is a great chap."[39] Kyne and Woods had been teammates in five successive Grand Finals (1935-39) sharing two premierships (1935-36).

37   Interview with Bernie Shannon, 2010
38   Interview with Jock Jr McHale
39   *The Argus*, May 18, 1950

Curtis, Wraith and Rush, three men who had served the Collingwood Football Club loyally for many years, all ended their direct association with the club. A new broom was sweeping through the club, though the pro-Kyne supporters on the committee would remain, including McHale.

Bernard Curtis and Daryl Wraith, sons of Harry and Frank, both say their fathers struggled to get over what happened to them during the 1950 Collingwood split. "It broke dad's heart," Bernard Curtis said. "He was shattered. He had given his life to the club for about 35 years and to be tipped out and then not even given the pleasure of a nice farewell was shattering for him. It probably made it a bit hard for them when Jock retired just before the start of the season. That wasn't ideal. I think my dad just assumed that Bervin Woods was the right person to take over. I suppose Phonse Kyne had the bigger name, but Bervin had served a very good apprenticeship. I think the most disappointing thing for my dad was that it wasn't settled behind closed doors."[40]

McHale remained on the committee yet still got a farewell of sorts when a gala night was held for him at Collingwood Town Hall in August 1950, where it was said that the club would honour the "King of Coaches". By that stage, at least, the dust had settled on a period in which the club had almost torn itself apart.

The Argus reported McHale was afforded a "tremendous reception"[41] and was presented with a cheque for £1,127. It was a remarkable night when three ruckmen he had coached—Syd Coventry, Phonse Kyne and Gordon Hocking—had helped to carry him off, wrapped in one of the club's premiership flags. At that stage, Collingwood had won 11 premierships, nine of them connected to McHale as player and coach.

Syd Coventry, one of the main speakers on the night, said: "His honesty of purpose, sincerity and straightforwardness were among the secrets of his success."

---

40 Interview with Bernard Curtis, 2010
41 *The Argus*, September 1, 1950

There was even a song written for the occasion—*Have You Heard of Jock McHale?*

Have you heard of Jock McHale, me boys, the pride of Collingwood?
Here's been out here for forty years and done a lot of good.
He's the finest coach we've ever had, the best we've ever seen,
And, 'twas he who did originate, the Collingwood Machine.

Oh, he taught them to kick, and he taught them how to punch the ball,
Turning on a trey bit in the centre of the ground.
There's been no history in the history of the League, me boys,
Whose football so consistently, opponents did confound.
Oh, he won the side 10 premierships,[42]
A record unsurpassed
And sorry were the Magpies when he turned it up at last.

He's been called the King of Coaches—a title well deserved:
In the Hall of Football fame his place will ever be reserved
When Jock came to Collingwood, nearly fifty years ago,
He couldn't even make the side, I'd like you all to know.
When he went into the centre, in his first year in the side.
He ran rings round Rod McGregor and he left him in a stride.

Yes, he still runs well, when the Brewery has a picnic day.
Dashing round the barrels in his knee-length shorts of black
Those grand old pants are part of his first uniform,
It's said that old Wal Lee is always asking for them back.
Still, he'll always be remembered, while the Magpies have their roost.
And he always seems to be around, to give the side a boost.

There's nothing more to say of him—just lift your glass of ale,
And join in wishing all the best, to dear old Jock McHale.[43]

---

42   Actually the 'poet' was wrong, it was nine as McHale missed 1903 through injury
43   Program for Jock McHale tribute night, August 31, 1950

CHAPTER 15

The Final Days

1951-1953

Jock McHale's contribution to Collingwood following his retirement as coach was significant. In 1950, he helped to move a motion to bring in a superannuation scheme for club secretary Gordon Carlyon, three other full-time employees, and four part-time employees. Carlyon recalled: "Jock asked me what sort of superannuation I had, and I said to him that I didn't have any. He said you should have it, and we ended up getting it."[1] Carlyon says McHale's influence—in this case for contributors outside the playing group—showed the measure of the man.

The Magpies had another football first in 1950 as well when it employed its first female employee, Pat Sanders. "Jock was not initially impressed," Pat Sanders said in 2010. "He didn't think women should be allowed at football clubs, but that was fair enough because he came from a different era. And he was still very much a man of that era when I met him. But he came to change his views on this and he got used to it, and probably thought it was a good idea in the end."[2]

Collingwood, under Phonse Kyne, was not too dissimilar to McHale's Collingwood but there were some subtle changes. McHale

---

1   Interview with Gordon Carlyon, 1995
2   Interview with Pat Sanders, 2010

remained on the match committee, and didn't shy away from making a statement at meetings. Carlyon noted some subtle differences: "Jock believed you made your moves at the selection table, and then you have full confidence in the selected team. In 1951 and 1952 Phonse used to like to delay the team until he heard the opposition's team, and Jock would fly right off his seat then. He said if you have to worry about other sides, you were half-beaten before you went into games."[3] He added: "They were very similar in their approach, but Phonse seemed to be a bit more co-operative with the players. Jock was a bit more stand-offish, but he had their respect."[4]

The Magpies struggled under Kyne in 1950, and that probably had as much to do with the difficult succession following McHale's rule. Kyne even returned for seven games from rounds 10 to 16, in an effort to try and lift the side, but Collingwood would eventually finish seventh. With a 9-9 record, the Magpies ended a game and percentage outside the final four, after losing two of their last three games. The Magpies would improve to finish second behind Geelong at the end of the home and away season the following year, with each having a 14-4 record. An 82-point thrashing by the Cats in the second semi-final opened their finals campaign, with Geelong's full-forward George Goninon kicking 11 goals, one more than Collingwood could score on the day. Collingwood led Essendon by 24 points at the last change in the following week's preliminary final, but a five goal to one last quarter saw the Bombers win by two points. Geelong, in the midst of a record-setting streak of 23 consecutive wins, would win the Grand Final by 11 points.

Carlyon was privy to a lesson in the power of McHale and Wren just before the start of the 1952 season. Melbourne was in the midst of a serious dry spell and Victoria Park was rock hard. The Collingwood

3   Interview with Gordon Carlyon, 1995
4   ibid

secretary said: "Phonse Kyne requested that I ask the groundsman, Mr Tom Bird (who incidentally played nine games with Collingwood in 1925 and 1928 under McHale), to have it watered for the last match practice. Mr Bird referred me to Mr Cohen, the Collingwood City Curator, who stated that he could not release men to do the job. At the committee meeting on the Tuesday night Phonse reported that he was afraid to have match practice because of the hardness of the oval. Jock McHale volunteered to request Mr Wren's assistance. The next morning I met Jock as arranged at the Carlton Brewery at 9.30am and together we drove to Mr Wren's office in Flinders Lane. We discussed the inability to get water on the ground, and left with Mr Wren saying he would see what could be done. I returned Jock McHale to the Carlton Brewery and drove to the ground at about 11am. I was greeted by the Mayor, the Town Clerk, the City Engineer, City Curators and six gardeners."[5]

Collingwood (after a season of 14 wins and five losses) was back in a Grand Final in 1952, the first time it had made a premiership playoff since 1939. McHale helped out wherever he could. The Magpies were a young group, with an average age of only 22 and 58 games, but they were no match for the Cats in the second semi-final (loss by 54 points), and after dispensing with Fitzroy in the preliminary final, again in the premiership decider. *The Argus* reported: "The Brains Trust of Collingwood—Jock McHale, Sid (sic) Coventry and Phonse Kyne—sat imperturbably inside the fence like three wise monkeys and in identical pose." The Cats won by 46 points.

Jock McHale turned 70 in December 1952. He was still keeping busy, though the milestone birthday meant that he would have to retire at the start of the following year after a lifetime service to Carlton and United Breweries. On March 31, 1953, he retired from the job that had always been there for him, over 51 years—first with McCracken's Brewery (starting in 1901), and predominantly Carlton and United (from 1907

---

5   Interview with Gordon Carlyon, 1999

onwards). His workmates presented McHale with a grandfather clock as well as a beer mug decorated in Collingwood colours.

CUB's *What's Brewing* magazine of June 1953 documented the retirement ceremony for McHale and other long-serving employees. It said: "We said farewell to one of our oldest members, Mr 'Jock' McHale. Mr McHale had a long and honourable connection with the company and was highly respected by all for his sterling qualities as a worker and as a friend and advisor to the men who worked under him. He was fair and forthright in all his dealings to each and everyone, and he will be greatly missed by all with whom he came into contact."[6]

At a function in the CUB boardroom 210 years of service by McHale and four other employees were celebrated grandly. McHale was presented with a keepsake gold wristwatch. Collingwood, too, had presented McHale with a magnificent pocket watch in early 1953, to mark his 50 seasons spent at the club.

At Collingwood's annual meeting, where he was presented with the pocket watch, president Syd Coventry warned members that "time marches on ... and that Jock may have to sever his connections with the club in the near future."[7]

The 1953 VFL season was an exceptionally good one in multiple ways. It was the year of Queen Elizabeth II's coronation and the year in which New Zealander Edmund Hillary with Sherpa Tensing conquered the previously unconquerable Mount Everest. And it was the year which Collingwood would finally conquer Geelong, one of the great teams of the era. Geelong had wrested *The Machine's*—and McHale's—record of 20 consecutive wins, taking it to 23 before the round 14 game between the two teams at Kardinia Park. It was a tight

---

6   *What's Brewing*, June 1953, A magazine for and by the employees of Carlton and United Breweries.

7   *The Sun*, March 5, 1953

contest all afternoon, with the Cats leading narrowly all day. But in a massive last term, Collingwood overran Geelong to create a massive upset and to draw some new life into a season that had looked to be the Cats' for some time. It was Collingwood's first win over Geelong since round 14, 1951, a spread of five matches.

The two teams again finished first and second, with the Magpies (14-4) just a game behind the Cats. Collingwood easily accounted for Geelong in the second semi-final by 30 points, and the Cats advanced to the Grand Final after an easy win over Footscray in the preliminary final to meet Collingwood. Even though they had won the past two games against a team considered one of the best for a number of years, there was still a fair bit of nervousness in the Collingwood camp ahead of the game. It had been 17 years since the last Magpies' premiership— and back then Jock McHale was coach and Phonse Kyne was a key forward in just his third season. In that period, the Magpies had lost four Grand Finals, with Kyne playing in three of them.

The silent figure of McHale, head bowed, seated and with his eyes fixed to the floor, his hat in his hands, caught the attention of Collingwood star Bob Rose in the dressing rooms an hour or so before the 1953 Grand Final. Pale and racked by nerves, the mood of the one-time coach, selector and patriarch of the club contrasted starkly with that of some of the younger members of the team, such as Lerrel Sharp and Des Healey, stretched out on the change tables reading comics. Rose said: "He (McHale) was as quiet as a mouse. He just sat there with his head bowed as if there had been a death in the family."[8]

McHale had always been on edge in finals. But there was even more strain with this one. He wasn't coaching, but the long premiership drought had left him exceptionally nervous before the game. A win would mean everything to him, and it might just repair a few relationships that had been damaged by the split from three years earlier.

---

8   *The Premiership's a cakewalk*, Glenn McFarlane and Richard Stremski, Spicers Papers, 1998

Huggy Buggy would reveal in *The Argus* just how big an impression McHale made on that Collingwood team that day, especially via one selection gamble. Buggy wrote: "Always a man of forthright views, he pressed strongly for the transfer of the second rover Ron Richards to the wing for the Grand Final against Geelong. He found himself in the minority of one on the club committee, but such never daunted Jock. He maintained that Richards would do a job on the wing in the absence of Jack Hickey, and he hammered his point doggedly. Finally, he won the selectors to his view, and Richards went to his wing."[9] Richards was one of Collingwood's best players.

Collingwood led at every stage, but the game—and the premiership—would be a tightly contested one from start to finish, except through the third term when the Magpies kicked away to a nice lead of 29 points at three-quarter-time. But even then McHale and Wren were not at ease. Each had sat through enough Grand Finals to know that. One good omen for Wren was the fact that his racehorse, Walu, won the Moonee Valley Stakes that day—wearing Magpie colours.

As expected from a great team, Geelong kept coming. At one stage earlier in the final term, the margin had been drawn back to 14 points. Fittingly, Rose, a player whom McHale would laud after the game as potentially the best he had seen in black and white, sealed the game, and the premiership with a great goal. He recalled later: "I had the horrible thought of what might have happened if I had missed. As it went through, somebody in black and white waved to me, and I returned the thumbs up."[10]

Collingwood may have managed only one goal to Geelong's three in the last term, but Rose's goal—his third for the day—was enough to secure the Magpies their first premiership since the 1936 victory over South Melbourne.

---

9   *The Argus*, October 6, 1953
10   *The Official Collingwood Illustrated Encyclopedia*, Michael Roberts and Glenn McFarlane, Slattery Publishing and Lothian, 2004

When the final bell rang out across the MCG, with the Magpies 12 points clear, it set in train a wave of celebrations that swept through the crowd. Many of them would try to sneak into the rowdy Collingwood dressing rooms.

The overwhelming emotion for McHale, rising 71, and for Wren, 82, was relief. In many ways this premiership validated McHale's firm belief that Kyne was the right choice to replace him; including this premiership, Kyne had coached Collingwood for 80 matches, for 54 wins, two Grand Finals and a premiership. His win-loss record to that point—67.5%—even exceeded McHale's career record.[11] Wren's reputation never really recovered from the publication of Frank Hardy's thinly disguised novel of 1950, *Power Without Glory*, but for him to see one more Collingwood flag must have warmed his cockles.[12]

McHale is asked to say a few words in the rooms; he climbs on a seat and begins his last address to the Collingwood Football Club. A tape recorder is produced as pandemonium prevails. McHale's breathless, emotionally charged voice is heard to crackle and then booms as he fights to speak over the roar of the celebrations.

He says: "A bit of order ... I just want to make an announcement— listen, order—Mr Jack Stewart, a great friend of Mr Wren's ... Mr Wren told him to come down and tell me personally to give the players £500." Then he switches back to what the victory means to him: "I've never been through a season in my life as I have this season,

---

11 Kyne would finish coaching Collingwood at the end of the 1963 season, finishing with a win-loss record of 151-121 (2 draws), for a win-loss percentage of 59 per cent. He also coached Collingwood to its unlikely win over Melbourne in the famous 1958 Grand Final—the victory for Collingwood that protected the club's record of four straight premierships set by The Machine (1927-30).

12 In 1951 Frank Hardy faced trial for criminal libel because of his depiction of the wife of Hardy's principle character "John West" having an affair. West was the character based on the life and times of John Wren. The case failed, as Hardy's defence was that the novel was a mix of fact and fiction.

particularly today. It has been the most thrilling season that I've ever had with the Collingwood team. Although I am not coach, (I'm) only helping out and giving a bit of guidance, (it's) the most thrilling feeling I've had in all the premierships. I've never been so much worked up as I have been this season, to get into the four, and for more reason than one to win the premiership for 'Phonsey' Kyne, and all the players connected to the Collingwood Football Club, and our worthy president (Syd Coventry) and our committee."[13]

They were among the last public words Jock McHale ever said. Perhaps, as in his own words, he was a little too "worked up" from the Grand Final triumph. So, too, was Wren. The Collingwood Football Club linked the two friends in life, and so it would be in death.

Other than his cameo in the winning rooms, McHale took no further part in the celebrations as he took ill soon after, suffering a heart attack in the days following the match. His health progressively got worse, though few people, other than close family and friends, knew of his plight. He remained intensely private to the end, and would die from the effects of the heart attack just eight days after the Grand Final victory, and those emotional words in victory, on October 4. June McHale recalled: "We thought he was indestructible, so it was a real shock when he died. He had pneumonia and heart failure."

Wren had a heart attack 36 hours after the game, and would be so ill that he was unable to attend Jock's funeral. He would succumb on October 26.

Following McHale's death, the tributes flowed for a man who had truly been a colossus of Australian sport for 50 years. Even those he had fallen out with in the 1950 succession split were quick to put aside any ill feelings to pay tribute. Frank Wraith told *The Herald*: "Nothing I can say can convey what a fine personality has been lost

---

13   Audio recording, Collingwood rooms, 1953 Grand Final. Listen to the audio at
      *http://www.slatterymedia.com/store/viewBook/jock---the-story-of-jock-mchale-
      collingwood-s-greatest-coach/media*

to Collingwood and to football."[14] Harry Curtis said: "He was one of the true Magpies ... he lived only for Collingwood."[15] And Bob Rush described Collingwood's "great loss".

The Collingwood Football Club was in the middle of their end of year trip to Tasmania when McHale passed away. The president, Syd Coventry, captain, Lou Richards, and coach Phonse Kyne, flew back for a huge funeral at St Therese's in Essendon, following by a burial service at Coburg cemetery. McHale would be laid to rest in the same plot as his son 'Frankie' (James Francis 1919) and his beloved daughter 'Jean' (Mary Jean 1934). More than 10 years later, in January 1964, Violet McHale, aged 80, would join them.

The Collingwood team itself marked McHale's service with a minute's silence on a roadside in Tasmania.

McHale was gone, but his legacy to the club would endure, as one of his former charges, Bruce Andrew, wrote in *The Sporting Globe:* "The Prince of Coaches, as he was so often called is gone, but the spirit he imbued into his teams is still there; as strong, if not stronger than ever. It is a tradition that will not die. While the 'arms' and 'legs' of his team have been replaced, the 'body'—that fanatical team spirit— has remained a foundation on which he built his football structure. He did not radiate enthusiasm or personality. He was a man of single purpose—a football fanatic whose only real interest was Collingwood and loyalty to Collingwood."[16]

---

14   *The Herald,* October 5, 1953
15   ibid
16   *The Sporting Globe,* October 7, 1953

The McHale Legacy

Writing *Jock* evoked some remarkable reflections—drawn, no doubt, from the knowledge that my grandfather was part of Jock McHale's most glorious period, the four premierships of 1927-30, as well as the 1935 flag. These were McHale's years, but also the heyday of Charlie Dibbs, a grandfather I never knew, but whose life and influences I now know intimately. Charlie died in 1960, nine years before I was born, but he imbued a love of Collingwood in my mother, Dawn, who passed on that beautiful legacy to her family, and to me.

Fortunately, I met—and corresponded with—a number of members of *The Machine* team as a teenager, and came to hear about the great Jock McHale, prompting an interest to learn more about Collingwood and football of that era. I was also lucky enough to meet other descendants of *The Machine* in more recent years when Michael Roberts and I wrote a book about the famous team.

As Bruce Andrew noted in his beautifully expressed obituary, Jock McHale's legacy to Collingwood, and to football, was extraordinary and permanent. Much of it still resonates almost 50 years after his death. I hope this book has explained what made the legendary coach tick, and what set him apart from other coaches of the time; and has also shown him as he was, a passionate believer in the game, and the club he loved; a husband and father, who endured heartbreak in a personal sense on more than one occasion; and a simple yet sometimes complex character who could both unite and divide.

Many at Collingwood believe McHale's legacy had been sorely neglected in official channels at VFL and AFL level for too long, but that has changed in recent years.

Incredibly, Jock McHale never received any recognition in his lifetime from the competition that he served in one capacity or another for 50 years. Even in the last year of his life, *The Argus's* Ken Moses wrote a public memo to the VFL: "He (McHale) has given 50 years of his life to the national game, all with Collingwood, and 40 of them (note: it was actually 38 seasons) as coach. You sent him a three-line letter congratulating him on his half century in the game. I take it you have run out of life memberships up your way."

There was no provision for coaches to become life members of the League at the time. It wasn't until 1977 that those rules were changed and McHale belatedly became a life member, 24 years after his death. He became a member of the Australian Football Hall of Fame on its inauguration in 1996, and a similar rule change to the Hall Of Fame charter in 2005 (allowing coaches to be elevated to Legend status), saw him made a Legend in 2005.

He was overlooked as coach of the AFL Team Of The Century, in favour of Melbourne's Norm Smith, who became the second coach elevated to Legend status in 2007. Smith had been a Collingwood supporter growing up, and often spent time at Victoria Park as a kid watching the great Jock McHale coach the Magpies. So, too, did another coaching genius, Hawthorn's John Kennedy.

It was no surprise that McHale was chosen as Collingwood coach for its Hall of Fame side. What would have surprised him, no doubt, was the fact that he was also named as the coach of the New South

Wales Team Of The Century, even though in his first five years of living in that state, he never picked up an Australian Rules football.

But perhaps the greatest posthumous honour that Jock McHale was to receive came in 2001 when the AFL decided to name the premiership medal for the winning coach in his honour—the Jock McHale Medal. Collingwood cheer squad identity Jeff "Joffa" Corfe came up with the suggestion, raised it with president Eddie McGuire and Dean Moore from the AFL saw the suggestion on a Magpie fan site, Nick's Collingwood Page.

The McHale Medal was backdated to coaches who had coached premiership teams from 1950 onwards, given McHale retired on the eve of that season. Previous winners were presented with the Premiership Coach's Medal.

McHale's name even featured in an AFL advertisement to launch the 2005 AFL season, with Collingwood champion Nathan Buckley declaring: "So help me Jock". Those who speak in almost reverential tones about McHale the coach would have liked that.

Jock's wife, Violet, outlived her devoted husband by a little more than 10 years. In the years after Jock's death, she liked nothing better than sitting in the room dominated by a photo of her late husband. She retained her love of football until her dying day, even writing into *The Sun* newspaper on March 23, 1962, saying: "My husband, the late James (Jock) McHale served Victorian football for 50 years, and was always in favour of publicising this great game. Now elderly, my only contact with football is through television and radio. Give us back those direct telecasts. Violet McHale, Melbourne." Her plea for live games would take until 2012 to be delivered, under the 2012-16 broadcasting agreement.

Jock jnr received a phone call from the club the day after his famous father died, telling him of the need for him to replace his father on the Collingwood board. A wealthy man via canny business dealings, Jock jnr continued the McHale family's contribution to Collingwood, giving of his time and money generously for many years, and even acting as a guarantor—along with John Wren's sons, John jnr and Joseph—for the club's social club building.

He also helped to facilitate his father's legacy in another way, commissioning renowned portrait artist Paul Fitzgerald to paint a powerful, famous portrait of McHale, which has been on display at the Collingwood Football Club offices ever since.

In some ways, it was fitting that Jock jnr was the man who unfurled the 1990 premiership flag in early 1991, prompting Harry Collier to say: "His father did that much for the club; it's nice to see the young fellow doing the job." At the time Harry was 83 and the "young fellow" Jock jnr, was 76. He was also instrumental in having Victoria Park renamed McHale Stadium in the late 1990s.

Jock jnr passed away in June 2003, aged 88.

One hundred years ago, at the end of the 1911 season, the Collingwood committee presented a keepsake kettle to the "brilliant and consistent centre, Mr Jim McHale, for his fine record of 165 matches in his nine years of service." He was then 29 years old, a few months away from another decision the club would make—appointing him as coach and captain of Collingwood. These were the formative years of the game, and the concept of coach was very different from that of today: in many ways, the captain was the true leader of the club, but McHale—and his great contemporary, Carlton's Jack Worrall— would change that.

Leadership, under the McHale model, came from the man on the bench—a leader as orator, a leader as motivator, a leader as the setter of policy for team and club.

It is fitting to end the story of Jock McHale in his own words, with his manifesto of the role of coach and club, written in 1925. It remains as emphatic today as it was then:

> There is more in football than merely kicking a ball about. You will discover this as your training progresses. If played in the proper spirit, this game brings out the very best that is in a boy.

It develops him morally and physically. It teaches him that to flinch spells cowardice. It teaches him, perhaps more than any other game does, the art of self-control. To be cool, with a level head, is absolutely essential. It teaches him to be unselfish and manly. All this may be summed up in one word—character—and if that is not worth developing, nothing is.

Acknowledgements

This book would not have been possible without the assistance and encouragement of a huge number of people, and I extend my sincere thanks to those who helped me in all stages of the production of this book.

The publisher of this book, Geoff Slattery, approached me with the idea of writing a biography of Jock McHale in late 2008, and he has played a pivotal role in the outcome. He has a passion for ensuring football's past is well documented and never forgotten, and his guidance and editorial assistance were invaluable.

The editor, Ashley Browne, worked tirelessly on this project, and was extremely patient and understanding. He was a tremendous support. Assistant editor Paul Daffey and pictures editor Justine Walker were also crucial, and I extend my thanks to everyone at The Slattery Media Group.

Family was the reason why I did this book (my grandfather, Charlie Dibbs, played under Jock McHale for 12 seasons), so it seems appropriate that my family played such a pivotal role in allowing me to reach the finish line. At times, it seemed as if the process was almost as long as Jock's career, so I thank my family for keeping me going through the difficult times.

My wife Christine is a passionate Magpie (*her* grandfather used to go to watch *my* grandfather play at Victoria Park) and her commitment to this project was remarkable. She also provided much needed guidance, research skills and proof reading, often until the early hours of the morning.

To my three little Magpies—Lachlan, Elise and Charlotte—thanks for keeping me sane through the tough times, and keeping me inspired through the good times. Thanks for being such great kids.

My mum, Dawn, was, as always, a tower of strength and I think she was more relieved than anyone when the final full stop went on the manuscript. She gave me a love of Collingwood and of family, and my late father, Bob, gave me a love of football and words. I could not be more grateful to either of them.

My sister, Deb, my brothers Robert and Gary, and the rest of the Craker and McFarlane clan, most of them Magpies, have always supported me in anything I have done. Thanks also to Rob, Nic, Lis and Jamie Craker for other help and babysitting duties.

My Aunty Robyn (Dawn's sister and Charlie's youngest daughter) was a big believer in this book, but sadly never got to see the final publication. Thanks also to Charlie and Pearl for making me a Magpie, and giving me a sense of family.

Thanks to my other family, Howard and Sylvia Leigh, for their support and friendship over many years,

I'd like to thank June McHale for her memories and hospitality, and for allowing me to document the life of her famous father-in-law. Other McHale/Gibbons family members kindly assisted me in this work, particularly the wonderful Mary Doyle, from Ireland, Austin Gibbons, John Finlay, Danny Hoban, John Murphy, John McHale and Aaron McHale (whose grandfather wrote a family history that was provided to me).

I'd like to thank club president Eddie McGuire and everyone at the Collingwood Football Club and, in particular, the Collingwood Football Archives Group, for their assistance. I'm extremely grateful to Tom Wanliss for allowing me to listen to his taped interviews with greats such as Harry Collier, Percy Bowyer, Bruce Andrew, Gordon

Carlyon, Bill Twomey and Neil Mann. Peter Furniss generously read the manuscript, while he and Bernie Murphy always provided great support. Others such as Joyce Draper, Pat Overend, Bob Beach and Janiene Hart helped me out on many Monday afternoons.

My frequent co-author Michael Roberts was outstanding in his support, guidance and friendship, never ceasing to answer my many questions, even though he was in the process of doing his own book. His many past works on the Collingwood Football Club were invaluable. Thanks mate.

Thank you also to Russell Holmesby who allowed me to sift through his archives, for pointing me in the right direction at times and for providing some invaluable information on Jock McHale's reserves coach, Hughie Thomas.

Richard Stremski kindly provided recordings of interviews with Jock McHale jnr, Bervin Woods and Roy Allen, as well as some photographs. His book, *Kill For Collingwood*, was a constant reference.

Other football historians and lovers of history have helped me, including the AFL's Col Hutchinson and Cameron Sinclair, Tony De Bolfo, David Allen, Rhett Bartlett, Ray Webster and the MCC Library volunteers, as well as historical societies of Coonabarabran, Warialda, Coburg and Brunswick.

I was lucky enough to speak with a number of people associated with Jock McHale, including some of the men who played under him or who were at the club when he was. They were Jack Pimm, Bernie Shannon, the late Norm Crewther, Peter Lucas, Ron Richards, Lou Richards, Murray Weideman, Jack Synon, Stan Smith, Ray Riddell and Fred Stabb.

Add to that the correspondence I was lucky enough to have with *The Machine* members and their families over many years.

Others who gave of their time and recollections include: the late Miriam Rumney and her daughter Jan Trew, Jack Coventry, Daryl Wraith, Bernard Curtis, Pat Sanders, Harold Thomas, Harold Smith, Paul Fitzgerald, John Wren III, Christopher Wren, Peter French,

Marc Fiddian, Brian Hansen, Maureen Lane, Rick Milne, Vicky Eldridge, Rod Prusa, George Firth, Stan Lord, Ted Ellen, Ron Secull and Carmen Saunders.

Thanks also to *The Sunday Herald Sun* and *Herald Sun* for allowing me to do this project, especially Damon Johnston and Jamie Tate, as well as Shane Crawford, Tony Sheahan and Darren Symes for keeping me amused and awake after many late nights and early mornings.

There were others who helped me in this time, and I thank everyone who assisted in whatever way they could. If I neglected to mention anyone by name, please accept my thanks.

Glenn McFarlane, 2011

Jock McHale

An Official Legend of the Australian Football Hall Of Fame

Born: December 12 1882, at Alexandria, New South Wales
Died: October 4, 1953, at Coburg, Victoria

THE PLAYER
Collingwood: 1903-1918, 1920: 261 games, 18 goals.
Honours:
Captain 1912-1913, 1917 (co-captain)
Premierships 1910, 1917
Victorian representative 1911 (four games)

THE COACH
Collingwood 1912-1949: 714 games, 467 wins, 237 loses,
10 draws, winning rate 65%.
Finals: 27 wins, 30 losses, two draws,
eight premierships (1917, 1919, 1927, 1928, 1929, 1930, 1935, 1936)
runners-up (1915, 1918, 1920, 1922, 1925, 1926, 1937, 1938, 1939)

Coach of the Collingwood Team of the Century (1997)
Member Australian Football Hall of Fame (1996)
Legend Australian Football Hall of Fame (2005)

There is more in
kicking a ball about
as your training [
the proper spirit, th
very best that is in
morally and physica
to flinch spells cow
perhaps more than a
art of self-control. T
head, is absolutely e
to be unselfish and
summed up in the or
if that is not worth